A GENERAL VIEW OF THE HISTORY
OF THE ENGLISH BIBLE

THE MACMILLAN COMPANY
NEW YORK · BOSTON · CHICAGO · DALLAS
ATLANTA · SAN FRANCISCO

MACMILLAN & CO., Limited
LONDON · BOMBAY · CALCUTTA
MELBOURNE

THE MACMILLAN CO. OF CANADA, Ltd.
TORONTO

A GENERAL VIEW OF THE HISTORY
OF THE ENGLISH BIBLE

BY

BROOKE FOSS WESTCOTT, D.D.

THIRD EDITION REVISED BY
WILLIAM ALDIS WRIGHT,
VICE-MASTER OF TRINITY COLLEGE, CAMBRIDGE

New York
THE MACMILLAN COMPANY
1927

Εὐλόγως ὁ Διδάσκαλος ἡμῶν ἔλεγεν

Γίνεσθε τραπεζῖται δόκιμοι.

First Edition, Crown 8vo. 1868,

Second Edition, Crown 8vo. 1872,

Third Edition revised by William Aldis Wright, 8vo. 1905

PREFACE.

IN the following Essay I have endeavoured to call attention to some points in the history of the English Bible which have been strangely neglected. The history of our Bible is indeed a type of the history of our Church, and both histories have suffered the same fate. The writers who have laboured most successfully upon them have in the main confined themselves to outward facts without tracing the facts back to their ultimate sources, or noticing the variety of elements which go to form the final result. As far as I know no systematic inquiry into the internal history of our Authorised Version has yet been made, and still no problem can offer greater scope for fruitful research. To solve such a problem completely would be a work of enormous labour, and I have been forced to content myself with indicating some salient points in the solution, in the hope that others may correct and supplement the conclusions which I have obtained. It is at least something to know generally to what extent Tindale and Coverdale made use of earlier versions, and to be able to refer to their sources most of the characteristic readings of Matthew's New Testament and of the Great Bibles[1].

---

[1] Perhaps I may be allowed to mention one or two collations which would certainly furnish some valuable results.

(1) A collation of the Grenville Fragment with the smaller Tindale's Testament of 1525.

(2) A collation of Tindale's Testaments of 1534 and 1535 with the New Testament in Matthew's Bible of 1537.

(3) A collation of Tindale's Pentateuchs of 1530 and 1534 with Matthew's Bible 1537, for which Mr Offor's MSS. in the British Museum would be available as a verification (see p. 208, n.).

(4) A collation of numerous select passages in the Great Bibles of 1539,

Even in the external history of our Bible much remains to be done. It seems scarcely credible that adequate inquiry will not shew from what presses Tindale's New Testament of 1535[1], Coverdale's Bible of 1535 and Matthew's Bible of 1537 proceeded. And it is impossible not to hope that Mr Brewer's researches may yet bring to light new documents illustrating the vacillating policy of Henry VIII. as to the circulation of the vernacular Scriptures.

It does not fall within my province to criticise other histories. I have used Mr Anderson's *Annals of the English Bible*, and the *Historical Account*[2] prefixed to Bagster's *Hexapla* (to which Mr Anderson does scant justice) with the greatest profit, and I desire to express generally my obligations to both essays. If I differ from them silently on any points I do so purposely, and in some cases I have even felt obliged to point out errors in them which were likely to mislead.

Absolute accuracy in an inquiry of so wide a range seems to be impossible, and everyone who is conscious of his own manifold mistakes would gladly leave the mistakes of others unnoticed ; but when writers like Mr Hallam and Mr Froude misrepresent every significant feature in an important episode of literary history, it seems necessary to raise some protest. Their names are able to give authority to fictions, if the fictions are unchallenged[3]........

April, 1540, and November, 1540, with a view to ascertaining how far the reaction in the last text extends, and whether it can be traced to any principle.

(5) A collation of the New Testaments of the Bishops' Bibles of 1568 and 1572.

[1] See p. 161, n., 1872.

[2] The *Historical Account* appears in two forms. That which I have used was drawn up (I am informed) by Dr S. P. Tregelles. In the later issue of the *Hexapla* this independent and valuable narrative was replaced by another written (it is said) by Mr Anderson, which I have not consulted. 1872. [It was written not by Mr Anderson, but by Dr John Stoughton.—W. A. W.]

[3] One example of this contagiousness of error, which is a fair specimen of a very large class, falls under my notice as these sheets are passing through the press. 'Tindale,' writes Mr Smiles, 'unable to get his New Testament

No apology, I trust, will be needed for the adoption of our ordinary orthography in quotations from the early versions ; and the extreme difficulty of revising proofs by the help of distant libraries must be pleaded as an excuse for more serious errors.

What I have done is for the most part tentative and incomplete, and many points in the history of the Bible are left wholly unnoticed. If my leisure would have allowed I should have been glad to examine the changes in the headings of the chapters and the marginal references, both before and after 1611, for their history involves many details of great interest. One question however in con-nexion with the Authorised Version I have purposely neglected. It seemed useless to discuss its revision. The revision of the original texts must precede the revision of the translation, and the time for this, even in the New Testament, has not yet fully come[1].

But however painful the sense of incompleteness and inaccuracy in such an essay as this must be, it has this advantage, that it bears witness almost on every page to

'printed in England, where its perusal was forbidden [?], had the first edition 'printed at Antwerp in 1526...A complete edition of the English Bible, 'translated partly by Tindale and partly by Coverdale, was printed at 'Hamburgh in 1535; and a second edition, edited by John Rogers, under 'the name of Thomas Matthew, was printed at Marlborow in Hesse in '1537...Cranmer's Bible, so called because revised by Cranmer, was pub-'lished in 1539-40.' *Huguenots*, p. 15, and note. London, 1867. Neither the first nor the second edition of Tindale's New Testament was printed at Antwerp. The Bible of 1535 was not partly translated by Tindale; and no competent bibliographer at present assigns it to the Hamburgh press. Matthew's Bible was in no sense a second edition of Coverdale's, of which, indeed, two editions were published in 1537, and the place where it was printed is as yet uncertain. 'Cranmer's Bible' was not revised by Cranmer, and the editions of 1539 and 1540 are quite distinct. With that of 1539 Cranmer had nothing to do till after it was printed. Thus every statement in the quotation is incorrect. Lewis's *History* has, I fear, much to answer for; but it is unpardonable to use it without verification.

[1] [The experience of the work of New Testament Revision during the last two years has shewn me that I was wrong in this opinion. Whatever may be the merits of the Revised Version it can be said confidently that, in no parallel case have the readings of the original text to be translated been discussed and determined with equal care, thoroughness and candour. 1872.]

the kindness of friends. It would have been far more imperfect than it is if I had not been allowed every facility for using the magnificent collections of Bibles in the British Museum, the University Library at Cambridge, and the Baptist College at Bristol. For this privilege and for similar acts of courtesy my warmest thanks are due to the Rev. H. O. Coxe, Bodley's Librarian at Oxford, Mr Bradshaw, University Librarian at Cambridge, Mr Bullen, of the British Museum, the Rev. Dr Gotch, Principal of the Baptist College, Bristol, Mr Aldis Wright, Librarian of Trinity College, Cambridge, Mr Francis Fry, Cotham, Bristol, and the late Rev. Dr Milman, Dean of St Paul's.

B. F. W.

HARROW,
Nov. 3, 1868.

NOTICE TO THE SECOND EDITION.

THE kindness of many friends has enabled me to issue this second edition of the *History of the English Bible* with considerable additions in different sections, but the book is substantially unchanged. Later researches have fully established the general results which I indicated as to the composite character of our present Authorised Version; and the labours of the New Revision have brought into clearer relief the merits and defects of the Scholars who successively fulfilled the office of Revisers in earlier times. Even now perhaps full justice has not been done to the exquisite delicacy of Coverdale and the stern fidelity of the Rhemists. But, not to dwell on the individual characteristics of former Revisers, it may fairly be said that they have marked a general method of proce-.dure which those who follow them are not likely to abandon. The changes in our Authorised Version which are still necessary are due for the most part to the claims of riper scholarship and more searching criticism, and not to any altered conception of the style and character most appropriate to a popular Version of the Holy Scriptures. That question most happily has been settled for ever.

One most remarkable discovery which has been made lately as to the early editions of the English Testament requires to be brought into special notice. Mr F. Fry has found the text of 'Tindale 1535' in an edition dated 1534 (see p. 161, n.). It is possible, therefore, that the misspelt copies may belong to a pirated reprint of Tindale's own work.

The admirable biography of Tindale by the Rev. R. Demaus appeared after my early sheets were printed off; but I owe to the kindness of the author several criticisms and corrections of which I have gladly availed myself. In expressing the hope that he will be encouraged to continue his exhaustive labours upon the great leaders of our Reformation, I say only what all must feel who have had occasion to profit by his researches.

To Mr F. Fry and Professor Moulton my warmest thanks are due. Both placed at my disposal extensive collections, which I have used only partially, yet, as I hope, in such a manner as to shew how highly I value the generosity which allowed me to gather the fruits of long and unattractive work[1].

B. F. W.

TRINITY COLLEGE, CAMBRIDGE,
  Nov. 7, 1872.

[1] As this last sheet is passing through the press I have noticed a very remarkable detail in the History of the English Bible, which seems to call for further investigation. In the Library of the House of Lords there is a draft of 'An Act for reducing of diversities of Bibles now extant in the 'English tongue to one settled Vulgar translated from the original.' The draft is not dated, but is referred to the reign of Elizabeth, and is certainly after 1560 from internal evidence. 'Great errors,' it is recited, 'arise and 'papistry and atheism increase from the variety of translations of Bibles, 'while many desire an authorised translation, which the Lords spiritual 'could complete had they power to compel assistance from students of the 'Universities. The Lords spiritual or any six of them (of whom the Arch-'bishop of Canterbury for the time being is to be one) may assemble, treat, 'and deal touching the accomplishment of the work, and may call for the 'assistance of students of either University, and pay them out of moneys 'to be levied on such cathedral churches or colleges as shall be thought 'requisite, and any temporal person may give gift or legacy for furtherance 'of the work.' I owe this abstract of the draft to the kindness of Mr R. W. Monro. [Mr Edmund Gosse, Librarian to the House of Lords, informs me that the MS. is now preserved in the Victoria Tower. It appears to have been a form for the first reading which was never proceeded with.—W. A. W.]

PREFACE TO THE THIRD EDITION.

AT the end of the year 1900, when Bishop Westcott was in Cambridge, I asked him why he did not bring out a new edition of his *History of the English Bible*, which had been long out of print. He explained that his own engagements left him no time for such a work, and other arrangements he had hoped to make had not been carried out, but he said, ' If you will do it, I will give 'you my materials.' After some consideration I consented, and on January 24, 1901, the Bishop wrote, ' It will be a very 'great pleasure to me if you undertake a new edition of 'the *History of the English Bible*. A conversation with 'you after a lecture which I gave at Cambridge on the 'question led me to write it. What then can be more 'appropriate than that you should complete it ? '

This to the best of my ability I have endeavoured to do. The plan of the work is unchanged. Every statement and every quotation have been verified. Such corrections as were necessary have been silently made, and all additions are placed in the notes in square brackets, sometimes for the sake of clearness with my own initials attached. The corrections, however, have been not merely of errors of the press or slips of the pen, but involve a rectification of the manner of reference to authorities. In estimating, for instance, the influence of Luther upon Tindale it is useless to quote the modern editions. Luther's New Testament as contained in his Bible of 1534 could have had no influence upon Tindale's version of 1525, and Luther's final edition of 1541 could not have affected Tindale's of 1534 and 1535. In like manner,

Tindale in 1525 could only have known of the New
Testament of Erasmus as it appeared in the first three
editions of 1516, 1519, and 1522, and it was not till 1534
that he could have used the edition of 1527. Similar
remarks apply to Coverdale. There is no doubt that the
translation of the New Testament in the Genevan Bible
of 1560 was affected by Beza's Latin Version, but this
could only have been as it appeared in 1556 and 1559.
The edition of Beza published in 1565 may have been
used for the Bishops' Bible of 1568, and the Latin renderings in the subsequent issues of 1575, 1576, 1582, 1585, 1589,
and 1598 could have been consulted by the translators of
the Authorised Version, but as the renderings vary it is
necessary to specify the edition in which they first appear.
In the previous editions of this History it seems that the
important fact of these variations was not sufficiently
recognized, and it has been my endeavour to reduce the
method of reference to these authorities to a system more
consistent with chronology. In the previous editions also
the spelling of the English quotations is modernized, but
though such a change may be tolerable in a merely
popular book I could not regard it as appropriate to the
work of a scholar of Bishop Westcott's reputation, and I
have therefore in most instances restored the ancient
forms, only regretting that I have not done so more completely. This change will cause no difficulty to intelligent
readers, while it will add an interest to the quotations
themselves.

The additions, such as the notes on the Tindale New
Testament of 1536 (p. 49), on the printing of the Coverdale
Bible (p. 57), on the influence of the French translations on Matthew (p. 170), on the editions of 1549 (p. 73),
on Tindale's connexion with the translation of the historical books in Matthew's Bible (p. 172), on the marginal
notes in Matthew (Appendix XI.), and others, explain
themselves. Appendix IX., on the revision of the
Authorised Version, has been expanded, and Appendices
XII. and XIII. have been added.

Since the last edition of this work in 1872 there have appeared other books on the same subject which may be consulted with advantage. Among these are *The English Bible* by Dr John Eadie (1876), *The History of the English Bible* by Dr W. F. Moulton (1878), *Our English Bible* by Dr Stoughton, *The Bibles of England* by Dr A. Edgar (1889), *English Versions of the Bible* by Dr Mombert (1890), and *The Evolution of the English Bible* by Mr H. W. Hoare (1901). More recently Dr Lupton has contributed an extremely valuable article on the English Versions to the supplementary volume of Hastings' *Dictionary of the Bible*, though he has unfortunately been led into error by mistaking the 1569 edition of the Great Bible for the Bishops' Bible in 4to of the same date.

I may take the opportunity of adding to what I have said (p. 19, note 2) of a Bible which in 1480 was in the possession of Edward the Fourth. Among the King's Privy Purse Expenses for that year is an item, ' For ' binding, gilding and dressing of a booke called the Bible ' xvjs,' and I have said that there is nothing to shew that this was an English Bible. Nor is there in this entry; but later in the same MS. (Harl. 4780) there is an inventory of the books belonging to the King at Richmond, and we find among them ' The Bible, in englissh,' so that no doubt there was a copy of the Wycliffite Version in the Royal Library.

With regard to the different title-pages of Coverdale's Bible of 1535 I have not been able to satisfy myself, owing to the uncertainty introduced by the so-called facsimiles. There are undoubtedly three title-pages which are genuine: one (in German type) in the Library of the Earl of Leicester at Holkham, with a list of the books on the reverse: one (English type) in the possession of the Marquess of Northampton: and one (English type) in the University Library, Cambridge, which has on the reverse the prayer here printed at p. 66. In one of the two copies in the British Museum there is a made-up title, partly genuine, but completed in facsimile by Harris from the title-page of the Bible printed for Berthelet by Petit and Redman in 1540. The other Museum copy, which is in the Grenville Library, has a facsimile title, resembling but differing from that in the Holkham copy, the original of which I have been unable to trace. Mr Fry had a facsimile made from the Holkham title, but without the list of books on the reverse. It is difficult therefore to place implicit confidence in facsimiles.

In conclusion I have to express my sincere thanks to all who have assisted me in this work: to His Grace the Archbishop of Canterbury for his kindness in allowing me to have a transcript made of the interesting manuscript in Lambeth Palace Library which is printed in Appendix XII.; to Dr Ginsburg for giving me free access to his fine collection of Bibles, which is especially rich in copies of Luther's and the Zürich Versions; to the officers of the British Museum for many courtesies and much assistance; to Mr H. F. Moule, to whom is largely due the excellent Catalogue of Bibles in the Library of the British and Foreign Bible Society, and to whom I am indebted for valuable suggestions; to the Librarian of the John Rylands Library, Manchester, for the readiness with which he has supplied me with information from the rich collection under his charge; to Mr Charles Sayle, of the University Library, Cambridge, for constant help; to Mr Cowley, of the Bodleian; to the Rev. Prebendary Maddison, Librarian of the Chapter Library, Lincoln, and to others who have materially lightened my labours.

WILLIAM ALDIS WRIGHT.

TRINITY COLLEGE, CAMBRIDGE,
  16th August, 1905.

ERRATUM.

p. 137, note[1], l. 18, *For* seyne *read* keyne.

CONTENTS.

INTRODUCTION.

pp. 3—8.

PAGES

Vernacular versions of Scripture among the first works of Christian
antiquity   3
Early Saxon Versions : Bede, Alfred, and others 5, 6
A pause in the work   6

CHAPTER I.

THE MANUSCRIPT ENGLISH BIBLE,

pp. 11—21.

Characteristics of the fourteenth century 11, 12
The Wycliffite Versions   12
Purvey's revision 13, 14
Perils of the work   15
Spirit of the translators   16
The progress of the work checked 17, 18
Manuscripts of the version still remaining 18, 19
The version secretly used in the xvith century . . .   20

CHAPTER II.

THE PRINTED BIBLE: EXTERNAL HISTORY,

pp. 24—121.

Position of the Bible at the beginning of the xvith century . .   24, 25

§ 1. TINDALE, pp. 25—54.

Tindale's early life : residence at London . . . .   25—29
Visits Hamburgh 1524 : Cologne 1525 . . . . .   29, 30
The first *New Testament* finished at Worms in two editions   31—33
Tidings of the work spread 33, 34
Copies of the translation received in England . .   35—37
The English New Testament at Cambridge . . . .   38—40
        „   „   at Oxford . . . .   40—42
Bp. Nix's Complaint   42
Archbp. Warham's assembly   43

	PAGES
Tindale translates the *Pentateuch*, 1530, 1	44
and the book of *Jonah*, 1534	44
Joye's New Testament	45, 46
Tindale's revised New Testament, 1534	47
Q. Anne Boleyn's copy	48
A New Testament printed in England, 1536	48
Tindale's martyrdom, 1536	49
His last revision of the New Testament, 1534, 1535 . .	50
Characteristics of Tindale	52—54

§ 2. COVERDALE, pp. 55—67.

Coverdale's connexion with More and Crumwell	55
His Bible printed, 1535. Different title-pages . . .	56—58
His account of his work	59—61
His Latin-English Testaments	62. 63
Coverdale's first edition not sanctioned by the king . . .	63
A council held by Crumwell (1537) in which the use of Scripture is discussed	64, 65
Coverdale's second edition printed in England, and published (1537) with the king's license	65, 66
The prefatory Prayer to this edition	66, 67

§ 3. MATTHEW (ROGERS), pp. 67—72.

Composite character of this Bible	67
Dedicated to Henry VIII.	69
Cranmer's joy at receiving it	69, 70
Licensed by the king	71

§ 4. THE GREAT BIBLE, pp. 73—83.

The revision undertaken by Coverdale	73
His account of his design	74—76
The commentary finally abandoned	78
Public use of the Bible	79—81
Feeling divided	81—83

§ 5. TAVERNER, pp. 83, 84.

His account of his work	84
Superseded by the Great Bible	84

§ 6. A TIME OF SUSPENSE, pp. 85—89.

The revision of the Bible suspended	85
Edward VI., his devotion to the Bible	86, 87
Sir J. Cheke's translation of St Matthew	88
The reign of Mary	89

§ 7. THE GENEVAN BIBLE, pp. 90—94.

The Genevan Testament (1557), and Psalms (1559) . . .	90, 91
The Bible	91
Becomes the popular English Bible	93
Archbp. Parker's judgment on it	94

§ 8. THE BISHOPS' BIBLE, pp. 95—102.

PAGES

Q. Elizabeth's relation to the English Bible 95, 96
Archbp. Parker plans a new revision 96
  Characteristics of the work 98
  Scholars engaged upon it 99
  Sanctioned for public use by Convocation 100
Displaces the Great Bible 102

§ 9. THE RHEIMS AND DOWAY VERSION, pp. 102—106.

Vernacular Versions of Roman Catholics 102
The English Version of the New Testament 103
The translators and annotators 104
The Old Testament 105

§ 10. THE AUTHORISED VERSION, pp. 107—121.

The English Bible at the accession of James I. 107
  Proposals for a revision 108
  The proposals carried out 110
  Choice of revisers 111
    Their qualifications 114
  Instructions for the revision . . . . 114—116
    The revisers' own account of the work . . . . 116—118
The revised Bible printed 119
A new revision proposed under the Commonwealth . . . 120

CHAPTER III.

THE INTERNAL HISTORY OF THE ENGLISH BIBLE,
pp. 125—278.

Materials available for a translation of the Bible at the beginning
  of the xvith century 126
  Greek, 127; Hebrew, 127; texts and translations . . 128—131

§ 1. TINDALE, pp. 131—161.

Tindale acquainted with Greek and Hebrew 131
  His independence in the New Testament; how far he used
    the Vulgate, 132; Luther, id.; Erasmus 135
  The quarto fragment 137
  His own statement 139, 140
  Comparison of the texts of 1525 and 1534 140
  Glosses of the edition of 1534 141
Revision of 1535 [1534, G. H.] 144
Influence of Luther on Tindale's writings 146
  On the short Prologues 149
  Differences 150

PAGES

Tindale's independence in the Old Testament 153
Revision of lessons from Old Testament 156
His permanent influence 157
Note. *Comparison of readings in Tindale's second and third
revisions* . . . . 158—161

§ 2. COVERDALE, pp. 161—169.

Coverdale's Bible, a secondary translation 161
His Old Testament based on the Zürich Version . . 163
His New Testament a revision of Tindale's 164
The value of his work 164
Note. *Examples of Coverdale's renderings in St Matthew* . . 167—169

§ 3. MATTHEW, pp. 169—179.

His Bible, a composite work, 169, edited by Rogers . . . 171
Jonah taken from Coverdale 171
Tindale's fragmentary translations neglected 175
The New Testament taken from Tindale, 1535 [1534, G. H.] 178

§ 4. THE GREAT BIBLE, pp. 179—207.

The revision of the Old Testament based upon Münster . . 179
Examination of Judges v. 28—30 181
„ Psalm li. 183
„ Psalms xix, xlii. 184
„ Isaiah liii. 186
Different revisions, 1539, 1540 April, 1540 November . . 192, 193
The revision of the New Testament based on Erasmus . . 195
The Vulgate and Complutensian texts used 197
The Psalter retained in the Prayer-Book 108
Note A. *Comparisons of readings in the representative editions of
the Great Bible* 203
Note B. *Various readings in the Psalters of the Great Bible* . 206

§ 5. TAVERNER, pp. 207—211.

Merits of the revision of the New Testament 208
Note. *Characteristic renderings of Taverner* 209

§ 6. THE GENEVAN BIBLE, pp. 212—230.

New Latin and other versions available 212
General character of the Version 214
Examination of 1 Kings iii. 5—10 214
„ Job xix. 23—28 215
„ Isai. ix. 2—7 217
„ Wisd. vii. 15—21, 27—30 219
„ Wisd. viii. 19—21 221
The revision of the New Testament based on Beza . . . 222

PAGES

Examination of Eph. ii. 12—18   224
        „   Rev. ii. 8—11   225
Special readings   227
Notes from the Genevan Bible   229

§ 7. THE BISHOPS' BIBLE, pp. 230—244.

General character of the revision   231
Examination of Isai. liii.   232
        „   Ps. xix.   235
Lawrence's Notes   237
Examination of Eph. iv. 7—16   238
The revision again revised in 1572   241
Notes from the Bishops' Bible   243

§ 8. THE RHEIMS AND DOWAY BIBLE, pp. 245—255.

The plan of the work   245
The peculiar value of the version   249
Specimens of the version : Dan. ix. 18—26   249
        „   „   Isai. ix. 6, 7   251
        „   „   Ps. xix. 8—13   251
        „   „   Ps. lvii. 9—12   252
Latin phrases adopted from it   253
Fidelity of the translators   253

§ 9. THE AUTHORISED VERSION, pp. 255—278.

New materials available   255
Use of the Genevan and Rhemish Versions 257, 273
Examination of Isai. liii.   258
        „   Wisd. vii. 15—21, 27—30   262
        „   the marginal renderings in Malachi . .   264
Revision of the New Testament   266
Examination of Hebr. xiii. 5—16   267
Use of Beza   269
Examination of the marginal renderings in St Mark . .   270
        „   changes in 1 John   272
General characteristics   274
Note. *Comparison of renderings in the Bishops' and Authorised
        Versions*   276

CONCLUSION.

pp. 279—284.

The different versions recognized in the Prayer-Book . . .   279
The English Bible compared with the Vulgate . . .   281
Words of the Translators   282

APPENDICES.

pp. 285—352.

		PAGES
I.	Specimens of the earlier and later Wycliffite Versions .	287
II.	Chronological List of Bibles	290
III.	Collation of 1 John in the three texts of Tindale . .	295
IV.	An examination of the sources of Coverdale's Notes .	298
V.	Specimen of notes from Tindale and Matthew . . .	306
VI.	Specimens of the Latin-English Testaments of Coverdale .	308
VII.	Passages from the Pentateuch and Historical Books in Tindale, &c.	311
VIII.	The relation of the Wycliffite to later Versions . .	316
IX.	The Revision of the Authorised Version	320
X.	Phrases in the Psalms marked in the Psalter of the Great Bible as additions from the Vulgate	333
XI.	Sources of the notes in Matthew's Bible	336
XII.	Notes on the Translators of the Authorised Version .	342
XIII	Rules for the translation of the Authorised Version reported to the Synod of Dort	351
	INDEX	353

INTRODUCTION.

THEN the boy sprang up from his knees, and ran,
Stung by the splendour of a sudden thought,
And fetched the seventh plate of graven lead
Out of the secret chamber, found a place,
Pressing with finger on the deeper dints,
And spoke, as 'twere his mouth proclaiming first,
'I am the Resurrection and the Life.

Whereat he opened his eyes wide at once,
And sat up of himself, and looked at us;
And thenceforth nobody pronounced a word:
Only, outside, the Bactrian cried his cry
Like the lone desert-bird that wears the ruff,
As signal he were safe, from time to time.

BROWNING, *Dramatis Personæ, A Death in the Desert.*

INTRODUCTION.

THERE is a famous saying, which dates from the times of persecution, that 'the blood of Martyrs is the seed of the 'Church.' It may be added in the like spirit that the voice of Holy Scripture is the spring and measure of individual faith. Both statements require to be modified in their application; but it remains generally true that the society which is founded by human devotion and labour, is quickened in its several members by the influence of the Word. So it is that the history of the vernacular Scriptures is in a great measure the history of personal faith. A people which is without a Bible in its mother tongue, or is restrained from using it, or wilfully neglects it, is also imperfect, or degenerate, or lifeless in its apprehension of Christian Truth, and proportionately bereft of the strength which flows from a living Creed.

In the first ages of the Church the translation of the Scriptures followed immediately on the introduction of Christianity to a nation of a new language. When the Gospel spread eastwards, a Syriac translation of the New Testament was one of the first monuments of its power. When it spread westwards, a Latin version preceded, as far as we know, all other literary efforts of the African Church. Ulfilas, the second bishop of the Goths, gave them the Scriptures in their own language. Miesrob, the framer of the Armenian alphabet, was the translator of the Armenian Bible; and the Slavonic version was due in part at least to the two brothers, Cyrillus and Methodius, who first reduced the Slavonic dialect to writing. The history of the Æthiopic and Egyptian Scriptures is probably similar, though it is more obscure; and it is most significant, that of these ancient versions, the greater part survive substantially the same in the public services of the nations which occupy the places of those for whom they were originally composed.

The original versions of Holy Scripture remain, but all else is changed. If we fix our eyes on the west only, we see the new-won empire of the Church desolated almost as soon as it was gained, by successive hordes of barbarian invaders, out of whom she was destined in the Providence of God to shape the forefathers of modern Europe. In less than ten years after Jerome completed his version of the Old Testament from the Hebrew (A.D. 400—404), Alaric took Rome (A.D. 410). Thenceforward a fresh work was to be achieved by Christianity, and by a new method. For a time the normal processes of Christianity were in abeyance: organization prevailed over faith. These new races were to be disciplined by act before they could be taught by the simple word. Thus the task of the translation of Scripture among the northern nations was suspended. The Latin Vulgate sufficed for the teachers, and they ministered to their congregations such lessons from it as they could receive.

But as soon as society was again settled, the old instinct asserted itself, and first, which is a just cause of pride, in our own island. As early as the eighth century, the Psalms were rendered into Anglo-Saxon; and about the same time, Bede, during his last illness, translated the Gospel of St John.

The narrative of the completion of this work is given by an eye-witness, Cuthbert, a scholar of Bede, in a letter to a fellow-scholar, and is in itself so beautiful a picture of the early monastic life, that it may be quoted in abstract. Bede had been ill for some weeks. About Easter (A.D. 735), he felt that his end was approaching, and looked forward to it with ceaseless gratitude, 'rejoicing that he was counted 'worthy thus to suffer.' He quoted much from Holy Scripture; and one fragment of Saxon poetry, which he recited and may have composed, was taken down by Cuthbert[1]. But he was chiefly busy with two English translations of Excerpts from Isidore, and of the Gospel of St John. Ascension-day drew near. His illness increased, but he only laboured the more diligently. On the Wednesday, his scribe told him that one chapter alone remained, but feared that it might be painful to him to dictate. 'It is 'easy,' Bede replied, 'take your pen and write quickly.' The work was continued for some time. Then Bede directed Cuthbert to fetch his little treasures from his casket (capsella), 'pepper, scarves (oraria) and incense,' that he might distribute them among his friends. And so he passed the remainder of the day till evening in holy and cheerful conversation. His boy-scribe at last found an opportunity to remind him, with pious importunity, of his unfinished task: 'One sentence, dear master, still remains 'unwritten.' 'Write quickly,' he answered. The boy soon said, 'It is completed now.' 'Well,' Bede replied, 'thou hast said the truth : all is ended. Take my head 'in thy hands, I would sit in the holy place in which 'I was wont to pray, that so sitting I may call upon 'my Father.' Thereupon, resting upon the floor of his cell, he chanted the *Gloria*, and his soul immediately passed away, while the name of the Holy Spirit was on his lips[2].

In the next century Alfred prefixed to his laws a translation of the Ten Commandments, and a few other fragments from the book of Exodus; and is said to have been engaged on a version of the Psalms at the time of his death (A.D. 901). In the tenth century, or a little later, the

---

[1] The original is given in Gale, *Hist. Angl. Script.* I. 152, and by Wright, *Biographia Literaria*, I. p. 21, from whom I borrow a literal translation · 'Before the necessary 'journey no one becomes more prudent 'of thought than is needful to him, to 'search out before his going hence what 'to his spirit of good or of evil after 'his death hence will be judged.'

[2] Cuthbert's letter is given in Bede's *Eccles. Hist.* Præf. c. ii. Tom. VI. p. 15, ed. Migne.

four Gospels were translated apparently for public use; and two interlinear translations, probably of an earlier date, into other English dialects, are preserved in Latin Manuscripts, which shew at least individual zeal[1]. Of the Old Testament, the Pentateuch, Joshua, Judges, Esther, and parts of other books were translated about the tenth century. All these translations, with the possible exception of Bede's[2], were only secondary translations from the Latin, but none the less they reveal the thoughts with which men's hearts were stirred. And there was no hindrance to their execution. On the contrary, the number of the labourers who took part in the work shews that it was of wide popularity.

But the effort was as yet premature. England had still to receive a new element of her future strength; and for her the time of discipline was not over. The Norman invasion, which brought with it the fruits of Romanic thought and culture, checked for a while the spontaneous development of religious life. Nevertheless fragmentary translations of Scripture into Norman-French shew that the Bible was popularly studied, and in the end the nation was

---

[1] One of these noble MSS. is in the British Museum (the Lindisfarne (St Cuthbert's) Gospels, *Cotton*, Nero, D. IV.); and the other is in the Bodleian (the Rushworth (Mac Regol's) Gospels, *Bodl.* D. 24 (now *Auct.* D. II. 19)). I am not acquainted with any satisfactory description of the MSS. of the common Anglo-Saxon Version; nor yet with any general account of the relation in which the several copies stand to one another. In this respect Thorpe's edition is most unsatisfactory. Three distinct types of the text of St Matthew with various readings from four other manuscripts have been published by Mr C. Hardwick (Cambridge, 1858), who so far finished the work begun by Mr J. M. Kemble. At present Mr W. W. Skeat is engaged on

completing an edition of the four Gospels, which will supply the critical introduction in which Mr Hardwick's work is wholly deficient. [Professor Skeat edited St Mark in 1871, St Luke in 1874, St John in 1878, and re-edited St Matthew in 1887. The MSS. are described in the Preface to the Gospel of St Mark.]

[2] Bede at least was acquainted with Greek, and in his *Retractationes* (*Act. Ap. Præf.*) he notices the variations of a Greek manuscript of the Acts which he had collated from the ordinary Latin text. From the readings cited there is every reason to believe that his manuscript was the Græco-Latin copy of the Acts in the Bodleian known as the *Codex Laudianus* (E_2). Compare Mill, *N. T. Prolegg.* 1022 ff.

richer by the delay[1]. Nor may it be forgotten even in this
relation that the insularity of the people furthered its
characteristic growth ; for while it remained outside the
Roman Empire yet it shared in the spiritual strength which
came at that time from an intimate union with the Roman
See. Thus the nation preserved throughout its progress
the features of its peculiar constitution, and at the same
time was brought within the influence of Catholic discipline
and sympathy. It would be out of place to follow out here
the action and reaction of these special and general powers
upon the English type of mediæval Christianity ; but the
recognition of their simultaneous working is necessary for
the understanding of the history of the English Bible. For
three centuries they acted with various and beneficent
results. At length in the 14th century the preparatory
work of the Papacy was ended and its dissolution commenced. The many nations and the many churches began
from that time to define their separate peculiarities and
functions. The time of maturity was now ready to follow
on the time of tutelage : a free development was sufficiently
prepared by a long discipline[2].

It is then at this point that the history of the English
Bible properly commences, a history which is absolutely
unique in its course and in its issue. And this history is
twofold. There is the external history of the different

---

[1] [The Canterbury Psalter (12th
cent.) in the Library of Trinity College, Cambridge, contains interlinear
translations in Anglo-Saxon and
Norman-French. The former of
these is written between the lines of
the Roman Psalter, and was edited
for the Early English Text Society
in 1889 by Mr F. Harsley. The
latter accompanies what is known
as Jerome's Hebrew Version, and
was edited in 1876 by M. Francisque
Michel, who had previously (1860)
edited another version from a MS.
in the Bodleian Library. Sir John
Spelman in 1640 published an edition
of the Anglo-Saxon Psalter from a MS.
in the possession of his father, with
the readings of three other copies.]

[2] No notice has been taken of the
metrical paraphrases and summaries
of parts of Scripture, as that of Cæd-
mon († c. 680) on parts of Genesis,
Exodus, and Daniel; of Orm (c.
1150) on the Gospels and the Acts;
and the 'Sowlehele' (c. 1250). These,
though they paved the way for translations of the Bible, cannot be reck-
oned among them. [See *Biblical
Quotations* in *Old English Prose
Writers*, by Professor A. S. Cook.
Two Series, 1898—1903.]

versions, as to when and by whom and under what circumstances they were made ; and there is the internal history
which deals with their relation to other texts, with their
filiation one on another, and with the principles by which
they have been successively modified. The external history
is a stirring record of faithful and victorious courage : the
internal history is not less remarkable from the enduring
witness which it bears to that noble catholicity which is the
glory of the English Church.

CHAPTER I.

THE MANUSCRIPT BIBLE.

Another race hath been and other palms are won.

WORDSWORTH, *Ode: Intimations of Immortality.*

CHAPTER I.

THE MANUSCRIPT BIBLE.

THE external history of the English Bible may be divided into two periods of not very unequal length, the first extending from the beginning of Wycliffe's labours to the publication of Tindale's New Testament in 1525, the second from that date to the completion of our present received version in 1611. The first of these will be the subject of the present chapter.

It has been already said that the 14th century was the first stage in the dissolution of the mediæval Church. Its character was marked by the corruption of the higher clergy, and the growth of independence in the masses of the people. Both facts favoured an appeal from custom and tradition to the written and unchanging Word. Moreover the last great progressive effort for the restoration of the Church—the establishment of the mendicant orders—had failed, but not before the people had been roused by the appeals which were addressed to them. Touched by a feeling of anxious suspense men turned with intense longing to the Bible, and in the first instance naturally to the Psalter, which has been in every age the fresh spring of hope in times of trial. Of this no less than three English versions in prose, dating from the first half of the 14th century, have been preserved[1]. But the work of

---

[1] Of these the most important is that by Richard Rolle, Hermit of Hampole. [The three MSS. mentioned by Lewis (*Hist. of Eng. Tr. of the Bible*, pp. 12—15) are apparently varieties of Richard Rolle's Psalter and Com-

translation did not long stop here. The years from 1345 to 1349 were full of calamities—pestilence and famine and war—which seemed to men already deeply stirred by the sight of spiritual evils to portend the end of the world. Other commotions followed not long afterwards which shewed the widespread disorganization of society. In France there was the terrible rising of the Jacquerie (1358); in Italy the momentary triumph and fall of Rienzi (1347—1354); a great schism (1378—1417) divided the forces of the Church; and Adrianople became (1360) the capital of a Turkish Empire in Europe built on the ruins of a Christian power.

In the meantime the general belief that some awful crisis was at hand found expression in England in the Tract on the *Last Age of the Church* (1356), which has been commonly though wrongly attributed to Wycliffe; and Wycliffe himself must have been influenced by a like expectation when he chose the Apocalypse as the subject of his first labours on the Bible. His translation of the Apocalypse was soon followed by a translation of the Gospels with a commentary, and at a later time by versions of the remaining books of the New Testament with a fresh rendering of the Apocalypse, so that a complete English New Testament was finished about 1380. To this a version of the Old Testament was soon added, which appears to have been undertaken by a friend of Wycliffe's, Nicholas de Hereford. The original manuscript of Nicholas is still preserved in the Bodleian, and offers a curious memorial of his fortunes. For having incurred the displeasure of his superiors, he was cited to appear in London in 1382, to answer for his opinions. He was excommunicated, and

mentary. This was edited in 1884 by the Rev. H. R. Bramley, and in 1895-6 other treatises by Rolle were published by C. Horstman. In 1891 Dr Karl Bülbring edited for the Early English Text Society *The Earliest Complete English Psalter* in the West Midland Dialect from two 14th cent. MSS. (Brit. Mus. Add. 17376, and Trinity College, Dublin, MS. A. 4. 4), and in 1904 Miss Paues published *A Fourteenth Century English Biblical Version*, containing portions of the New Testament, from 14th cent. MSS.]

left England shortly afterward, breaking off his translation
in the middle of Baruch (iii. 20), where the manuscript
ends abruptly.   The work was afterwards completed, as it
is supposed, by Wycliffe, who thus before he died in 1384
had the joy of seeing his hope fulfilled and the Scriptures
circulated in various forms among his countrymen.

Like the earlier Saxon translations, Wycliffe's translation was made from the Latin Vulgate, and from the text
commonly current in the 14th century, which was far from
pure.   It was also so exactly literal that in many places
the meaning was obscure.   The followers of Wycliffe were
not blind to these defects, and within a few years after his
death a complete revision of the Bible was undertaken by
John Purvey, who had already become notorious for his
opinions, and had shared in the disgrace of Nicholas de
Hereford[1].

Purvey has left, in a general Prologue, an interesting
account of the method on which he proceeded in his
revision, which is marked by singular sagacity and judgment.   He had, as will be seen, clear conceptions of the
duties of the critic and of the translator, and the comparison
of his work with Wycliffe's shews that he was not unable
to carry out the design which he formed.   After enumer-
ating several obvious motives for undertaking his task, he
continues : ' For these resons and othere, with comune
' charite to saue alle men in oure rewme, whiche God wole
' haue savid, a symple creature [so he calls himself] hath
' translatid the bible out of Latyn into English.   First, this
' symple creature hadde myche trauaile, with diuerse
' felawis and helperis, to gedere manie elde biblis, and
' othere doctouris, and comune glosis, and to make oo
' Latyn bible sumdel [somewhat] trewe[2]; and thanne to

---

[1] Purvey's copy is still preserved
at Dublin.   The Latin MSS. which
Purvey used exhibit many different
readings from Wycliffe's, but they
are not different in character.   Both
translations contain the interpolations
in the books of Samuel. *e.g.* 1 Sam.

v. 6, x. 1, &c.
[2] The collation of manuscripts must
have been very partial and scanty.
Thus in 1 John ii. 14 all the copies of
Purvey's translation read ' *brithren*,'
i.e. fratres for *patres*, a blunder of
which I can find no trace in Bentley's

'studie it of the newe, the text with the glosse...; the
'thridde tyme to counseile with elde gramariens...; the iiij.
'tyme to translate as cleerli as he code to the sentence
'[sense], and to haue manie gode felawis and kunnynge at
'the correcting of the translacioun. First it is to knowe,
'that the best translating is...to translate after the sentence,
'and not oneli aftir the wordis, so that the sentence be as
'opin, either openere, in English as in Latyn, and go not
'fer from the lettre...In translating into English, many
'resolucions moun [may] make the sentence open, as an
'ablatif case absolute may be resoluid into these thre
'words, with couenable [suitable] verbe, *the while, for, if...*
'and...*whanne*...Also a participle of a present tens...mai
'be resoluid into a verbe of the same tens, and a coniunc-
'cioun copulatif...Also a relatif, which mai be resoluid
'into his antecedent with a coniunccioun copulatif...Also
'whanne riȝtful construccioun is lettid [hindered] bi rela-
'cion, I resolue it openli: thus where...*Dominum formi-*
'*dabunt adversarij ejus* shulde be Englishid thus bi the
'lettre, *the Lord hise aduersaries shulen drede*, I Englishe it
'thus bi resolucioun, *the aduersaries of the Lord shulen*
'*drede him*...At the bigynnyng I purposide, with Goddis
'helpe, to make the sentence as trewe and open in English
'as it is in Latyn, either more trewe and more open than it
'is in Latyn; and I preie, for charite and for comoun
'profyt of cristene soulis, that if ony wiys man fynde ony
'defaute of the truthe of translacioun, let him sette in the
'trewe sentence and opin of holi writ...for...the comune
'Latyn biblis haue more nede to be correctid, as manie as
'I haue seen in my lif, than hath the English Bible late
'translatid[1].'...As might be expected the revised text dis-

collations of English MSS. of the Vulgate. The clause is omitted by Wycliffe, as by many Latin MSS.

[1] *Prologue*, c. xv. p. 57. Mr Froude's statement (which is retained in his last edition, 1870) that the second version, based upon Wycliffe's, was 'tinted more strongly with the 'peculiar opinions of the Lollards,' is, as far as I have compared the two, wholly without foundation. The differences are exactly those which the Prologue describes. It need not be said that it was not made 'at the 'beginning of the fifteenth century' (*History of England*, III. p. 77). [The Lollard opinions are in Purvey's *Prologue*, not in his version.]

placed the original version, and in spite of its stern pro-
scription in a convocation in 1408 under the influence of
Archbishop Arundel[1], it was widely circulated through all
classes till it was at last superseded by the printed versions
of the 16th century[2].

But this first triumph of the English Bible was not
won without a perilous struggle. One or two contemporary
notices of the state of feeling over which it was achieved
and of that again out of which it sprung are of deep
interest. Thus a scholar writes when asked to teach the
ignorant the contents of the Gospel: 'Brother, I knowe
'wel that I am holde by Crystis lawe to parforme thyn
'axinge, bote natheles we beth now so fer yfallen awey
'fram Cristis lawe, that if Y wolde answere to thyn axingus
'I moste in cas vnderfonge the deth; and thu wost wel,
'that a man is yholden to kepe his lyf as longe as he
'may[3].' Many think it amiss, says Wycliffe, 'that men
'schulden knowe Cristus lyfe, for thenne prestus schullen
'schome of hyre lyues, and specyaly these hye prestus, and

---

[1] See p. 17.

[2] The translation included all the
Apocryphal Books except 2 Esdras.
The *Epistle to the Laodicenes* was not
included in Wycliffe's or Purvey's
translation, but was added afterwards
in some MSS. The texts of the
original translation and of the revision are generally uniform.

It is scarcely necessary to add that
Sir T. More's statement that 'the
' Holy Bible was translated [into En-
'glish] long before Wycliffe's days' is
not supported by the least independent
evidence. He may have seen a MS.
of Wycliffe's version, and (like Lambert, see p. 24) have miscalculated
the date. Bp. Bonner (for instance)
had a copy [now at Lambeth], and
there was a fine one at the Charterhouse [now in the Bodleian]. See
p. 19. Compare Tindale's *Answer
to More*, III. p. 168 (Parker Soc. ed.).
[In Dec. 1868 Henry Bradshaw

wrote to Dr Westcott: ' There is one
' thing that I could wish you had
' mentioned in your first chapter, for
' though I have never seen it remarked
' anywhere, it has long struck me as
'being very remarkable; I mean the
' apparent fact that the English Wy-
' cliffite version seems so much to
' have superseded the Latin. I have
' examined scores of English copies of
' Latin Bibles, and I have never seen
' a XVth century copy, never a copy
' which could be put later in execution
' than the completion of the English
' version. I dare say there are such
' copies, but I don't think my ex-
' perience is likely to be exceptional,
' and as such it is a thing worth noting
' in the history of the English Bible,
' as showing how little effect the pro-
' scription had.']

[3] Forshall and Madden, *Wycliffe's
Bible*, Pref. p. xv. n.

'for they reuersen Crist bothe in worde and in dede. Yet there was a vigorous party to which the reformers could trust. 'On comfort,' he adds, 'is of knyghtes, that they 'saueren muche [care much for] the gospel, and haue wylle 'to rede in Englysche the gospel of Cristys lyf[1].' But the fear of death and the power of enemies could not prevail against the spirit in which the work was wrought.

'Cristen men,' one says, 'owe moche to traueile ny3t 'and day aboute text of holy writ, and namely the gospel 'in her modir tunge, sithe Jhesu Crist, very God and very 'man, tau3t this gospel with his owne blessid mouth and 'kept it in his lyf[2].' 'I besek and with alle my hert pray 'them that this werk redyn,' writes Wycliffe, in the preface to his *Harmony of the Gospels*, 'that for me thei pray the 'mercy of God, that I may fulfylle that is set in the 'draghing of this boke ; and that he at whos suggestyon 'I this werke began, and thei that [this] werk redyn, and 'alle cristen men with me, thurgh doynge of that that is 'wrytyn in this bok, may com to geder to that blisse 'that neuer salle ende[3].' And Purvey when he revised Wycliffe's work knew well what was required of the interpreter of Scripture. 'He hath nede to liue a clene 'lif, and be ful deuout in preiers, and haue not his wit 'ocupied about worldli thingis, that the Holi Spiryt, Autour 'of wisdom, and kunnyng [knowledge], and truthe, dresse 'him in his werk and suffre him not for to erre...Bi this 'maner,' he concludes, 'with good liuyng and greet traueil, 'men moun come to trewe and cleer translating, and trewe 'vndurstonding of holi writ, seme it neuere so hard at the 'bigynnyng. God grante to us alle grace to kenne wel, 'and kepe wel holi writ, and *suffre* ioiefulli sum peyne for 'it at the laste[4].'

The last words were not allowed to remain without fulfilment. As long as the immediate influence of Wycliffe lasted the teaching of his followers was restrained within reasonable bounds. Times of anarchy and violence fol-

---

[1] *Wycliffe's Bible*, l. c.
[2] Id. p. xiv. n.
[3] Id. p. x. n.
[4] Id. Prologue, p. 60.

lowed, and spiritual reform was confounded with the destruction of society. The preachers of the Bible gave occasion to their enemies to identify them with the enemies of order; and the reestablishment of a strong government led to the enactment of the statute *De hæretico comburendo* (2 Hen. IV), which was soon put in force as a powerful check on heresy. It is impossible to determine whether the Wycliffite Bible was among 'the books' mentioned in the preamble of the act by which the Lollards were said to excite the people to sedition[1]. Later parallels make it likely that it was so; but it was not long before the Version was directly assailed.

In a convocation of the province of Canterbury held at Oxford under Archbishop Arundel in 1408, several constitutions were enacted against the party of the Reformation. The one on the use of the vernacular Scriptures is important both in form and substance. 'It is a danger-'ous thing,' so it runs, 'as witnesseth blessed St Jerome, 'to translate the text of the holy Scripture out of one 'tongue into another; for in the translation the same 'sense is not always easily kept, as the same St Jerome 'confesseth, that *although he were inspired* (etsi inspiratus 'fuisset), yet oftentimes in this he erred; we therefore 'decree and ordain that no man hereafter by his own 'authority (auctoritate suâ) translate any text of the 'Scripture into English or any other tongue, by way of 'a book, pamphlet, or treatise; and that no man read any 'such book, pamphlet, or treatise, now lately composed 'in the time of John Wycliffe or since, or hereafter to be 'set forth in part or in whole, publicly or privately, upon 'pain of greater excommunication, until the said trans-'lation be approved by the ordinary of the place, or, if 'the case so require, by the council provincial. He that 'shall do contrary to this shall likewise be punished as 'a favourer of heresy and error[2].'

---

[1] The preamble is quoted by Mr Froude, *History of England*, II. 20.
[2] Foxe, *Acts and Monuments*, III. 245 (whose translation I have generally followed). The original Latin is given in Wilkins' *Concilia*, III. 317.

Four years after came the insurrection and death of Sir John Oldcastle. A new and more stringent act was passed against heresy (2 Hen. V), and the Lollards as a party were destroyed. But the English Bible survived their destruction. The terms of the condemnation under Archbishop Arundel were explicit, but it was practically ineffectual. No such approbation as was required, so far as we know, was ever granted, but the work was still transcribed for private use ; and the manuscripts are themselves the best records of its history[1].

Of about one hundred and seventy copies of the whole or part of the Wycliffite versions which have been examined, fifteen of the Old Testament and eighteen of the New belong to the original version. The remainder are of Purvey's revision, which itself has in some very rare cases undergone another partial revision. Of these not one-fifth are of an earlier date than Arundel's condemnation[2]. The greater part appear to have been written between 1420 and 1450 ; and what is a more interesting fact, nearly half the copies are of a small size, such as could be made the constant daily companions of their owners. Others again are noticeable for the rank of those by whom they were once possessed. One belonged to Humphrey, the 'good' duke of Gloucester[3]: another to Henry VI, who gave it to the Charterhouse[4]: another (apparently) to Richard III[5]; another to Henry VII (?), another to Edward VI[6]; and another was presented to Queen Eliza-

---

[1] Two names however are connected too closely with Wycliffe to be omitted altogether. John of Gaunt vigorously supported Wycliffe in his endeavours to circulate an English version of the Bible, and after his death successfully opposed a Bill brought into the House of Lords, 1390, to forbid the circulation of the Scriptures in English (*Hist. Acc.* p. 33). Anne of Bohemia also, according to the testimony of Archbishop Arundel, 'constantly studied the four 'Gospels in English' (Foxe, III. 202,

ed. Townshend). The subsequent conduct of Arundel is not inconsistent with the belief that this version was Wycliffe's.

[2] [In a copy of the New Testament in the Library of Emmanuel College, Cambridge, there is a note ' Finished ' 1382, this copy taken 1397.']

[3] [Brit. Mus. Eg. MSS. 617, 618.]

[4] [Bodl. 2249.]

[5] [Forshall and Madden, Pref. p. lxiii.]

[6] This copy is now in the University Library at Cambridge (Mm. II. 15),

beth as a new-year's gift by her chaplain[1]. There are yet
other copies with interest of a different kind[2]. One probably was that of Bp. Bonner[3]: another records in a hand
of the 16th century, that 'this ancient monyment of holy
'scripture dothe show, how the Lord God in all ages and
'tymes wold haue his blessed woorde preserved for the
'comforte of his elect children and church in all tymes
'and ages, in despyte of Sathane[4].'

and R. Crowley printed from it the
General Prologue in 1550, 'the
'Originall whereof is founde written
'in an olde English Bible,' so he
writes on the title-page, 'bitwixt the
'olde Testament and the Newe.
'Whych Bible remaynith now in ye
'Kyng his maiesties Chamber.'

The book retains a binding apparently of the age of Edward VI,
which bears stamped on one side
Verbum Domini and on the other
manet in aeternum.

Part of Crowley's notice to the
reader is worthy of being quoted:
'[This Prologue] was at ye fyrste
'made common to fewe men yt wolde
'and were able to optayn it. But
'nowe it is made commen to all
'menne, that be desyrouse of it.
'Forget not therfore, [gentle reader,]
'to take it thanckfully, to vse it
'Christenly, and to esteme it of no
'lesse value than a most preciouse
'iewell, fyrst framed by the Diuine
'wisdome of gods spirite poured vpon
'the fyrste Autoure, preserued by
'goddis mercyfull prouidence, and
'nowe offered vnto the by God hym-
'selfe, that thou hongring the perfecte
'knowledge of goddis worde shuldest
'not be destitutid of so necessarye a
'meane to attayne to the same.'

[1] [Forshall and Madden, Pref.
p. xxxix.]

[2] [In the Chapter Library, Westminster, there is a copy, written
about 1450, which was given by the
Duchess of Richmond, Surrey's sister,
to Henry Fitz Alan, Earl of Arundel,
and by him in September, 1576, to
Richard Wiclif. In the Wardrobe
Accounts of Edward IV (1480) there
is an item for binding his Bible, but
nothing to shew whether it was Latin
or English, or possibly French.]

[3] [Lambeth 25.]

[4] [Forshall and Madden, Pref. p.
lx.] But it must be observed that in
spite of the wide circulation of the
English Version the Latin Vulgate
remained the Bible of those who
could read, just as afterwards in
Cranmer's time. One interesting memorial of this remains. The 'Per-
'sones Tale' in Chaucer (c. 1386—
1390) abounds in passages of the Bible
in English. The Latin 'catch-word'
is very rarely given; and in no one
case have I observed a real coincidence
with either of the Wycliffite versions.
On the contrary, the renderings differ
from them more than might have been
expected in contemporary versions of
the same Latin text; and the same
text (*e.g.* Acts iv. 12) is turned differently in different places. One or two
examples are worth quoting.
'Allas! I caytif man, who shal
'delivere me fro the prisoun of my
'caytif body?' (Rom. vii. 24).
'An avaricious man is in the thral-
'dom of idolatrie' (Eph. v. 5).
'Go, quod Iesu Crist, and have na-
'more wil to sinne' (John viii. 11).

Thus the books themselves speak to us and witness of the work which they did[1]. In fact, they help us to understand Foxe's famous testimony that in 1520...'great 'multitudes...tasted and followed the sweetness of God's 'holy Word almost in as ample manner, for the number 'of well-disposed hearts, as now...Certes, the fervent zeal 'of those Christian days seemed much superior to these 'our days and times, as manifestly may appear by their 'sitting up all night in reading and hearing; also by 'their expenses and charges in buying of books in English, 'of whom some gave five marks [equal to about £40 in 'our money], some more, some less for a book: some gave 'a load of hay for a few chapters of St James or of St 'Paul in English...To see their travails, their earnest seek- 'ings, their burning zeal, their readings, their watchings, 'their sweet assemblies...may make us now in these days 'of free profession, to blush for shame[2].' So Foxe wrote in 1563, and after three centuries the contrast is still to our sorrow[3].

[1] The editors of the Versions quote two instances of copies given to churches for ecclesiastical use at York (1394) and Bristol (1404): Forshall and Madden, Pref. p. xxxii. n.

[The Wycliffite origin of the translation of the Bible was never seriously questioned till, in an article on the Pre-Reformation English Bible in the *Dublin Review* for July, 1894, Father (now Abbot) Gasquet propounded the theory that the so-called Wycliffite Version was· in reality the orthodox version mentioned by Sir Thomas More and others, which was sanctioned by the Church and the use of which was conditionally permitted. This view was subjected to criticism by Mr F. D. Mathew in the *English Historical Review* for January, 1895, by Dr F. G. Kenyon in *Our Bible and the Ancient Manuscripts*, 1895, and by a writer in the *Church Quarterly Review* for October, 1900,

and January, 1901, with the result that the Wycliffite origin of the translations which came into existence in the 14th century has been reestablished. Abbot Gasquet has no doubt brought into greater prominence the fact that the version was found where it could hardly have been except by express permission of the Church, but it is remarkable that notwithstanding such permission it was never allowed to be printed. Perhaps this may have been because some taint of Wycliffite heresy was believed to be attached to it. In Germany, France, Italy, and Spain, translations from the Vulgate into the vernacular languages of those countries existed many years before the Reformation.]

[2] Foxe, *Acts and Monuments*, IV. 217 f.

[3] [The later of the Wycliffite Versions of the New Testament was printed by Lewis in 1731, and re-

printed by Baber in 1810. The earlier version was published by Pickering in 1848 from a MS. in the possession of Mr Lea Wilson and afterwards in the collection of Lord Ashburnham. The text in Bagster's *Hexapla* (1841) is of the later version, from a MS. which belonged successively to the Duke of Sussex, Mr Lea Wilson. and the Earl of Ashburnham. But the great authority on the subject of the Wycliffite translations is the monumental work of Forshall and Madden in four volumes quarto, Oxford, 1850, which contains both versions of the Old and New Testaments and Apocrypha, with an elaborate critical apparatus, preface, and glossary. Reprints from this edition of the New Testament (1879) and of the Poetical Books, Job—Song of Solomon (1881), were edited for the Clarendon Press by Professor Skeat.]

CHAPTER II.

THE PRINTED BIBLE.

This is the doctrine simple, ancient, true;
  Such is life's trial, as old earth smiles and knows.
If you loved only what were worth your love,
Love were clear gain and wholly well for you:
  Make the low nature better by your throes!
Give earth yourself, go up for gain above!

BROWNING, *Dramatis Personæ, James Lee's Wife*, VII. 2.

CHAPTER II.

THE PRINTED BIBLE.

THE general testimony of Foxe to the circulation of the English Scriptures at the beginning of the 16th century, which has been just quoted, is illustrated by several special incidents, which he records. These, however, shew at the same time that the circulation and study of the manuscripts was both precarious and perilous. 'I did once,' says Lambert in 1538, 'see a booke of the Newe Testamēt '(which was not vnwryttē by my estimation this C. yeres) 'and in my minde right wel translate after thexample of 'that which is red in the Church in Laten. But he that 'shewed it me said, he durst not be known to haue it by 'him, for many hadde bene punished afore time for keping 'of such as conuict of heresy[1].' And that this fear was not ungrounded may be seen by the registers of the dioceses of Norwich and Lincoln, which contain several examples of men charged before the bishops with the offence of reading or perusing 'the New Law' (that is, the New Testament) in English[2].

But meanwhile a momentous change had passed over Western Europe. 'Greece,' in the striking language of an English scholar, 'had risen from the grave with the New 'Testament in her hand'; and the Teutonic nations had welcomed the gift. It had been long felt on all sides that

---

[1] Foxe, *Acts and Monuments*, v. 213. I have quoted from the text of the edition 1563 (March 20: ? 1564), p. 559.

[2] Foxe, *ib*. IV. 217 ff.

the Latin Bible of the mediæval Church could no longer satisfy the wants of the many nations of a divided world Before the end of the 15th century Bibles were printed in Spanish, Italian, French, Dutch, German and Bohemian ; while England as yet had only the few manuscripts of the Wycliffite versions.   But, like Wycliffe's, these were only secondary versions from the Vulgate.   The Hebrew text of the Old Testament was published as early as 1488, though very few except Jews could use it ; but the Greek text of the New Testament was not yet printed. Scholars however were being duly trained for the work of direct translation.   The passionate declamation then current against Hebrew and Greek shews that the study of both was popular and advancing[1].   And England, though late to begin, eagerly followed up the 'new learning[2].' From 1509 to 1514 Erasmus was Professor of Greek at Cambridge, and, as appears probable, it was the fame of his lectures which drew there William Tindale about the year 1510[3], to whom it has been allowed more than to any other man to give its characteristic shape to our English Bible.   And the man, as we shall see, was not unworthy of the glorious honour for the attainment of which indeed he lived equally and died.

§ 1   TINDALE.

With Tindale the history of our present English Bible begins[4] ; and for fifteen years the history of the Bible is almost identical with the history of Tindale.   The fortunes of both if followed out in detail are even of romantic interest.   Of the early life of Tindale we know nothing.

[1] See Chap. III.

[2] According to Erasmus, England was second only to Italy and in advance of France and Germany.   Erasmus himself studied Greek at Oxford. Compare Hallam, *Introduction to Lit. of Europe*, I. pp. 269 f.

[3] [This is not now so probable since the discovery of an entry in the Oxford Register by which it appears that William Hichyns, who is supposed to be Tindale, took his M.A. degree in 1515.]

[4] See Appendix VIII.

He was born about 1484[1], at an obscure village in Gloucestershire[2], and 'brought up from a child,' as Foxe says, in the University of Oxford, where he was 'singularly 'addicted to the study of the Scriptures[3].' From Oxford he went to Cambridge, and after spending some time there, as we have noticed, he returned about 1520 to his native county as tutor in the family of Sir John Walsh of Little Sodbury.   Here he spent two years, not without many controversies, in one of which he made his memorable declaration to 'a learned man' who 'said we were 'better be without God's laws than the Pope's': 'I defy 'the Pope and all his laws'; and said, 'If God spare my 'life, ere many years I will cause a boy that driveth the 'plough shall know more of the Scripture than thou 'doest[4].'   The boast was not an idle phrase.   Erasmus,

[1] [Probably later.] The dates in Tindale's life up to his coming to London in 1522-3 are fixed only approximately and by conjecture. There is no adequate external evidence to determine them exactly, but the amount of error cannot be great.   I may refer by anticipation to a promised *Life of Tyndale* by the Rev. R. Demaus [published in 1871], as certain to exhaust all the information on the subject which is left to us.

[2] The exact place is uncertain, but it was near Nibley Knoll, one of the Cotswold hills, on which a monument has lately been erected to his memory. Mr F. Fry informs me that 'there 'are Tindales now in those parts'; and further that 'Hunt's Court, 'where Tindale is said to have been 'born, did not come into the posses- 'sion of the Tindale family till later.' Tindale was known also by the name Hutchins (Hychins, Hochin), which had been assumed, it is said, by his great-grandfather; and in official documents he is described by both titles: *e.g.* in the *Articles against Munmouth*, Strype, *Eccles. Mem.* I.

488. [Demaus (ed. 2) was of opinion that all the evidence is in favour of Melksham Court, in the parish of Stinchcombe, being the home of Tindale's family.]

[3] He studied in Magdalen Hall, called *Grammar* Hall from the labours of Grocyn, W. Latimer, and Linacre there in favour of classical learning (Anderson, I. 26). [He probably took the degree of M.A. in 1515.] Mr Fry informs me that the MS. quoted in the *Historical Account*, p. 41 n., purporting to contain translations by Tindale ('W.T.') from the New Testament and dated 1502, was unquestionably a forgery. The MS. was afterwards burnt [in 1865 at Sotheby's, when the sale of Offor's Library had begun]; but the facsimile of a single page, for the sight of which I am indebted to Mr Fry, seems absolutely conclusive as to its spuriousness.

[4] This passage is given according to the first edition (1563), p. 514. In the later editions the form of the last sentence is turned into the oblique: *Acts and Monuments*, V. 117.

had published the Greek Testament for the first time,
with a new Latin version, in 1516, before Tindale left
Cambridge; and Tindale must have been acquainted with
the effect which its introduction there had immediately
produced[1]. At the same time, as he tells us, he 'had
'perceaued by experyence, how that it was impossible to
'stablysh the laye people in any truth, excepte y⁰ scripture
'were playnly layde before their eyes in their mother
'tonge, that they might se the processe, ordre and mean-
'inge of the texte'...'Which thinge onlye,' he says, 'moved
'me to translate the new testament[2].'

When his enemies grew so powerful as to endanger
his patron, 'I gat me,' he says, to 'London.' 'If I might
'come to the Bishop of London's service'—Tunstall's, of
whose love of scholarship Erasmus had spoken highly—
'thought I, I were happy.' By this time he knew what
his work was, and he was resolutely set to accomplish it[3].

[1] One memorable instance of its influence is seen in the narrative of Bilney, afterwards martyred in 1531, who was first roused to a lively faith by reading in Erasmus' edition, 1 Tim. i. 15, as he narrates in touching words in a letter addressed to Tunstall: Foxe, *Acts and Monuments*, IV. 635. Bilney's Latin Bible is still preserved [in the Library of Corpus Christi College, Cambridge], with many passages marked, and among them the one on which he dwelt most in the night before his death. Anderson, I. p. 301. [The Librarian, Mr C. W. Moule, informs me that the volume is a small folio copy of the Vulgate printed at Lyons in 1520 at the expense of Antony Koberger, and presented to the College in 1588 by Robert Willon, Rector of Wilbraham Parva and formerly Fellow. See Masters's *History of Corpus*, ed. Lamb, p. 321. W.A.W.] It is not indeed unlikely, as has been pointed out by the author of the *Historical Account* (p. 44), that the saying of Tindale given above

was suggested by a phrase in the *Exhortation* of Erasmus. 'I would,' he writes, 'that the husbandman at 'the plough should sing something 'from hence [the Gospels and Epi-'stles].'

[2] *Preface to Genesis* [*Pentateuch*], p. 394 (Park. Soc.).

[3] No phrase could more completely misrepresent Tindale's character than that by which Mr Froude has thought right to describe him at this time—'the young dreamer' (II. 30). Tindale could not have been much less than forty years old at the time, and he was less of a 'dreamer' even than Luther. From the first he had exactly measured the cost of his work; and when he had once made his resolve to translate the Scriptures, he never afterwards lost sight of it, and never failed in doing what he proposed to do.

I do not think that the phrase 'fiery young enthusiast,' which Mr Froude has substituted for 'young 'dreamer' in his last edition is much happier, though it certainly indicates a very different character. 1870.

At the same time he was prepared to furnish the bishop
for whose countenance he looked with an adequate test
of his competency.   The claim which he preferred was
supported by a translation of a speech of Isocrates from
the Greek.   'But god,' he continues, and the story can
only be given fitly in his own words, 'sawe that I was
'begyled, ād that that councell was not the nexte way
'vnto my purpose'—to translate the Scriptures—'And
'therfore he gate me no favoure in my lordes sight. Wher-
'uppon my lorde answered me, his house was full: he had
'mo thē he coude well finde, and advised me to seke in
'london, wher he sayd I coude not lacke a service.'

The bishop's prediction was fulfilled in a way which
he could not have anticipated.   Tindale had indeed already
found a friend ready to help him in an alderman of London,
Humphrey Munmouth.   Munmouth, who was afterwards
(1528) thrown into the Tower for the favour which he had
shewn Tindale and other reformers, has left an interesting
account of his acquaintance with him in a petition which
he addressed to Wolsey to obtain his release.   'I heard
'[Tindale],' he writes, ' preach two or three sermons at
'St Dunstan's-in-the-West in London', and after that I
'chanced to meet with him, and with communication I
'examined what living he had.   He said he had none at
'all, but he trusted to be with my lord of London, in his
'service, and therefore I had the better fantasy to him.
'Afterward [when this hope failed, he]...came to me again,
'and besought me to help him ; and so I took him into my
'house half a year ; and there he lived like a good priest as
'methought.   He studied most part of the day and of the
'night at his book ; and he would eat but sodden meat by
'his good will, nor drink but small single beer.   I never
'saw him wear linen about him in the space he was with

[1] It is not known when Tindale was admitted to Holy Orders; but it is at least clear from the silence of Sir T. More that he was not the W. Tindale who is said to have 'made 'profession in the monastery of the 'Observants at Greenwich in 1508'; for More does not fail to taunt Joye and Jerome, who had belonged to that monastery, with being renegade friars, while he brings no such charge against Tindale.

'me. I did promise him ten pounds sterling to pray for
'my father and mother their souls and all Christian
'souls. I did pay it him when he made his exchange
'to Hamburgh[1].'

This time of waiting was not lost upon Tindale. In
the busy conflicts and intrigues of city life he learnt
what had been hidden from him in the retirement of the
country. 'In london,' he continues, 'I abode almoste an
'yere, and marked the course of the worlde...and vnder-
'stode at the laste not only that there was no rowme
'in my lorde of londons palace to translate the new
'testament, but also that there was no place to do it in
'all englonde...[2]'

So he left his native country for ever, to suffer, as he
elsewhere says, 'poverty, exile, bitter absence from friends,
'hunger and thirst and cold, great dangers and innumerable
'other hard and sharp fightings[3],' but yet to achieve his
work and after death to force even Tunstall to set his name
upon it.

Tindale's first place of refuge was Hamburgh. This
free city, like Antwerp, offered great advantages to religious
exiles; and at a later period we find Coverdale also living
there for some months[4]. At the same time, as no press
was yet established at Hamburgh, Tindale may not have
remained there during the whole of the year 1524, if, as
appears likely, he published the Gospels of St Matthew and
St Mark separately at that date[5]. Among other places,
Wittenberg, where Luther was then living, was easily
accessible, and it is not unlikely that Tindale found some
opportunity of seeing the great leader with whom the work
of the Reformation was identified. The fact of a passing
visit would explain satisfactorily the statement of Sir T.

---

[1] Foxe, IV. 617. App. to Strype,
Eccles. Mem. [vol. I. part 2], No.
89.

[2] *Preface to Genesis*, p. 396 (Park.
Soc. ed.).

[3] Report of Vaughan to Henry VIII,
quoted by Anderson, I. 272.

[4] See p. 30, note 6.

[5] The separate publication of these
Gospels appears probable from the
evidence adduced by Anderson, I.
153, 183, but the references may be
to the (Cologne) quarto edition. See
p. 33, n. I.

More[1], while the more exact account of Spalatinus[2], who makes no mention of Luther, leads to the belief, on all grounds the most probable, that Tindale, though acquainted with Luther's writings and ready to make use of them[3], lived independently, with his fellow-exiles, at Hamburgh[4] or elsewhere, till his chosen work was completed. In the next year (1525) Tindale went to Cologne, and there began to print the translation of the New Testament, which he had by that time completed[5]. It was a time of sore trial for the Reformers. Luther's marriage troubled some. His breach with Karlstadt alienated others. The rising of the peasants furnished a ready pretext to the lukewarm for confounding the new doctrines with revolutionary license. But Tindale laboured on in silence, and ten sheets of his Testament were printed in quarto when his work was stopped by the intrigues of Cochlæus, a relentless enemy of the Reformation[6].

[1] *Dialogue*, Book III. ch. 8. 'It 'is to be cōsydered that at the tyme 'of this translacyon, Hychens [Tin-'dale] was with luther in Wytten-'berge, & set certayne glosys in the 'mergent, framed for the settynge 'forthe of the vngracyous secte. By 'saynt Iohan quod your frende yf that 'be trewe that Hychens were at that 'time wyth Luther, it is a playne 'token that he wrought som what 'after his counsayle...Very trewe quod 'I. But as touchynge the confederacye 'betwene Luther and hym [it] is a 'thynge well knowen and playnly 'confessed, by soche as hauè ben 'taken and conuycted here of heresye 'comynge frome thens....'
To this Tindale's reply is simply: 'When he saỳth "Tyndall was con-'"federate with Luther," that is not 'truth.' This statement is of course consistent with the fact of a visit to Luther. Sir T. More's information was without doubt derived from Cochlæus. See also the letter of Lee, p. 34.
[2] See below, p. 35, n.

[3] See below, Chap. III.
[4] Tindale's close connexion with Hamburgh appears at a later time in the circumstantial statement of Foxe that 'at his appointment Coverdale 'tarried for him there and helped him 'in the translating of the whole five 'books of Moses, from Easter to 'December, in the house of a wor-'shipful widow Mistress Margaret 'van Emmerson, anno 1529...' [Foxe, v. 120.]
[5] Fryth did not join him till 1528; and there is no evidence that either his amanuensis Roye, or Joye, if he was with him at the time, had any independent part in the translation. See below, Ch. III. The date of the printing of the New Testament is established by the use of a woodcut as the frontispiece to St Matthew which was afterwards cut down and used in an edition of Rupert of Deutz, finished June 12, 1526. A facsimile of each of these woodcuts is given in Mr Arber's edition of the fragment.
[6] The one fragment of this edition which remains (see below, p. 37) has

It is a strange and vivid picture which Cochlæus, who is the historian of his own achievement, draws of the progress and discovery of the work[1]. The translation of 'the New 'Testament of Luther'—so he calls it—was, in his eyes, part of a great scheme for converting all England to Lutheranism. The expense, as he learnt, was defrayed by English merchants; and their design was only betrayed by their excess of confidence. But though Cochlæus was aware of the design, he could not for some time find any clue to the office where it was being executed. At last becoming familiar with the printers of Cologne while engaged on a book to be published there, he heard them in unguarded moments boast of the revolution which would be shortly wrought in England. The clue was not neglected. He invited some of them to his house, and plying them with wine learned where three thousand copies of the English Testament were being worked off, for speedy and secret distribution through England. He took immediate measures to secure the aid of the authorities of the city for checking the work. The printers were forbidden to proceed, but Tindale and Roye taking their printed sheets with them escaped to Worms by ship. Cochlæus —it was all he could then do—warned Henry, Wolsey, and Fisher of the peril to which they were exposed, that so they might take measures 'to prevent the importation of the 'pernicious merchandise.'

Meanwhile Tindale pursued his work under more favourable circumstances. The place to which he fled was already memorable in the annals of the Reformation. It was then not much more than four years since the marvellous scene

been photo-lithographed and published with an excellent introduction by Mr E. Arber (London, 1871), who has printed at length with great exactness and illustrated by careful notes the original records bearing upon the early life and work of Tindale.

[1] Mr Arber has given at length (*l. c.* pp. 18 ff.) the three passages, from works dated respectively 1533, 1538, 1549, in which Cochlæus mentions the transaction: the last account, from *De Actis et Scriptis M. Lutheri*, pp. 132 ff., is in every respect the most detailed. Cochlæus thinks that Henry VIII was as much indebted to him for the information as Ahasuerus to Mordecai, though he gave him no acknowledgment for the service.

when Luther entered Worms (1521) to bear witness before
the Emperor. But within that time the city had 'become
'wholly Lutheran[1].' So Tindale found a safe retreat there,
and prepared two editions of his New Testament instead of
one. The edition, which had been commenced at Cologne,
was in quarto and furnished with marginal glosses. A
description of this had been sent to England by Cochlæus,
and therefore, as it seems, to baffle his enemies Tindale
commenced a new edition in small octavo without glosses.
This octavo edition was finished first. In a short epistle
to the reader, which is placed at the end, the translator
apologizes for 'the rudnes off the worke' then first accomplished : 'Count it' he says 'as a thynge not havynge his
'full shape, but as it were borne afore hys tyme, even as a
'thīg begunne rather then fynesshed. In tyme to come (yf
'god have apoynted vs there vnto) we will geve it his full
'shape : and putt out yf ought be added superfluusly : and
'adde to yff ought be oversene thorowe negligence : and
'will enfoarce to brynge to compendeousnes, that which is
'nowe translated at the lengthe, ād to geve lyght where it
'is requyred, and to seke ī certayne places more proper
'englysshe, and with a table to expoūde the wordes which
'are nott cōmenly vsed, and shewe howe the scripture
'vseth many wordes, which are wother wyse vnderstonde of
'the cōmen people : ād to helpe with a declaracion where
'one tonge taketh nott another. And will endever oure
'selves, as it were to sethe it better, and to make it more
'apte for the weake stomakes : desyrynge them that are
'learned, and able, to remember their duetie, and to helpe
'there vnto : and to bestowe vnto the edyfyīge of Christis
'body (which is the cōgregacion of them that beleve) those
'gyftes whych they have receaved of god for the same
'purpose. The grace that cometh of Christ be with thē
'that love hym.' The whole book then closes with the
characteristic words : 'praye for vs.'

The words just quoted in part describe the general

---

[1] Anderson, I. p. 64, quoting Cochlæus (plebs pleno furore Lutherizabat)
and Seckendorf.

Prologue and glosses with which the quarto edition was furnished, and Tindale appears to have lost no time in completing this interrupted work[1]. Both editions reached England without any indication of the translator's name[2] early in 1526; and, as might have been expected, the quarto edition first attracted attention, while for a short time the undescribed octavo escaped notice.

Before the books arrived Henry VIII had received a second warning of the impending danger from his almoner Lee, afterwards archbishop of York, who was then on

---

[1] The quarto edition was commenced by Quentel. The octavo was printed by P. Schoeffer, the son of one of the first great triumvirate of printers. The same printer, it has been conjectured, completed the quarto; but of this there is no direct evidence, as the Grenville Fragment contains only sheets A—H, while A—K were printed by Quentel. There is not however any reasonable doubt that the quarto edition was completed about the same time as the first octavo, and therefore it seems likely that it was completed at Worms and by Schoeffer. Two editions, a large and a small, one with and one without glosses, made their appearance simultaneously in England Three thousand copies of the first sheets of the quarto were struck off and six thousand is said to have been the whole number of New Testaments printed. Moreover it is not likely that Tindale would allow the sheets which he rescued to lie idle. On the other hand, as Mr F. Fry reminds me, there is no direct evidence that the quarto edition was printed at Worms or printed in 1525, or that the Cologne sheets were used in this edition. But on the whole the conjectural interpretation of the facts which I have ventured to give seems to me to be correct. It is of course possible that

'the chapters of Matthew' referred to by Necton as in his possession before the Testaments may refer to these sheets, and not to another separate publication of that Gospel. Strype, *Mem.* I. 2, p. 63 See also Mr Arber, *l. c.* pp. 26–7. 1871. For specimens of the Glosses, see App. v.

[2] Tindale's name was attached to the *Parable of the Wicked Mammon* in 1528, and he there gives his reasons for printing his New Testament anonymously. 'The cause why I set my 'name before this little treatise and 'have not rather done it in the New 'Testament is, that then I followed 'the counsel of Christ, which exhort- 'eth men (Matt. vi.) to do their good 'deeds secretly, and to be content 'with the conscience of well-doing 'and that God seeth us; and patiently 'to abide the reward of the last day 'which Christ hath purchased for us: 'and now would I fain have done 'likewise, but am compelled otherwise 'to do.' (*To the Reader*, p. 37, ed. Park. Soc.) He wished to separate his own writings distinctly from the violent satires of W. Roye. In speaking simply of 'the New Testament' it seems evident that Tindale included the two editions, quarto and octavo. In the revised edition (1534) his name was added.

the Continent. Writing to the king from Bordeaux on Dec. 2nd, 1525, Lee says: ' Please it your highness moreover to 'understand that I am certainly informed, as I passed in 'this country, that an Englishman your subject, at the 'solicitation and instance of Luther, with whom he is, hath 'translated the New Testament into English, and within 'few days intendeth to arrive with the same imprinted in 'England. I need not to advertise your grace what infection 'and danger may ensue hereby if it be not withstanded. '.This is the next way to fulfil your realm with Lutherians.' And then he adds, ' All our forefathers, governors of 'the Church of England, hath with all diligence for-'bid and eschewed publication of English Bibles, as 'appeareth in constitutions provincial of the Church of 'England[1]...'

The account which reached Lee's ears had travelled far and was inaccurate in its details; but the swiftness with which it reached him is a proof of the interest which Cochlæus' discovery excited. Another notice of Tindale's translation which appears in the diary of a German scholar under August 1526 is more truthful and full of interest. After mentioning other subjects of conversation at the dinner table, as the war with the Turks, the exhaustion of the bishops by the peasants' war, the literary troubles of Erasmus, he adds, one told us that '6000 copies of the 'English Testament had been printed at Worms. That it 'was translated by an Englishman who lived there with two 'of his countrymen, who was so complete a master of seven 'languages, Hebrew, Greek, Latin, Italian, Spanish, English, 'French, that you would fancy that whichever one he spoke 'was his mother tongue. He added that the English, in 'spite of the active opposition of the king, were so eager 'for the Gospel as to affirm that they would buy a New

---

[1] For this letter I am indebted to Mr Froude, *Hist. of England*, II. 31. It is given more accurately by Mr Arber, *l.c.* p. 37. [Cotton MSS. Vesp. C. III. fol. 211.] At the same date Lee writes also to Wolsey to the same effect, informing him that he had written to the king. Brewer, *State Papers*, No. 1802. [Hen. VIII. vol. IV. part 1, p. 805.]

'Testament even if they had to give a hundred thousand
'pieces of money for it[1].'

The reception of the books in England answered to
these anticipations. They were eagerly bought, and as
eagerly proscribed and sought out for destruction. Sir T.
More fiercely attacked the translation as ignorant, dis-
honest and heretical[2]. In the autumn Tunstall and Warham
issued mandates for the collection and surrender of copies[3].
Tunstall attacked it in a Sermon at Paul's Cross, and professed to have found 3000 errors in it: 'and truly,' writes
one [Lambert] who heard him, 'my heart lamented greatly
'to hear a great man preaching against it [the New Testa-
'ment], who shewed forth certain things that he noted for
'hideous errors to be in it, that I, yea, and not only I, but
'likewise did many other, think verily to be none[4].'

---

[1] Etiamsi centenis millibus æris sit
redimendum. Diary of Spalatinus
under 'Sunday after St Laurence's
'Day, 1526,' given in Schelhorn,
Amæn. Liter. IV. 431 (ed. 1730).
The enumeration of languages is
'Hebraicæ, Græcæ, Latinæ, Italicæ,
'Hispanicæ, Britannicæ, *Gallicæ*.'
The passage is misquoted in the life
of Tindale prefixed to the edition of
Park. Soc. with '*Dutch*' (*i.e.* German)
for 'French' (p. xxx. n.). The error
is important, for if the printed reading
be correct, it is unlikely that Tindale
had spent a long time at Wittenberg
with Luther.

[2] His great charge was the disregard of 'ecclesiastical terms,' 'church,
'priest, charity, grace, confess, pen-
'ance,' for which Tindale substituted
'congregation, elder, love, favour,
'knowledge, repentance.' Tindale's
reply is full of interest.

A similar charge against the translation was made by R. Ridley (uncle
of N. Ridley). Writing in Feb. 1527
to [Henry Golde] the chaplain of
Archbp. Warham, he says: 'By this
'translation shall we losse al thies
'cristian wordes *penaunce, charite*,

'*confession, grace, prest, chirche*, which
'he alway calleth a congregation,
'quasi turcharum et brutorum nulla
'esset congregatio, nisi velit illorum
'etiam esse ecclesiam; *Idololatria*
'callith he worshippyng of images....
'Ye shal not neede to accuse this
'translation. It is accused and damn-
'ed by the consent of the prelates
'and learned men, and commanded
'to be brynt, both heir and beyonde
'the see, wher is many hundreth of
'tham brynt; so that it is to layt now
'to ask reson why that be condemned,
'and which be the fawtes and er-
'rours...' (Arber, pp. 52 ff. Anderson,
I. 153 ff.). [Cotton MSS. Cleop. E.
v. fol. 362 *b*.]

[3] Oct. 24, 1526. Foxe, *Acts and
Monuments*, p. 449 (ed. 1563). Anderson, I. p. 118. Arber, pp. 50 ff.

[4] Foxe, *Acts and Monuments*, v.
213. Tunstall returned in April 1526.
[Roye in his *Rede me and be nott wrothe*
mentions the three thousand errors
which Tunstall professed to have
found. Cochlæus (*Acta et Scripta
Martini Lutheri*, Moguntiæ, 1549,
p. 135) says 'supra duo milia de-
'pravationum.']

The attack of Tunstall appears to have been the result of a deliberation of the Cardinal and the bishops. In a preface added to the English translation of Henry VIII's answer to Luther's letter of 1525 it is said in the name of the king that he had 'with the deliberate aduyse of......
'Thomas lorde Cardynall......and other reuerende fathers
'of the spyritualtye, determyned......[Tindale's] vntrue
'translatyons to be brenned, with further sharppe correction
'and punisshment against the kepars and reders of the
'same......¹.' Roye, in his *Brief Dialogue*, gives an account of the discussion which issued in this condemnation, and represents at least the popular opinion as to the parts played by the several actors². The betrayal of the New Testament is compared with the betrayal of Christ. The part of Judas is assigned to Standish, bishop of St Asaph. The Cardinal 'spake the words of Pilat, Sayinge, I fynde 'no fault therin.' But the argument of 'bisshop Cayphas' [Tunstall] prevailed, who pleaded that it was better that the Gospel be condemned than their estate contemned; and so the Cardinal and all the bishops decided that the book should be burnt.

The decision being once made was vigorously carried out. Copies of the New Testament were bought up and burnt in Antwerp and London and Oxford³. Diplomacy was invoked to restrain the printers. But all was in vain. The tide was fairly flowing and it could not be checked. A formidable popular organization was ready in England to welcome the books and to spread them. Numerous agents were employed both in importing them from Holland and in circulating them. There is even something quaintly

¹ The preface is given at length by Mr Arber, pp. 48 f. The date of the book 'cannot be long after the be-'ginning of 1527' (Arber).
² The passages are printed in full by Mr Arber, pp. 29 ff.
³ ...nuper cum summa ejus laude et gloria auditum est, Majestatem suam sacrum B[ibliæ] codicem, qui ad pervertendum pias fidelium simplicium mentes a perfidis abominandæ sectæ Lut[heranæ] sectatoribus vernaculo sermone depravatus, et ad ejus regnum delatus fuerat, justissime comburi fecisse (Campeggio to Wolsey, Nov. 21, 1526. Arber, p. 49). Compare also Anderson, I. p. 214, Arber, pp. 49 ff., and below pp. 39, 41.

human in the spirit of the trader which shewed itself in
this sacred work.   One John Tyball came with a friend to
London (1526) to buy one of Tindale's New Testaments.
After giving some proof of their sincerity they shewed 'the
'Friar Barnes of certain old books that they had, as of four
'Evangelists and certain epistles of Peter and Paul in
'English.   Which books the said Friar did little regard,
'and made a twit of it and said "a point for them! for they
'"be not to be regarded toward the new *printed* Testament
'"in English.   For it is of more cleaner English."   And
'then the said Friar Barnes delivered to them the said
'New Testament in English...and after...did liken the
'New Testament in Latin to a cymbal tinkling and brass
'sounding[1].'   Thus by 1530 swiftly and silently six editions,
of which three were surreptitious, were dispersed, and
Tindale could feel that so far his work was substantially
indestructible.   He had anticipated its immediate fate.
'In burning the New Testament,' he wrote soon after the
book reached England (1527), 'they did none other thing
'than that I looked for, no more shall they do if they burn
'me also, if it be God's will it shall so be.   Nevertheless in
'translating the New Testament I did my duty and so do
'I now...[2].'   Yet so fierce and systematic was the persecution both now and afterwards, that of these six editions,
numbering perhaps 15,000 copies, there remains of the first
one fragment only, which was found about thirty years ago[3],
attached to another tract, of the second, one copy, wanting
the title-page, and another very imperfect[4]; and of the

---

[1] Deposition of John Tyball, Strype's *Memorials*, I. 131, App. I. part 2, xvii. p. 55.

[2] Preface to *Parable of the Wicked Mammon*, p. 44 (Parker Soc. ed.).

[3] [In 1834, Anderson, Index List.] Now in the Grenville Library in the British Museum. See p. 30, n. 6.

[4] The first, which is in the Library of the Baptist College at Bristol, has been reproduced in facsimile by Mr Fry: the second is in the Library of St Paul's, London. The Bristol copy has richly illuminated capitals, and was evidently designed for a wealthy purchaser. Marginal references are also added, perhaps by the illuminator, which are generally but not always identical with those in the edition of 1534. A very few notes in Latin and English were added by an early hand, but they are of no special in-terest.

others, two or three copies, which are not however satisfactorily identified[1].

Two characteristic incidents will be sufficient to shew
the strength and weakness of the popular movement to
which the origin and circulation of the translation was due.

The Eastern Counties, which took an active part on
the popular side in the barons' war and in the great revolution, seem to have been most ready to welcome the New
English Testament. Nearly all the places out of London
mentioned in direct connexion with the first circulation of
the books lie in this district, as Norwich, Bury, Colchester.
And Cambridge, which had enjoyed the teaching of
Erasmus, was early and deeply leavened by the 'new
learning.' Bilney, Latimer, and Barnes, men of distinction
in the University and not young students, were its representatives. Their position made them bold. On Christmas
Eve, 1525, Barnes preached a sermon in which he criticized
among other things the luxury of Wolsey. This personal
attack gave force to the accusation against him, which
after a little delay was laid before the Cardinal. A messenger came early in February of the next year to search
for heretical books, but his visit was anticipated by private
information. The books were placed carefully beyond his
reach, but he arrested Barnes. With such an offender the
process was short and simple. After he had appeared
before the court the choice was left him of abjuration or
the stake. A bitter struggle revealed his present weakness, and on the next Sunday in company with some
German traders—'Stillyard men'—committed 'for Luther's
'books and Lollardy[2],' he performed a memorable penance

---

[1] Of these three editions one was
printed by Endhoven, and the two
others by Ruremonde, but all at
Antwerp: Anderson, I. 129—133;
163—165. The Dutch copy in the
Library of Emm. Coll. Cambridge
[printed in 1538 without the name of
place or printer], as Dr Cotton points
out, is Coverdale's and not Tindale's

version. It is very probable that
other editions [besides the six which
Anderson mentions] existed of which
no trace has yet been discovered.

[2] An abstract of the depositions of
these men (Feb. 8, 1526) is given by
Brewer, *Calendar of State Papers*,
Henry VIII, No. 1962 [vol. IV.
part 1, p. 884].

in St Paul's[1]. 'The Cardinal had a scaffold made on the
'top of the stairs for himself, with six-and-thirty Abbots,
'mitred Priors and Bishops, and he in his whole pomp
'mitred, which Barnes spake against, sat there enthronised,
'his chaplains and spiritual doctors, in gowns of damask
'and satin, and he himself in purple, even like a bloody
'antichrist. And there was a new pulpit erected on the
'top of the stairs also for [Fisher] the Bishop of Rochester,
'to preach against Luther and Dr Barnes; and great baskets
'full of books standing before them within the rails, which
'were commanded after the great fire was made before
'the Rood of Northen[2] there to be burned; and these
'heretics after the sermon to go thrice about the fire and
'to cast in their faggots.' The ceremony was duly enacted.
Barnes humbly acknowledged the mercy which he had
received, and the obnoxious books were burnt. 'And so
'the Cardinal,' Foxe continues with grave humour, 'de-
'parted under a canopy with all his mitred men with him,
'till he came to the second gate of Paul's; and then he
'took his mule and the mitred men came back again[3].'

The tidings of this scene and of Fisher's sermon reached
Tindale. 'Mark, I pray you,' he wrote not long afterwards, 'what an orator he [Rochester] is, and how vehe-
'mently he persuadeth it! Martin Luther hath burned
'the pope's decretals: a manifest sign, saith he, that he
'would have burned the pope's holiness also, if he had
'had him! A like argument, which I suppose to be
'rather true, I make: Rochester and his holy brethren
'have burnt Christ's Testament: an evident sign verily,
'that they would have burnt Christ Himself also, if they
'had had Him[4].' But so it was that for a while the per-

[1] This took place Feb. 11, 1526.
The narrative is given by Foxe, *Acts
and Monuments*, v. 414 ff. See Demaus' *Life of Latimer*, pp. 49 ff.
[2] The crucifix, that is, 'towards
'the great north door...whereunto
'oblations were frequently made,
'whereof the dean and canons had

'the benefit.' Dugdale, *History of
St Paul's*, p. 15 (ed. 1818).
[3] Foxe, *Acts and Monuments*, v.
418.
[4] *Obedience of a Christian Man*
(A.D. 1528), p. 221, ed. Parker Soc.
I owe the passage to Mr Anderson,
I. p. 107. It is possible indeed that

secution triumphed. The faith of the confessors was not yet purified and strengthened.

From Cambridge and London we pass to Oxford. One of the first and most active distributors of Tindale's Testaments was Thomas Garret, curate of All Hallows, Cheapside. It seems that he had been engaged some time in circulating them at Oxford and elsewhere before the suspicion of the government was roused. At last, in Feb. 1528[1], tidings of his labours reached Wolsey, and search was made for him in all London. It was found that he was then 'gone to Oxford to make sale of [the 'books] there to such as he knew to be the lovers of the 'Gospel,' for this was not his first labour of the kind. A messenger was despatched thither to apprehend him, but the timely warning of a friend gave him an oppor-tunity of escaping. But 'after that he was gone a day's 'journey and a half he was so fearful that his heart would 'no other but that he must needs return again unto 'Oxford.' He was immediately apprehended, but again escaped from custody and sought out his friend Dalaber, who has recorded the story. With 'deep sighs and plenty of tears, he prayed me,' Dalaber writes, 'to help to convey 'him away; and so he cast off his hood and his gown, 'wherein he came unto me, and desired me to give him 'a coat with sleeves, if I had any; and told me that he 'would go into Wales, and thence convey himself into 'Germany, if he might. Then I put on him a sleeved 'coat of mine, of fine cloth in grain, which my mother 'had given me. He would have another manner of cap 'of me, but I had none but priest-like, such as his own 'was. Then kneeled we both down together on our knees, 'lifting up our hearts and hands to God, our heavenly

Tindale may be speaking here of the burning of Luther's translations, which were found in possession of the Hanse merchants; for it is not certain that the English Testaments were burnt till after Tunstall's sermon (*i.e.* after April, 1526). See p. 35.

[1] Mr Demaus has pointed out to me that this is certainly the date of Garret's apprehension. At the same time there can be no doubt that his connexion with Oxford commenced at an earlier time, and probably in 1526.

'Father, desiring him, with plenty of tears, so to conduct
'and prosper him in his journey, that he might well escape
'the danger of all his enemies, to the glory of his holy
'name, if his good pleasure and will so were. And then
'we embraced, and kissed the one the other...and so he
'departed from me apparelled in my coat....' But when
Garret thus fled others remained behind not unworthy to
carry on his work. 'When he was gone down the stairs
'from my chamber,' Dalaber continues, 'I straightways
'did shut my chamber-door, and went into my study
'shutting the door unto me, and took the New Testament
'of Erasmus' translation in my hands, kneeled down on
'my knees, and with many a deep sigh and salt tear, I did
'with much deliberation read over the tenth chapter of
'St Matthew his Gospel; and when I had so done, with
'fervent prayer I did commit unto God that our dearly
'beloved brother Garret, earnestly beseeching him in and
'for Jesus Christ's sake, his only begotten Son our Lord,
'that he would vouchsafe not only safely to conduct and
'keep our said dear brother from the hands of all his
'enemies; but also that he would vouch endue his tender
'and lately-born little flock in Oxford with heavenly
'strength by his Holy Spirit, that they might be well
'able thereby valiantly to withstand, to his glory, all their
'fierce enemies; and also might quietly, to their own salva-
'tion, with all godly patience bear Christ's heavy cross,
'which I now saw was presently to be laid on their young
'and weak backs, unable to bear so huge a one, without
'the great help of his Holy Spirit. This done, I laid
'aside my books safe....' Within a short interval Garret
was brought back to Oxford. By this time numerous
discoveries had been made. Forbidden books had been
found carefully secreted. The Cardinal's College, which
had received a large infusion of Cambridge men, was
deeply infected with the new heresy. But for the moment
old influences were too powerful. The 'lately-born flock'
was not ripe for the trial. Before many days were over
Garret and Dalaber took a principal part in a public act

of penance in company with Fryth and Taverner and
Coxe and Udall and Ferrar and many others destined
to play an important part in the coming struggle of the
Reformation.   One detail of their punishment was to
throw a book into a fire kindled at Carfax.   The procession passed away, the fire died out, the books were
consumed, and such was the end of the first appearance
of Tindale's New Testament at Oxford[1].

Twelve years later (1540) Barnes and Garret were
martyred together, two days after the execution of
Crumwell.

Even within a short time this zeal of persecution
brought out into greater prominence the extent of the
movement against which it was directed.   One of those
who had originally (June, 1527) contributed money for
the purpose of buying up Tindale's Testaments was Nix,
bishop of Norwich[2].   This singular plan for stopping the
sale of the books having failed, Nix wrote three years
afterwards in deep distress to Archbishop Warham to
obtain some more effectual interference in the matter.   His
letter is in every way so quaint and characteristic that
it must be quoted in its original form:

' I am accombred with such, as kepith and redith these
'arronious boks in Englesh......My Lorde, I have done that
'lieth in me for the suppresion of suche parsons; but it
'passith my power, or any spiritual man for to do it.   For
'dyverse saith openly in my Diocesse, that the Kings
'grace wolde, that they shulde have the saide arroneous
'boks......And they [with whom I confer] say, that wher-
'somever they go, they here say, that the Kings pleasure
'is, the Newe Testament in English shal go forth, and
'men sholde have it and read it.   And from that opinion
'I can no wise induce them but I had gretter auctoritie
'to punyshe them, than I have.   Wherefore I beseiche
'your good Lordshep...that a remedy may be had.   For
'now it may be done wel in my Diocesse: for the Gentil-

---

[1] The original history is given by   [2] His letter is given by Anderson,
Foxe, v. 421 ff., and App. No. VI.   I. p. 158.

'men and Commenty be not greatly infect; but marchants,
'and suche that hath ther abyding not ferre from the See...
'There is a Collage in Cambrige, called Gunwel haule
'[Gonville Hall], of the foundation of a Bp. of Norwich.
'I here of no clerk, that hath commen ought lately of
'that Collage, but saverith of the frying panne, tho he spek
'never so holely¹'....

The fears and wishes of Nix were probably shared by
a large party in England, and ten days after he wrote an
imposing assembly was convened by Archbishop Warham,
at which the errors of Tindale and his friends were
formally denounced, and a bill drawn up to be published
by preachers. In this it was stated, among other things,
that, in spite of the widespread feeling to the contrary,
it was not part of the King's duty to cause the Scriptures
to be circulated among the people in the vulgar tongue.
And that he 'by th' advise and deliberation of his
'counceill, and the agrement of great learned men, thinkith
'in his conscience that the divulging of this Scripture at
'this tyme in Englisshe tonge, to be committed to the
'people...shulde rather be to their further confusion and
'destruction then the edification of their soules².' Thus in
the very condemnation of the vernacular Bible, the general
demand for it is acknowledged, and a translation is only
deferred till a more convenient opportunity, which was
nearer at hand than More or Tunstall could have imagined.
Even in Warham's assembly 'there were' on Latimer's
testimony 'three or four that would have had the Scripture
'to go forth in English.' 'The which thing also your
'grace,' so he writes to the King, 'hath promised by your
'last proclamation: the which promise I pray God that
'your gracious Highness may shortly perform, even to-
'day before to-morrow. Nor let the wickedness of these
'worldly men detain you from your godly purpose and
'promise³.'

---

¹ Strype's *Cranmer*, 695 f. App. XII.   fol. 360.]
The letter is dated May 14th. [The   ² Wilkins' *Concilia*, III. 736.
original is Cotton MS. Cleop. E. 5,   ³ Foxe, VII. 509.

Thus the first battle for the Bible was being fought in England. Meanwhile the work had advanced one step further abroad. Very early in the same year it is likely that Tindale continued his work by publishing separately translations of Genesis and Deuteronomy. It is not known when the other books of the Pentateuch were printed The earliest edition which contains the five books has at the end of Genesis the date '1530, the 17th of January.' Perhaps however this may indicate, according to our style, Jan. 1531;' and there is no evidence to shew when the whole collection was issued, or indeed whether it was issued as a whole. The marginal glosses with which these translations are annotated are full of interest and strongly controversial. The spirit and even the style of Luther is distinctly visible in them. In the directness and persistency of their polemics against Rome they differ much from the glosses in the quarto Testament. Thus Tindale finds in the ceremonies of the Jewish Church the origin of the Romish rites (note on Ex. xxviii.). For example, on Ex. xxix. 37, he adds, 'Toch not the chalyce nor the 'altare stōne, nor holy oyle and holde youre hande out off 'the fonte' On Ex. xxxvi. 5, he writes : 'when wil the 'Pope saye hoo, and forbid to offere for the bylding of 'saint Peters chyrch: and when will our spiritualtie saye 'hoo, and forbid to geue thē more londe, ād to make moe 'fūdacions? neuer verely vntill they haue all.' Even Tindale too could descend to a pleasantry like Luther Thus on Ex. xxxii. 35, he remarks, 'The popis bull sleeth moo 'thā Aarons calfe...' The tonsure is criticized Levit. xxi. 5, 'Of the hethē preastes therfore toke our prelates the 'ensample off their balde pates.' One grim touch of satire may be added, Deut. xi. 19, 'Talk of them [the Lord's 'words] when thou sittest in thine house.' 'Talke of 'robynhod saye oure prelates.'

In the same year (1531), in all probability, the book of Jonah[1] with an important Prologue appeared, but no more

---

[1] Of this a single copy was found at Ickworth [in 1861] by [the late] Lord   A. Hervey [afterwards Bishop of Bath and Wells], which was reproduced in

of Tindale's work on the Old Testament was published
during his lifetime, except the 'Epistles from the Old
'Testament,' which were added to the revised edition of
his New Testament. For in the midst of his constant
perils and anxieties from within and from without Tindale
found time to revise his New Testament carefully. The
immediate occasion for the publication of his work was
the appearance of an unauthorised revision in August 1534,
by George Joye. The demand for the New Testaments,
which appears to have slackened since 1530, was again
so great that three surreptitious editions were printed at
Antwerp in that year[1]; and Joye undertook to revise the
sheets of a fourth edition. In doing this he made use, as
he says, of the Latin text, and aimed at giving 'many
'words their pure and native signification.' The title of
the book is singularly affected[2], and the alterations were

facsimile by Mr F. Fry, 1863. [It is
now in the British Museum.] For a
comparison of the version with that
of Coverdale, see p. 68. The book
was denounced by Stokesley, Dec. 3,
1531, and in 1532 Sir T. More speaks
of 'Jonas made out of Tindale.' Mr
Fry has called my attention to these
references.

[1] [According to Joye (*An Apology
to W. Tindale*, ed. Arber, 1882,
pp. 20–1), writing in November
1534, two pirated editions were sold
off more than a year before, the first
having apparently been issued soon
after (Joye says 'a non aftir') the
appearance of Tindale's translation.
A third was printed in the course of
1534, and Joye was asked but declined
to correct it. The fourth edition
which gave great offence to Tindale
was edited by Joye and was published
in August 1534.]

[2] The new Testament as it was
written, and caused to be written, by
them which herde yt. Whom also
oure saueoure Christ Iesus commaunded that they shulde preach it vnto al
creatures.

At the end of the New Testament
is this colophon:

Here endeth the new Testament,
diligently ouersene and corrected, and
prynted now agayn at Antwerpe, by
me wydowe of Christoffel of Endoue
In the yere of oure Lorde .M.CCCC.
and .XXXIIII, in August.

One copy only of this edition is
known, which is in the Grenville
Library in the British Museum.

It is not true, as is commonly said,
that Joye 'expunged' the word 're-
'surrection' from his New Testament.
It stands in such critical passages as
Acts i. 22; iv. 2; xvii. 18, 32, &c.;
1 Cor. xv. 12, &c.; nor did Tindale
bring this charge against him, but
that 'throughout Matthew, Mark and
'Luke perpetually, and often in the
'Acts, and sometimes in John, and
'also in the Hebrews, where he find-
'eth this word "Resurrection," he
'changeth it into the "life after this
'"life," or "very life," and such like,
'as one that abhorred the name of
'the resurrection.' (*W. T. yet once
more to the Christian reader*, in the
N.T. of 1534.) Thus in Matt. xxii.

such as to arouse the just indignation of Tindale, whose
name however is nowhere connected with the version.
Among other new renderings Tindale specially notices
that of '*the life after this*' for '*resurrection*.' Still Joye
does not avoid the word 'resurrection'; and if this were
the only change, the particular substitution would be of
little moment in the connexion where it occurs, but comparatively few paragraphs are left wholly untouched as far
as I have examined the book.   One continuous passage
will exhibit Joye's mode of dealing with the text.   The
words in italics are variations from Tindale :

'That *thing* (om. T.) which was from the beginning
'declare we unto you, (add. *concerning* T. 1st ed.) which we
'have heard, which we have seen with our eyes, which
'we have looked upon, and our hands have handled ;
'*even that same thing which is* (*of the word of* T.) life. For
'*that* (*the* T.) life appeared, and we have seen *it* (om. T.),
'*wherefore we* (*and* T.) bear witness and shew unto you
'that eternal life, which was with the Father and appeared
'unto us.   That *same thing* (om. T.) which we have seen
'and heard declare we unto you, that ye may have fellow-
'ship with us, and that our fellowship may be with the
'Father and His Son Jesus Christ[1].'   (1 John i. 1—3.)

Several of the changes noticed are suggested by the
Vulgate ; others are due apparently only to a mistaken
effort to obtain clearness : none mark a critical examin-

23, 30, we read 'life after this'; xxii.
31, 'the life of them that be dead.'

So also Luke xx, 27, 33, 36 (children
of that life).   John v. 29 is translated
'and shall come forth, they that have
'done good unto the very life. And
'they that have done evil into the life
'of damnation.' In John xi. 24, 25
the word 'resurrection' is retained.
From these examples it is obvious
that Joye's object was simply exe-
getical in the particular passages which
he altered, and that he had no desire
to expunge the idea or the word 're-
'surrection' from his version.   Later

writers have not dealt justly with him.

[1] In John i. 1—18 the following
noticeable variations occur ;

1 *that* Word : and God *was that
Word*. 4 life (om *the*). 5 darkness
(om. *the*). 10 and the world (om.
yet). 11 *into* his own and his (om.
own) received. 15 bare witness of
him, saying. 16 *favour for favour*
17 *favour and verity*.

In Ephes. i. again these are found :
5 that we should be *chosen to be*
heirs. 6 in *his* beloved *son*. 8 wisdom
and *prudency*. 13 the Gospel of your
health. 18 what *thing* that hope is.

ation of the original. But Joye knew that Tindale was studying the Greek afresh for his revised edition, which he had had some time in hand, and so he might well be said not to have 'used the office of an honest man.' However Tindale's own work was ready in the November of the same year. The text was not only revised, but furnished also with short marginal notes. Prologues were added to the several books[1]; the beginnings and endings of the lessons read in Church were marked; and a translation of 'the Epistles taken oute of the olde testament, 'which are red in the church after the vse of Sals-'burye vpon certen dayes of the yere,' which include a large number of fragments from the Old Testament and the Apocrypha, classed together by Tindale under one head[2]

---

[1] On the relation of these Prologues to Luther's, see Chap. III.

[2] The relation of the 'Epistles' containing translations of the Old Testament to the text of Tindale's continuous translation will be noticed afterwards. The following is (I hope) an accurate list of them. Gen. xxxvii. 6—22; Ex. xii. 1—11; xx. 12—24; xxiv. 12—18; Lev. xix. 1—18; Num. xx. 2—13; 1 Kings xvii. 17—24; xix. 3—8; Prov. xxxi. 10—31; Cant. ii. 1—14; Is. i. 16—19; ii. 1—5; vii. 10—15; xi. 1—5; xii. 1—6; xlix. 1—7; li. 1—8; liii. 1—12; lviii. 1—9; lx. 1—6; lxii. 6—12; Jerem. xvii. 13—18; xxiii. 5—8 (wrongly given xxxiii.); Ezek. i. 10—13; xviii. 20—28; xxxvi. 23—28; Joel ii. 12—19; 23—27; iii. 17—21; Hos. xiv. 1—9 (wrongly given xiii.); Amos ix. 13—15; Zech. ii. 10—13; viii. 3—8; Mal. iii. 1—4. From the Apocrypha, Esther xiii. 8—18; Wisd. v. 1—5; Ecclus. xv. 1—6; xxiv. 7—15; 17—22; xliv. 17; xlv. 4 (part); li. 9—12. In his reference to these, Mr Anderson is singularly unhappy. He omits six of the chapters from which the passages are taken (he does not give the verses), and of those which he gives, six are wrong, from a confusion of x and v. He suppresses all the passages from the Apocrypha and converts Esther xiii. (apocryphal) into Esther viii. (canonical). He argues from the publication of these passages, 'that there were other chapters in 'manuscript' (I. p. 570), wholly neglecting to notice that these lessons were a definite collection from the service book. It is not generally worth while to note mistakes, but this error deserves to be signalized, because it does not spring from inaccuracy, but apparently in some degree from want of candour, for Mr Anderson labours to shew that Tindale would not have translated the Apocrypha. [This is hardly just to Anderson. He undoubtedly made mistakes in his account of the passages from the Old Testament translated by Tindale, but he omitted the references to the Apocrypha, not because he laboured to shew that Tindale would not have translated it, but because, regarding it as it is still regarded in Scotland, he did not concern himself with the history of its translation.

One of the few copies of this edition which have been preserved is of touching interest. Among the men who had suffered for aiding in the circulation of the earlier editions of the Testament was a merchant-adventurer of Antwerp, Mr Harman, who seems to have applied to Queen Anne Boleyn for redress. The Queen listened to the plea which was urged in his favour, and by her intervention he was restored to the freedom and privileges of which he had been deprived. Tindale could not fail to hear of her good offices, and he acknowledged them by a royal gift. He was at the time engaged in superintending the printing of his revised New Testament, and of this he caused one copy to be struck off on vellum and beautifully illuminated. No preface or dedication or name mars the simple integrity of this copy   Only on the gilded edges in faded red letters runs the simple title *Anna Regina Angliæ*[1].

The interest of the Queen in the work of Tindale appears to have extended yet further[2]: an edition of his revised New Testament, the first volume of Holy Scripture printed in England, appeared in the year in which she was put to death (1536), and from the press of a printer with whom her party was connected[3]. Tindale, who suffered in

For this reason in giving an account of the Authorised Version he omits the Company appointed to revise the Apocrypha, and mentions them only in a footnote, as distinguished from those 'engaged upon the Sacred Text.' In the last Revision, only one of the Scotch members of the Companies took an active part in the revision of the Apocrypha. W. A. W.]

[1] The copy was bequeathed to the British Museum by the Rev. C. M. Cracherode in 1799, but I have been unable to learn its previous history. It may have been 'bound in blue 'morocco' when it was presented to Anne Boleyn, as Mr Anderson says (I. 413), though it is very unlikely: the present binding is obviously of the 18th century [and is stamped with the arms of Mr Cracherode].

The shield on the title-page is filled with the arms of France and England quarterly. The first quarter is defaced, and the outline of the wood-engraving below is mixed with the charge. The capitals [at the beginning of the several books] are exquisitely illuminated.

[2] The 'lady Anne' had at an earlier time had a perilous adventure from lending to one of her ladies a copy of Tindale's *Obedience of a Christian Man*. The narrative is quoted in Tindale's *Works*, I. p. 130 (Parker Soc. ed.) [from Strype, *Eccl. Mem.* I. 172].

[3] This was not T. Berthelet, as is commonly supposed, but T. Godfray. This fact has been ascertained beyond all doubt by Mr Bradshaw. The engraved border, on the evidence of which the work has been assigned to

the same year, may have been martyred before the book was finished, but at least he must have been cheered with the knowledge of its progress. He had worked for thirteen years in exile by foreign instruments, and now in his last moments he was allowed to rejoice in the thought that his labour had found its proper home in his own land. For this end he had constantly striven: for this he had been prepared to sacrifice everything else; and the end was gained only when he was called to die.

It is impossible to follow in detail the circumstances of Tindale's betrayal and martyrdom, yet the story is well worth pondering over. Some of the life-like touches in Foxe's narrative bring out the singleness of the character of the man whom he worthily called 'for his notable 'pains and travail an apostle of England.' One work had absorbed all his energy, and intent on that he had no eye for other objects. The traitor by whose devices he was taken (May, 1535) seemed to him, in spite of warnings,

Berthelet, was used by Godfray before it passed into Berthelet's possession; and there is no evidence that Berthelet used it as early as 1536.

['It is doubtful,' says Mr Jenkinson (*Early English Printed Books in the University Library, Cambridge*, III. p. 1730), 'whether this represents 'Mr Bradshaw's final opinion.' It is certain that the border in question was used by Berthelet in 1530 in a book printed by him, 'Gravissimæ '...Italiæ et Galliæ Academiarum 'censuræ—de veritate illius proposi-'tionis...quod ducere relictam fratris 'mortui...sit de iure divino.' Again, it is found in another book also printed by him, *Kotser codicis R. Wakfeldi*, which must have been issued between 1533 and 1536, because of the references in it to Queen Anne Boleyn. According to Leland (*De viris illustribus*) Berthelet also printed an edition of Chaucer. (See Tyrwhitt's *Chaucer*, App. to Pref.)

If this is Thynne's edition of 1532, 'Printed by Thomas Godfray,' which has the same border on the title-page, it may throw some light on the relation between Godfray and Berthelet. From the undated edition (? 1550) which is said to have been 'printed 'by' each of the four booksellers, Bonham, Kele, Petit, and Toye, it is clear that 'printed by' sometimes meant 'printed for,' and therefore Thynne's edition may have been printed by Berthelet for Godfray. However this may be, it is not improbable that Tindale's New Testament of 1536, which has the same border, was printed by Berthelet, and it is certain, from the evidence given above, that Mr Bradshaw was mistaken in supposing that Berthelet did not use the border so early as 1536.]

The edition ends with the significant words, 'God saue the kynge, and all 'his well wyllers.'

honest, handsomely learned and *very conformable.*' He
even furnished him with money, 'for in the wily subtilties
'of this world he was simple and inexpert.'   But in defence
of himself Tindale needed no counsel ; even by an adversary
he was called 'a learned, pious and good man': his keeper,
and his keeper's daughter, and others of his keeper's household were won over by him to his belief.   His last prayer
when fastened to the stake (Oct. 1536) witnessed equally to
his loyalty and his faith : ' *Lord ! open the King of England's*
'*eyes.*'

Before his imprisonment Tindale revised his New Testament once again for the press.   This last edition contains
one innovation in the addition of headings to the chapters
in the Gospels and Acts, but not in the Epistles ; and is
without the marginal notes, which were added to the
edition of 1534. But it is chiefly distinguished by the pecu-
liarity of the orthography, which has received a romantic
interpretation.   Tindale, as we have seen, had affirmed that
'he who followeth the plough' should in a few years have
a full knowledge of the Scripture, and from the occurrence
of such words as *maester, faether, moether, stoone,* in this
edition it was concluded by a biographer that in his last
years he adapted his translation to 'the pronunciation of
'the peasantry.'   The conjecture seemed plausible and it is
scarcely surprising that it has been transformed by repetition into an acknowledged fact.   It is however not borne
out by an examination of the book itself.   Whatever may
be the explanation of the orthography it is evident from
its inconsistency that it was not the result of any fixed
design.   Nay more, there is not the least reason to suppose
that some of the forms are provincial, or that the forms as
a whole would make the language plainer to rustics.   The
headings too, which have been also supposed to have been
designed 'to help to the understanding of the subjects
'treated of,' just fail when on that theory they would be
most needed[1].

---

[1] Two copies of this edition are known. That which I have used is in the University Library at Cambridge. [The other is in the Library

But though this pleasant fancy of the literal fulfilment
of an early promise must be discarded, Tindale achieved in
every way a nobler fulfilment of it. Instead of lowering
his translation to a vulgar dialect, he lifted up the common
language to the grand simplicity of his own idiom. ' It
' pleased God,' as he wrote in his first Prologue, ' to put
' [the translation] in his mind,' and if we look at his life and
his work, we cannot believe that he was left without the
Spirit of God in the execution of it. His single honesty is
beyond all suspicion. ' I call God to recorde,' so he writes
to Fryth in the Tower, 1533, ' against ye day we shall
' appear before our Lord Iesus, to geue a recknyng of our
' doings, that I neuer altered one sillable of Gods word
' agaynst my cōscience, nor would this day, if all that is in
' the earth, whether it be pleasure, honour or riches, might
' be geuen me[1].' Not one selfish thought mixed with his
magnificent devotion. No treacherous intrigues ever shook
his loyalty to his king : no intensity of distress ever obscured
his faith in Christ. ' I assure you,' he said to a royal

of Exeter College, Oxford, and there
is a fragment in the British Museum.]
The orthography in the Table of the
four Evangelists and the Prologue to
the Romans which follows (not displaced by the binder) offers no marked
peculiarities. In sheet A we find
*aengell, waeye, faether, maeke, waere,
saeyde, moether, aroese, beholde, toeke,
harde* (heard), &c., &c. In B, *maester,
mother, moether, father, sayd,* or *sayde*
(consistently), *fayth, stoede,* &c. In C,
*sayde, angels, moether, harde, maester,
master, father,* &c. In D, *faether,
moether, mother, sayde, hearde,* &c.
In F on one side, *faether, moether,
broether,* and on the other, *angels,
sayde, daye, brother, told, hearde,*
&c. In Y and Z we have almost consistently *faeyth, saeyde, hoepe, almoest,
praeyer,* &c. Yet again in b *prayer,*
&c. In the headings of the Epistles
we have *saynct* and *saeynct.* Some
spellings certainly belong to a foreign
compositor, *thongs* (tongues, 1 Cor.

xiii.) [but twice in the same page
tonges]; *thaugh* (taught). Some I
cannot explain, *caled* (called), *holly*
(holy), which forms are consistently
used. Of possible explanations none
seems more likely than that the copy
was read to a Flemish compositor (at
Brussels? or Malines?) and that the
vowels simply give the Flemish equivalents of the English vowel sounds.
See note at the end of the section,
p. 54.

The text is carefully revised, as will
be shewn afterwards, and the chapter
headings are simply transferred from
the table of the Gospels and Acts in
the Testament of 1534. Mr F. Fry
has since found substantially the same
text in an edition dated 1534 (G. H.),
i.e. probably 1535, January—March.
[Mr Fry's copy, now in the Library
of the Bible Society, has a title-page
with the date 1535.]

[1] Tindale's *Works,* p. 456 (ed.
1573).

envoy[1], 'if it would stand with the king's most gracious
'pleasure to grant only a bare text of the Scripture to be
'put forth among his people, like as is put forth among
'the subjects of the emperor in these parts [the Nether-
'lands], and of other Christian princes, be it of the transla-
'tion of what person soever shall please his majesty, I shall
'immediately make faithful promise never to write more,
'nor abide two days in these parts, after the same; but
'immediately repair into his realm, and there most humbly
'submit myself at the feet of his royal majesty, offering my
'body, to suffer what pain or torture, yea, what death his
'grace will, *so that this be obtained*.' His life had seemed
friendless, but his one dearest companion (Fryth) may
interpret the temper common to them both. 'Doubt not,'
he writes from the Tower to his desolate congregation, 'but
'that god...shal so prouide for you, that ye shall haue an
'hundred fathers for one, an hūdred mothers for one, an
'hundred houses for one, and that in this lyfe, *as I haue
'proued by experience*[2].' We dilute the promise by our comments: these martyrs proved it in their lives.

The worth of Tindale as a scholar must be estimated
by his translation, which will be examined afterwards. Of
the spirit in which he undertook the great work of his life
something has been said already. To the end he retained
unchanged, or only deepened and chastened his noble for-
getfulness of self in the prospect of its accomplishment,
with a jealous regard for the sincere rendering of the Scriptures. Before he published the revised edition of 1534 he
had been sorely tried by the interference of Joye, which
might, as he thought, bring discredit to the Gospel itself.

---

[1] Vaughan's dispatch (1531) quoted
by Anderson, I. p. 278. Fryth's language (1533) is to the same effect:
'This hath bene offered you, is offered,
'and shall be offered: Graunt that the
'word of God, I meane yᵉ text of
'Scripture, may go abroad in our
'English toung, as other nations
'haue it in their tounges, and my

'brother William Tyndall, and I haue
'done, & will promise you to write
'no more. If you wil not graunt this
'condition, then will we be doing
'while we haue breath, and shew in
'few wordes that the Scripture doth in
'many: and so at the lest saue some.'
Fryth's *Works*, p. 115 (ed. 1573).

[2] *Id.* p. 82.

The passage with which he closes his disclaimer of Joye's
edition reflects at once his vigour and its tenderness. There
is in it something of the freedom and power of Luther, but
it is charged with a simple humility which Luther rarely if
ever shews....' My part,' Tindale writes, ' be not in Christ if
' mine heart be not to follow and live according as I teach,
' and also if mine heart weep not night and day for mine
' own sin and other men's indifferently, beseeching God to
' convert us all and to take his wrath from us and to be
' merciful as well to all other men, as to mine own soul,
' caring for the wealth of the realm I was born in, for the
' king and all that are thereof, as a tender-hearted mother
' would do for her only son.

'As concerning all I have translated or otherwise
' written, I beseech all men to read it for that purpose I
' wrote it: even to bring them to the knowledge of the
' Scripture. And as far as the Scripture approveth it,
' so far to allow it, and if in any place the word of God
' disallow it, there to refuse it, as I do before our Saviour
' Christ and His congregation. And where they find faults
' let them shew it me, if they be nigh, or write to me if they
' be far off: or write openly against it and improve it, and
' I promise them, if I shall perceive that their reasons con-
' clude I will confess mine ignorance openly.

'Wherefore I beseech George Joye, yea and all other
' too, for to translate the Scripture for themselves, whether
' out of the Greek, Latin or Hebrew. Or (if they will
' needs)...let them take my translations and labours, and
' change and alter, and correct and corrupt at their pleasures,
' and call it their own translations and put to their own
' names and not to play bo-peep after George Joye's
' manner...But I neither can nor will suffer of any man,
' that he shall go take my translation and correct it without
' name, and make such changing as I myself durst not do,
' as I hope to have my part in Christ, though the whole
' world should be given me for my labour[1].'

[1] 'W. T. yet once more to the   1534. I cannot find this address in
'Christian Reader' in the N.T. of   my copy of Tindale's *Works* published

by the Parker Society. Part of it is given in the *Life*, pp. lxii. ff.

The Grenville fragment of Tindale's first quarto Testament with glosses has been perfectly reproduced in photo-lithography by Mr E. Arber, London, 1871.

The first octavo has been printed: (1) by Mr Offor [1836], but this edition, though verbally accurate, is wholly untrustworthy in spelling; and (2) in facsimile by Mr F. Fry [1862] with most scrupulous exactness.

The revised edition of 1534 (M. Emperour) is given in Bagster's *Hexapla*, carefully and well, as far as I have observed.

The final revision of 1535, 1534 G. H. has not yet been published as a whole or in a collation, though it is from this that Tindale's work has passed directly into our Authorised Version. [The edition of 1535 is probably an unauthorised reprint.]

NOTE to p. 51.

Mr F. Fry has made an ample collection of the spellings peculiar to or characteristic of the edition of 1535. By the help of this, which he most kindly communicated to me, I have drawn up the following table of the substitutions of vowel sounds. They seem to me to fall (as Mr W. A. Wright has suggested) under the general description which Bosworth has given of the peculiarities of the Flemish orthography: *Anglo-Saxon Dictionary*, p. cxi. The unequal distribution of the peculiarities to which attention has been called already (p. 51, note) is a most important fact in this connexion. [See Fry on Tindale's N.T., 1878, pp. 63–5.]

ae for a
　abstaeyne, aengell, awaeke, caeke, caese, faether, graece, maester, raether, shaell, greaet

ae for ay
　vaele (vayle 1534)

ae for ea
　aete (eate), paerle (pearl), recaeve (receave 1534), swaerdes (sweardes 1534)

ae for e
　belaeved (beleved 1534), decaevable (decevable 1534), dekaeye (dekeye 1534), naedeth (nedeth 1534)

oe for o
　aboede, accoerde, almoest, anoether, aroese, avoeyde, boedy, boeke, broether, choese, coelde, hoepe, moether, roese

oe for ou
　foere (foure 1534)

oe for e
　knoeled (kneled 1534)

oó for o
　boones, coostes (costes), hoow, loo (lo), moore, moost, oone, oonly, oons (once), roope, thoorow, whoo, whoose

ye for y
　abyede (abyde 1534)

ey for e
　agreyment (agrement 1534)

ee for e
　heere, preest (prest), spreede (sprede 1534), teell, theese

ea for a
　eare (are)

ie for y (i)
　bliend

ea for e
　streates (stretes), fealde (felde 1534), hear (her), neade (nede 1534)

ae for ay
　chaene (chayne 1534), counsael (counsayle 1534)

ue for u
　crueses, ruele, ruelers

§ 2. COVERDALE.

Tindale's character is heroic. He could see clearly the
work to which he was called and pursue it with a single
unswerving faith in GOD and in the powers which GOD
had given him. It was otherwise with Miles Coverdale,
who was allowed to finish what Tindale left incomplete.
The differences of the men are written no less on their
features than on their lives. But our admiration for the
solitary massive strength of the one must not make us
insensible to the patient labours and tender sympathy of
the other[1]. From the first Coverdale appears to have
attached himself to the liberal members of the old party
and to have looked to working out a reformation from
within through them. As early as 1527 he was in intimate
connexion with Crumwell and More[2]; and in all probability it was under their patronage that he was able to
prepare for his translation of Holy Scripture. How long
he thus laboured we cannot tell[3]. In 1529 he met Tindale
at Hamburgh[4], and must have continued abroad for a considerable part of the following years up to 1536. In the
meantime a great change had passed over England since

Some sounds are expressed in different ways, especially 'o.' Thus we
have *aloene* and *aloone; boeldely* and
booldly; boethe and *booth; coete* and
coote; hoeme and *hoome; loeke* and
louke (*loke* 1534); *noene* and *noane;
stoene* and *stoone; thoese* and *thoose;
whoem* and *whoom.* So also we have
theare and *theere; tought* and *thaught*
(*taught*).

Other exceptional forms are tappe
(top), touth (to the 1534), waere and
woere (where), woeld (would), te
(the), mouny (money).

[1] The later Puritanism of Coverdale
is consistent with this view of his
character. He was a man born rather
to receive than to create impressions.

[2] Anderson, I. p. 186.

[3] In an undated letter to Crumwell
he says, evidently in reference to some

specific 'communication' from him,
'Now I begin to taste of Holy Scrip-
'tures...Nothing in the world I desire
'but books as concerning my learning:
'they once had, I do not doubt, but
'Almighty God shall perform that in
'me which he of his plentiful favour
'and grace hath begun.' Anderson
fixes this in 1531. The letter however
from style seems to be nearly contemporary with another addressed to
Crumwell in 1527. [*State Papers,*
I. 383.]

[4] Foxe, *Acts and Monuments,* V.
120. I see nothing derogatory to
Tindale or improbable in Foxe's explicit statement that at this time
Coverdale helped him in translating
the Pentateuch; though on such a
point Foxe's unsupported statement
is not sufficient evidence.

the 'Bill' of 1530[1]. At the close of 1534 a convocation
under the presidency of Cranmer had agreed to petition
the king that he would 'vouchsafe to decree that the Scrip-
'tures should be translated into the vulgar tongue, by some
'honest and learned men, to be nominated by the king, and
'to be delivered to the people according to their learning[2].'
Crumwell, who must have been well aware of the turn
which opinion had taken, seems now to have urged
Coverdale to commit his work to the press.   At any rate
by 1534 he was ready, 'as he was desired,' 'to *set forth*'
(*i.e.* to publish) his translation[3], and the work was finished
in October, 1535.

But up to the present time the place where it was
printed is wholly undetermined, though most bibliographers
agree that it was printed abroad.   Various conjectures have
been made, but when examined minutely they are found to
be unsupported by any substantial evidence.   The woodcuts and type are certainly not those used by Egenolph of
Frankfort, to which however they bear a very close resemblance[4].   On the other hand, no book printed by Froschover
of Zurich has yet been found with more than the two larger
kinds of type used in Coverdale's Bible[5].   The question is
further complicated by the fact that the title-page and

[1] See p. 43.

[2] Strype, *Cranmer*, p. 34 (ed. 1812).
It is uncertain whether it was after
this resolution (as seems most likely),
or not till after the corresponding
resolutions of 1536, that Cranmer endeavoured to engage the bishops in a
translation or revision of the English
Bible [New Testament], of which
attempt Strype has preserved an
amusing anecdote: *Cranmer*, p. 48.
Strype says that Cranmer took 'an
'*old* English translation which he
'divided into nine or ten parts...to
'be sent to the best learned bishops
'and others, to the intent they should
'make a perfect correction thereof.'
It has been argued that the epithet
'old' can only refer to a copy of the

Wycliffite version—as if that were
available for such a purpose; but in
point of fact the epithet is not found
in Foxe's MSS. [Harl. MS. 422,
Plut. lxv. E fol. 87], to which Strype
refers as the authority for his account.

[3] The date is added in the edition
of 1550.   The words do not imply
that he commenced it then.

[4] Mr F. Fry on *Coverdale's Bible of
1535*, p. 32.   On this point I have
satisfied myself completely.

[5] Mr Fry, *l.c.* p. 28.   It is right to
add that I am convinced, on internal
grounds, that Froschover was the
printer, though at present no satisfactory direct evidence of the fact can
be adduced.   Froschover, it may be
added, printed the edition of 1550.

preliminary matter were reprinted in a different (English) type[1], and the five remaining title-pages represent three

Dr Ginsburg informs me that he has complete typographical proof that the Bible was printed by Froschover. [See the article on Coverdale by Mr Tedder in the *Dict. of Nat. Biography*.]

[In the Catalogue of the Caxton Exhibition in 1877 the late Henry Stevens of Vermont propounded (pp. 86—90) a theory that the Bible of 1535 was printed at Antwerp by Jacob von Meteren at his own cost, and that the translation was his work, Coverdale occupying the humbler position of corrector of the press. This theory would have been grotesque but for the fact that it was adopted by the authorities of the British Museum in their Catalogue, in which Antwerp is given as the place of printing and Van Meteren as the printer, without a hint that these were in any way doubtful. All this cobweb is spun out of the simple statement by Simeon Ruytinck, in his Leven van Emanuel van Meteren (E. van Meteren, *Nederlandische Historie*, 1614, fol. 672), that his father, Jacob van Meteren, had in his youth learnt the art of printing and had shewn especial zeal in defraying the expenses of translating and printing the English Bible in Antwerp, employing for the purpose a learned student, Miles Coverdale by name. This is probably what Ruytinck heard, not quite accurately, from Emanuel; but in a document in the possession of the Dutch Church, Austen Friars, Emanuel himself in 1610 deposes, 'That he was brought to England 'Anno 1550, in King Edward's the 6 'dayes, by his Father, a furtherer of 'reformed religion, and he that caused 'the first Bible at his costes to be 'Englisshed by Mr Myles Coverdale 'in Andwarp, the w'h his father, with

'Mr Edward Whytchurch, printed 'both in Paris and London.' (See Introduction to the Registers of the Dutch Reformed Church, by W. J. C. Moens, 1884.)

There is nothing in either of these statements to imply anything so absurd as that the first English Bible was translated by a Dutchman, and the only safe inference that can be drawn from them is that Jacob van Meteren found means which enabled Coverdale to carry out his work of translation at Antwerp. So far the two accounts agree. But according to Ruytinck the printing also was done at Antwerp, whereas Emanuel van Meteren places it at Paris and London. This fact, together with the introduction of the name of Edward Whitchurch, makes it probable that the English Bible with which Jacob van Meteren had to do was rather Matthew's of 1537 or the Great Bible of 1539 and not Coverdale's of 1535.

Whitchurch's initials are conspicuous in the Bible of 1537, and he was on intimate terms with Rogers, for it was to his house that Rogers appears to have come on his return to England in 1548. He was also associated with Grafton in printing the Great Bible.

In estimating the value of Emanuel van Meteren's evidence, it must be remembered that his knowledge could only have been derived from hearsay, for he was not born till 1535.

No trace of Jacob van Meteren has been found among the Antwerp printers.]

[1] Probably, as Mr Fry shews, by Nycolson: *l.c.* p. 20. In the same way the title-page and preliminary matter of the edition of 1550 printed abroad were cancelled, and a new title-page, &c. printed in England substituted in their place.

distinct issues, two in 1535, and one in 1536. Two copies[1] have a title-page corresponding to the body of the book, dated 1535, and one[2] of them preserves a single page of the original preliminary matter. Another copy[3] has a title-page in English type, corresponding to the English preliminary matter, dated also 1535. The two other title-pages are printed in English type, but with the date 1536[4]. Thus there can be no reason to doubt that the book was issued both with the foreign and English title-pages, &c.[5], though it may still be doubted whether the English title-page, &c. belong to 1536 or to 1535[6].

One important difference between the foreign and English title-pages must be noticed. In the former it is said that the book is 'faithfully and truly translated out of 'Douche [German] and Latyn in to Englishe': in the latter the sources of the version are left unnoticed, and it is said simply to be 'faithfully translated into English.' It is possible that the explanatory words taken in connexion with some further details in the original prologue may have been displeasing to the promoters of the edition[7], and that a new and less explicit title-page, &c. was substituted for

[1] [One in the British Museum, imperfect, the other in the Library of the Earl of Leicester at Holkham.]

[2] [At Holkham.]

[3] [The Marquess of Northampton's.]   [4] See App. II.

[5] The fragment of the foreign printed Prologue offers only one important variation from the corresponding part of the English Prologue: Mr Fry, *l.c.* p. 18.

It is of course impossible to determine the cause of the suppression of the foreign title-page and Prologue. Coverdale may have explained too much in detail 'the Douche and 'Latyn' sources from which he borrowed to suit the wishes of his patrons or publishers. The change in the title-page suggests the conjecture, which is however otherwise unsupported.

[6] It is possible (as has been suggested to me) that when some copies of the English title-page had been struck off with the date 1535, corresponding to the imprint, this date was afterwards changed in the setting of the page to 1536 to suit the actual time of the English issue; so that the two title-pages belong really only to one issue. The only difference observable in the facsimiles of the two title-pages is the inversion of one of the ornaments on the side of BIBLIA.

[7] [The less subtle explanation of Stevens (*Bibles in the Caxton Exhibition*, p. 70) is probably the true one. The title is in a woodcut border, and when the two lines of the quotation from Joshua were added, space had to be provided for them by omitting some of the preceding words.]

the first. However this may have been, the statement
itself, as will be seen afterwards, was literally true, and
Coverdale describes clearly enough in the existing prologue the secondary character of his work[1].

Coverdale indeed disclaims the originality which friends
and detractors have alike assigned to him. And it is in
this that the true beauty and truth of his nature are seen.
He distinctly acknowledges that he could but occupy for a
time the place of another; nay he even looks to this as the
best fruit of his labours that he should call out a worthier
successor to displace himself. 'Though it [Scripture],'
he writes, 'be not worthely ministred vnto the [Christian
'reader] in this translacyon (by reason of my rudnes);
'Yet yf thou be feruēt in thy prayer, God shal not onely
'sende it the in a better shappe, *by the mynistracyon of*
'*other that beganne it afore* [Tindale], but shall also moue
'the hertes of them, which as yet medled not withall, to
'take it in hande, and to bestowe the gifte of theyr vnder-
'stondynge theron[2].'...

Yet in the meantime he saw that there was something
for him to do. It was a noble end if he could secure that
Holy Scripture should be 'set forth' (as he was able to
obtain) 'with the Kynges most gracious license.' And so
plainly disclosing his motives he says...'whan I cōsydered
'how greate pytie it was that we shulde wante it so longe,
'& called to my remembraunce yᵉ aduersite of them, which
'were not onely of rype knowlege, but wolde also with all
'theyr hertes haue perfourmed yᵗ they beganne, yf they
'had not had impediment......these and other reasonable
'causes consydered I was the more bolde to take it in

---

[1] The supposition that the publication of the work was delayed by the
fall of Q. Anne Boleyn is quite base-
less. The substitution of the name of
Q. Jane without any other alteration
in the edition of 1537 is like that of the
name of Edward VI for Henry VIII
in the edition of 1550. The appro-
priateness of epithets was not much
considered by early editors. Mr Fry
has shewn, *l.c.* pp. 10 ff., that all the
dedications found in copies of the first
edition with Q. Jane's name belong to
the edition of 1537.

[2] Coverdale's *Prologe vnto the
Christen Reader.*

'hande. And to helpe me herin, I haue had sondrye
'translacions, not onely in latyn, but also of the Douche
'[German] interpreters: whom (because of theyr synguler
'gyftes & speciall diligence in the Bible) I haue ben the
'more glad to folowe for the most parte, accordynge as I
'was requyred. But to saye the trueth before God, it was
'nether my laboure ner desyre, to haue this worke put in
'my hande: neuertheles it greued me y^t other nacyōs
'shulde be more plenteously prouyded for with ye scripture
'in theyr mother tongue, then we: therfore whan I was
'instantly requyred, though I coulde not do so well as
'I wolde, I thought it yet my dewtye to do my best, and
'that with a good wyll[1].'

Some good indeed he did hope might permanently
remain from his work. As the faithful and honest interpretation of one man it might serve as a kind of comment
to another version.

'...So maye dyuerse translacyons,' he writes 'vnderstonde
'one another, & that in the head articles & grounde of
'oure most blessed faith, though they vse sondrye wordes.
'wherfore me thynke we haue great occasyon to geue
'thanks vnto God, that he hath opened vnto his church the
'gyfte of interpretacyon & of pryntying, and that there
'are now at this tyme so many, which with soch diligēce
'and faithfulnes interprete the scripture to the honoure of
'god and edifyenge of his people......For the which cause
'(acordyng as I was desyred)[2] I toke the more vpon me to
'set forth this speciall translacyon, not as a checker, not as
'a reprouer, or despyser of other mens translacyons (for
'amonge many as yet I haue founde none without occasyon
'of greate thankesgeuynge vnto god) but lowly & faythfully
'haue I folowed myne interpreters, & that vnder correcyon.
'And though I haue fayled eny where (as there is noman
'but he mysseth in some thynge) loue shall constyrre all to
'ye best without eny peruerse iudgment...Yf thou [reader]
'hast knowlege therfore to iudge where eny faute is made

[1] Coverdale's *Prologe*.   [2] In the edition of 1550 is added 'in 1534.'

' I doute not but thou wilt helpe to amende it, yf loue be
' ioyned with thy knowlege.   Howbeit wherin so euer I can
' perceaue by my selfe, or by the informacyon of other, that
' I haue fayled (as it is no wonder) I shall now by the helpe
' of God ouerloke it better & amende it[1].'

The translation of Tindale went forth to the world
without any dedication or author's name. All that was
personal was sunk in the grandeur of the message opened
to Englishmen. But it could not be so with Coverdale's.
His object was to bring about the *open* circulation of the
Scriptures, and that could only be by securing the king's
favour. To this end the work was dedicated to Henry VIII
in language which to us now is in many parts strangely
painful, though it was not out of harmony with the taste
and peculiar circumstances of the time[2].

...' I thought it my dutye,' he says, ' and to belonge
' vnto my allegiaunce, whan I had translated this Bible, not
' onely to dedicate this translacyon vnto youre hyghnesse,
' but wholy to commytte it vnto the same: to the intent
' that yf any thynge therin be translated amysse (for in
' many thynges we fayle, euen whan we thynke to be sure)
' it may stōde in youre graces handes, to correcte it, to
' amende it, to improue it, yee & cleane to reiecte it, yf
' youre godly wysdome shall thynke it necessary.'   But
even so the spirit of the humble and true scholar asserts
itself. For he continues, ' And as I do with all humblenes
' submitte myne vnderstondynge and my poore translacyon
' vnto yᵉ spirite of trueth in your grace, so make I this
' protestacyon (hauyng God to recorde in my cōscience),
' that I haue nether wrested nor altered so moch as one
' worde for the mayntenaūce of any maner of secte: but
' haue with a cleare conscience purely & faythfully translated
' this out of fyue sundry interpreters, hauyng onely the
' manyfest trueth of the scripture before myne eyes[3].'...

---

[1] *Prologe vnto the Christen Reader*.
[2] The Dedication of the Authorised
Version is even more painful and less
capable of excuse. It seems strange
that this should hold its place in our
Bibles while the noble Preface is
universally omitted.
[3] *An Epistle vnto the Kynges
hyghnese.*

Still acting on the broad principle of 'becoming all 'things to all men,' Coverdale afterwards (1538) revised his New Testament, according to the Latin and published it with the Vulgate in parallel columns[1]. His great object was to interpret the Latin itself to some who used it ignorantly, and also to shew openly the substantial identity of Scripture in different languages. Many disparaged this translation or that...'as though,' he says, 'the holy goost 'were not the authoure of his scripture aswell in the 'Hebrue, Greke, French, Dutche, and in Englysh, as in 'Latyn. The scripture & worde of God is truly to euery 'Christē man of lyke worthynesse and authorite, in what 'language so euer the holy goost speaketh it. And ther- 'fore am I, and wyl be whyle I lyue (vnder youre moost 'gracious fauoure and correction)'—he is still addressing Henry VIII—'alwaye wyllynge and ready to do my best 'aswel in one translation, as in another[2].' And thus in the

[1] Of this *Latin-English Testament* there are three editions. The first was printed by Nycolson 1538 and dedicated to Henry VIII. This was executed while Coverdale was in Paris and disowned by him on the ground that 'as it was disagreeable to my 'former translation in English, so 'was not the true copy of the Latin 'text observed' (*Remains*, p. 33). Accordingly he revised it, weeding out 'the faults that were in the Latin 'and English before' (*id.*), and printed a new edition in Paris in the same year, which was published by Grafton and Whitchurch, and dedicated to Lord Crumwell. Nycolson however put forth another impression of his edition under the name of John Hollybushe (1538).

It is probable that Coverdale simply left instructions with the printer as to how the work should be done, not foreseeing the difficulties which would arise, and that the printer engaged Hollybushe to superintend the work, which Coverdale when he saw it dis-

avowed. Coverdale's own Testament is an adaptation of his version to the Latin. Hollybushe's is a new version from the Latin on the basis of Coverdale's. Specimens are given in App. VI.

The titles of the two principal editions are the following:

The newe testament both Latine and Englyshe ech correspondent to the other after the vulgare text, communely called S. Ieroms. Faythfully translated by Myles Couerdale Anno M.CCCCC.XXXVIII....Printed in Southwarke by Iames Nicolson. Set forth wyth the Kynges moost gracious licence.

The new testamen both in Latin and English after the vulgare texte: which is red in the churche. Translated and corrected by Myles Couerdale : and prynted in Paris, by Fraunces Regnault. M.CCCCC.XXXVIII. in Nouembre...Cum gratia & privilegio regis.

[2] *Memorials of Myles Coverdale* (1838), p. 97.

particular case of translations from different texts he re-affirms his general principle of the utility of various transla-tions, applied before to various renderings of the same text ...'for thy part, most gentle reader, take in good worth 'that I here offer thee with a good will, and let this present 'translation be no prejudice to the other, that out of the 'Greek have been translated before, or shall be hereafter. 'For if thou open thine eyes and consider well the gift of 'the Holy Ghost therein, thou shalt see that one translation 'declareth, openeth, and illustrateth another, and that in 'many places one is a plain commentary unto another[1].'

It is very difficult to ascertain the exact relation in which the first edition of Coverdale's Bible stood to the civil authority. There can be no doubt that it was under-taken by the desire of Crumwell, and its appearance may have been hastened by the change of feeling which found expression in the resolutions of Convocation in 1534, though it could not have owed its origin to them. But when it was finished in October 1535 Crumwell appears to have been unable to obtain a definite license from the king, or it may be that he thought it more prudent to await the publication of the book. So much is certain that the first edition went forth without any distinct royal sanction. The book was not suppressed, and this was all[2]. But Convocation was not satisfied; and in 1536 they again petitioned that a new translation might be undertaken. Nothing however was

---

[1] *Remains*, p. 36. (*Parker Soc.*)

[2] On the whole it seems best to refer Coverdale's account of the reference of 'his Bible' by the King to the Bishops to the Great Bible. See p. 76, n. 1. [But if Fulke's account (*Defence of the English Translations of the Bible*, p. 98, Parker Soc. ed.) is correct, Coverdale in his sermon at Paul's Cross spoke of having twice revised his translation since it was submitted to the King. These two revisions would be apparently the Great Bible of 1539 and the edition of April 1540. In this case the Bible presented to the King must have been that of 1535. According to Coverdale, the Bishops to whom it was referred said there were many faults in it, but admitted there were no heresies. 'Then,' said the King, 'in God's 'name let it go abroad among our 'people,' and accordingly the 4° edition printed by Nycolson in 1537 bore on the title-page, 'Set forth with 'the Kinges moost gracious licence.' After this it is hardly likely that the Great Bible also would be referred to the Bishops.]

done; but the relation in which the king stood to the Papal See had already given greater importance to the public recognition of the supremacy of Scripture.

So it happened that when a council was held in the next year under the presidency of Crumwell, as vicar-general, to determine certain articles of faith, the varieties of opinion about Scripture found vigorous expression. Alexander Ales has left a vivid account of the meeting which has been transcribed by Foxe. 'At the king's 'pleasure all the learned men, but especially the bishops, 'assembled, to whom this matter seemed chiefly to belong '......The bishops and prelates attending upon the coming 'of Crumwell, as he was come in, rose up and did obeisance 'unto him as to their vicar-general, and he again saluted 'every one in their degree, and sat down in the highest 'place at the table, according to his degree and office......' Thereupon Crumwell opened the discussion by sketching in a short speech the king's purpose and commands. He will not, he said, 'admit any articles or doctrine not con-'tained in the Scripture, but approved only by continu-'ance of time and old custom, and by unwritten verities, 'as ye were wont to do......His majesty will give you high 'thanks, if ye will set and conclude a godly and a perfect 'unity: whereunto this is the only way and mean, if ye 'will determine all things by the Scripture, as God com-'mandeth you in Deuteronomy; which thing his majesty 'exhorteth and desireth you to do.' On this 'the bishops 'rose up altogether giving thanks unto the king's majesty '......for his most godly exhortation......' There was less unanimity afterwards. The discussion turned upon the Sacraments. Cranmer wisely urged moderation and accuracy of definition. Ales, at the invitation of Crumwell, proceeded to investigate the meaning of the word. Stokesley, bishop of London, interrupted him as he was examining the opinions of the fathers, and was in turn checked by Fox of Hereford, who reminded both that 'they were 'commanded by the king that these controversies should 'be determined only by the rule and judgment of the

'Scripture.' Then specially addressing the bishops he
continued......'The lay people do now know the holy
'Scripture better than many of us; and the Germans have
'made the text of the Bible so plain and easy, by the
'Hebrew and Greek tongues, that now many things may
'be better understood without any glosses at all than by all
'the commentaries of the doctors. And, moreover, they
'have so opened these controversies by their writings, that
'women and children may wonder at the blindness and
'falsehood that have been hitherto.. ...Truth is the daughter
'of time, and time is the mother of truth; and whatsoever
'is besieged of truth cannot long continue; and upon
'whose side truth doth stand, that ought not to be thought
'transitory, or that it will ever fall...' But Stokesley, hard
pressed in the argument, replied to Ales with inconsiderate
warmth...,..'Ye are far deceived if ye think that there is
'none other word of God but that which every souter and
'cobbler doth read in their mother tongue. And if ye
'think that nothing pertaineth unto the Christian faith,
'but that only that is written in the Bible, then err ye
'plainly with the Lutherans'......'Now when the right noble
'lord Crumwell, the archbishop, with the other bishops, who
'did defend the pure doctrine of the Gospel, heard this,
'they smiled a little one upon another, forasmuch as they
'saw him flee, even in the very beginning of the disputation,
'unto his old rusty sophistry and unwritten verities......'
'Thus, through the industry of Crumwell, the colloquies
'were brought to this end, that albeit religion could not
'wholly be reformed, yet at that time there was some
'reformation had throughout all England[1].'

In the meantime the first edition of Coverdale's Bible
was exhausted. The fall and death of Queen Anne, which
had seemed likely to be fatal to the cause of the reformers,
had not stayed the desire for the vernacular Scriptures
which sprang from popular and not from political impulses.
The feeling of the clergy and the bishops was indeed

[1] Foxe, *Acts and Monuments*, v. 378—384.

divided on the question, but even among them the king
could find sufficient support to justify a decided step in
directly authorising the publication of the English Bible[1].
Two editions of Coverdale's translation, in folio and quarto,
'overseen and corrected,' were published by Nycolson in
Southwark in 1537, and for the first time the quarto has
'Set forth with the Kinges moost gracious licence.' The
name of Queen Jane was substituted for that of Queen
Anne in the dedication without further change, and at
length the English Bible was not only tacitly overlooked
but distinctly allowed to circulate freely Coverdale,
through Crumwell's influence, had established a precedent,
and successors were found at once to avail themselves of it.

The revised edition of Coverdale differs slightly in text
and arrangement from that of 1535. One significant addition is worthy of notice, a prayer to be used before reading
the Bible   'Because that whan thou goest to studye in
'holy scripture thou shuldest do it with reuerence, therfore
'for thyn instruccyon and louynge admonicyon therto, the
'Reuerende father in God, Nicolas[2], Bysshoppe of Salis-
'bury hath prescrybed this prayer folowinge, taken out of
'the same.

"O Lorde God almyghtye which longe ago saydest by
"the mouth of Iames thyne Apostle Yf ony of you lacke
"wysdome, let hym aske it of God......Heare my peticyon
"for this thy promes sake.   Haue mercy vpon me, &
"gracyously heare me for IESUS CHRI[S]TES sake our
"LORDE. which lyueth and rayneth with thee, his father &
"the holy goost, worlde with out ende.   Amen."

'After the ende of ony Chapter (yf thou wylt) thou
'mayest saye these verses folowynge

---

[1] According to Foxe, Crumwell, as Vice-gerent, issued in 1536 an injunc-tion that by Aug. 1 every church should be provided with 'a book of 'the whole Bible, both in Latin, and 'also in English...for every man that 'will, to look and read thereon...,' (Foxe, *Acts and Monuments*, v. 167.)

It is however certain that this injunc-tion was not *published* The original draught may have contained the pro-vision, which is the more likely as it is not similar in form to the corre-sponding injunction of 1538.

[2] [Shaxton.]

" Leade me (O LORDE) in thy waye, & let me walke in
"thy trueth. Oh let myne heart delyte in fearynge thy
"name.

" Ordre my goynges after thy worde, yᵗ no wyckednesse
"rayne in me.

" Kepe my steppes within thy pathes, lest my fete turne
"into ony contrarye waye."¹

§ 3 MATTHEW (ROGERS).

Coverdale, we have seen, looked earnestly for the dis-
placing of his own work by another. His prayers and the
prayers of his readers were answered sooner than he could
have hoped. Tindale, at the time of his martyrdom, had
published of the Old Testament the Pentateuch and book
of Jonah, with a few detached pieces, being 'Epistles from
'the Old Testament according to the use of Salisbury,'
including Lessons from Ecclesiasticus and Wisdom². But
he had left in manuscript, according to universal belief, a
version of the books from Joshua to 2 Chronicles inclusive,
which came into the hands of his friend John Rogers. This
work was not to be lost; so Rogers, by the help of an
unknown fellow-labourer, Thomas Matthew, or simply under
this assumed name³, put together a composite Bible made

¹ [This prayer is also found on the
back of the title of a copy of the Bible
of 1535 which is in the Cambridge
University Library.] Coverdale's
Bible of 1535 has been reprinted by
Bagster, London, 1838; and, as far
as I can judge, the reprint has been
very well executed. [It was made
from a copy then in the library of the
Duke of Sussex, and now in my possession (W. A. W.)]

² This alone is sufficient to refute
Anderson's supposition that Tindale,
if he had lived, would not have been
guilty of printing the Apocryphal with
the Canonical Books. [See p. 47.]

³ In the former edition I expressed
myself strongly against the identification of John Rogers and Thomas
Matthew. The name Thomas Matthew stands at the end of the dedication and the initials I.R. at the end
of the Exhortation to the study of
Scripture. In the official sentence
Rogers is described as 'Johannes
'Rogers alias Mathew, presbyter
'secularis' (Foxe, Acts, ed. 1563, p.
1029), and the earliest writers assume
the identity of Rogers and Matthew.
Compare Strype, Mem. III. 1, p. 288.

It is of course quite possible that
the identification simply expressed the
known responsibility of Rogers for the
Bible called Matthew's. Compare
Chester's Life of J. Rogers (London,
1861), pp. 47 f., 55 f., 113. At the

up of Tindale's translation from Genesis to 2 Chronicles, and his revised New Testament of 1535 (or 1534 G. H.)[1], with the remainder of the Old Testament including Jonah[2], and the Apocrypha from Coverdale. The expense of the work was defrayed by two citizens of London, R. Grafton and E. Whitchurch, and it was printed abroad[3]. It was

same time it must be observed that the Christian name as well as the surname is changed, and the earliest evidence does not recognize this change.

[1] This will be shewn afterwards, c. II. § 3.

[2] A copy of Tindale's translation of Jonah was found in 1861 by Lord A. Hervey, bound up in a volume of tracts. [See p. 44.] It has been published with the Prologue and Coverdale's version by Mr F. Fry in facsimile (1863). As some writers still venture to say that Matthew gives Tindale's and not Coverdale's version, it may be worth while to indicate the various readings of one chapter (chap. ii.).

TINDALE.	COVERDALE (MATTHEW).
1 *bowels*	1 *belly*
2 ye bowels of the fish	2 the fishes **belly**
and + *he* sayde	om. *he*
tribulacion	*trouble*
answered	*herde*
3 + *For* thou hadest	3 om. *For*
and all thy	*yee* all **thy**
4 + *&°* I thought	4 I thought
5 water	5 waters
vn to	to
soule *of me*	soule
6 + *And* I wēt	6 om. *And*
vn to	to
+ *on euery syde* for e.	om. *on euery syde*
And yet thou	*But* thou
lorde	+ *O* Lorde
broughtest	hast brought
thought **on**	thought *vp*on
7 in	7 *with*in
8 *obserue*	8 *holde of*
haue forsakē	*wil·forsake*
him that was mercifull vn to them	*his mercy*
9 sacrifice + *vn to the*	9 + *do the* sacrifice
that sauinge	*for why? saluacion*

It is certain however that Coverdale's version was not independent of Tindale's, as indeed this collation itself would shew.

[3] The place of printing has not yet been determined. Grafton's account of the work is given in Strype's *Cranmer*, App. xx.

ready for publication in 1537, and furnished with a dedication to Henry, drawn up in terms exactly similar in tenor to those which have been already quoted ; ' for vnto whom,' Matthew asks, 'or in to whose proteccyon shulde the defence ' of soche a worck be soner cōmytted (wherin are contayned ' the infallyble promeses of mercy...wyth the whole summe ' of Christyanitye) then vnto his maiestye, which not onely ' by name and tytle, but most euydently & openly, most ' Christenly & wyth most Godly pollicye, dothe profess ' the defence therof.' And as men's thoughts were now anxiously turned to the future—it was shortly before the birth of Edward VI—he concludes 'The euerliuyng Lord... ' blesse you at thys present wyth a sonne, by youre most ' gracyous wyfe Quene Iane, which may prosperously & ' fortunately raygne, and folowe the godly steppes of his ' father...'

Whether Cranmer was privy to the preparation of this edition or not is uncertain[1], but it is evident that the authors of it had good reason to be assured that he would welcome its appearance. The first tidings of its arrival in England is contained in a letter which he addressed to Crumwell[2]. 'My especial good lord...,' he writes, ' these ' shall be to signify unto the same, that you shall receive by ' the bringer thereof a bible in English, both of a new ' translation and of a new print, dedicated unto the king's ' majesty, as farther appeareth by a pistle unto his grace in ' the beginning of the book, which in mine opinion is very ' well done, and therefore I pray your lordship to read the ' same. And as for the translation, so far as I have read ' thereof, I like it better than any other translation hereto- ' fore made ; yet not doubting but that there may and will ' be found some fault therein, as you know no man ever

---

[1] An impression is an intangible argument, but to me Cranmer's letter appears to be that of a man who was not taken by surprise by the new Bible. It is further to be remarked that Grafton (who joined in the publication) was acquainted with the contents of Cranmer's letter to Crumwell of Aug. 13th, and wrote to Crumwell with a present of six Bibles on the same day that Cranmer wrote the second letter of thanks. Cranmer's *Works*, p. 346 n. (ed. Park. Soc.).

[2] Letter 194 (ed. Park. Soc).

'did or can do so well, but it may be from time to time
'amended.   And forasmuch as the book is dedicated unto
'the king's grace, and also great pains and labour taken in
'setting forth of the same; I pray you, my Lord, that you
'will exhibit the book unto the king's highness, and to
'obtain of his grace, if you can, a licence that the same may
'be sold and read of every person, without danger of any
'act, proclamation, or ordinance, heretofore granted to the
'contrary, until such time that we the bishops shall set
'forth a better translation, which I think will not be till
'a day after doomsday[1].   And if you continue to take such
'pains for the setting forth of God's word, as you do,
'although in the mean season you suffer some snubs, and
'many slanders, lies, and reproaches for the same, yet one
'day He will requite altogether...'   He was not long in
waiting for the news of Crumwell's success.   In little
more than a week he thanks him for that he 'hath not only
'exhibited the bible...to the king's majesty, but also hath
'obtained of his grace, that the same shall be allowed by
'his authority to be bought and read within this realm...[2]';
and he continues, 'you have shewed me more pleasure
'herein, than if you had given me a thousand pound...[3].'
Nor was he satisfied with this first acknowledgment.   A
fortnight afterwards he writes again : 'These shall be to
'give you most hearty thanks that any heart can think,
'and that in the name of them all which favoureth God's
'word, for your diligence at this time in procuring the
'king's highness to set forth the said God's word and his
'gospel by his grace's authority.   For the which act, not
'only the king's majesty, but also you shall have a per-
'petual laud and memory of all them that be now, or
'hereafter shall be, God's faithful people and the favourers
'of his word[4].'

   The work which Crumwell had achieved was certainly
one which required great address.   The Preface to the

---

[1] See p. 56, n. 2.
[2] It may have been at this time
that Crumwell obtained the license

for Coverdale's Bible also: p. 66.
[3] Letter 197.
[4] Letter 198.

Bible, to which Cranmer specially called his attention, may have smoothed his way; but the king could not have been ignorant that the translation was in part the very work of Tindale, which he had by the advice of his council condemned more than once. The Prologue to the Romans had been condemned separately and was not to be easily overlooked, and the most superficial inspection would have shewn the boldness of the notes with which the text was copiously furnished[1]. It is impossible to tell what considerations availed with Henry. He may have been glad to act independently of the bishops. But however this may have been, by Cranmer's petition, by Crumwell's influence, and by Henry's authority, without any formal ecclesiastical decision, the book was given to the English people, which is the foundation of the text of our present Bible. From Matthew's Bible—itself a combination of the labours of Tindale and Coverdale—all later revisions have

---

[1] The notes in Matthew are distributed not quite equally throughout the Old and New Testament. [Many of them are from Lefèvre's French Bible of 1534. See Appendix XI. for examples from each book.] The commentary on the Psalms is the most elaborate. On the Apocryphal books I have noticed only a few various readings (2 Esdr. iv.: Tob. xii.: Ecclus. xxxiii.: 2 Macc. ii.), and two notes: one on 2 Macc. iv. 'Olympiades: These were kepte euery 'fiftye yeare (sic),' where 'fiftye' [=fifþe] is a misprint for Coverdale's 'fifth'; and the other of considerable interest on 2 Macc. xii. [expanded from Olivetan]. 'Judge upon this 'place whether the opinion hath been 'to pray for the dead, as to be bap-'ised for them, 1 Cor. xv., which 'thing was only done to confirm the 'hope of the resurrection of the dead, 'not to deliver them from any pain. 'S. Paul did not allow the ceremony 'of Christening for the dead, no more 'doth any place of the canonical

'scripture allow the ceremony of 'offering for the dead. Furthermore: 'This whole book of the Maccabees, 'and especially this second, is not 'of sufficient authority to make an 'article of our faith, as it is before 'sufficiently proved by the authority 'of S. Jerome in the prologue of the 'books called Apocrypha.' [The Prayer of Manasses is taken literally from Olivetan.]

One or two other notes may be quoted: John vi. 33. 'The word of 'the Gospel which is Christ, is the 'true and lively bread of heaven that 'giveth life to the whole world.' [From Lefèvre's French Bible of 1534.] John v. 2. ' *Slaughter house.* 'The Greek hath *sheep house*, a place 'where they killed the beasts that 'were offered.' James ii. 24. '*Jus-* '*tified*, that is, is declared just, is 'openly known to be righteous, like 'as by the fruits the good tree is 'known for good. Otherwise may 'not this sentence be interpreted...'

been successively formed. In that the general character and mould of our whole version was definitely fixed. The labours of the next seventy-five years were devoted to improving it in detail.

Matthew's Bible must have been eagerly welcomed. In the same year in which it was imported a scheme was made for reprinting it in England in a smaller form by ' Douche men living within this realm,' ' for covetous-' ness[1]' Grafton, who had ventured a large sum upon the original edition, which consisted of fifteen hundred copies, begged Crumwell for protection, and suggested that he might command in the king's name ' that every curate have ' one of them...yea and that every Abbey should have ' six...yea,' he adds, ' I would none other but they of the ' Papistical sort should be compelled to have them. It does not appear what answer Crumwell gave His action at least was effectual ; for there is no reason to think that the reprint was ever executed[2]. Grafton and Whitchurch were reimbursed for their expenditure ; and in the next year they were ready to embark in a new enterprise, which was designed to supplant their first, and was undertaken under the direct patronage of Crumwell[3].

[1] Grafton's *Letter to Crumwell*, Strype, *Cranmer*, App. xx. [Cotton MS Cleop. E. 5, fol. 325.] Grafton speaks in undue disparagement of ' the ' former [Coverdale's] Bibles, which ' have neither good paper, letter, ink, ' nor correction.' [This may refer to the pirated reprints of Tindale's N.T.]

[2] Taverner's Bible does not answer fully to the description ; otherwise it might be supposed that this ' smaller ' edition was meant.

On the other hand Mr F Fry informs me that ' Mr Lenox has the ' centre of a first title and last leaf of ' a Matthew which he considers to ' belong to the pirated edition,' and that he himself has ' two leaves which ' may be of it.' [I have no information with regard to the title and last leaf in Mr Lenox's Library, but the other two leaves mentioned by Mr Fry, which are now in the Library of the Bible Society, are not what he supposed them to be In the copy of Matthew's Bible in the Cambridge University Library they are inserted in their proper place in the Apocrypha, foll. 12, 13, and were apparently reprinted to make good a defective quire. They are distinguished by the use of the comma instead of the virgule, but the differences in the text are trifling, and shew that the leaves were not cancelled on account of any error I have not at present found another copy in which the reprinted leaves occur in their place W A. W.]

[3] Matthew s Bible was reprinted in 1549 (Raynalde and Hyll), and again in 1551 for several publishers (Cotton.

§ 4. THE GREAT BIBLE (CRUMWELL, CRANMER, TUNSTALL AND HEATH).

It is indeed evident that Crumwell's zeal for the circulation of the vernacular Scriptures could not be satisfied with the license which he had obtained for the Bibles of Coverdale and Matthew. The first was imperfect in its conception : the second was burdened with notes and additions which could not fail sooner or later to call out bitter antagonism. Under these circumstances he appears to have applied to Coverdale, who was in England in the early part of 1538, to undertake the charge of a new edition on the basis of Matthew's, but with a more complete critical collation of the Hebrew and Latin texts than had been hitherto attempted. Grafton and Whitchurch had earned by their former work the privilege of undertaking the conduct of this, but the resources of the English press were not adequate to carry it out as Crumwell wished. And so

p. 27 n.). It was also revised by E. Becke, and his altered text was published in 1549 by Daye and Seres (both folio and 8vo). I have not however examined the texts of these editions at any length, but a cursory collation shews considerable differences in the reproductions both of Matthew and of Becke's revision, which extend alike to text and notes. An edition by Daye, 1551 (with 3 Macc.), gives the Old Testament text of Taverner, though it is called ' Matthew's.'

[The editions of 1549 printed by Raynalde and Hyll, and of 1551 by Hyll alone, for 'certayne honest men ' of the occupacyon,' are little more than reprints of Matthew's Bible of 1537, with the addition of Tindale's prologues to some of the books. The edition of 1549 has the prologues to the books of the Pentateuch, Jonah, and the Epistle to the Romans, but not those to the New Testament, the Gospels or the other Epistles, while they are all given in the edition by Hyll in 1551.

Becke's edition of 1549 by Daye and Seres and that of 1551 by Daye alone contain all Tindale's prologues. The notes from Matthew are considerably altered in both, but in the 1549 edition the text is not substantially changed. In 1551 Becke with slight alterations adopted Taverner's text of the Old Testament except in Deut. xxxii.—Joshua xiii. and the Psalms. He added the third book of Maccabees, and gave a new translation of 3 Esdras, Tobit, and Judith (see Dore's *Old Bibles*, 2nd ed. pp. 144 &c.). Becke had nothing to do with the edition printed by Hyll in 1551, as stated in the account given of him in the *Dictionary of National Biography*.

In the book of Revelation in Becke's edition of 1549 the woodcuts are accompanied by descriptions in doggerel verse. In the edition of 1551 woodcuts and verse are omitted.]

about Lent Coverdale proceeded with Grafton to Paris to superintend the printing there. A license was obtained from Francis for the execution of the work[1], which was commenced on a splendid scale by Regnault. Coverdale pressed forward the enterprise with all haste, for even from the first they were 'dayly threatened,' and looked 'ever 'to be spoken withall.' By September he could inform Crumwell that 'Youre Lordshippes worke of the Bible... 'goeth well forwarde, and within few monethes, will drawe 'to an ende, by the grace of Allmightie God.' Three months later when the text was almost finished the danger of interruption to the printing became imminent. Coverdale conveyed as much of the Bible as was ready to Crumwell by the help of Bishop Bonner, ambassador at Paris, that 'if these men proceed in their cruelness against us, and 'confiscate the rest yet this at the least may be safe[2].' In four days more the expected inhibition came An order from the Inquisitor-general for France forbade the further progress of the work and the removal of the printed sheets. Coverdale and Grafton made their escape, but not long after returned to Paris and conveyed presses, types and workmen to London, and even rescued a large quantity of the condemned sheets—'four great dry-vats' full—which had been sold to a tradesman as waste-paper, instead of being burnt. Thus that which had seemed to be for the hindrance of Crumwell's design really forwarded it permanently in a wonderful manner by introducing into England the materials and men best suited to carry it out. The Bible, henceforth known as the *Great Bible*[3], was finished in April, but without the critical and explanatory com-

---

[1] The license granted by Francis is given by Strype, *Cranmer*, p. 756, App. xxx. [Cotton MS. Cleop. E. 5. p. 326]. After the permission to print and export is added the provision: 'Dummodo quod sic imprimetis et 'excudetis sincere et pure, quantum 'in vobis erit, citra ullas privatas aut 'illegitimas opiniones, impressum et 'excussum [excusum] fuerit....' This clause was of course sufficiently wide to admit of the interference of the Inquisition.

[2] Coverdale's *Remains* (Parker Soc.), p. 497. [Harl. MS. 604, p. 98.]

[3] I have ventured to keep this name as a general title for the group of Bibles, including Crumwell's Bible (1539) and the six later issues with Cranmer's Preface (1540-1), though

mentary which Coverdale had designed[1]. While the revision
was going forward he had set 'in a pryvate table the
'dyversitie of redinges of all textes [Hebrew, Chaldee,
'Greek, Latin], with such annotacions, in another table, as
'shall douteles delucidate and clear the same, as well with-
'out any singularyte of opinions, as all checkinges and
'reprofes[2].' And when it was drawing to a close, he writes
regretfully: 'Pitie it were, y^t the darck places of ye text
'(vpon which I haue allwaye set a hande ☞) shulde so
'passe vndeclared. As for anye pryuate opynion or con-
'tencious words, as I wyll vtterly avoyde all soche, so wyll
'I offre ye annotacions first to my sayd lord of herdford
'[Bonner], to ye intent y^t he shall so examen ye same, afore

it must be carefully borne in mind
that these seven issues do not give
the same text, however like they may
be externally. The text of 1539 is
quite distinct from that of April, 1540,
and this again from that of November,
1540, 1541, which is in the main the
text of the later reprints. Compare
Chap. III.

[1] A copy of this edition on vellum
designed for Crumwell and described
by Coverdale himself, is now in the
Library of St John's College, Cambridge.

It is worthy of remark that this
Bible has no dedication. The title-
page—said to have been designed
by Holbein—represents (at the top)
the king giving the Bible (Verbum
Dei) to Crumwell and Cranmer: they
in turn (on the sides) distribute it
among ecclesiastics and laymen: at
the bottom a crowd is listening to a
preacher. Labels with various texts
&c. issue from the mouths of the chief
figures. The composition includes
many other details and will repay a
careful examination. It is well described in the *Historical Account*,
pp. 91, 92.

The reference of 'Coverdale's Bible'
to the Bishops by the king, and their

confession that there were no heresies
to be maintained thereby, appears to
refer to this edition (Fulke, p. 98).
[But see p. 63, note 2.]

In a preliminary explanation of
signs some account is given of the
delay in the publication of the notes:
'We haue also (as ye may se) added
'many handes both in the mergent
'of this volume and also in the text,
'vpon the which, we purposed to
'haue made in the ende of the Byble
'(in a table by them selues) certen
'godly annotacions: but forsomoch
'as yet there hath not bene soffycient
'tyme minystred to the kynges moost
'honorable councell, for the ouersight
'and correccyon of the sayde annota-
'cyons, we wyll therfore omyt them,
'tyll their more conueniēt leysour,
'doynge now nomore but beseke the,
'most gentle reader, that when thou
'commest at soch a place where a
'hande doth stande...& thou canst
'not attayne to the meanynge and
'true knowledge of that sentence,
'then do not rashly presume to make
'any priuate interpretacyon therof:
'but submyt thy selfe to the iudge-
'ment of those that are godly learned
'in Christ Jesu.'

[2] *State Papers*, I. 576.

'they be put in prynte, yf it be y^r lordshippes good pleasure, 'y^t I shall do so.' But Coverdale's regret was ineffectual. The various marks which he designed remained in the text of several editions of the Great Bible, but nothing more than a general explanation of their import was ever given. The volume of 'annotations' was deferred till a more convenient occasion, which never came. But in the mean time a complete English text of the Scriptures was provided for public use, which, by an injunction framed beforehand, Crumwell, as the king's vice-gerent, required should be set up in some convenient place in every church throughout the kingdom before a specified day[1]. 'A 'domino factum est istud' is the worthy motto with which it concludes[2].

There is no evidence to shew that Cranmer had any

[1] There cannot be the least doubt that the 'Bible of the largest volume 'in English' was the edition being prepared in Paris. No one who has seen Coverdale's, Matthew's, and Crumwell's Bibles together would hesitate as to the application of the description: the Bible and the injunction corresponded and were both due to the same man. I cannot agree with Mr Anderson in supposing Matthew's Bible to have been intended: II. 34, in spite of Strype, *Cranmer*, I. 117. The date by which the Bible was to be procured was left blank. At the time when the injunctions were drawn up the interruption of the printing could not have been definitely foreseen. Similar proclamations were issued by the king in May, 1540, immediately after the publication of the second (Cranmer's) Great Bible; and again in May, 1541, after the publication of the fourth, which bore the names of Tunstall and Heath. Anderson, II. pp. 131, 142

It may be added that Cranmer in his injunctions for the clergy of the diocese of Hereford (between May and November, 1538) requires that every one 'shall have, by the first day 'of August next coming (1539?), as 'well a whole bible in Latin and 'English, or at the least a new 'testament of both the same lan- 'guages, as the copies of the king's 'highness' injunctions.' These injunctions were probably issued after September, and the date fixed in 1539. Cranmer, *Works*, II. p. 81.

[2] One passage which occurs at the end of the Introduction is worthy of being quoted, and it seems characteristic of Coverdale:

'With what judgment the books of 'the Old Testament are to be read.

...' The books of the Old Testament 'are much to be regarded because they 'be as it were a manner of founda- 'tion, whereunto the New Testament 'doth cleave and lean, out of the 'which certain arguments of the New 'Testament may be taken. For there 'is nothing shewed in the New Tes- 'tament, the which was not shadowed 'before in the figures of Moses' Law, 'and forespoken in the revelations of 'the Prophets, some things even evid- 'ently expressed...'

share in the first preparation of the Great Bible, or
even that he was acquainted with the undertaking. The
selection of Coverdale for the execution of the work,
and Coverdale's correspondence, distinctly mark it as
Crumwell's sole enterprise. But Cranmer was not slow in
furthering it. By the autumn of the same year arrangements were completed for the printing of a new edition
in London with the help of the materials obtained from
Paris; and the archbishop had drawn up a preface for it,
which he had transmitted to Crumwell for the approbation
of the king. By a strange coincidence Crumwell received
from Henry on the very day on which Cranmer wrote
to him to make a final decision about the price, &c.[1], the
absolute right of licensing the publication of Bibles in
England for five years. Thus all difficulties were removed
from the way, and the Bible with the Preface of the
archbishop was finished in April, 1540. Two other editions
followed in the same year (July: November, the title-page
is dated 1541): and three more in 1541 (May: November:
December). These six editions all have Cranmer's prologue, but the third and fifth bear the names of Tunstall
and Heath upon the title-page, who are said to have
'overseen and perused' the translation 'at the command-
'ment of the kinges highnes.' The cause of this nominal
revision is obvious. Crumwell had been disgraced and
executed in July. The work which he had taken so
much to heart was naturally suspected; and thus the
open sanction of two bishops, prominent among the party
opposed to him, was required to confirm its credit. And
so it was that at last by a strange irony 'my lord of
'London' authorised what was in a large part substantially

[1] 'If your lordship hath known the
'king's highness' pleasure concerning
'the preface of the bible which I sent
'to you to oversee, so that his grace
'doth allow the same, I pray you
'that the same may be delivered
'unto the said Whitchurche unto
'printing, trusting that it shall both
'encourage many slow readers and
'also stay the rash judgments of them
'that read therein.' Cranmer to
Crumwell, Letter 264, Nov. 14th,
1539. From the long interval which
elapsed before the completion of the
Bible—five months—it appears likely
that little was actually done before
Cranmer was assured of the king's
favour.

the very work of Tindale, which he had before condemned
and burnt[1].

The variations in the texts of these editions of the
Great Bible will be considered afterwards. But one important change was made in the original design of the
book which requires to be noticed now.   Coverdale, as
we have seen, looked upon the notes as an important
part of the work, and the reference to them was retained
through three editions[2]. With the fall of Crumwell all
hope of publishing a commentary disappeared, and the
'pointing hands' were removed.   It is not difficult to
understand the objections to Coverdale's design, and a
narrative which Foxe has preserved will explain the influence which led to its suppression.

'Not long after [the death of Crumwell],' he writes,
'great complaint was made to the king of the translation
'of the Bible, and of the preface of the same; and then
'was the sale of the Bible commanded to be stayed, the
'bishops promising to amend and correct it, but never
'performing the same.   Then Grafton was called, and first
'charged with the printing of Matthew's Bible, but he,
'being fearful of trouble, made excuses for himself in all
'things.   Then was he examined of the great Bible, and
'what notes he was purposed to make: to the which he
'answered, that he knew none.   For his purpose was, to
'have retained learned men to have made the notes; but
'when he perceived the king's majesty and his clergy
'not willing to have any, he proceeded no further.   But

[1] The expense of these editions
was defrayed, as seems certain, by
'Antony Marler a haberdasher' of
London, who presented to Henry a
magnificent copy on vellum [of the
edition of April, 1540] with an autograph inscription, which is preserved
in the British Museum. Mr Anderson
quotes a minute of the Privy Council
bearing on his privileges with regard
to the sale, dated April, 1541 (II. p.
142), and a patent for printing the

Bible alone for four years: March,
1542 (II. p. 152).

[2] Of April, 1539: April, 1540:
July, 1540. After this the ☞—the
reference to *notes*—was omitted.

For the relation between the texts
of the several issues of the Great
Bible see Chap. III. § 4. I cannot
tell by what surprising oversight Mr
Anderson describes Crumwell's Bible
as being *Matthew's* text.

'for all these excuses, Grafton was sent to the Fleet, and
'there remained six weeks, and before he came out was
'bound in three hundred pounds, that he should neither
'sell, nor imprint nor cause to be imprinted any mo
'Bibles until the king and the clergy should agree upon
'a translation. And thus was the Bible from that time
'stayed, during the reign of king Henry VIII.[1]'

The publication of the Great Bible and the injunction
for its free exhibition in the parish churches marked a
memorable epoch. The king in a declaration appointed
'to be read by all curates upon the publishing of the
'Bible in English' justly dwelt upon the gravity of the
measure. He commanded 'that in the reading and hear-
'ing thereof, first most humbly and reverently using and
'addressing yourselves unto it'—the curate is speaking to
his congregation—'you shall have always in your re-
'membrance and memories that all things contained in
'this book is the undoubted will, law, and commandment
'of Almighty God, the only and straight means to know
'the goodness and benefits of God towards us, and the
'true duty of every Christian man to serve him accord-
'ingly...And if at any time by reading any doubt shall
'come to any of you, touching the sense and meaning
'of any part thereof; that then, not giving too much to
'your own minds, fantasies and opinions, nor having
'thereof any open reasoning in your open taverns or
'alehouses, ye shall have recourse to such learned men as
'be or shall be authorised to preach and declare the same.
'So that avoiding all contentions and disputations in
'such alehouses and other places...you use this most high
'benefit quietly and charitably every of you, to the edify-
'ing of himself, his wife and family...[2].'

Among others Bp Bonner 'set up Six Bibles in certain
convenient places of St Paul's church,' after the king's
proclamation in May, 1540[3], with an admonition to readers

---

1 Foxe. *Acts and Monuments*, v.   XXIII. [Cotton MS. Cleop. E. 5,
p. 412   p. 327.]
     2 Strype's *Cranmer*, II. 735–6, App.   3 See p. 76, n. 1.

to bring with them 'discretion, honest intent, charity, 'reverence and quiet behaviour. That there should no 'such number meet together there as to make a multitude. 'That no exposition be made thereupon but what is de- 'clared in the book itself. That it be not read with 'noise in time of divine service; or that any disputation 'or contention be used at it[1].' It is scarcely surprising that the novelty of the license granted to the people should have led them to neglect these instructions. Bonner was forced, as he pleads, by the great disorders created by the readers to issue a new admonition in which he threatened the removal of the Bibles. 'Diverse wilful 'and unlearned persons,' he writes, 'inconsiderately and 'indiscreetly...read the same especially and chiefly at the 'time of divine service...yea in the time of the sermon 'and declaration of the Word of God...Wherefore this is 'eftsoons of honest friendship to require and charitably 'to desire and pray every reader of this Book that either 'he will indeed observe and keep my former advertisement 'and friendly admonition adjoined hereunto...either else to 'take in good part and be content that the said Bibles 'for the said abuses be taken down, for assuredly, the fault 'and disorder herein not amended but increased, I intend, 'being thereunto enforced, upon right good considerations, 'and especially for the said abuses, to take down the said 'Bibles, which otherwise I would be right loth to do, con- 'sidering I have been always and still will be by God's 'grace right glad that the Scripture and Word of God 'should be well known and also set forth accordingly[2].'

The popular zeal for reading the Scriptures was not always manifested thus inconsiderately. In a public document drawn up to justify the position of the English Church in 1539[3] great stress is laid upon the revolution

---

[1] Strype's *Cranmer*, I. 121. [The Admonition is printed in the Catalogue of the Library of the British and Foreign Bible Society, vol. I. p. 25.]

[2] Foxe, *Acts and Monuments*, v. App. 14.

[3] A Summary Declaration of the Faith, Uses and Observations in England (dated 1539). Collier, *Ecclesiastical History*, II. *Collection of Records*, 47.

in common habits which was thus effected. 'Englishmen
'have now in hand in every Church and place, almost
'every man the Holy Bible and New Testament in their
'mother tongue instead of the old fabulous and fantastical
'books of the *Table Round, Launcelot du Lac*, &c., and
'such other, whose unpure filth and vain fabulosity the
'light of God has abolished utterly.'

One narrative, which is derived from actual experience,
will illustrate the feelings of the time. It was taken by
Strype from a manuscript of Foxe.

'It was wonderful to see with what joy this book of
'God was received not only among the learneder sort and
'those that were noted for lovers of the reformation, but
'generally all England over among all the vulgar and
'common people; and with what greediness God's word
'was read and what resort to places where the reading
'of it was. Every body that could bought the book or
'busily read it or got others to read it to them if they
'could not themselves, and divers more elderly people
'learned to read on purpose. And even little boys flocked
'among the rest to hear portions of the holy Scripture
'read. One William Maldon happening in the company
'of John Foxe, in the beginning of the reign of Q. Eliza-
'beth, and Foxe being very inquisitive after those that
'suffered for religion in the former reigns, asked him if he
'knew any that were persecuted for the Gospel of Jesus
'Christ that he might add it to his Book of Martyrs. He
'told him he knew one that was whipped by his own
'father in king Henry's reign for it. And when Foxe
'was very inquisitive who he was and what was his name,
'he confessed it was himself; and upon his desire he wrote
'out all the circumstances. Namely that when the king
'had allowed the Bible to be set forth to be read in all
'Churches immediately several poor men in the town of
'Chelmsford in Essex, where his father lived and he was
'born, bought the New Testament and on Sundays sat
'reading of it in the lower end of the Church: many
'would flock about them to hear their reading: and he

'among the rest, being then but fifteen years old, came
'every Sunday to hear the glad and sweet tidings of the
'Gospel. But his father observing it once angrily fetched
'him away and would have him say the Latin Matins with
'him, which grieved him much. And as he returned at
'other times to hear the Scripture read, his father still
'would fetch him away. This put him upon the thoughts
'of learning to read English that so he might read the
'New Testament himself; which when he had by diligence
'effected he and his father's apprentice bought the New
'Testament, joining their stocks together, and to conceal
'it laid it under the bedstraw and read it at convenient
'times. One night his father being asleep he and his
'mother chanced to discourse concerning the crucifix, and
'kneeling down to it and knocking on the breast then
'used, and holding up the hands to it when it came by on
'procession. This he told his mother was plain idolatry...
'His mother enraged at him for this said, "Wilt thou not
'worship the cross which was about thee when thou wert
'christened and must be laid on thee when thou art dead ?"
'In this heat the mother and son departed and went to
'their beds. The sum of this evening's conference she
'presently repeats to her husband; which he impatient
'to hear and boiling in fury against his son for denying
'worship to be due to the cross, arose up forthwith and
'goes into his son's chamber and, like a mad zealot, taking
'him by the hair of his head with both his hands pulled
'him out of the bed and whipped him unmercifully. And
'when the young man bore this beating, as he related,
'with a kind of joy, considering it was for Christ's sake
'and shed not a tear, his father seeing that was more
'enraged, and ran down and fetched an halter and put it
'about his neck, saying he would hang him. At length
'with much entreaty of the mother and brother he left
him almost dead[1].'

It would be impossible to paint in more vivid colours

---

[1] Strype's *Cranmer*, I. 91, 92. [Harl. MS. 590, fol. 77.]

the result of the first open reading of the English Bible, and the revelation which it made of the thoughts of many hearts. Classes and households were divided. On the one side were the stern citizens of the old school to whom change seemed to be the beginning of license: on the other young men burning with eager zeal to carry to the uttermost the spiritual freedom of which they had caught sight. And between them were those to whom all they had been taught to reverence was still inestimably precious while yet they could not press to extremity those by whom the old tenets were assailed.

§ 5.   TAVERNER.

While Crumwell was hurrying forward his Bible in Paris, another edition was being printed in London. This also was based on Matthew, and seems to have been executed in considerable haste. The editor was a layman and a lawyer, R. Taverner, who had a great reputation as a Greek scholar. At an earlier time he was one of the students of 'Cardinal College,' Oxford, who had suffered persecution upon the first circulation of Tindale's New Testament [see p. 42]. He was acquainted with Crumwell, and by his influence the king appointed him to be one of his clerks of the signet. In the reign of Edward VI he had a special license to preach, and a quaint account[1] has been preserved of the studiously unclerical habit— with a velvet bonnet and damask gown, and gold chain and sword—in which he discharged the duty. It was his humour also, as we are told[1], 'to quote the law in Greek.' These little touches are important, for they throw no small light upon the spirit in which he accomplished his revision. In one respect he stands above his predecessors. His Dedication to Henry is couched in language full at once of respect and manliness. He gives the king due credit for what he had done and speaks with modesty of

[1] [In Wood's *Athenæ Oxonienses.*]

his own labours :...'This one thing I dare full well affirme
'that amonges all your maiesties deseruinges...your highnes
'neuer did thing more acceptable vnto god, more profitable
'to yᵉ auaūcemēt of true christianitie, more displeasaūt to
'the enemies of the same, & also to your graces enemies,
'then when your maiestie lycenced and wylled the moost
'sacred Byble conteynyng the vnspotted and lyuely worde
'of God to be in the Englysh tong set forth to your
'hyghnes subiectes...

. 'Wherfore the premisses wel cōsidered, forasmoch as
'yᵉ printers herof were very desirous to haue this most
'sacred volume of the bible com forth as faultlesse &
'emendatly, as the shortnes of tyme for the recognising
'of yᵉ same wold require, they desired me your most
'hūble servāt for default of a better lerned, diligētly to
'ouerloke & peruse the hole copy...Whiche thynge ac-
'cordyng to my talent I haue gladly done.

'These therfore my simple lucubraciōs & labours, to
'whō might I better dedicate, thē vnto your most ex-
'cellēt & noble maiestie, yᵉ only authour & grounde nexte
'God of this so highe a benefite vnto your graces people,
'I meane that the holy scripture is communicate vnto
'the same.'

Taverner's Bible (like Crumwell's) was published in
1539, in two editions, folio and quarto[1]. It is furnished
with a marginal commentary based upon Matthew's, but
shorter, and containing some original notes. In the same
year in which his Bible was printed, Taverner likewise
put forth two editions (quarto and octavo) of the New
Testament through another printer but the same publisher;
but the appearance of the Great Bible must have checked
the sale of his works. The Bible and the New Testament
were each reprinted once, and his Old Testament was
adopted in a Bible of 1551 [see p. 73, note]. With these
exceptions his revision appears to have fallen at once into
complete neglect.

---

[1] [The existence of the quarto edition mentioned by Cotton is doubtful.]

§ 6. A TIME OF SUSPENSE.

After the publication of the Great Bible (1539—1541) the history of the English Version remains stationary for a long time. Nothing was done to amend it and severe restrictions were imposed upon its use. In 1542 a proposition was made in convocation in the king's name for a translation of the New Testament to be undertaken by the Bishops. The books were portioned out, but Gardiner brought the scheme to an end by pressing the retention of a large number of Latin terms which would practically have made a version such as the Rhemish one was afterwards[1]. As this condition was obviously inadmissible, the king, by Cranmer's influence, resolved to refer the translation to the two Universities. Convocation was no more consulted on the subject, and the Universities did nothing.

In the next year Parliament proscribed all translations bearing the name of Tindale, and required that the notes in all other copies should be removed or obliterated. At the same time it was enacted that no women (except noble or gentle women), no artificers, apprentices, journeymen, serving-men, husbandmen, or labourers, should read to themselves or to others, publicly or privately, any part of the Bible under pain of imprisonment. Three years later (1546) the king repeated the prohibition against Tindale's books with many others and included Coverdale's New Testament in the same category. Thus the Great Bible alone remained unforbidden, and it was probably at this time that the great destruction of the earlier Bibles and Testaments took place. And even where the book has been preserved, the title-page has been in many cases destroyed that the true character of the volume might escape the observation of a hasty inquisitor.

[1] The list of words is a very strange one. With words like *ecclesia, pœnitentia, pontifex, peccatum, hostia, pascha, impositio manuum, confessio,* which have a dogmatic significance, are others which are practically proper names like *Christus, zizania, didrachma, tetrarcha,* and others again which have apparently no special force, as *simplex, dignus, ejicere, oriens, tyrannus.* [See Fuller's *Church History,* Cent. XVI, Book v. p. 238 (ed. 1655).]

For the proclamation was not allowed to remain idle. The party of the 'old learning' even outran the letter of the edict. This had enjoined 'the burning of certain 'translations of the New Testament,' but, 'they were so 'bold as to burn the whole Bible, because they were of 'those men's, Tindale's or Coverdale's, translation ; and 'not the New Testament only.' Nay more, they were anxious to escape from the responsibility which they had incurred by sanctioning the Great Bible. Tunstall and Heath, who had been 'appointed to overlook the trans-'lation' at the time of Crumwell's execution, and had 'set their names thereunto, when they saw the world 'somewhat like to wring on the other side denied it ; and 'said they never meddled therewith[1].'

But in the midst of this reaction Henry died (Jan. 28, 1547). The accession of Edward restored the reforming party to power, and the young king himself is said to have shewn a singular devotion to the Bible. According to some the English Bible was first used at his coronation[2]. 'When three swords were brought,' so Strype writes[3], 'signs of his being king of three kingdoms, he 'said, there was one yet wanting. And when the nobles 'about him asked him what that was, he answered, *The* '*Bible*. "That book," added he, "is the Sword of the 'Spirit, and to be preferred before these swords..." And 'when the pious young king had said this, and some other 'like words, he commanded the Bible with the greatest 'reverence to be brought and carried before him.' However this may have been, the work of printing the English Scriptures was carried on during his reign with great activity. Thirty-five Testaments and thirteen[4] Bibles were published in England in the six years and a half for which he occupied the throne. The public use of them was made

---

[1] *A Supplication of the poor Commons*, printed in Strype's *Eccles. Memorials*, 1. 608 ff.

[2] The fact is not mentioned in the order of the Coronation printed by Burnet, and in part by Strype, *Cran-*mer, 1. 202 ff.

[3] *Eccles. Mem.* II. 35, on the authority of Bale *de Viris Illustr.* [See Camden's *Remaines* (ed. 1614), p. 294.]

[4] [Fourteen in Anderson's list.]

the subject of special admonition and inquiry. Among
the injunctions issued by the king (1547) on his accession
was one requiring that all beneficed persons 'shall provide
'within three months next after this visitation, one book
of the whole Bible of the largest volume in English ; and
'within one twelve months next after the said visitation,
'the Paraphrasis of Erasmus also in English upon the
'Gospels, and the same set up in some convenient place
'within the...Church..., whereas their parishioners may
'most commodiously resort unto the same and read the
'same.' And again, 'that they shall discourage no man
'(authorized and licensed thereto) from the reading any
'part of the Bible, either in Latin or in English, but shall
'rather comfort[1] and exhort every person to read the
'same, as the very lively word of God, and the special
'food of man's soul that all Christian persons are bound
'to embrace, believe and follow, if they look to be saved[2].'
In the next year Cranmer instituted inquiries into the
fulfilment of these injunctions in his articles for the visitation of the diocese of Canterbury[3], further asking 'whether
'...priests being under the degree of a bachelor of divinity
'have of their own the New Testament both in Latin
'and English and the Paraphrase of Erasmus upon the
'same.'

But beyond this nothing of moment was actually
achieved with regard to the English Version of the Scriptures. At this crisis the constitution of the English
Church and the remoulding of the Service-books were of
more urgent importance than the revision of the Bible ;
but Cranmer did not overlook this work. In 1549 Fagius
and Bucer were appointed by his influence to professor-
ships at Cambridge, and during their stay with him at
Lambeth, before they entered on their work there, 'the
'archbishop himself directed of what subject matter their
'lectures should be. As it had been a great while his pious

---

[1] [So Cardwell, *Doc. Ann.* (ed. 1);   9. Comp. p. 25.
'conform' ed. 2.]   [3] Cranmer's *Works*, II. p. 155.
[2] Cardwell's *Doc. Ann.* [ed. 2] I.   Compare pp. 161; 81.

'and most earnest desire that the Holy Bible should come
'abroad in the greatest exactness and true agreement with
'the original text, so he laid this work upon these two
'learned men. First that they should give a clear plain
'and succinct interpretation of the Scripture according to
'the propriety of the language; and secondly illustrate
'difficult and obscure places and reconcile those that
'seemed repugnant to one another. And it was his will
'and his advice that to this end and purpose their public
'readings should tend...Fagius, because his talent lay in
'the Hebrew learning, was to undertake the Old Testa-
'ment; and Bucer the New...Fagius entered upon the
'Evangelical prophet Esaias and Bucer upon the gospel
'of the Evangelist John, and some chapters in each book
'were dispatched by them. But it was not long but both
'of them fell sick, which gave a very unhappy stop to
'their studies[1].' Nothing indeed is here said of an immediate revision of the authorised Bible, but the instructions point to the direction in which the great archbishop's
thoughts were turned.

Meanwhile a fragment of a version of the New Testament—the Gospel of St Matthew and the beginning of
St Mark—was completed by Sir John Cheke—at one time
professor of Greek at Cambridge and tutor to Edward VI.
He seems to have aimed at giving a thoroughly English
rendering of the text, and in this endeavour he went to
far greater lengths of quaintness than Taverner. Thus he
coins new words to represent the old 'ecclesiastical' terms
for which More and Gardiner contended most earnestly:
frosent (apostle): *biword* (parable): *gainbirth* (regeneration): *uprising* or *gainrising* (resurrection): *tablers* (money-
changers): *tollers* (publicans): *freshman* (proselyte): and
uses strange participial forms: *gospeld* (xi. 5): *devild* (viii.
28): *moond* (iv. 24); and even *crossed* for crucified. The
fragment remained in manuscript till quite lately[2], and it is
not certain that it was designed for publication. As it will

[1] Strype's *Cranmer*, 1. 281.
[2] Edited by the Rev. James Goodwin, Cambridge, 1843.

not be necessary to revert to it again, a specimen may be given to shew its general style :

'At that time Jesus answered and said : I must needs, 'O Father, acknowledge thanks unto Thee, O Lord of 'heaven and earth, which hast hidden these things from 'wise and witty men, and hast disclosed the same to babes; 'yea and that, Father, for such was thy good pleasure 'herein. All things be delivered me of my Father. And 'no man knoweth the Son but the Father, and he to whom 'the Son will disclose it. Come to me all that labour 'and be burdened and I will ease you. Take my yoke on 'you and learn of me, for I am mild and of a lowly heart. 'And ye shall find quietness for yourselves. For my yoke 'is profitable ($\chi\rho\eta\sigma\tau\acute{o}s$) and my burden light.' (Matt. xi. 25—30.)

In the reign of Mary no English Bible was printed. Rogers and Cranmer were martyred : Coverdale with difficulty escaped to the Continent: the bones of Fagius and Bucer were burnt; but no special measures appear to have been taken for the destruction of the English Scriptures, or for the restriction of their private use. The public use of them in churches was necessarily forbidden. Proclamations against certain books and authors were issued, but no translations of the Old or New Testament were (as before) mentioned by name. Copies of the Bible which had been set up in churches were burnt ; but they were not sought out or confiscated. Evidently a great change had come over the country since the time of Henry VIII. And in the mean time though the English press was inactive the exiles abroad were busy, and at the close of Mary's reign a New Testament was printed at Geneva, which was the first step towards a work destined to influence very powerfully our Authorised Version. The origin of this must now be traced.

§ 7. THE GENEVAN BIBLE.

It is unnecessary to dwell upon the disastrous discussions at Frankfurt which divided the English exiles of Mary's reign. The task of continuing the revision of the Bible fell naturally to the non-conforming party who retired to Geneva, the active centre of the labours of Calvin and Beza. Among them was W. Whittingham, who married Calvin's [wife's] sister[1]; and it is to him in all probability that we owe the Genevan Testament[2], which appeared in 1557 [in Roman type], with an Introductory Epistle by Calvin. The reviser's own address to the reader is anonymous, but it is definitely personal, and claims the work for a single man, and no one seems more likely than Whittingham to have undertaken it.

'As touchīg the perusing of the text,' he writes, 'it was 'diligently reuised by the moste approued Greke examples, 'and conference of translations in other tonges, as the 'learned may easely iudge, both by the faithful rendering of 'the sentence, and also by the proprietie of the wordes, and 'perspicuitie of the phrase. Forthermore that the Reader 'might be by all meanes proffited, I haue deuided the text 'into verses and sectiōs[3], according to the best editions in 'other langages....And because the Hebrewe and Greke 'phrases, which are strange to rendre in other tongues, and 'also short, shulde not be to harde, I haue sometyme inter-'preted them, without any whit diminishing the grace of

[1] [The inscription on Whittingham's tomb in Durham Cathedral described him as 'maritus sororis Johannis 'Calvini theologi.' But it is clear that his wife was not Calvin's sister, for in her will 'Loys Jaqueeman' is mentioned as her father. She must therefore in all probability have been his wife's sister. Calvin married a widow, Idelette de Buren, and her maiden name is not recorded. But the inscription which was contemporary admits of no other interpretation.]

[2] [Printed in 1841 in Bagster's *Hexapla*, and again separately in 1842.]

[3] The diyision into verses was first given in Stephens' Gr. Lat. Test. of 1551. See Tregelles, *An Account of the Printed Text...* p. 33. The use of supplemental words is found in Münster's O.T. 1534, but the italics are said to have been borrowed by the reviser of 1557 from Beza's Testament of 1556. A different type was employed in the Great Bible to mark readings borrowed from the Vulgate, *e.g.* 1 John v 7.

'the sense, as our lāgage doth vse them, and sometyme
'haue put to [added] that worde, which lacking made the
'sentence obscure, but haue set it in such letters as may
'easely be discerned from the cōmun text.'

The attractiveness of the book was enhanced by a
marginal commentary, in which the author boasts that to
his knowledge he has 'omitted nothing vnexpounded,
'wherby he that is anything exercised in the Scriptures of
'God, might iustely cōplayn of hardenes.' It was at least
far more complete than any yet available for the English
reader. So it was that the edition received a ready
welcome and soon found its way to England. It was,
however, only the beginning of a larger enterprise. Within
a few months after it was finished, a thorough revision of
the whole Bible was commenced, and was continued 'for
'the space of two yeres and more day and night.' The
striking difference between the translation of the New
Testament in this complete edition of the Bible (1560) and
the separate New Testament (1557)[1], is a signal proof of
the amount of independent labour bestowed upon the work.
The names of those who were engaged upon it are not
given, but they were several and perhaps not the same
during the whole time. The accession of Elizabeth broke
up the society in part, but 'Whittingham with one or two
'more, being resolved to go through with the work, did
'tarry at Geneva an year and an half after Q. Elizabeth
'came to the Crown[2].' These were probably Gilby and

---

[1] See Chap. III. § 6. The acknowledged importance of this work of
revision is further shewn by the fact
that the text of the edition of 1557
was never reprinted. It was at once
superseded by the more complete
work undertaken very shortly after
its appearance Compare Mr F Fry,
Journal of Sacred Literature, July,
1864 [also printed separately]. The
separate New Testament of 1560 [of
which a copy is in the Library of
Lambeth Palace] gives, as Mr Fry

has shewn, the text of the translation
in the Bible and not that of the New
Testament of 1557. [Before the
Geneva Bible appeared in 1560 a
separate edition of the Psalms from
the Bible Version was issued in
1559. Of this only two copies are
known to exist. one in the Library
of the Earl of Ellesmere, Bridgewater
House, and the other in my own
possession. W. A. W]
[2] Wood's *Athenæ Oxon.* s. v. Whittingham.

Sampson[1]. Under their care the Bible was finished in 1560, and dedicated to Q. Elizabeth in bold and simple language without flattery or reserve.

'The eyes of all that feare God in all places beholde 'your countreyes,' thus they address the Queen, 'as an 'example to all that beleue, and the prayers of all the 'godly at all tymes are directed to God for the preserua-'tiō of your maiestie. For considering Gods wonderful 'mercies toward you at all seasons, who hath pulled you 'out of the mouthe of the lyons, and how that from your 'youth you haue bene broght vp in the holy Scriptures, the 'hope of all men is so increased, that thei cā not but looke 'that God shulde bring to passe some wōderful worke by 'your grace to the vniuersal comfort of his Churche. There-'fore euen aboue strēgth you must shewe your selfe strong 'and bolde in Gods matters...This Lord of lordes & King 'of kings who hath euer defended his, strengthē, cōfort and 'preserue your maiestie, that you may be able to builde vp 'the ruines of Gods house to his glorie, the discharge of 'your conscience, and to the comfort of all them that loue 'the comming of Christ Iesus our Lord[2].'

The cost of the work was defrayed by members of the congregation at Geneva, 'whose hearts God touched' to encourage the revisers 'not to spare any charges for the 'fortherance of suche a benefite and fauour of God'; and one of those most actively engaged in this service was John Bodley, the father of the founder of the Bodleian Library, who received afterwards from Elizabeth a patent for the exclusive right to print the revision in England for seven years[3]. A folio edition was published by him in the next year[4], but this was printed at Geneva, and he does not

---

[1] This is well established by Anderson, II. pp. 320 f.

[2] The aim of the book was indicated by the original title of the address to the reader, which was 'To our be-'loved in the Lord the brethren of 'England, Scotland, Ireland, &c.' This superscription was altered in 1578 to 'To the diligent and Christian 'reader,' and afterwards to 'To the 'Christian reader.' (Comp. Anderson, II. 356–7.)

[3] Anderson, II. 324.

[4] The first title is dated 1562, but the title of the New Testament is dated 1561, and the Preface April,

appear to have availed himself afterwards of the privilege, though the patent may have helped the sale of the work.

The form in which the Bible was published marked its popular destination. Its size—a moderate quarto—offers a marked contrast to the ponderous folios of Coverdale, Matthew and the Great Bible. With the same view the text was printed for the first time in Roman letter; and the division of the chapters into verses was introduced[1]. A marginal commentary also was added, pure and vigorous in style, and, if slightly tinged with Calvinistic doctrine, yet on the whole neither unjust nor illiberal[2].

It was not therefore surprising that from the time of its first appearance the Genevan Bible became the household Bible of the English-speaking nations ; and it continued to be so for about three-quarters of a century It was never sanctioned for public use in churches ; but the convenience of its form and the simple clearness of its notes gained it a wide popularity with the mass of the people[3].

1561. No printer's name is attached to the book. One other edition was printed at Geneva in 1569, by J. Crispin. [Some copies have the date 1570 on the title. It is this edition which has the Calendar taken from the French Bible printed by Francois Estienne in 1567.]

[1] [A kind of fatality seems to attend those who write about the history of the English Bible. In the article on Whittingham in the *Dictionary of National Biography* we are informed that in the Geneva Bible of 1560 'the 'old black letter was abandoned for '*Italian* characters.' It is printed in Roman type. It is also said that 'the 'Apocrypha was for the first time 'omitted,' which is not the fact, 'as 'were the names and days of saints 'from the calendar prefixed.' There was no calendar prefixed. These errors are partially corrected in the volume of *Errata*, where we are told to substitute 'Roman' for 'Italian,' and for the words 'omitted...prefixed'

to read 'differentiated, as regards its 'authoritative value, from the rest of 'the Old Testament.' Here is a new error, for this differentiation is already to be found in Matthew's Bible of 1537 and in Coverdale's of 1535.]

[2] [The woodcuts in the books of Exodus, 1 Kings, and Ezekiel were evidently in the first instance prepared for a French Bible, and are to be found in that of 1560, printed at Geneva in folio by Antoine Rebul. The Arguments of the books of Job and the Psalms are taken almost literally from the French Bible of 1559 printed by Barbier and Courteau, while the Arguments to Isaiah and Jeremiah shew traces of the same origin. The translators evidently made considerable use of this version.]

[3] [In the *Historical Catalogue of Bibles* in the Library of the British and Foreign Bible Society, p. 61, it is estimated that between 1560 and 1644 at least 140 editions of the Genevan Bible or Testament appeared.]

And the intrinsic merits of the book justified its popularity; for it was not without cause that the revisers say when reviewing their work: 'we may with good conscience 'protest, that we haue in every point and worde, according 'to the measure of that knollage which it pleased almightie 'God to giue vs, faithfully rendred the text, and in all hard 'places moste syncerely expounded the same. For God is 'our witnes that we haue by all meanes indeuored to set 'forthe the puritie of the worde and right sense of the 'holy Gost for the edifying of the brethren in faith and 'charitie.'

Thus it came to pass that the revision found a ready welcome even from those who were not predisposed in its favour. Some time after the 'Bishops' Bible' was undertaken, Bodley applied to Cecil for an extension of his patent. The secretary consulted Parker before replying to the request. Parker's answer is conceived in a generous spirit. He and the bishop of London [Grindal] 'thought 'so well of the first impression [of the Bible] and the review 'of those who had since travailed therein, that they wished 'it would please him [Cecil] to be a means that twelve 'years' longer term might be by special privilege granted 'him [Bodley], in consideration of the charges by him 'and his associates in the first impression, and the review 'since sustained ; and that though one other special Bible 'for the Churches were meant by them to be set forth, as 'convenient time and leisure hereafter should permit, yet 'should it nothing hinder but rather do much good to have 'diversity of translations and readings.......'

[1] Strype's *Parker*, 1. 412. One other revision of the New Testament must be classed with the Genevan versions, that by Lawrence Tomson, which was professedly based on Beza, and contained a new Commentary, translated in the main from his. This was published in 1576, and dedicated to F. Walsingham and F. Hastings; and became so popular that it was frequently substituted for the Genevan revision in the editions of the Genevan Bible.

Tomson repeats the promise of the Genevan editor with regard to the Commentary with even greater emphasis: 'I dare avouch it, and whoso 'readeth it, shall so find it, that there 'is not one hard sentence, nor dark 'speech nor doubtful word, but is so 'opened, and hath such light given 'it, that children may go through

§ 8   THE BISHOPS' BIBLE.

The Genevan revision was, as has been seen, the work of exiles whose action was unfettered by considerations of national policy.   A work was comparatively easy for them which was not possible in the English Church.   The commencement of Queen Elizabeth's reign was beset by many of the same difficulties which had occupied the great reformers on the accession of Edward VI.   In the face of these it was not likely that measures would be taken for the revision of the English Bible.   It was enough at first to restore what had been already once established.   The injunctions which were issued by the Queen (1559) were closely moulded on those which had been put forth by Edward VI, and contained the same charge for the provision of a copy 'of the whole Bible of the largest volume' to be set up in some convenient place in each church. No limitation however was now added to the general encouragement to read the Scriptures ; but it was said significantly that all should 'read the same *with great* '*humility and reverence,* as the very lively word of God[1].'

The concessions thus made fell in with the general desire of the people.   This was shewn in a characteristic manner during the progress of the Queen from the Tower to Westminster on her accession to the throne.   Various symbolic greetings were devised to welcome her on the way ; and one above all seems to have attracted popular interest.   At the 'Little Conduit in Cheape' a pageant was prepared 'and it was told her Grace that there was placed 'Time.'   "Time ?" quoth she, "and Time hath brought me 'hither."'   And with Time also was 'Truth the daughter

---

'with it, and the simplest that are 'may walk without any guide, without 'wandering and going astray.'

[1] Cardwell, *Doc. Ann.* (ed. 2) I. 214.   In the Injunctions of 1547 it is said, 'They [the parsons, vicars, &c.] 'shall discourage no man, *authorized* '*and licensed thereto,* from the reading

'any part of the Bible either in Latin 'or in English...'   In the Injunctions of 1559 the words in italics are omitted.   Cardwell, *Doc. Ann.* (ed. 2) I. pp. 9, 214.   On the other hand, the words in italics in the text are not contained in the Injunctions of 1547.

'of Time,' who held a book in her hand upon the which was written 'Verbum veritatis,' the word of Truth—the Bible in English—'which she delivered to the Queen. But 'she, as soon as she had received the book kissed it, and 'with both her hands held up the same and so laid it upon 'her breast with great thanks to the city therefor'—'to the 'great comfort,' it is added afterwards, 'of the lookers-on[1].'

It is likely indeed that in this respect the zeal of the Queen was suspected to be cooler than that of many about her. 'On the morrow of her coronation,' so Bacon writes, 'it being the custom to release prisoners at the inaugura-'tion of a prince...one of her courtiers...besought her with 'a loud voice, That now this good time there might be four 'or five principal prisoners more released; those were the 'four Evangelists and the apostle St Paul, who had been 'long shut up in an unknown tongue, as it were in prison, 'so as they could not converse with the common people. 'The Queen answered very gravely, That it was best first 'to inquire of them whether they would be released or 'no[2].'

Thus at first the Great Bible was allowed to retain its place as the authorised Bible for ecclesiastical use, but the wide circulation of the Genevan edition made its defects generally known, and Parker, who was naturally inclined to biblical studies, as soon as an opportunity offered, took measures for the review of the old translation. This was about 1563–4. The method which he followed has been described by Strype. 'The Archbishop,' he writes, 'took 'upon him the labour to contrive and set the whole work 'a going in a proper method, by sorting out the whole 'Bible into parcels..., and distributing those parcels to able 'bishops and other learned men, to peruse and collate each 'the book or books allotted them: sending withal his 'instructions for the method they should observe; and they 'to add some short marginal notes for the illustration or 'correction of the text. And all these portions of the

---

[1] Nichols' *Progresses*, I. pp. 13 ff., 27.

[2] Bacon, *Collection of Apophthegms*, § 1 [from Rawley's *Resuscitatio*, 1660].

'Bible being finished and sent back to the archbishop, he
'was to add the last hand to them and so to take care for
'printing and publishing the whole[1].'

Among those whose help he sought was Sandys, bishop
of Worcester. Sandys strongly urged the necessity of the
work. 'Your Grace,' he says, 'should much benefit the
'Church in hastening forward the Bible which you have in
'hand those that we have be not only false printed but
'also give great offence to many by reason of the depravity
'in reading.' In another letter which accompanied his revision of the portion of Scripture assigned to him, he
explains more at length the ground of his opinion.
'According to your Grace's letter of instruction I have
'perused the book you sent me and with good diligence;
'having also in conference with some other considered of
'the same in such sort, I trust, as your Grace will not
'mislike of. .... In mine opinion your Grace shall do well
'to make the whole Bible to be diligently surveyed by
'some well learned before it be put to print......which
'thing will require a time. *Sed sat cito si sat bene.* The
'setters forth of this our common translation followed
'Munster too much, who doubtless was a very negligent
'man in his doings and often swerved very much from the
'Hebrew......[2].'

Other fragments of correspondence shew some of the
difficulties with which Parker had to contend. Guest,
bishop of Rochester, in returning the book of Psalms which
had been sent to him for correction, gives a singular view
of the duties of a translator. 'I have not,' he says, 'altered
'the translation but where it gave occasion of an error.
'As at the first Psalm at the beginning I turn the præter-
'perfect tense into the present tense, because the sense is
'too harsh in the præterperfect tense. Where in the New
'Testament one piece of a Psalm is reported I translate it
'in the Psalms according to the translation thereof in the
'New Testament, for the avoiding of the offence that may
'rise to the people upon divers translations......[3].'

[1] Strype's *Parker*, I. 414.   [2] *Id.* I. 415, 6.   [3] *Id.* I. 416.

Again, Cox, bishop of Ely, writing in May, 1566, says,
'I trust your Grace is well forward with the Bible by this
'time. I perceive the greatest burden will lie upon your
'neck, touching care and travail. I would wish that such
'usual words as we English people be acquainted with
'might still remain in their form and sound, so far forth as
'the Hebrew will well bear, ink-horn terms to be avoided.
'The translation of the verbs in the Psalms to be used
'uniformly in one tense......¹.'

However, in spite of all difficulties, the work went forward, and the Bishops' Bible, as it was called, appeared in
1568 in a magnificent volume, printed by R. Jugge 'cum
privilegio regiæ majestatis.' No word of flattery disfigures
the book. It is even without a dedication. But a portrait
of the Queen occupies the centre of the engraved title-
page, and others of Leicester and Burleigh occur before the
book of Joshua and the Psalms. At the end is an elegant
couplet on the device of the pelican feeding her young :

> Matris ut hæc proprio stirps est satiata cruore.
> Pascis item proprio, Christe, cruore tuos.

It was not by these signs only that Parker shewed his
true sense of the character of the task which he had undertaken. The revisers, speaking through him in the Preface,
express a noble consciousness of the immensity of their
labour. 'There be yet,' they say, quoting the words of
John Fisher, once bishop of Rochester, 'in the gospels
'very many darke places, whiche without all doubt to the
'posteritie shalbe made muche more open. For why should
'we dispayre herein, seing the gospell was deliuered to this
'intent, that it might be vtterly vnderstanded of vs,
'yea to the very inche. Wherfore, forasmuche as Christe
'sheweth no lesse loue to his Churche now, then hitherto
'he hath done, the aucthoritie wherof is as yet no whit
'diminished, and forasmuch as that holy spirite [is]
'the perpetuall keper and gardian of the same Church,
'whose gyftes and graces do flowe as continually and as

¹ Strype's *Parker*, I 417   Comp II 212 ff.

'abundantly as from the beginning: who can doubt but
'that such thinges as remayne yet vnknowen in the gospell,
'shalbe hereafter made open to the latter wittes of our
'posteritie, to their cleare vnderstanding?' They felt then
that their labour was provisional, and that the Spirit had
yet further lessons in His Word to teach to later ages.

It is not certainly known by whom the whole revision
was actually made. Initials are placed at the end of some
of the books, and this, Parker says, was done by his own
wish that the several scholars might be 'more diligent, as
'answerable for their doings.' But it seems evident from
the manner in which the initials are distributed that they
do not indicate all the contributors[1]. They do not stand
at the end of groups of books which might naturally be
supposed to have been given to one reviser. Once the
same initials are repeated in consecutive books. Some
names too are certainly passed over. Lawrence, for
example[2], had a considerable part in the revision of the
New Testament, and his initials nowhere occur. Of the
revisers who can be probably identified eight were bishops,
and from them the revision derived its popular title[3].

---

[1] This is indeed implied in Parker's own language; see p. 100, n. 1.

[2] See Ch. III. § 7

[3] The initials given are the following (for the identifications I am indebted mainly to the *Historical Account*). At the end of the Pentateuch W. E. = W. Exoniensis, William Alley, Bp. of Exeter:

of 2 Samuel R. M. = R. Menevensis, Richard Davies, Bp. of St David's:

of 2 Chronicles E. W. = E. Wigornensis, Edwyn Sandys, Bp. of Worcester:

of Job A. P. *C.* = Andrew Pearson, canon of Canterbury:

of the Psalms T. B. ? Thomas Becon: [It may be doubted whether the initials T. B. are those of Thomas Becon, who disclaims any special knowledge of Greek and may therefore be presumed not to have been much

of a Hebrew scholar. They may possibly indicate Thomas Bickley, one of Parker's chaplains, and afterwards Bp. of Chichester.]

of the Song of Solomon A. P. *E.* = Andrew Perne, canon of Ely:

of Lamentations R. W. = R. Wintonensis, Robert Horne, Bp. of Winchester:

of Daniel T. C. L. = T. Cov. & Lichf., Thomas Bentham, Bp. of Lichfield and Coventry:

of Malachi E. L. = E. Londinensis, Edmund Grindal, Bp. of London:

of Wisdom W. C. = William Barlow, Bp. of Chichester, omitted in some copies:

of 2 Maccabees *J. N.* = J. Norvicensis. John Parkhurst, Bp. of Norwich

of the Acts R. E. = R. Eliensis, Richard Cox, Bp. of Ely: 7—

When the edition was ready for publication Parker endeavoured to obtain through Cecil a recognition of it by the Queen. The revision did not, he pleaded, 'vary much 'from that translation which was commonly used by public 'order, except when the verity of the Hebrew and Greek 'moved alteration, or when the text was by some negli-'gence mutilated from the original.' His design was to secure a uniform text for public use, and in some places the Genevan revision was now publicly read, which seemed to be an infringement of ecclesiastical discipline, and yet the Great Bible could not be honestly maintained[1]. There

of Romans R. E. (as before):
of 1 Corinthians G. G. = Gabriel Goodman, dean of Westminster.

In the copy of the edition of 1568 which I have used the letters A. P. C. do not occur after Proverbs. Mr F. Fry tells me that he has 'both 'leaves of this edition, one with A. P. 'C., and one without.' [These are now in the Library of the Bible Society.]

To the other books no initials are appended. [But in ed. 1568 we find M. C. under the initial letters of Genesis, Exodus, the Gospel of St Matthew, the Second Epistle to the Corinthians, the Epistle to the Galatians (in some copies), Ephesians, Philippians, Colossians, 1 and 2 Thessalonians, 1 and 2 Timothy, Titus, Philemon, and the Hebrews, which may indicate that the revision of these books was superintended by the Archbishop himself. Similarly to the initial letters of 1 Peter v., 2 Peter iii., 1 John v., 3 John, Jude, and Rev. xxii. are attached the initials H. L., which may be those of Hugh Jones, Bishop of Llandaff, who was a friend of Parker's, and perhaps took up what had been assigned to the Bishop of Lincoln.]

[1] Parker's words are important as describing the care which was spent upon the edition, and the objects for which it was designed: 'Because I 'would you knew all,' he writes to Cecil [5 Oct. 1568], 'I send you a 'note to signify who first travailed in 'the divers Books; though after them 'some other perusing was had; the 'letters of their names be partly 'affixed in the end of their Books; 'which I thought a policy to shew 'them, to make them more diligent, 'as answerable for their doings...The 'Printer hath honestly done his dili-'gence; if your honour would obtain 'of the Queen's highness that this 'edition might be licensed, and only 'commended in public reading in 'Churches, to draw to one uniformity, 'it were no great cost to the most 'parishes, and a relief to him for his 'great charges sustained.' (*Biblioth. Sussex.* II. pp. 311 f.) He presses for the grant of the Queen's license 'as well for that in many churches 'they want their Books, and have 'long time looked for this; as for 'that in certain places, be publicly 'used some translations which have 'not been laboured in your realm, 'having inspersed divers prejudicial 'notes which might have been also 'well spared.' (*Id.* II. p. 313.) [The list of translators given in Parker's letter to Cecil (*Parker Correspondence*, pp. 334-6, ed. Parker Soc.) does not exactly correspond with that given in

is no evidence to shew whether the Queen returned any answer to his petition. The action of Convocation however was decided, and cannot have been in opposition to the royal will. It was ordered in the 'Constitutions and 'Canons Ecclesiastical' of 1571 that 'every archbishop and 'bishop should have at his house a copy of the holy Bible 'of the largest volume as lately printed at London......and 'that it should be placed in the hall or the large dining 'room, that it might be useful to their servants or to 'strangers[1].' It was also enjoined that each Cathedral should have a copy[2]; and the same provision was extended 'as far as it could be conveniently done' to all churches[3].

These injunctions however do not seem to have been rigorously carried out; and sixteen years afterward Arch-

---

the previous note. The Archbishop himself undertook Genesis, Exodus, the first two Gospels, and 2 Corinthians—Hebrews. Andrew Pierson (Cantuariæ) was responsible for Leviticus and Numbers as well as Job and Proverbs, and Deuteronomy was the only part of the Pentateuch entrusted to Alley, Bishop of Exeter. Joshua—2 Samuel were given to Davies, Bishop of St David's; Kings and Chronicles to Sandys, Bishop of Worcester; Ecclesiastes and Canticles to Andrew Perne (Cantabrigiæ), Dean of Ely; Isaiah, Jeremiah, and Lamentations to Horne, Bishop of Winchester; Ezekiel and Daniel to Bentham, Bishop of Lichfield and Coventry; the Minor Prophets to Grindal, Bishop of London; Esdras, Judith, Tobit, and Wisdom to Barlow, Bishop of Chichester; Ecclesiasticus, Susanna, Baruch, and Maccabees to Parkhurst, Bishop of Norwich; Luke and John to Scambler, Bishop of Peterborough; Acts and Romans to Cox, Bishop of Ely; 1 Corinthians to Goodman, Dean of Westminster; the Canonical Epistles and Apocrypha to Bullingham, Bishop of Lincoln. No mention is made of the translator of the Psalms, and the books from Ezra to Esther are not assigned to any one. The Sum of the Scripture, the Tables of Christ's line, the Argument of the Scriptures, the first Preface to the Whole Bible, the Preface to the Psalter, and the Preface to the New Testament, were written by the Archbishop.]

[1] Quivis archiepiscopus et episcopus habebit domi suæ sacra Biblia in amplissimo volumine, uti nuperrime Londini excusa sunt, et plenam illam historiam quæ inscribitur 'Monumenta 'martyrum,' et alios quosdam similes libros ad religionem appositos. Locentur autem isti libri vel in aula vel in grandi cenaculo ut et ipsorum famulis et advenis usui esse possint (Cardwell, *Synodalia*, I. p. 115).

[2] Cardwell, *l.c.*

[3] Ædituus curabunt...ut sacra Biblia sint in singulis Ecclesiis in amplissimo volumine (si commode fieri possit) qualia nunc nuper Londini excusa sunt...(Cardwell, *Synodalia*, I. p. 123).

bishop Whitgift took measures for their better observance. Writing to the Bishop of Lincoln, he says: 'whereas I am 'credibly informed that divers as well parish churches as 'chapels of ease, are not sufficiently furnished with Bibles, 'but some have either none at all, or such as be torn and 'defaced, and yet not of the translation authorized by the 'synods of bishops: these are therefore to require you 'strictly in your visitations or otherwise to see that all and 'every the said churches and chapels in your diocese be 'provided of one Bible or more, at your discretion, of the 'translation allowed as aforesaid.......And for the perform-'ance thereof I have caused her highness' printer to imprint 'two volumes of the said translation of the Bible afore-'said, a bigger and a less...both which are now extant and 'ready[1].'

There is no evidence to shew how far this new effort was successful in securing exclusively for the Bishops' Bible public use in churches. The revision did not at least gain any such hold upon the clergy as to lead even them to adopt it alone privately, and when Martin assailed the English versions (1582) he takes the Great Bible, or the Bishops' or the Genevan indifferently; and Fulke in his answer does not claim absolute precedence for any one of them. But while the Genevan Bible held its ground, there can be no doubt that the Great Bible was soon entirely displaced by the Bishops'; and no edition of it appears to have been printed after 1569.

§ 9. THE RHEIMS AND DOWAY VERSION.

The wide circulation and great influence of the reformed versions of the Bible made it impossible for the Roman Catholic scholars to withstand the demand for vernacular translations of Scripture sanctioned by authority in their churches. The work was undertaken not as in itself either necessary or generally desirable, but in special considera-

---

[1] Cardwell. *Documentary Annals* (ed. 2), II. 31 f.

tion of the circumstances of the time[1].   So it came to pass
that 'since Luthers reuolt...diuers learned Catholikes, for
'the more speedy abolishing of a number of false and
'impious translations put forth by sundry sectes, and for
'the better preseruation or reclaime of many good soules
'endangered thereby, haue published the Bible in the
'seuerall languages of almost all the principal provinces of
'the Latin Church' in the sixteenth century[2].   The design
of an English Version formed part of the systematic plan
for winning back England to the Papacy, which was shaped
and guided by the energy and skill of [Cardinal] Allen.
The centre of Allen's labours was the seminary which he
first established at Douai (1568), and afterwards transferred
temporarily to Rheims (1578).   And it was in this seminary that the Rhemish Version, as it is commonly called,
was made.

The history of the Rhemish Version has not yet been
traced in contemporary records[3]; but the prefaces to the
Old and New Testaments explain with perfect clearness
the objects and method of the translators.   They professed
to find the cause of the troubles of England in the free
handling of the deep mysteries of Scripture which led men
to 'contemne or easily passe ouer all the moral partes.'   'If
'our new Ministers had had [that sense of the depth and
'profundity of wisdom...], this cogitation and care that these
'and all other wise men haue, and euer had, our countrie
'had neuer fallen to this miserable state in religion, & that
'vnder pretence, colour, and coutenance of Gods word:
'neither should vertue and good life haue bene so pitifully
'corrupted in time of such reading, toiling, tumbling and
'translating the booke of oure life and saluation...[4].'   The
text of these new translations, they plead, was full of alterations, transpositions, new pointings; the authorship and

---

[1] *Preface to the Rhemish Testament.*
[2] *Id.*
[3] Collections for the bibliographical
history of the version have been made
by Dr Cotton in his *Rhemes & Doway*
...Oxford, 1855. [The latest and most

valuable contribution to this subject is
by Dr J. G. Carleton, *The part of
Rheims in the making of the English
Bible*, 1902.]
[4] *Preface to the Rhemish New Testament.*

authority of whole books were questioned ; old terms and forms were abandoned ; the language was dealt with as freely as if it were the language 'of Liuie, Virgil, or 'Terence.' 'We therfore,' they continue, 'hauing com-'passion to see our beloued countrie men, with extreme 'danger of their soules, to vse onely such prophane transla-'tions, and erroneous mens mere phantasies, for the pure 'and blessed word of truth, much also moued therevnto by 'the desires of many deuout persons : haue set forth, for 'you (benigne readers) the new Testament to begin withal, 'trusting that it may giue occasion to you, after diligent 'perusing thereof, to lay away at lest such their impure 'versions as hitherto you haue ben forced to occupie[1]'

A controversial commentary formed a necessary part of the undertaking. It was pleaded that 'though the text, 'truely translated, might sufficiently, in the sight of the 'learned and al indifferent men...controule the aduersaries 'corruptions...yet...somewhat to help the faithful reader in 'the difficulties of diuers places, we [the editors] haue also 'set forth reasonable large ANNOTATIONS, thereby to shew '...both the heretical corruptions and false deductions, & 'also the Apostolike tradition, the expositions of the holy 'fathers, the decrees of the Catholike Church and most 'auncient Coūcels : which meanes whosoeuer trusteth not, 'for the sense of holy Scriptures, but had rather folow his 'priuate judgmēt or the arrogāt spirit of these Sectaries, he 'shal worthily through his owne wilfulnes be deceiued...[2]'

The names of those who performed the work are no-where given in connexion with it, but internal evidence leaves no doubt that the chief share in the translation was undertaken by Gregory Martin, sometime fellow of St John's College, Oxford, a scholar of distinguished attain-ments both in Hebrew and Greek. Upon renouncing Protestantism Martin had studied for some years at Douai and then after an interval of travel settled at Rheims as one of the readers of divinity in the English College there.

[1] *Preface to Rhemish N.T*   [2] *Id.*

Other scholars were probably associated with Martin in the task of translation or in the composition of the notes. It is said that Dr Allen himself, Dr R. Bristow, formerly a fellow of Exeter College, and Dr J. Reynolds, formerly a fellow of New College, among others, assisted Martin in revising his translation. More particularly also the notes on the New Testament have been attributed to Dr Bristow, and those on the Old Testament to Dr Worthington. However this may be, Martin clearly identified himself with the work in a treatise which he published on the '*Manifold corruptions of the Holy Scriptures by the heretikes*' (Rhemes, 1582), very shortly after the appearance of the first instalment of the new version[1]. Yet it may be concluded from a comparison of the annotations with this treatise that Martin's work lay in the version and not in the commentary. His labours, as it seems, proved fatal to him. He died in the same year in which the books appeared to which he had devoted his life.

When the New Testament was published the whole version had been 'long since' finished though the publication was delayed 'for lacke of good meanes[2].' This 'one 'general cause,' the 'poor estate [of the favourers of the 'version] in banishment[3],' delayed the appearance of the Old Testament till 1609–10 (Douai). The complete work cannot have had an extensive circulation. It was reprinted in 1635 (Rouen), and then not again for one hundred and fifteen years, when it was revised by Dr R. Challoner (1749–50); and this revision has formed the basis of the later editions[4].

The New Testament, as might have been expected, attracted more attention. It was reprinted at Antwerp

---

[1] The priority of the publication of the New Testament is shewn by a reference to it in the Preface to the *Discoverie of the manifold corruptions* ...(p. 63, Parker Soc. reprint). On the other hand the *Discovery* was already composed when the Preface to the New Testament was written:

Margin to § 21.

[2] *Preface to the New Testament.*

[3] *Preface to the Old Testament.*

[4] Cotton, *l. c.* pp. 47 ff. The standard edition is said to be that 'revised 'and corrected' under the sanction of Dr Troy, 1791.

in 1600 and 1621, and again (at Rouen?) in 1633, though not afterwards for more than a hundred years[1]. But it obtained a still larger circulation by the help of its opponents. The annotations called for an answer A powerful party in England urged Cartwright to prepare one[2]. Difficulties however were interposed in his way and his reply was not published in a complete form till 1618, fifteen years after his death. In the mean time Fulke, who answered Martin's book on the 'Corruptions 'of Holy Scripture,' answered his edition of the New Testament also (1589)[3]. He printed the Rhemish and Bishops' (revised 1572) version in parallel columns, and added to the Rhemish notes, which he gave at length, the refutation or qualifications which they seemed to require. This book became very popular, and the Rhemish Testament gained in this way a wide currency which it would not otherwise have enjoyed. But questions of scholarship or textual criticism are wholly subordinated in this examination to larger topics of controversy. At the same time the scriptural vocabulary was, as we shall see afterwards, insensibly increased, and even Bacon goes aside to praise 'the discretion and tenderness of the Rhemish 'translation,' which ever distinguished the Christian grace 'charity' (ἀγάπη) from 'love' (ἔρως)[4].

---

[1] In the mean time two other Roman Catholic translations of the New Testament from the Vulgate were made, one by Dr Nary (1718, see Dr Cotton, *l.c.* pp. 37 ff.) ; and the other by Dr Witham (1730, see Dr Cotton, *l.c.* pp. 41 ff.).

[2] Strype, *Whitgift,* I. 482; *Annals*, III. i. 287 ff.

[3] Other editions of this book were published in 1601, 1617, 1633. In the account of Fulke prefixed to the Parker reprint of his answer to Martin an edition is assigned also to the year 1580 by a surprising mistake.

[4] In his tract *Concerning the Liturgy.* [*Letters and Life*, ed. Spedding, III. 118.] This reference I owe to Mr Plumptre.

§ 10. THE AUTHORISED VERSION.

There were, as we have seen, during the latter part of Elizabeth's reign two rival English Bibles[1], the Bishops', which was sanctioned by ecclesiastical authority for public use[2], and the Genevan, which was the common Bible of the people and even of scholars. If we may judge from the editions published, the circulation of the latter was more than quadruple that of the former, and the convenient forms in which it appeared marked its popular destination. There are only seven editions of the Bishops' Bible in quarto; all the others (eleven) are in folio; and no small edition was printed after that prepared by authority in 1584. Of the Genevan Bible, on the other hand, there are between 1568 and 1611 sixteen editions in octavo, fifty-two in quarto, and eighteen in folio[3].

[1] It would be interesting to determine the texts followed by the Elizabethan divines. On this the editions of the Parker Society, as far as I have examined them, give no help. Mr Anderson gives a few examples, II. 338. [According to Anderson the Geneva Bible was quoted by Gervase Babington, Bishop of Worcester, in his *Annotations on the Five Books of Moses*, and by George Abbot, afterwards Archbishop of Canterbury, in his *Commentary on Jonah* (1600). To these may be added John King, afterwards Bishop of London, in his *Lectures on Jonas* (1594). In an article on the Authorisation of the English Bible in *Macmillan's Magazine* for October, 1881, the present Archbishop of Canterbury shews that the Geneva version was used by Bishop Andrews in sermons preached in 1618, 1622, 1623, and 1624; by Bishop Laud in 1621; by Bishop Carleton in 1624; by Bishop Hall in 1613 and 1624; and by Dean Williams in 1624. In Hall's *Meditations* the headings are from the Authorised Version, but the quotations are almost always from the Geneva. The Archbishop examined more than fifty sermons preached between 1611 and 1630, and found that the texts of 27 were taken from the Geneva and only five from the Bishops' Bible. An independent examination which I made of the Sermons of Bishop Andrews, ranging from 1589 to 1624, proved that a very large majority of his texts were taken from the Genevan Bible, and that though he was one of the translators of the Authorised Version, he seldom preached from it. The text of his Funeral Sermon by Bishop Buckeridge in 1626 was taken from the Bishops' Bible.]

[2] Fulke describes it on the title-page of his Text of the New Testament, &c., 1589, as 'the Translation '...commonly used in the Church of ' England,' and at the beginning of the text ' the translation of the Church ' of England.'

[3] This calculation is only approximately true. Mr F. Fry informs me

This rivalry was in every way undesirable; and in the conference on ecclesiastical matters which was held at Hampton Court shortly after the accession of James I, the authorised version of the Bible was brought forward as one of the things 'amiss in the Church.' The conference had no official or constitutional character, and was summoned by the king's proclamation, who had not yet himself been recognized as king by Parliament. But though it proved ineffectual in all other points, we owe to it our present Bible. The question was brought forward by Dr Reynolds, President of Corpus Christi College, Oxford, who quoted several mistranslations from the authorised Bibles[1]. 'My Lord of London (Bancroft) 'well added: That if every man's humour should be fol- 'lowed there would be no end of translating. Whereupon 'his Highness wished that some special pains should be 'taken in that behalf for one uniform translation—pro- 'fessing that he could never yet see a Bible well translated 'in English; but the worst of all his Majesty thought the 'Geneva to be—and this to be done by the best learned 'in both the Universities; after them to be reviewed by 'the bishops and the chief learned of the Church; from 'them to be presented to the Privy Council; and lastly 'to be ratified by his royal authority; and so this whole 'Church to be bound unto it and none other. Marry

that he has altogether sixty-six editions in quarto, including those of later date, and that the whole number must be at least seventy. [See p. 93, note 3.]

[1] Gal. iv. 25; Pss. cv. 28, cvi. 30.

The account given in the Preface to the Authorised Version is somewhat different from, though reconcileable with, Barlow's. 'The very Historicall 'trueth is, that vpon the importunate 'petitions of the Puritanes, at his 'Maiesties comming to this Crowne, 'the Conference at Hampton Court 'hauing bene appointed for hearing 'their complaints: when by force of 'reason they were put from all other 'grounds, they had recourse at the 'last, to this shift, that they could 'not with good conscience subscribe 'to the Communion booke, since it 'maintained the Bible as it was there 'translated, which was as they said, 'a most corrupted translation. And 'although this was iudged to be but 'a very poore and emptie shift; yet 'euen hereupon did his Maiestie be- 'ginne to bethinke himselfe of the 'good that might ensue by a new 'translation, and presently after gaue 'order for this Translation which is 'now presented vnto thee.'

'withal he gave this caveat, upon a word cast out by my
'lord of London, that no marginal notes should be added,
'having found in them which are annexed to the Geneva
'translation, which he saw in a Bible given him by an
'English lady, some notes very partial, untrue, seditious,
'and savouring too much of dangerous and traitorous
'conceits. As for example, Ex. i. 19; 2 Chron. xv. 16[1].'

Nothing further was done at the conference, and the
ecclesiastical authorities do not appear to have been
anxious or even ready to engage in the proposed revision[2] Bancroft had expressed what was probably a very
general feeling, and in the Convocation which followed
shortly afterwards (March—July, 1604) it was enjoined
that every parish as 'yet unfurnished of the Bible of
'the largest volume[3]' should provide one within a convenient time, so that it seems unlikely that they even
expected that it would be speedily carried out. But

---

[1] Barlow's *Sum and Substance of
the Conference*...(printed in Cardwell's
Hist. of Conferences), pp. 187–8.

Mr Anderson claims for Dr Reynolds the honour of having proposed
originally that the translation should
be 'without any marginal notes' (II.
371). But the passage of Galloway
which he quotes, so far from professing
to give Reynolds' own scheme, gives
'the heads which his Majesty would
'have reformed at this time.' 'Sun-
'dry,' he continues, 'as they favoured,
'gave out copies of things here con-
'cluded: whereupon myself took oc-
'casion, as I was an ear and eye
'witness, to set them down, and
'presented them to his Majesty, who
'with his own hand mended some
'things, and eked other things which
'I had omitted. Which corrected
'copy with his own hand I have, and
'of it have sent you herein the just
'transumpt word by word..' The
conclusion in question is: 'That a
'translation be made of the whole
'Bible, as consonant as can be to the
'original Hebrew and Greek; and

'this to be set out and printed without
'any marginal notes, and only to be
'used in all Churches of England in
'time of Divine Service' (Cardwell,
Hist. of Conferences, pp. 213, 214).

[2] Still in the note which was made,
apparently by Bancroft himself of
'things as shall be reformed,' occurs
'One uniform translation of the Bible
'to be made, and only to be used in
'all the churches of England' (Cardwell, *Hist. of Conferences*, p. 142).

[3] Canon 80. From a comparison
with Whitgift's injunctions (p. 102) the
reference is probably to the Bishops'
Bible. But Dr Reynolds' quotations
from the Great Bibles 'allowed in
'the reign of Henry VIII and Ed-
'ward VI,' as still publicly used,
shew that these had not been done
away with or forbidden.

It is worthy of notice that in
Archbp. Bancroft's visitation articles
of 1605 the 'Bible of the greatest
'volume' is not mentioned as in the
corresponding articles of Cranmer
and Whitgift (§ 48. Cardwell's *Doc.
Ann.* ed. 2, II. 110).

about the same time the king had matured his scheme.
It is not known in what manner the scholars to be entrusted with the revision were selected It appears however that some were submitted to the king who approved
of the choice, and the list was complete by June 30th.
The undertaking was no doubt really congenial to James'
character, and Bancroft writing to Cambridge on that day
to hasten on its execution adds, 'I am persuaded his
'royal mind rejoiceth more in the good hope which he
'hath for the happy success of that work, than of his
'peace concluded with Spain[1]' Three weeks afterwards
(July 22nd) the king wrote to Bancroft, who was acting as
representative of the vacant see of Canterbury, announcing
that he had 'appointed certain learned men, to the number
'of four and fifty, for the translating of the Bible,' and
requiring him to take measures whereby he might be
able to recompense the translators by church preferment.
'Furthermore,' he adds, 'we require you to move all our
'bishops to inform themselves of all such learned men
'within their several dioceses, as, having especial skill in
'the Hebrew and Greek tongues, have taken pains in their
'private studies of the Scriptures for the clearing of any
'obscurities either in the Hebrew or in the Greek, or
'touching any difficulties or mistakings in the former
'English translation, which we have now commanded to be
'thoroughly viewed and amended, and thereupon to write
'unto them, earnestly charging them and signifying our
'pleasure therein that they send such their observations
'either to Mr Lively, our Hebrew reader in Cambridge,
'or to Dr Harding, our Hebrew reader in Oxford, or to
'Dr Andrews, dean of Westminster, to be imparted to the
'rest of their several companies; that so our said intended
'translation may have the help and furtherance of all our
'principal learned men within this our kingdom[2].'

Having provided in this manner for the future remu-
neration of the scholars whose services he had engaged,

[1] [Quoted by Anderson, II. 372, from Lewis.]   [2] Cardwell, *Doc. Annals* (ed. 2), II. 84.

the king was equally prudent in endeavouring to obtain the means of defraying their immediate expenses. These 'his majesty,' it is said, 'was very ready of his most 'princely disposition to have borne, but some of my lords, 'as things now go, did hold it inconvenient'; so 'he re-'quested the bishops and chapters to contribute toward 'this work,' with the additional stimulus that 'his majesty 'would be acquainted with every man's liberality.' Bancroft in communicating this notice to the different dignitaries to whom it applied, adds, 'I do not think that a thousand 'marks will finish the work,' so that the amount of the tax might not be left altogether in uncertainty[1]. But in spite of the royal request nothing seems to have been subscribed, and from the life of one of the translators it appears that they received nothing but free entertainment in the colleges till some of them met in London for the final revision of the work[2].

It does not appear in what way the actual selection of the revisers was made, but it is most likely that names were suggested by the universities and approved by the king. There is also some discrepancy as to the number engaged upon the work. The king speaks of fifty-four, and only forty-seven names appear upon the list. It is possible that some were originally appointed who did not in the end take any part in the revision, or that a committee of bishops was chosen as an independent group of revisers ; but no satisfactory solution of the difficulty has yet been proposed[3]. The delay, however, which took place in the commencement of the revision is sufficient to account for its existence ; for though the preliminaries were settled before the end of 1604, the revision does not appear to have been seriously undertaken till 1607[4]. The

[1] Cardwell, *l. c.* 87 ff.

[2] Walker's *Life of Boys*, quoted by Anderson, II. 381. [See p. 118.]

[3] Of the bishops, Bancroft, though not among the translators, is said to have 'altered the translation in four-'teen places' to make it 'speak the pre-'latical language,' and to have been

'so potent' in pressing his corrections that there was no contradicting him (Dr Hill quoted by Mr Anderson, II. 378).

[4] Some of the revisers may indeed have begun their work at once. Thus Boys is said to have worked for four years before the final revision, which

death of Mr Lively in 1605 was no doubt a grave check to the progress of the scheme, and it is not hard to imagine other obstacles which may have hindered it.

When at length the whole plan was ready for execution, the translators were divided into six companies, of which two met respectively at Westminster, Cambridge, and Oxford, and the whole work was thus divided among them[1].

Westminster.	Dr L. Andrews, Dean of Westminster. Dr J. Overall, Dean of St Paul's. Dr A. de Saravia, Canon of Canterbury. Dr R. Clark, Fellow of Christ's Coll., Camb. Dr J. Layfield, Fellow of Trin. Coll., Camb. Dr R. Teigh, Archdeacon of Middlesex. Mr F. Burleigh, Pemb. Hall, Camb., D.D. 1607 Mr Geoffrey King, Fellow of King's Coll., Camb. Mr Thompson, Clare Hall, Camb.[2] Mr Bedwell.	Genesis to 2 Kings inclusive.

took nine months (*Life*, quoted by Anderson, II. 381). But the translators fix about two years and three-quarters as the length of time spent on the revision. See p. 116.

[1] This list is taken chiefly from Dr Cardwell's reprint of Burnet's list (*Doc. Annals*, ed. 2, II. 140 ff.). It is only approximately correct, and does not suit exactly the date 1604, as Barlow was not then Dean of Chester, nor 1607, when Mr Lively was dead. [Barlow was installed Dean of Chester 12 June, 1602, and in May, 1605, was elected Bishop of Rochester. Lively died in the beginning of May, 1605. The list is therefore correct for 1604.] Two other names, Dr J. Aglionby and Dr L. Hutton, are given elsewhere, in place of Dr Eedes and Dr Ravens. See Cardwell, *l.c.* ed. 2, p. 144 n. [and Wood's *Hist. and Ant. of the Univ. of Oxford*, ed. Gutch, II. 283]. The spelling of the names, it scarcely need be added, varies considerably. [According to Clark's *Register of the University of Oxford*, vol. II. part 1, p. 141 (quoted by Dr Lupton in his article on the English Versions in Hastings' *Dictionary of the Bible*), on '14 May 1605 Arthur Lakes, 'M.A. New College was allowed 'B.D. and D.D., deferring the exer- 'cises for both; because engaged on 'the translation of the New Testament 'at London.' In a letter from Bishop Bilson to Sir Thomas Lake (*Calendar of State Papers*, Domestic Series, 19 April, 1605), also quoted by Dr Lupton, George Ryves of New College (D.D. 1599) is mentioned as a translator. These names are not in the usual lists. I have not found that similar dispensations were granted at Cambridge, but 'about 1605 there 'was a decree of the Chapter of York 'to keep a residentiary's place for 'Andrew Byng, as he was then oc- 'cupied in translating the Bible.' (*Notes and Queries*, 3rd Series, IV. 380.)]

[2] On Richard Thomson ('Dutch 'Thomson') see a collection of ma-

Cambridge.	Mr Lively, Fellow of Trin. Coll. Mr Richardson, afterwards Master of Trin. Coll. Mr Chatterton, Master of Emm. Coll. Mr Dillingham, Fellow of Christ's Coll. Mr Harrison, Vice-Master of Trin. Coll. Mr Andrews, afterwards Master of Jesus Coll. Mr Spalding, Fellow of St John's. Mr Byng, Fellow of St Peter's Coll.	1 Chron. to Eccles. inclusive.
Oxford.	Dr Harding, Pres. of Magd. Coll. Dr Reynolds, Pres. of Corpus Christi Coll. Dr Holland, afterwards Rector of Ex. Coll. Dr Kilbye, Rector of Lincoln Coll. Dr Miles Smith, Brasenose Coll. Dr R. Brett, Fellow of Lincoln Coll. Mr Fairclough, Fellow of New Coll.	Isaiah to Malachi.
Cambridge.	Dr Duport, Master of Jesus Coll. Dr Branthwait, Master of Caius Coll. Dr Radcliffe, Fellow of Trin. Coll. Dr Ward, afterwards Master of Sid. Coll. Mr Downes, Fellow of St John's Coll.[1] Mr Boys, Fellow of St John's Coll.[2] Mr Ward, Fellow of King's Coll.	The Apocry- pha.
Oxford.	Dr T. Ravis, Dean of Ch. Ch. Dr G. Abbot, Dean of Winchester. [Dr R. Eedes, Dean of Worcester.] Dr G. Thompson, Dean of Windsor. Mr (Sir H.) Savile, Provost of Eton. Dr Perin, Fellow of St John's Coll. [Dr Ravens, Fellow of St John's Coll.] Dr Harmer, Fellow of New Coll.	The four Gospels, Acts, Apoca- lypse.
Westminster.	Dr W. Barlow, Dean of Chester[3]. Dr Hutchinson, Archdeacon of St Alban's. Dr John Spencer, Pres. of Corp. Chr. Coll. Ox. Dr Roger Fenton, Fellow of Pemb. Hall, Camb. Mr Michael Rabbett, Trin. Coll. Camb. Mr Sanderson, Balliol Coll. Oxford, D.D. 1605. Mr Dakins, Fellow of Trin. Coll. Cambridge.	Romans to Jude inclusive.

terials for a memoir by the Rev. J. E. B. Mayor in *N. and Q.* 2 S. ix. 155 ff.; 237 ff.

[1] On Mr Andrew Downes see Mr Mayor's edition of Baker's *History of St John's College*, pp. 598 f.

[2] On Mr John Bois see Mr Mayor, *l.c.*

[3] [An interesting document in the Lambeth Palace Library contains

Of these scholars many (as Andrews, Overall, Savile, and Reynolds) have obtained an enduring reputation apart from this common work in which they were associated. Others, whose names are less familiar, were distinguished for special acquirements requisite for their task. Lively, Spalding, King, and Byng were successively professors of Hebrew at Cambridge, and Harding and Kilbye at Oxford. Harmer and Perrin were professors of Greek at Oxford, and Downes at Cambridge; Bedwell was the most distinguished Arabic scholar of the time. Saravia was an accomplished modern linguist. Thompson (Camb.), Chatterton, Smith, and Boys were equally distinguished for their knowledge of ancient languages. It is one sign of the large choice of Hebraists which was offered at the time that Boys, who was especially famous for oriental learning, was originally employed upon the Apocrypha.

No doubt can be entertained as to the ability and acquirements of the revisers. At the same time care was taken to check individual fancies. Their duty was accurately defined in a series of rules which were drawn up probably under the direction of Bancroft. These provide for an elaborate scheme of revision as well as furnish general directions for the execution of the work[1].

1. 'The ordinary Bible read in the Church, commonly 'called the Bishops' Bible, to be followed, and as little 'altered as the truth of the original will permit.

2. 'The names of the prophets and the holy writers, 'with the other names of the text to be retained as

---

some notes on the translators of the Authorised Version which are printed in Appendix XII All that can be ascertained about them from internal evidence is that they were written by a member of Emmanuel to a member of Trinity, perhaps Thomas Hill, Master of the College, who came from Emmanuel. The writer took his degree in 1621, and so was a younger contemporary of the translators, and the document appears to have been written not long before

1650. It is in some places difficult to decipher.]

[1] The text of the rules varies in different books. I have followed Burnet, *Hist. of Reformation*, II. App. p. 368, No. 10 (ed. 1681), who quotes '*ex MS. D. Borlase.*'

An account of the rules given by the English Delegates to the Synod of Dort reduces the final number of the rules to seven. Anderson, II. 377. [See Appendix XIII.]

'nigh as may be, accordingly as they were vulgarly
'used.

3. 'The old ecclesiastical words to be kept, viz. the
'word *Church* not to be translated *Congregation*, &c.

4. 'When a word hath divers significations, that to be
'kept which hath been most commonly used by the most
'of the ancient fathers, being agreeable to the propriety
'of the place and the analogy of the faith.

5. 'The division of the chapters to be altered either
'not at all or as little as may be, if necessity so require.

6. 'No marginal notes at all to be affixed, but only
'for the explanation of the Hebrew or Greek words which
'cannot, without some circumlocution, so briefly and fitly
'be expressed in the text.

7. 'Such quotations of places to be marginally set
'down as shall serve for the fit reference of one Scripture
'to another.

8. 'Every particular man of each company to take
'the same chapter or chapters; and having translated or
'amended them severally by himself where he thinketh
'good, all to meet together, confer what they have done,
'and agree for their parts what shall stand.

9. 'As any one company hath dispatched any one
'book in this manner, they shall send it to the rest to be
'considered of seriously and judiciously, for his majesty
'is very careful in this point.

10. 'If any company, upon the review of the book
'so sent, doubt or differ upon any place, to send them
'word thereof, note the place, and withal send the reasons;
'to which if they consent not, the difference to be com-
'pounded at the general meeting, which is to be of the
'chief persons of each company at the end of the work.

11. 'When any place of special obscurity is doubted of,
'letters to be directed by authority to send to any learned
'man in the land for his judgment of such a place.

12. 'Letters to be sent from every bishop to the rest
'of his clergy, admonishing them of this translation in
'hand, and to move and charge as many as being skilful

'in the tongues and having taken pains in that kind, to
'send his particular observations to the company either
'at Westminster, Cambridge, or Oxford.

13. 'The directors in each company to be the Deans
'of Westminster and Chester for that place; and the king's
'professors in the Hebrew or Greek in either university.

14. 'These translations to be used when they agree
'better with the text than the Bishops' Bible : viz. Tindale's,
'Matthew's, Coverdale's, Whitchurch's, Geneva.

15. 'Besides the said directors before mentioned, three
'or four of the most ancient and grave divines in either
'of the universities, not employed in translating, to be
'assigned by the Vice-Chancellor upon conference with
'[the] rest of the Heads to be overseers of the translations,
'as well Hebrew as Greek, for the better observation of
'the fourth rule above specified[1].'

It is impossible to tell how far all these provisions
were adhered to. Almost all that is certainly known of
the proceedings of the revisers is contained in the noble
preface which the printers have removed from modern
editions of the Bible. In this Dr Miles Smith, afterwards
Bishop of Gloucester, writing in the name of his fellow-
labourers, gives some account of the time which was spent
upon the revision, and of the manner and spirit in which
it was executed. 'Neither did we,' he says, 'run ouer the
'worke with that posting haste that the *Septuagint* did,
'if that be true which is reported of them, that they
'finished it in 72. days...... The worke hath not been
'hudled vp in 72. dayes, but hath cost the workemen, as
'light as it seemeth, the paines of twise seuen times
'seuentie two dayes and more' (about two years and nine
months). 'We are so farre off,' he writes again, 'from
'condemning any of their labours that traueiled before
'vs in this kinde, either in this land or beyond sea, either
'in King *Henries* time or King *Edwards* (if there were

---

[1] This last rule appears to have been   *Historical Account*, p. 153 [Bagster's
added afterwards, when the practical   *Hexapla*, ed. 1841].

'any translation, or correction of a translation in his time)
'or Queene *Elizabeths* of euer-renoumed memorie, that
'we acknowledge them to haue beene raised vp of God,
'for the building and furnishing of his Church, and that
'they deserue to be had of vs and of posterity in euer-
'lasting remembrance'...... Still, 'let vs rather blesse
'God from the ground of our heart, for working this
'religious care in him [the King], to haue the translations
'of the Bible maturely considered of and examined. For
'by this meanes it commeth to passe, that whatsoeuer is
'sound alreadie (and all is sound for substance, in one or
'other of our editions, and the worst of ours farre better
'then their [the Romanists'] autentike vulgar) the same
'will shine as gold more brightly, being rubbed and
'polished; also, if any thing be halting, or superfluous,
'or not so agreeable to the originall, the same may bee
'corrected, and the trueth set in place...' And thus,
summing up all briefly, he says, 'Truly, (good Christian
'Reader,) we neuer thought from the beginning, that we
'should neede to make a new Translation, nor yet to make
'of a bad one a good one......but to make a good one
'better, or out of many good ones, one principall good
'one, not iustly to be excepted against: that hath bene
'our indeauour, that our marke. To that purpose there
'were many chosen, that were greater in other mens eyes
'then in their owne, and that sought the truth rather then
'their own praise....... Neither did wee thinke much to con-
'sult the Translators or Commentators, *Chaldee*, *Hebrewe*,
'*Syrian*, *Greeke*, or *Latine*, no nor the *Spanish*, *French*,
'*Italian*, or *Dutch* [German][1]; neither did we disdaine to

[1] Selden, in his *Table Talk*, has given a similar account of the proceeding of the translators, which he may have received from someone who was engaged in the work: 'The 'English Translation of the Bible is 'the best Translation in the World 'and renders the Sense of the Origi-'nal best, taking in for the English 'Translation the Bishops' Bible as 'well as King James's. The Trans-'lation in King James' time took an 'excellent way. That part of the 'Bible was given to him who was 'most excellent in such a tongue (as 'the Apocrypha to Andrew Downs) 'and then they met together, and 'one read the Translation, the rest 'holding in their hands some Bible, 'either of the learned Tongues, or

'reuise that which we had done, and to bring back to the
'anuill that which we had hammered: but hauing and
'vsing as great helpes as were needfull, and fearing no
'reproch for slownesse, nor coueting praise for expedi-
'tion, wee haue at the length, through the good hand
'of the Lord vpon vs, brought the worke to that passe
'that you see.'

When the revision was completed at the different
centres, 'two members were chosen from each company[1]'
to superintend the final preparation of the work for the
press in London, and 'Three copies of the whole Bible
'were sent there, one from Cambridge, a second from
'Oxford, and a third from Westminster[2].' It is not likely
that this committee did more than arrange the materials
which were already collected; but whatever their work
was, it was completed in nine months, and the whole
labour of the revision was thus brought to a successful
end[3].

'French, Spanish, Italian, &c.: if
'they found any fault they spoke,
'if not he read on' (*Table Talk*, p. 20,
ed. 1868).

[1] As the revisers were 'six in all,'
it is evident that by 'company' we
must understand 'centre': *i.e.* Oxford,
Cambridge and Westminster.

[2] Walker's *Life of Boys* [in Peck's
Desiderata Curiosa], quoted by Anderson, II. 381.

[3] It is remarkable that none of the
many copies of the Bishops' Bible
used for the revision have yet been
discovered. There is an interesting volume in the Bodleian Library
(Bishops' Bible, Barker, 1602), which
has been commonly but certainly
wrongly supposed to be one of the
copies prepared for the press. The
text is corrected throughout some
books to the Royal Version; and in
some cases letters are attached (g, j, t)
which appear to indicate the sources
from which the corrections were derived. Mr J. Wordsworth, Fellow of

Brasenose [now Bishop of Salisbury],
has kindly given me the following summary of the extent of the corrections:

Gen. i.—xxv. with g, j, t, and perhaps another letter.

Gen. xxvi. to Joshua inclusive with
g (j again from Deut. xxxii. to end).

Judges—Is. iv. corrected without
added letters; and so also

Jer. i.—iv.

Ezech. i.—iv.

Dan. i.—iv.

The Minor Prophets.

St Matthew, St Mark, St Luke.

St John xvii. to end.

There are also two notes on Eph.
iv. 8, 2 Thess. ii. 15.

From collations which I owe to
the great kindness of the Rev. H. O.
Coxe, the Bodleian Librarian, it is
certain that 'g' marks corrections
obtained from the Genevan Version.
The materials which I have are not
as yet sufficient to identify 't' and
'j.' [They are probably Tremellius
and Junius.]

The revised version appeared at length from the press of R. Barker, in 1611. The book is said to be 'Newly 'Translated out of the Originall Tongues; And with the 'former Translations diligently compared and reuised, by 'his Maiesties speciall Commandement.' A further notice adds that it is 'Appointed to be read in Churches.' From what has been said, it will appear with what limitations the first statement must be interpreted. The second is more difficult of explanation; for no evidence has yet been produced to shew that the version was ever publicly sanctioned by Convocation or by Parliament, or by the Privy Council, or by the king. It gained its currency partly, it may have been, by the weight of the king's name, partly by the personal authority of the prelates and scholars who had been engaged upon it, but still more by its own intrinsic superiority over its rivals. Copies of the 'whole Bible of the largest volume and 'latest edition' are required to be in churches by the Visitation Articles of Laud 1622 (St David's), 1628 (London). In the Scotch Canons of 1636 it is said still more distinctly that 'the Bible shall be of the translation 'of King James' (Cap. 16, § 1). Similar provisions are, I believe, contained in the Visitation Articles of London 1612, and Norwich 1619; but these I have been unable to see.

The printing of the Bishops' Bible was at once stayed when the new version was definitely undertaken. No edition is given in the lists later than 1606[1], though the New Testament from it was reprinted as late as 1618 or

The history of the book is un-known; but the occurrence of the reference-letters is at least a certain proof that it was not designed for the press. In all probability it con-tains simply a scholar's collation of the Royal and Bishops' texts, with an attempt to trace the origin of the corrections.

The corrections throughout the O. T. are apparently in the same hand: those in the N.T. are in a different hand and 'considerably more ' modern.'

[1] [An edition of 1606 is mentioned in the Catalogue of the Duke of Sussex's Library, but this is probably an error and the Geneva Bible of that year was intended. A copy of this was sold when the Duke's Library was dispersed.]

1619[1]. So far ecclesiastical influence naturally reached.
But it was otherwise with the Genevan Version, which was
chiefly confined to private use.   This competed with the
King's Bible for many years, and it was not till about
the middle of the century that it was finally displaced.
And thus, at the very time when the monarchy and
the Church were, as it seemed, finally overthrown, the
English people by their silent and unanimous acceptance
of the new Bible gave a spontaneous testimony to the
principles of order and catholicity of which both were
an embodiment.

Some steps indeed were taken for a new version during
the time of the Commonwealth.   The Long Parliament
shortly before it was dissolved (April, 1653) made an order
that 'a Bill should be brought in for a new translation
'of the Bible out of the original tongues,' but nothing
more was done at that time[2].   Three years afterwards the
scheme was revived, and Whitelocke has preserved an
interesting account of the proceedings which followed.

'At the grand committee [of the House] for Religion,
'ordered That it be referred to a sub-committee to send
'for and advise with Dr [Brian] Walton, Mr Hughes,
'Mr [Edmund] Castle, Mr [Samuel] Clark, Mr Poulk[3],
'Dr [Ralph] Cudworth, and such others as they shall think
'fit, and to consider of the Translations and impressions
'of the Bible, and to offer their opinions thereon to this
'Committee; and that it be especially commended to
'the Lord Commissioner Whitelocke to take care of this
'business.

'This committee often met at Whitelocke's house, and
'had the most learned men in the Oriental tongues to
'consult with in this great business, and divers excellent
'and learned observations of some mistakes in the Trans-
'lations of the Bible in English; which yet was agreed

[1] [See Dore's *Old Bibles*, 2nd ed.,
pp. 278—79. In Fulke's *Defence of
the English Translations* it was reprinted as late as 1633.]

[2] Lewis, *History of Translations*,
354.

[3] Mr J. E. B. Mayor informs me
that this can be nothing but an error
for Mr [Matthew] Poole.

'to be the best of any Translation in the world; great 'pains was taken in it, but it became fruitless by the ' Parliament's Dissolution[1].'

With this notice the external history of the English Version appropriately ends[2]. From the middle of the seventeenth century, the King's Bible has been the acknowledged Bible of the English-speaking nations throughout the world simply because it is the best. A revision which embodied the ripe fruits of nearly a century of labour, and appealed to the religious instinct of a great Christian people, gained by its own internal character a vital authority which could never have been secured by any edict of sovereign rulers[3].

---

[1] Whitelocke, *Memorials* (ed. 1682), p. 645.

[2] Since the first edition of this book appeared the work of revision has been resumed [1872]. See App. IX.

[3] The labours of Hugh Broughton on the English Bible ought not to be passed over without notice. This great Hebraist violently attacked the Bishops' Bible, and sketched a plan for a new version which his own arrogance was sufficient to make impracticable. He afterwards published translations of Daniel, Ecclesiastes, Lamentations, and Job, and offered his help towards the execution of the royal version. His overbearing temper, as it appears, caused him to be excluded from the work; but his printed renderings were not without influence upon the revisers: e.g. Dan. iii. 5. Lewis, *Hist. of Translations*, 297 ff.

CHAPTER III.

THE INTERNAL HISTORY OF THE ENGLISH BIBLE.

Oh, if we draw a circle premature
Heedless of far gain,
Greedy for quick returns of profit, sure
Bad is our bargain !
Was it not great? did not he throw on God,
(He loves the burthen)—
God's task to make the heavenly period
Perfect the earthen.....
That low man seeks a little thing to do,
Sees it and does it :
This high man, with a great thing to pursue,
Dies ere he knows it......
That has the world here—should he need the next,
Let the world mind him !
This throws himself on God, and unperplext
Seeking shall find Him......
Lofty designs must close in like effects :
Loftily lying,
Leave him—still loftier than the world suspects,
Living and dying.

BROWNING, *Dramatis Personæ*, *A Grammarian's Funeral.*

CHAPTER III.

THE INTERNAL HISTORY OF THE ENGLISH BIBLE.

SUCH in a general outline was the external history of the English Bible. We have still to inquire how it was made? with what helps? on what principles? by what laws it was modified from time to time? and how far our authorised version bears in itself the traces of its gradual formation? To some of these questions only tentative or imperfect answers can be rendered at present; yet it is something to clear the way to a fuller investigation; and when once the novelty and complication of the problems become evident, it cannot fail but that a combination of labour will achieve their complete solution. Hitherto nothing has been done systematically towards the work. A few vague surmises and hasty generalizations have gained unchallenged currency and stopped thorough search; yet when viewed simply in its literary aspect, the history of the growth of the authorised text involves a more comprehensive and subtle criticism, and is therefore filled with a deeper interest, than any similar history. Each revision stands in a definite relation to a particular position of the English Church, and may be expected to reflect its image in some degree. Moreover we possess the work at each stage of its structure and not only in its final completeness. Each part can be examined as it was first planned and executed, and not only as it was finally incorporated into a more complex whole. We can even determine the materials out of which it was raised, and the various resources of which its authors could avail themselves at each point of their task.

For us the result stands now amidst the accumulated treasures of later researches. But if we would appreciate it rightly in itself we must once again surround it by the conditions under which it was obtained.

The close of the 15th century sealed a revolution in Europe. The ecclesiastical language of the West had given place to or at least admitted into fellowship the sacred languages of the East. It was in vain that the more ignorant of the clergy denounced Greek and Hebrew as the fatal sources of heathenism and Judaism; it was vain that they could be popularly represented as emblems of apostate peoples of GOD while the Latin symbolized the faithful: the noblest and most far-seeing scholars, lay or cleric, recognized in the new learning a handmaid of religion, and took measures for its honourable admission into the circle of liberal education. In his University at Alcala the great Cardinal Ximenes made provision for the teaching of Hebrew and Greek with Latin, and consecrated the study in his noble Polyglott. At Louvain a foundation for the like purpose was added to the University about 1516 by Busleiden. Wolsey appears to have contemplated a similar course in his College at Oxford, where he founded in 1519 a chair of Greek[1]. When complaints were made, Henry, acting no doubt under his inspiration, enjoined that 'the study of the Scriptures in the original languages 'should not only be permitted for the future, but received 'as a branch of the academical institution[2].' The work of Wolsey was left unfinished, but it is not without interest to find among his canons two, John Fryth and Richard Taverner, who became afterwards distinguished for their labours in the translation of Scripture, and at least seven others who were sufferers by the first persecution which followed after the introduction of Tindale's New Testament[3]. Thus everywhere men were being disciplined for rendering the original text of the Bible into the

[1] Bp. Fox had founded one two years earlier, in 1517.

[2] Anderson, I. 26.

[3] Compare the lists given by Anderson, I. pp. 86, 95.

living languages of Europe, and at the end of the first quarter of the 16th century sufficient materials were gathered for the accomplishment of their office.

The appliances for the independent study of the Greek of the New Testament and the Septuagint Version of the Old were fairly adequate. Grammars were in wide circulation, of which the earliest was that of Lascaris (Milan, 1476), and the most enduring that of Clenardus (Louvain, 1530). In the interval between the appearance of these, numerous others were published in Italy, France, and Germany[1]. The first lexicon of Craston (1480) was republished in a more convenient form by Aldus (1497) and supplemented by the important collections of Guarino (Phavorinus) in his *Etymologicum Magnum*. But these and all other earlier lexicons were eclipsed by the so-called *Commentaries* of Budæus (Paris, 1529), a true *Thesaurus* of Greek, which still remains a vast monument and store-house of learning. The very names of many of the great German scholars shew the passion with which the study was pursued. Melanchthon (*Schwarzerd*), Œcolampadius (*Hausschein*), Capnio (*Reuchlin*), Erasmus (*Gerhard*), Ceratinus (*Horn*), are memorable instances to prove the power of Greek to furnish home names to the Teutonic nations. And though England can boast of no original Greek works till a later time, yet Croke, a scholar of Grocyn, first introduced a thorough knowledge of the language into northern Germany, where, it is said, he was received 'like a heavenly messenger[2].'

The pursuit of Hebrew was not less flourishing in the North. In Italy Greek had been welcomed at first as a new spring of culture. Beyond the Alps Greek and Hebrew were looked upon as the keys to Divine Truth. So it was that while Greek languished in Italy and Hebrew scarcely gained a firm footing among the mass of students; in Germany both were followed up with an

---

[1] One at *Wittenberg* in 1511. [Panzer, *Ann. Typ.* IX. 68, 17.]   [2] Hallam, *Introd. to Literature*, I. 268 n.

'ardent zeal which for good alike and for evil is yet fruitful
in great issues.   An Italian of the early part of the 16th
century instinctively marked the spiritual difference of the
North and South when he observed that in Germany
Hebrew was prized in the same manner as Latin in Italy.
Thus the early translators of the Old Testament found
materials already fitted for their use.   The first Hebrew
grammar was composed by Pellican (1503).   This was
followed by that of Reuchlin, with a dictionary, in 1506.
Another by S. Münster appeared in 1525, who published
also a Chaldee grammar in 1527. Pagninus, the translator
of the Bible, added a new dictionary in 1529.   The great
Complutensian Polyglott (published 1520, finished 1517)
contained a Latin translation of the Targum of Onkelos
and a complete Lexicon to the Hebrew and Chaldee
texts, with a Hebrew grammar.

In the mean time, while all the chief classical authors
had been published, the original texts and some of the
ancient versions of Holy Scripture had also become
accessible.   The Latin Vulgate is supposed to have been
the first book printed (c. 1455), and this first edition was
followed by a multitude of others, in some of which, and
notably in the Latin text of the Complutensian Polyglott,
old manuscripts were used.

The Hebrew of the Old Testament was first published
completely at Soncino in 1488.   Many other editions
followed, which were crowned by the great Rabbinical
Bibles of Bomberg in 1517 and 1525 : these were furnished
with the Targums and the commentaries of the greatest
early Jewish scholars.   Complete Latin translations from
the Hebrew were made by Sanctes Pagninus (1527), and
by Sebast. Münster (1534-5).   Considerable portions were
rendered afresh in Latin by Zwingli and Œcolampadius;
and single books by many writers before 1535.   The
Septuagint was contained in the Complutensian Polyglott,
and in a distinct text in the edition of Aldus 1518.   The
Greek Testament appeared for the first time many years
after the Latin and Hebrew texts, edited by Erasmus

with a new Latin translation in 1516[1]. A second edition
followed in 1519: a third, which may be considered his
standard edition, in 1522; and others in 1527, and 1535.
An edition from the press of Aldus with some variations
appeared together with the Septuagint in 1518. The
Complutensian Polyglott printed in 1514, in which there
is an independent text of the New Testament, was not
published till 1520. Other editions followed soon after
which have little or no independent value.

It remains only to characterize generally the critical
value of these editions. The Hebrew text of the Old
Testament edited by [Jacob] Ben Chayim (1525) is substantially good. Indeed as Hebrew Manuscripts all belong
to a comparatively late recension the extent of real variation between them is limited. The Latin texts accessible
in the first half of the 16th century were indifferent.
The Greek texts of the New Testament, and this is most
important, were without exception based on scanty and
late manuscripts, without the help of the oriental versions
and the precious relics of the Old Latin. As a necessary
consequence they are far from correct, and if the variations
are essentially unimportant as a whole, yet the errors in
the text of our English Testament inherited from them
are considerably more important than the existing errors
of translation.

Such were the materials which the first great Reformers
found to help them in their work of rendering the original
Scriptures into their own languages. Before the English
labourers entered the field it was already occupied.
Numerous students in Germany had translated separate
books when Luther commenced the work which he was
enabled to carry to a successful end. Luther's New
Testament appeared in 1522 as the fruit of his seclusion
in the Wartburg, and, like Tindale's, anonymously. The
Pentateuch followed in 1523. The Historical books and the
Hagiographa in 1524. The Prophets at various intervals

---

[1] In the same year appeared his
edition of St Jerome, the most important of the Fathers for a translator
of the Bible.

(Jonah in 1526) afterwards ; and the whole work in 1534.
The second revised edition did not appear till 1541. But
in the meanwhile a band of scholars at Zurich, including
Zwingli, Pellican, and Leo Juda, had taken Luther's work
as the basis of a new translation up to the end of the
Hagiographa, and completed it by an original translation
of the Prophets and the Apocrypha. This was published
in fragments from 1524—1529, and first completely in two
forms in the latter year. It was republished in 1530, and
with a new translation of the Hagiographa in 1531, and
often afterwards[1]. Another German Bible with an original
translation of the Prophets appeared at Worms in 1529[2].
The French translation of Lefevre (Faber Stapulensis)
was made (1523—1534) from the Vulgate, and was not
an independent work : that of Olivetan (Neuchâtel, 1535)
is said to have been based in the Old Testament on
Sanctes Pagninus, and in the New on Lefèvre[3].

The works of the first German translators, or at
least of Luther, must then be added to those previously
enumerated as accessible to Tindale[4] during the execution

---

[1] The editions which I have used
are those of 1530 and 1534. I have
not been able to consult the small
edition of 1529 with glosses [they are
but few]; nor have I collated the two
editions or determined how far the
translation in the earlier books differs
as a whole from Luther's. The difference in isolated passages is very considerable.

[2] This edition I have not used. [It
is substantially a reprint of the 16mo.
Zurich Bible of 1527-9 (see Panzer,
*Entwurf einer vollständigen Geschichte
der deutschen Bibelübersetzungen D.
Martin Luthers*, 2te Ausg., p. 254,
&c.).]

[3] I have not examined Lefèvre's
translation; and am ignorant also of
the real character of Bruccioli's Italian
version (1530—1532), which is said to
have been made from the original.
[The marginal notes in the 1534

edition of Lefèvre were largely used
in Matthew's Bible of 1537. In the
Old Testament Bruccioli is dependent
greatly on Pagninus.]

[4] The Wycliffite Versions do not
seem to have exercised any influence
on the later English Versions, unless
an exception be made in the case
of the Latin-English Testament of
Coverdale mentioned above. The
coincidences of rendering between this
and Purvey are frequently remarkable,
but as both literally reproduce the
Vulgate I have been unable to find
(so far as I have examined them) any
certain proof of the dependence of one
on the other.

As far as Tindale is concerned—
and his work was the undoubted basis
of the later revisions—his own words
are sufficient: 'I had,' he says in the
New Testament (1525), 'no man to
'counterfet [imitate], nether was

of his Version of the New Testament. Luther's name was indeed at the time identified with the idea of vernacular versions of Scripture, and it is not surprising that More affirmed that Tindale's work was a translation of Luther's, an assertion in which he has been followed by writers who have less excuse[1]. What Tindale's version really was we have now to inquire.

§ 1. TINDALE.

All external evidence goes to prove Tindale's originality as a translator[2]. He had, as we have seen, formed his purpose of translating the New Testament before he could have heard of Luther's[3], and in the year in which that appeared (1522) went up to London with a translation from Isocrates as a proof of his knowledge of Greek. His knowledge of Hebrew and Greek is also incidentally attested by the evidence of Spalatinus[4], of his opponent Joye[5], and yet more clearly by the steady confidence with which he deals with points of Hebrew and Greek philology when they casually arise. Thus after defending his rendering of *presbyteros* (elder), *charis* (favour), *agape* (love), &c. against Sir T. More he says (1530): 'These 'things to be even so Mr More knoweth well enough: for

'holpe with englysshe of eny that 'had interpreted the same, or soche 'lyke thīge ī the scripture before-'tyme.' (*Epistle to the Reader*, 1. p. 390, Parker Soc. ed.) See p. 140 and App. VIII.

[1] Hallam's account is so amazing from the complication of blunders which it involves that it deserves to be quoted as a curiosity. 'From this 'translation [Luther's], and from the 'Latin Vulgate, the English one of 'Tyndale and Coverdale, published 'in 1535, or 1536, is avowedly taken. '...That of 1537, commonly called

'Matthews's Bible, from the name of 'the printer, though in substance the 'same as Tyndale's, was superintend-'ed by Rogers...' (*Introd. to Lit.* 1. 373.) It is impossible that he could have examined any one of the books of which he thus summarily disposes.

[2] For the part which Joye had in the work of preparing the translation see *Preface to the Parable of the Wicked Mammon.*

[3] See above, p. 26.
[4] See above, p. 35 n.
[5] Anderson, 1. 397.

'he understandeth the Greek, and he knew them long
'ere I¹.' Again in an earlier work he writes (1528): 'The
'Greeke tounge agreeth more with the English then wyth
'the Latin. And the properties of the Hebrue tounge
'agreeth a thousand tymes more wyth the Englishe, then
'wyth the Latyn².'

But the translation of the New Testament itself is the
complete proof of its own independence. It is impossible
to read through a single chapter without gaining the
assurance that Tindale rendered the Greek text directly,
while he still consulted the Vulgate, the Latin translation
of Erasmus, and the German of Luther. Thus taking
a chapter at random we find in Eph. iv. the following
certain traces of the peculiarities of the Greek which are
lost in the Vulgate and the translations made from it.

   2 in...*longe sufferynge, forbearīge* one another...cum pa-
      tientia supportantes...with *pacience supportinge* ech
      other...(Wycliffe, Rheims).
   4 *even* as...sicut...as (Wycliffe, Rheims).
   8 *and* hath geven...dedit...he ȝaf...(Wycliffe, Rheims).
  17 as *wother* gentyls...sicut et...as hethene men (Wycliffe),
      as *also* the Gentiles (Rheims).
  27 *backbyter...diabolo...the deuel* (Wycliffe, Rheims).
  29 *filthy* cōmunicacion......sermo *malus......yuel* word
      (Wycliffe): *naughtie* speache (Rheims).
   — butt thatt whych is good to edefye wíth all, *when
      nede ys...*sed si quis bonus ad ædificationem *fidei...*
      but if ony is good to the edificacioun *of feith* (Wycliffe);
      but if there be any good to the edifying *of the faith*
      (Rheims).

And so again Tindale's rendering of vv. 5, 12, 14, 22
might come from the Greek but hardly from the Latin.
On the other hand it is evident that he had the Vulgate
before him, and that he owed to it the rendering '*blind-*

---

¹ *Answer to Sir T. More*, III. p. 23   Compare *Answer to More*, p. 75.
(ed. Park. Soc.).   *Prologue to St Matthew*, I. p. 468
² *Obedience of a Christian Man*   (Park. Soc.).
(Pref. to Reader, p. 102, ed. 1573).

'*ness* of their hearts' (cæcitatem), which has wrongly retained its place in the Authorised Version.

From Luther the same chapter differs in the entire complexion of the rendering and unequivocally in the interpretation of the following passages :

5 *Let ther be but* one lorde...Ein Herr...

13 tyll we everychone (*in the* vnitie of fayth...) growe vppe vnto a parfayte man...bis dass wir alle *hinan kommen zu einerlei* glauben...*und* ein vollkommener Mann *werden*...

21 as *the trueth is* in Iesu...wie in Iesu *ein rechtschaffenes Wesen* ist.

24 in *ryghtewesnes, and true holynes*...in *rechtschaffener Gerechtigkeit und Heiligkeit*...

A continuous passage will place the substantial independence of Tindale in a still clearer light[1].

VULGATE.	TINDALE (1525).	LUTHER (Dec. 1522).
13 Nunc autem in Christo Jesu vos qui aliquando eratis longe, facti estis prope in sanguine Christi.	13 *But nowe in Christ Iesu, ye* whych a whyle agoo *were farre off, are made neye by the bloude off Christ.*	13 Nu aber yhr die yhr ynn Christo seyt, vnd weyland ferne gewesen, seyt nu nahe worden durch das blut Christi.
14 Ipse enim est pax nostra, qui fecit utraque unum, et medium parietem maceriæ solvens,	14 *For he is oure peace,* whych *hath made* off *both wone ād hath broken doune the wall* ī the myddes, that was a stoppe *bitwene vs,*	14 Denn er ist vnser fride, der aus beyden eyns hat gemacht, und hat abbrochen die mittelwand, die der zawn war zwischen vns,
15 inimicitias in carne sua,	15 and hath also put awaye thorowe *his flesshe,* the cause	15 nemlich die feyndschafft, damit, das er hat durch ṣeyn

[1] The Italics in Tindale mark what is preserved in the Authorised Version. The only difference which I have observed between the editions of 1525 and 1534 is the omission in the latter of the words *in the midst* in v. 14.

VULGATE.	TINDALE (1525).	LUTHER (Dec. 1522).
legem mandatorum decretis evacuans,	of hatred (thatt is to saye, *the lawe of cōmaundement con-tayned in* the lawe writtē)	fleysch auffgehaben das gesetz der gepot, so fern sie schrifft-lich verfasset waren.
16 ut duos condat in semetipso in unum novum homi-nem, faciens pacem, et reconciliet ambos, in uno corpore Deo per crucem, inter-ficiens inimicitias in semetipso.	16 *for to make of twayne wone newe mā in hym silfe, so makynge peace. and to reconcile bothe vnto god in one body* throwe his *crosse,* ād slewe hattred *ther-by* ·	16 auff dass er aus zweyen eynen newen menschen schaffte, ynn yhm fride zu-machen, vnd das er beyde versuncte mit Got yn eynem leybe, durch das creutz, vnd hat die feyndschafft todtet durch sich selbs,
17 Et veniens e-vangelizavit pacem vobis, qui longe fu-istis, et pacem iis qui prope;	17 *and cam and preached peace to you which were afarre of, and to them that were neye.*	17 vnd ist komen, hat verkundiget ym Evangelio, den fri-den euch, die yhr ferne waret, vnd denen, die nahe waren.
18 Quoniam per ipsum habemus ac-cessum ambo in uno Spiritu ad Patrem.	18 *For thorowe hym we bothe have an* open waye in, in *one sprete vnto the father.*	18 Denn durch yhn haben wyr den zu-gang all beyde ynn einem geyst, zum vater.
19 Ergo jam non estis hospites et ad-venæ, sed estis cives sanctorum et domestici Dei,	19 *Nowe therfore ye are no moare stran-gers ād foreners: but* citesyns *with the saynctes, and of the housholde of god .*	19 So seyt yhr nu nicht mehr geste vnd frembdling, son-dern burger, mit den heiligen, vñ Gottis haussgenossen,
20 Superædificati super fundamentum Apostolorum et Pro-	20 *and are bilt apō the foundacion oj the apostles ād pro-*	20 erbawet auff den grund der Apostel vnd der propheten,

VULGATE.	TINDALE (1525).	LUTHER (Dec. 1522).
phetarum, ipso summo angulari lapide Christo Jesu;	*phetes, Iesus Christ beynge the* heed *corner stone,*	da Iesus Christus der ecksteyn ist,
21 In quo omnis ædificatio constructa crescit in templum sanctum in Domino,	21 *ī whom* every *bildynge* coupled *togedder, groweth vnto ā holy tēple in the lorde,*	21 auff wilchen, wilcherley baw yñ eynander gefugt wirt, der wechst, zu eynem heyligen tempel ynn dem herrn,
22 in quo et vos coædificamini in habitaculum Dei in Spiritu.	22 *ī whō* ye *also are bilt togedder,* and made *an habitacion* for *god* ī *the sprete.*	22 auff wilchen auch yhr mit erbawet werdet, zu eyner behausung Gottis im geyst.

There is, however, one other authority who had greater influence upon Tindale than the Vulgate or Luther. The Greek text of the New Testament published by Erasmus, which Tindale necessarily used, was accompanied by an original Latin version in which Erasmus faithfully rendered the text he had printed. This translation is very frequently followed by Tindale. Thus in the phrases already quoted from Eph. iv.[1] three at least seem to be due to Erasmus, 27 *backbiter, calumniatori* (Erasm.); 29 *filthy* communication, sermo *spurcus* (Erasm.); *id.* when *need is,* quoties *opus est* (Erasm.). But on the other hand, any chapter will shew important differences between Erasmus and Tindale, not always indeed in Tindale's favour, but sufficient at least to prove that he exercised a free judgment both in the general character and in the details of his version. A collation of Col. ii. offers the following considerable variations:

ERASMUS (1516).	TINDALE (1534).
1 *Nam* volo	I wolde (so Luther)
quantum *certamen*	what *fyghtinge* (*kampff* L.)
faciem meam	my *parson* (*person* L.)

[1] See p. 132.

Erasmus (1516).	Tindale (1534).
2 cum fuerint compacti in omnes divitias *certæ persuasionis intelligentiæ*	*and* knet togedder (so L.) in all ryches *of full vnderstondynge* (zu allem reychthum des volligen verstands L. 1522)
et patris	the father (L. 1522, 1534)
6, 7 ita in eo ambulate radicati et superstructi	so walke, roted and bylt in him (so wandelt...und seyt gewurtzelt L.)
11 *dum* exuistis *corpus peccatorum* carnis	*by* puttinge (*durch* Abl. L.) the *sinfull boddy* of the flesshe (des sundlichen leybes ym fleysch L.)
in circumcisione Christi (mit L.)	thorow the circumcision *that is in* Christ
12 per fidem operationis Dei	thorowe fayth, *thãt is wrought by* the operacion of god (durch den glawben den Got wircket L.)
13 per delicta et per præputium (ynn den sunden vnd ynn der...L.)	*in* synne *thorow* the vncircumcision (*in* sin *and in* the... 1525)
14 quod erat contrarium nobis *per decreta* (welche durch satzung entstund L. 1534)	that was agaynst vs, *contayned in the lawe written* (*made* in... 1525) [durch schrifftlich satzung erweyset L. 1522]
16 *vos judicet*	*trouble youre consciences* (euch gewissen machen L.)
aut novilunii (so L.)	*as* the holydaye of the newe mone
17 quæ sunt umbra (so L.) — corpus autem Christi	which are *nothinge but* shaddowes but the body is *in* Christ (so L.)
18 ne quis *vobis palmam intervertat, volens in humilitate, et superstitione angelorum*	Let no man *make you shote at a wronge* (*marke*), *which after his awne ymaginacion walketh in the humblenes and holynes of angels* (*Last euch niemand das zill verrucken...*L.) (om. *and holiness* 1525 [but added in Errata])

ERASMUS (1516).	TINDALE (1534).
23 *in superstitione ac humilitate animi et læsione corporis sui, non in honore quopiam, ad expletionem carnis*	*in chosen holynes and humblenes, and in that they spare not the body, and do the flesshe no wor-shype vnto his nede* (so L.[1])

A careful examination of the quarto fragment furnishes a most complete and unequivocal proof of Tindale's independence as a translator. We shall see afterwards[2] that he availed himself fully of Luther's notes for his own glosses, but he deals with the text as one who passed a scholar's judgment upon every fragment of the work, unbiassed by any predecessor. As nearly as I can calculate he differs from Luther in about two hundred places in the chapters contained in the fragment, Matt. i.—xxii. 12. Some examples will shew the extent and character of the differences:

TINDALE (1525).	LUTHER (Dec. 1522).
ii. 7 the tyme of the starre that appered [unlike Eras-mus]	wenn der stern erschynen were

[1] This last verse offers one of the most remarkable coincidences between Luther and Tindale which I have noted. Luther's version is: durch selbsterwählte Geistlichkeit und Demuth und dadurch dass sie des Leibes nicht verschonen, und dem Fleisch nicht seine Ehre thun zu seiner Nothdurft. [The version of Luther which is here given is that which is found in modern editions and is substantially the same as that in the edition of 1534. In place of the clause 'dem Fleisch nicht seine Ehre thun' all the editions down to 1525 which I have consulted have, with slight differences of spelling, 'an das fleysch seyne kost wenden.' As Tindale's rendering 'do the flesh no worship' is in his edition of 1525, it does not appear that he took it from Luther.] The version in the Witten-berg Latin Bible [printed in Luther's *Sämtliche Schriften*, ed. Walch, vol. XIV.] is quite different [in superstitione et humilitate, et non parcendo corpori, nec honorem ei habendo, quantum carni satis est]. In a number of passages taken almost at random where Tindale differs considerably from Luther I have noted that he agrees with Erasmus in Lu. xi. 36, 40; xix. 43. John ii. 9; x. 12. Acts iii. 16. 2 Cor. xi. 8. Gal v. 18 Eph. v. 16; and differs from Erasmus in Luke xix. 42 John xi. 2 Acts iii. 20. Rom. ix. 11, 28 Gal. v. 5 Col. iii. 9. Other differences exist between the texts of 1525, 1534 in [Col. ii.] *vv.* 10, 13, 14, 16, 18, 20. In five places the latter text approaches Luther more nearly than the earlier: in one the converse holds.

[2] See p. 146, n. 2.

TINDALE (1525).	LUTHER (Dec. 1522).
vii. 29 he taught them as one havynge power [like E.]	er prediget gewaltiglich
xii. 18 my sonne [like E.]	mein knecht
xiii. 13 for though they se, they se nott: and hearynge they heare not: nether vnderstonde	denn mit sehenden augen sehen sie nicht, vnd mit horenden orē horen sie nicht, deñ sie verstehē es nicht
— 38 the evyll mans chyldren are the tares	das vnkraut sind die kinder der bosheyt
— 57 there is no prophet with out honoure save..	Eyn Prophet gillt nyrgend weniger denn…
xvi. 7 sayinge: we have brought [like E.]	sie…sprachen, das wirts seyn, das wyr…
xix. 17 there is none good but wō, and that is god [like E.]	Niemant ist gut, denn nur der eynige Gott [the Strasburg edition of 1524 reads: denn nur der ewig got]
xxi. 20 Howe soone is the fygge tree wyddred awaye [E quomodo continuo aruit 1516]	Wie ist der feigen bawm so bald verdurret?

On the other hand there are passages (perhaps ten in all) where Luther's judgment has evidently swayed Tindale. Of these the most remarkable are:

ii. 18 On the hilles	Auf dem gebirge
vi. 25 from the ten cetes	von [L. 1522: aus 1534] den zehen stedtē
xi. 25 I prayse Thee	ich preysse Dich
xv. 9 which is nothynge but mens preceptes	die nichts denn menschen gepot sind
— 13 all plantes	alle pflantzen
xxi. 15 Hosianna	Hosianna

It does not seem necessary to bring forward any further evidence of the originality of Tindale's first labours on the New Testament[1]. The samples given are fair

---

[1] It is greatly to be regretted that Mr F. Fry did not add to his facsimile of the small Testament of 1525 a collation of the Grenville quarto fragment. The conclusion which Mr Anderson draws from the spelling as

specimens of the whole work. And in his later labours
Tindale continued to follow to the end the sure path on
which he had deliberately entered. The revised edition
of 1534 expressly claims upon the title-page to be
'diligently corrected and compared with the original
'Greek.' In the address 'to the Reader,' Tindale explains his work more in detail. 'Here thou hast (moost

to the priority of the quarto (I. 70)
is hasty and unsatisfactory. The
spelling in both editions is very inaccurate. In the Sermon on the Mount
I have noted among other variations
the following which are more or less
characteristic. The differences in
text are very slight, and in no one
case (except in the misprint VI. 24)
does the quarto edition give a reading which has been preserved in the
edition of 1534. So far therefore the
quarto text seems to have been cursorily revised before it was reprinted
at Worms. But a complete collation
of the text is desirable.

1525. COLOGNE.	1525. WORMS.
Matt. v. 1 wen	when
—mouth	mought
3 thers	theirs
4 mourne	morne
11, 45 evle vii 11	yvell, vii. 11 evyll
13 but añ yf	but and if
15 all those	all them (all 1534)
17 other the	or the (so 1534)
26 vtmoost forthynge	vtmost farthīge
29 in to	in tho
39, 42 turne vii. 6	tourne
40 clooke	cloocke
44 cursse	coursse
45 for vi. 2, 7 &c.	ffor
—oniuste	iniuste
vi. 5 Verely	Vereley
7 thinke	thincke
13 Lede	Leede
19 moththes	mothes
20 to gyddre	to gedder
—ner yet moththes corrupte	nor mothes corupe (om. yet 1534)
21 hertͭ (so ypocrytͭ, &c.)	hertes
23 boddy	body
24 lene to the (so 1534)	lene the
—that other	the other (so 1534)
26 nether	neder
—thē (them)	then
27 thought	tought
vii. 2 with that same	with the same (so 1534)
6 pierles	pearles

'deare reader) the new Testamēt or covenaunt made wyth
'vs of God in Christes bloude. Which I have looked over
'agayne (now at the last) with all dylygence, and com-
'pared it vnto the Greke, and have weded oute of it many
'fautes, which lacke of helpe at the begynninge and over-
'syght, dyd sowe therin. If ought seme chaunged [charged
'1536] all to gether agreynge with the Greke, let the fynder
'of yᵉ faute consider the Hebrue Phrase or maner of
'speche lefte in the Greke wordes. Whose preterperfectence
'and presenttence is ofte both one, and the futuretence
'is the optative mode also, and the futuretence is ofte the
'imperatyve mode in the actyve voyce, and in the passyve
'ever. Lykewyse person for person, nombre for nombre,
'and an interrogacion for a cōdicionall, and soch lyke is
'with the Hebrues a comen vsage. I have also in manye
'places set lyght in the mergent, to vnderstonde the text
'by. If anye man fynde fautes ether with the trāslacion
'or ought besyde (which is easyer for manye to do, then
'so well to have translated it them selves of their awne
'pregnant wyttes, at the begynnynge withoute forensample)
'to the same it shalbe lawfull to trāslate it them selves and
'to put what they lust therto. If I shall perceave ether
'by my selfe or by the informacion of other, that ought
'be escaped me, or myght be more playnlye translated,
'I will shortlye after cause it to be mended. Howbeit in
'manye places, me thynketh it better to put a declaracyon
'in the margent, then to runne to farre from the text.
'And in manye places, where the text semeth at the fyrst
'choppe harde to be understonde, yet yᵉ circūstāces
'before and after, and oftē readinge together, maketh it
'playn ynough...'

A comparison of the texts of the first and second
editions fully bears out the description which Tindale here
gives of his work. To take one example only: of the
thirty-one changes which I have noticed in the later
version of 1 John, about a third are closer approximations
to the Greek: rather more are variations in connecting
particles or the like, designed to bring out the argument

of the original more clearly; three new readings are
adopted; and in one passage it appears that Luther's
rendering has been substituted for an awkward paraphrase.
Yet it must be remarked that even in this revision the
changes are far more frequently at variance with Luther's
renderings than in accordance with them[1].

The importance of the New Testament of 1534, which
is altogether Tindale's noblest monument, gives a peculiar
interest to the short glosses with which it is furnished.
Though these do not throw much light upon the translation
itself, yet they give such a lively image of the character
of Tindale that a few specimens of them cannot be out
of place even in a history of the text[2]. Generally they
are pregnant with pithy comments on the passage with
which they deal, designed to guide the reader to its spirit,
and Bengel himself is not more terse or pointed. Such
for example are the following[3]:

'Whē ought is sayde or done, that shuld moue to
'pryde: he dassheth thē in the tethe with his deathe &
'passion.

'A couenaunt to them that loue the worde of God to
'wynne other with worde ād dede: and another to them
'that loue it not, that it shalbe their destruccion.

'Adams disobedyēce dampned vs all yer we oureselues
'wrought euell. And Christes obedience saueth us all, yer
'we oure selues worke anye good. [Luther.]

'God choseth of his awne goodnes and mercye: calleth
'thorow yᵉ gospell: iustifieth thorow faith and glorifieth
'thorow good workes.

'If a mā haue the gyfte, chastite is good, the more

---

[1] These variations are given in detail in App. III.

[2] It is difficult to say why these
marginal glosses and those on the
Pentateuch were not included in the
collected edition of Tindale's works.
Nothing that he has written is more
characteristic.

[3] I have made no attempt to conceal what appear to me to be errors
in Tindale's teaching. The passages
quoted fairly reflect his whole style.
Those who take account of the circumstances under which he had to
work will not pass a severe judgment
on unguarded or one-sided statements.

'quyetlye to serue God. For ye maryed haue ofte moch
'trouble: but if the mynde of the chast be cumbred with,
'other worldly busynes, what helpeth it? & if the maryed
'be the moare quyet mynded therby, what hurteth it
'Nether of it selfe is better then the other, or pleaseth god
'more thē the other   Nether is outewarde circumcision or
'outewarde baptyme worth a pynne of them selues, saue
'that they put vs in remēbraunce to kepe the covenaunt
'made betwene vs & God.

  'Fayth maketh vs sōnes and of the nature of christ,
'ād bindeth eche to haue other in the same reuerēce that
'he hath Christ.

  'Where true faith in Christ is, ther is loue to ye ney-
'boure And faith and loue maketh vs vnderstonde all
'thinges. Fayth vnderstondeth ye secretes of god & the
'mercie that is geuen her in Christ And loue knoweth
'hir dutie to hir neyboure, ād can interprete all lawes &
'ordinaūces & knoweth how farre forth they are to be
'kept & whē to be dispensed with.

  'By oure workes shall we be iudged: for as the in-
'uisible fayth is, soche are the workes by which the fayth
'is sene.

  'We be ye churche: & the obedyence of ye harte is
'ye spirituall sacrifice. Bodilye sacrifice must be offered
'to our neyboures, for yf thou offerest it to god thou
'makest a bodylie ydole of him.

  'Now yf anye that is not mercyfull beleueth to haue
'mercye of god he deceaueth him selfe: because he hath
'no Goddes worde for him   For godes promise partayneth
'to ye mercifull onlye: & true faith therfore is knowen
'by hir dedes.

  'Angell is a greke worde & signifieth a messenger.
'And all the angelles are called messengers, because they
'are sent so ofte from god to mā on message: euen so
'prophetes, preachers and the prelates of the churche are
'called angelles: that is to saye messengers, because their
'offyce is to bringe the message of god vnto the people
'The good angelles here in this booke are the true

'bysshopes and preachers, and the euell angelles are the
'heretyckes and false preachers which euer falsifye gods
'worde, with which the churche of Christ shalbe thus
'miserablye plaged vnto the ende of the worlde, as is
'paynted in these fygures.'

In other places Tindale calls attention emphatically
to the substance of a text, often by a single word, and
again by a brief note, as :

'God is not knowē as a father, but thorow christ.

'God dwelleth not in temples or churches made with
'hādes.

'Prayer & fastynge go to gether.

'Searche the scriptures for by thē may ye trye all
'doctrine.

'To haue pleasure in another mannes synne is greater
wyckednes then to synne thy selfe.

'Eternall lyfe is the seruinge of Christ.

'He is strōge that cā beare another mannes weakenes.'

Sometimes, though rarely, the gloss is simply explanatory :

'Love is yᵉ signe yᵗ the synnes are forgeven her.

'This John is the same Marcke, that wryte the gospel
of Marcke.

These syluerlinges which we now and then call pence
'the Iues call sicles, ād are worth a .x.pēce sterlynge.

'Th[at] is thou shalt kyndle him & make him to
loue.

'Bysshopes and elders is all one & an officer chosen to
'gouerne the congregaccion in doctryne ād liuinge.'

In a very few cases the gloss takes a polemical character,
but still without bitterness :

'Go not frō house to house as freers do.

'To speake with tonges or with the spirite, is to
'speake that other vnderstonde not, as prestes saye their
'seruyce.

'A good lesson for monkes & ydle freers.' [Comp.
Luther.]

In one passage only I have noticed a mystical interpretation which is foreign to the general complexion of Tindale's notes[1]:

'Nyght: when the true knowledge of Christ, how he 'onlie iustifieth, is lost: then can nomā worke a good 'worke in the sight of god, how gloriouse soeuer his 'workes apere.'

In his Preface to the edition of 1534, Tindale had expressed his readiness to revise his work and adopt any changes in it which might be shewn to be improvements. The edition of 1535 [or G. H. 1535, 1534] is a proof of his sincerity[2]. The text of this exhibits a true revision and differs from that of 1534, though considerably less than the text of 1534 from that of 1525[3]. Sometimes

[1] It is right to add that I have not examined whether the glosses are suggested by any earlier commentaries.

[2] Is it this edition to which Joye refers in his *Apology* (p. 4)? Tindale agreed, as he writes, 'that we shulde 'with one accorde in his next testa-'ment then in printing in the stede 'of this vncharitable pistle [added 'to the edition of 1534]...salute the 'reders with one comon salutacion 'to testifye our concorde.' The *Apology* is dated Feb. 27, 1535. It may be added that some of Joye's criticisms in his *Apology* on Tindale's renderings are of interest. Thus he objects to his translation in Mark xii. 26, where he plays 'boo pepe withe the 'tencis as he englissheth *resuscitan-*'tur [the word given by Erasmus 'for the *resurgant* of the Vulgate] '*shal ryse agen,* and not *are reuiued* 'or *resuscited*...' (p. 13) ... 'or they *ar* '*all redy alyue* (he saith not that 'they *shalbe alyue* or *shall ryse agayne* 'as [Tindale] in hys diligent last cor-'reccion turneth the present tence 'into the future: and the verbe passiue 'into a neuter to stablissh his errour 'thus corrupting the text' (p. 15). Again he objects to the rendering in

Rom. i. 4 *synce the tyme that Iesus Christ oure Lorde rose agayne from deeth,* where he says that Tindale has mistaken 'what *Ex eo* [the rendering 'of Erasmus again] there sygnifyeth' (p. 94). In 1 Cor. xiv. 14 he maintains that *spiritus* 'signifyeth...the 'breathe, and voice of our tongue...' and not spirit (p. 95). Throughout he appeals only to the Latin. [In 1904 the British Museum acquired a copy of Joye's New Testament, hitherto unknown, the colophon of which is dated 9 January, 1535. It is described by Mr A. W. Pollard in *The Library* for Jan. 1905.]

[3] In 1 John I have noted sixteen variations from the text of 1534 as against thirty-two in that of 1534 from the original text. From the great inaccuracy of the edition 'finished' 1535 it is often difficult to decide what are printers' errors and what intentional changes. The changes in the Gospels and Acts are (if I may trust a very limited collation) fewer than those in the Epistles. The variations in 1 John are given at length in App. III.

In the different Epistles the number of variations is considerable. In the Epistle to the Ephesians. neg-

the changes are made to secure a closer accordance with the Greek[1]: sometimes to gain a more vigorous or a more idiomatic rendering[2]: sometimes to preserve a just uniformity: sometimes to introduce a new interpretation[3]. The very minuteness of the changes is a singular testimony to the diligence with which Tindale still laboured at his appointed work[4]. Nothing seemed trifling to him, we may believe, if only he could better seize or convey to others the meaning of one fragment of Scripture[5].

Tindale's first Testament was without notes: so too was his last. The short Prologues to the four Evangelists are printed separately before each Gospel. The contents of the tables for the Gospels and the Acts are prefixed in detail before each chapter. The marginal references of the edition of 1534 are generally preserved. But with these exceptions the simple text of the New Testament is given without any addition except the list of books on the reverse of the [second] title-page, and the Epistles from the Old Testament at the end[6]. Thus Tindale

lecting undoubted misprints, I have noted only the following: i, 1 Jesu (Jesus); 20 *the dead* (*deeth*); ii. 1 you haeth he quickened (hath qu. you); iii. 11 purposed *to* (p. *in*); iv. 11 *and* some teachers (om.); iv. 16 of *him-selfe* (*it* silfe); vi. 20 messenger (*a* m.). Compare p. 178, n. 1.

[1] Matt. vi. 34 the daye (for *for* the daye). Mark xvi. 19 *sate him* doune (for *is set* doune). 1 Cor. xv. 10 add *yet*. Eph. iv. 11 add *and* some teachers.

[2] Mark xvi. 11 *though* they herde —*yet* they beleued it not (for *when* they herde—they beleved it not). Rom. xii. 13 *be readi* to harboure (for *diligently* to harboure). 2 Cor. vi. 18 be *my* sonnes (for be *vnto me* sonnes).

[3] Eph. iv. 16 the edyfyinge of *him-selfe* (for the edyfyinge of *it silfe*).

[4] One change is of considerable interest in connexion with the early associations of Tindale. In the edition of 1534 (and so in that of 1536)

the Epistle for St Catharine's day is that given in the Hereford Missal with which Tindale would be familiar in Gloucestershire. In the edition of 1535 the Epistle is given correctly from the Sarum Missal. [See p. 157, note 1.]

[5] See note at the end of the Section.

[6] A duplicate of the tables for the Gospels and Acts printed with another list of books on a page of a different size (36 not 38 lines) stands at the beginning of the volume. This is followed by the prologue to the Romans printed again in a different sized page (37 lines). But there is nothing to shew that these were originally intended to form part of the same book. They are severally contained in separate sheets with distinct signatures. The watermarks of the paper, as far as I can make out, are distinct, and the type in which the

ended as he had begun His last Testament was a final
appeal to the King and to the English people If the
text could gain currency it was enough, as he had re-
peatedly declared[1].

Tindale, as we have seen, both in his first translation
and in his two subsequent revisions of the New Testament,
dealt directly and principally with the Greek text. If he
used the Vulgate or Erasmus or Luther it was with the
judgment of a scholar His complete independence in
this respect is the more remarkable from the profound influence which Luther exerted upon his writings generally.
The extent to which Tindale silently incorporated free
or even verbal translations of passages from Luther's
works in his own has escaped the notice of his editors.
To define it accurately would be a work of very great
labour, but the result, as exhibiting the points of contact
and divergence in the opinions of the two great reformers,
would be a most instructive passage in the doctrinal
history of the time Tindale's ' Prologue' to his quarto
Testament, his first known writing, almost at the beginning
introduces a large fragment from Luther's Preface to the
New Testament. There is indeed a ring in the opening
words which might have led any one familiar with Luther's
style to suspect their real source ' Euāgeliō (that we cal
' the gospel) is a greke worde, & signyfyth good, mery,
' glad and ioyfull tydingę, that maketh a mannes hert glad,
' and maketh hym synge, daunce and leepe for ioye. As
' when Davyd had kylled Golyath the geaūt, cam glad
' tydingę vnto the iewes, that their fearfull and cruell enemy
' was slayne, and they delyvered oute of all daunger ; for
' gladnes were of, they songe, daunsed, and wer ioyfull[2].'

Prologue is printed does not appear
to me to range with that used in the
body of the book, though extremely
like it. Moreover, and this is most
worthy of notice, the orthography of
the two preliminary pieces presents
none of the marked peculiarities by
which the translation itself is gene-

rally characterized. Even 'called'
and 'Holy' are spelt according to
common usage. [See p 50, note.]

[1] See above, p. 53.

[2] Luther: Euangelion ist eyn grie-
chisch wort vnd heyst auff deutsch
gute botschafft, gute meher, gutte new
zeyttung, gut geschrey, davon man

The famous Prologue to the Romans (1526) is, as is
well known, for the most part a paraphrase or a translation of Luther's Preface. Like the Preface to the New
Testament this writing of Luther's also had been translated into Latin (1523), and Tindale's version seems at
one time to follow the German and at another time the
Latin text. Some phrases, as every Christian man must
'exercise himself therein [the Epistle to the Romans] *as*
'*with the daily bread of the soul*[1],' and 'God judgeth *after*
'*the ground of the heart*......therefore *his* law *requireth the*
'*ground of the heart* and love from the bottom thereof, and
'is not content with the outward work only, but *rebuketh*
'*those works* most of all *which spring not* of love *from*
'*the ground* and low bottom *of the heart*...[2],' shew clearly
that Tindale could not have been unacquainted with the
German; and on the other hand the general complexion
of the Prologue is more like the Latin translation than the

singet, saget und frolich ist, Gleich
als do Dauid den grossen Goliath
vberwand, kam eyn gut geschrey, vnd
trostlich new zeytūg vnter das Iu-
disch volck, das yhrer grewlicher feynd
erschlagen, und sie erloset, zu freud
vnd frid gestellet weren, *dauon sie
sungen vñ sprungen vnd frolich
waren.* The Latin translation of the
passage in the Wittenberg Bible [see
p. 137, note 1] may be added: Est
enim Euangelium Græca uox signifi-
cans *bonum seu lætum nuncium*, et
tale quidem quod summa omnium
gratulatione accipitur atque prædica-
tur, *Vnde uoluptas et læticia in hominum animis excitatur.* Nam quemadmodum cum Dauid magnum illum
Gygantem Goliath uicerat, lætum
nuncium ad populum Iudaicum per-
ferebatur, crudelissimo ipsorum hoste
occiso, a quo cum essent liberati nullo
non genere læticiæ atque gaudij per-
fundebantur, Sic et Euangelium siue
Nouum Testamentum &c. The passages italicised mark apparently
special coincidences with Tindale's
rendering.

The translation of Luther extends
from 'the Old Testament is a book—
'shall never more die.' (pp. 8—10, ed.
Parker Soc.).

The glosses exhibit the same powerful influence of Luther. Of the ninety-
one glosses (as I count them) which
appear in the quarto fragment forty-
eight are taken in whole or in part
from Luther's notes, and the remaining forty-three are original.

[1] p. 484 (ed. P. S.). Das sie eyn
Christen mensch...damit vmbgehe, als
mit teglichen brod der seelen. The
Latin has nothing which exactly corresponds.

[2] p. 485 (ed. P. S.). Got richtet
nach des hertzen grund, darumb
foddert auch sein gesetz des Herzen
grund, vnd lessit yhm an wercken
nicht benugen, sondern straft viel
mehr die werck on herzens grund
gethan...The Latin runs: Deus uero
cum sit Cardiognostes, iudicat secundum internos motus cordis, Proinde
et lex Dei requirit cor et affectus,
neque impletur externis operibus, nisi
hilari corde et toto affectu fiant.

German original, and many parts are unequivocally derived from it.   Thus the clauses 'thou understandest not...how '*that it* [the *law*] *cannot be fulfilled and satisfied but with* '*an unfeigned love and affection, much less can it be fulfilled* '*with outward deeds and works only*'[1]...; and again, 'if the 'Law were fleshly *and but man's doctrine*, it might be 'fulfilled...with outward deeds[2]'; and, once more, 'Such 'a new heart and *lusty courage* unto the law-ward canst 'thou never come by *of thine own strength* and enforce-'ment, *but by the operation and working of the Spirit*[3]'; have nothing which directly corresponds with them in the German.   Similar instances might be multiplied indefinitely, but the conclusion even from these seems to be inevitable that Tindale used the Latin by preference while he was able also to avail himself of the German.

The coincidences between Tindale's Exposition of the Sermon on the Mount and that of Luther, though fewer, are even more worthy of notice.   Luther's Expository Sermons were delivered in 1530, and printed in 1532, but they were not translated into Latin till 1533.   On the other hand Tindale's Exposition was printed in 1532. He must then have used the German edition of Luther, or perhaps even notes taken by some friend or by himself. The coincidences which are comparatively rare are still verbal and at the same time tacit.   Two examples will be sufficient to indicate their character.

Gerechtickeit mus an diesem ort nicht heissen, die Christliche heubt gerechtigkeit, dadurch die person frum und angenem wird fur Gott.   Denn ich habe vor gesagt, das diese

Righteousnes in this place is not taken for the principalle righteousnes of a christen mã, thorow which the parson is good and accepted before God. For these .VIII. poyntes are but gesetz leyplich were....

[1] p. 486.   ...quomodo non nisi affectu [lex] impleatur, ipsemet non satis tenes.   Tantum autem abest, ut lex externis operibus impleatur aut iustificet, ut etiam...   For this there is nothing in the German.

[2] *Id.*   Si lex esset carnalis *aut moralis doctrina tantum.* . Wenn das

[3] p. 487.   Talem vero nóvum et *ardentem ac hilarem cordis affectum* non *ex tuis ullis viribus* aut meritis, *sed* sola *operatione et afflatu spiritus* consequere.   For this the German has simply Eyn solchs hertz gibt niemant, deñ Gots geyst. ..

acht stuck nichts anders sind,
Denn eine lere von den früch-
ten vnd guten wercken eines
Christen, vor welchen der
glaube zuuor mus da sein, als
der bawm und heubstuck...
daraus solche stuck alle wach-
sen vnd folgen mussen. Darumb
verstehe hie die eusserlich Gerechtigkeit fur der welt, so wir
vnter vns gegen ander hallten...

Wie er ir Almosen vnd beten
gestrafft hat, so straffet er auch
hie ir fasten...wie sie des
Almosen...misbraucht haben...
also haben sie auch des fastens
misbrauchet vnd verkeret, nicht
fur iren leib im zwang und
zucht zu hallten...sondern von
den leuten gesehen zu werden...das man sich wundern
vnd sagen müsste, O das sind
treffliche heiligen, die da...
gehen inn grawen röcken, den
kopff hengen, sawr vnd bleich
sehen &c. wenn die nicht gen
himel komen, wo wollen wir
andern bleiben?

doctryne
of the frutes and workes of a
christen mā

before which the faythe must
be there:...ād as a tre out of
which all soche frutes ād workes
must sprynge.

Wherfore vndrestande here
the outwarde righteousnes before the worlde and true and
faythfull dealynge eche with
other...

As above of almose and
prayer: euen so here Christ
rebuketh the false entent and
ypocresye of fastynge. That
they sought prayse of that worke
that was ordeyned for to tame
the fleshe, and vsed soche
fassiōs, that all the world myght
knowe that they fasted, to
prayse them and to saye:

O what holye men are these;
how pale and pytifull looke they
euen lyke deethe, hangynge
downe their heedes...If these
come not to heauen, what shall
become of vs poore wretches
of the worlde?

But it is in the shorter Prologues to the several books
of the New Testament first published in 1534 that the
character of the dependence of Tindale on Luther is best
seen. Luther has no special Prologues to the Gospels;
but Tindale at the close of his Prologue to St Matthew,
which is an extensive essay, reproduces in a modified
form Luther's famous judgment on the relative worth of
the apostolic books in his Preface to the New Testament:

'...Paul's Epistles with the Gospel of John and his first
' Epistle, and the first Epistle of St Peter, are most pure
' Gospel and most plainly and richly describe the glory
' of the grace of Christ[1].' Tindale on the other hand has
no Preface to the Acts or to the Apocalypse, while
Luther has to both. With these exceptions all Tindale's
Prologues correspond generally in character and form with
Luther's, and every one besides that to 1 Corinthians is
framed out of or with reference to them. And further, as
these short Prologues were not included in the Wittenberg
Bible, nor, as far as it appears, separately translated, it
follows that Tindale must have become thoroughly familiar
with German during his long residence at Marburg, if he
was not so before.

As the Prologues are interesting on every account it
will be worth while to draw out a little more in detail
the coincidences and differences thus generally described.
The Prologues to 2 Corinthians, Ephesians, Philippians,
Colossians, 1, 2 Thessalonians, 1, 2 Timothy, Titus, Philemon, 1, 2 Peter, 1, 2, 3 John, are almost entirely taken from
Luther, but in nearly all cases in a compressed form That
to the Galatians incorporates a large piece of Luther's, but
is fuller Those to St James and St Jude are independent
in treatment and conclusion, but distinctly traceable to
Luther's. That to the Hebrews is a sustained argument
against Luther.

The changes are in all cases worthy of notice. One
of the omissions at least is strikingly significant. In the
Preface to Philemon Luther has a startling allegorical
application of the circumstances to the history of the

---

[1] p. 477 (ed. P. S.). With this
Luther's original judgment may be
compared: Summa, Sanct Johannis
Evangeli vnd seyne erste Epistel,
Sanct Paulus Epistel, sonderlich die
zu den Romern, Galatern, Ephesern,
vnd Sanct Peters erste Epistel, das
sind die bucher, die dyr Christum
zeygen vnnd alles leren, das dyr zu
wissen nott vnnd selig ist, ob du schon
keyn ander buch noch lere nummer
sehest noch horist. Darumb ist Sanct
Jacob Epistel eyn rechte stroern
Epistel gegen sie, den sie doch keyn
Euãgelisch art an yhr hat. The
wisdom with which Tindale avoids
the bold negativism of Luther is most
worthy of notice.

Redemption.   Even as Christ has dealt for us with GOD,
'so St Paul deals for Onesimus with Philemon.   For
'Christ emptied Himself of His right and overcame the
'Father with love and meekness, so that He must lay
'aside His wrath and right, and receive us to favour,
'for Christ's sake, who thus earnestly intercedes for us
'and takes us to Him so tenderly.   For we are all His
'Onesimuses if we only believe it.'   Of this characteristic
passage there is no trace in Tindale.   In other places
Tindale omits the temporal applications with which Luther
delighted to animate his teaching[1] and tempers the per-
emptoriness of his exposition by a fuller reference to the
text itself.   Two examples will be sufficient to make his
general method clear.

Am andern leret er wie fur dem Jungsten tag, das Romisch reych zuuor mus vntergehen,

In the seconde he sheweth that the last daye shuld not come, *tyll there were fyrst a departinge (as some men thynke) from vnder the obedyence of the Emperour of Rome,* and that Antichrist shuld set vp him selfe in the same place, as GOD: and deceaue the vnthankfull worlde with false doctrine, and with false & lyenge myracles *wrought by the workinge of Satan,*

vnd der Endchrist sich fur Got auffwerfen ynn der Christenheyt, vnd mit falschen leren vnd zeychen die vnglewbige welt verfuren,

bis das Christus kome vnd vestore yhn durch seyne herliche zukunfft, vnd mit eyner geystlichen predigt zuuor todte.

vntil Christ shuld come & slee him with his glorious commynge and spirituall preachinge of the worde of GOD.

Am dritten thut er ettliche ermanung, vnd sonderlich, das sie die mussigen, die sich nicht mit eygener hand erneren, straffen, vnd wo sie nicht sich bessern, meyden sollen, *wilchs*

In the thyrde he geueth them exhortacion & warneth thē to rebuke the ydle that wolde not laboure with their handes, and auoyde their cōpanie yf they wolde not mende[2].

---

[1] Luther's Preface to 1 Corinthians is full of special applications to the time, and this fact probably accounts

for Tindale's independence.

[2] Prologue to 2 Thessalonians.

gar hart widder den ytzigen
geystlichen stand lautt.

Summa, das erst Capitel
zeigt, wie die Christenheit stehen solt zur zeit des reinen
Evangelii.   Das ander Capitel
zeigt wie sie zur zeit des Bapsts
vnd menschen lere stehen
würde.   Das dritte, *wie hernach*
die leute beide Evangelion vnd
alle lere verachten, vnd nichts
gleuben werden.   Und das gehet
jtzt in vollem schwang, bis
Christus kome.

Finallie The fyrst Chapter
sheweth how it shuld goo in
the tyme of the pure & true
Gospell.   The seconde, how it
shuld goo in the tyme of the
pope and mennes doctrine. The
thyrde, *how at the last men*
shuld beleue nothinge ner feare
GOD at all[1].

Tindale's independence is however best seen in his
treatment of the disputed books which Luther placed in
a second rank.   His Prologue to the Hebrews is a careful
examination of the arguments which Luther urged against
its apostolic authority, and while he leaves its authorship
uncertain and will not 'think it to be an article of any
'man's faith,' yet he decides 'that this epistle ought no
'more to be refused for a holy godly and catholic than
'the other authentic scriptures.'   He even uses Luther's
image but to a different end :

Ob er (the author) wol nicht
den grund legt des glawbens,
wie er selbs zeuget...so bawet
er doch feyn drauff, golt, sylber,
edelsteyne   Derhalben vns
nicht hyndern sol, *ob villeicht*
etwas holtz stro, oder hew, mit
vnter gemenget werde, sondern
solche feyne lere mit allen
ehren auffnemen, On das man
sie den Apostolischen Episteln
nicht aller dinge gleychen mag.

now therfore.. though this
epistle.. laye not the grounde
of the fayth of Christ, yet it
buyldeth conynglye theron pure
golde, syluer, & preciouse
stones...

And seinge the epistle a-
greeth to all the rest of the
scripture, yf it be indifferētlye
loked on, how shuld it not be
of auctoryte and taken for holye
scrypture ?

---

[1] Prologue to 2 Peter.

The Epistles of St James and St Jude are dealt with in the same manner and with the same result. Of the former, Tindale writes: 'Though this Epistle were refused 'in the old time and denied of many to be the Epistle 'of a very Apostle, and though also it lay not the founda-'tion of the faith of Christ...yet because it setteth up 'no man's doctrine...and hath also nothing that is not 'agreeable to the rest of the Scriptures, if it be looked 'indifferently on, methinketh it ought of right to be 'taken for Holy Scripture[1].' Of the latter: 'As for the 'Epistle of Judas though men have and yet do doubt of 'the author, and though it seem also to be drawn out 'of the second epistle of S. Peter, and thereto allegeth 'Scripture that is nowhere found; yet seeing the matter 'is so godly and agreeing to other places of Holy Scrip-'ture, I see not but that it ought to have the authority of 'Holy Scripture[2].' [*Doctr. Treat.*, Park. Soc. pp. 525, 531.]

The standard which Tindale sets up may be a precarious one, but yet it differs widely from the bold subjectivity of Luther, which practically leaves no basis for the Canon but the judgment of the individual reader.

No one who has followed thus far Tindale's mode of dealing with the New Testament can doubt that in the Old Testament he would look first to the Hebrew text, 'which,' he writes, 'is most of need to be known[3]'; and a crucial test at once offers itself. An Appendix to his New Testament of 1534 contains, as we have seen [p. 47],

---

[1] Luther writes thus: Die Epistel Sanct Iacobi, wie wol sie von den alten verworffen ist, lobe ich vñ halt sie doch fur gut, darumb das sie gar keyn menschen lere setzt vñ Gotts gesetz hart treybt. Aber dz ich meyn meynüg drauff stelle, doch on ydermanns nachteyl, acht ich sie fur keyns Apostel schrifft...Darumb wil ich yhn nicht haben ynn meyner Bibel ynn der zal der rechten hewbt-bucher, wil aber damit niemant weren, das er yhn setz und hebe, wie es yhn gelustet, denn viel guter spruch sonst drynnen sind.

[2] Luther: Die Epistel aber Sanct Iudas kan niemant leugnen, das eyn ausstzog odder abschrifft ist aus S. Peters ander Epistel...Vnd furet auch spruch vnd geschicht die yñ der schrifft nyrgend stehen...Darumb ob ich sie wol preysze, ists doch eyn vnnotige Epistel vnter die hewbt-bucher zu rechnen, die des glawbens grund legen sollen.

[3] *Answer to More*, p. 75 (ed. Parker Soc.).

'The Epistles taken out of the Old Testament...after the
'use of Salisbury.' Among these are passages from books
which he had not published at that time, even if he had
translated them, and from others which he certainly never
translated. In the service-books they were of course
given in Latin, and it would be most obvious, therefore,
to turn them from the Vulgate text. If however in this
case Tindale took the Hebrew as his basis, and not the
Latin, and still less Luther, we may be sure that he
followed the like course in his continuous translations.
And so it is: though he keeps the explanatory words
which in some cases introduce or round off the lesson,
yet the lesson itself is rendered from the original Hebrew.
Two examples will be sufficient to make it plain that it
is so. In a very simple passage, 1 Kings xvii. 17 ff., the
following variations occur where Tindale strives to keep
close to the Hebrew against the Vulgate:

18 my *synne*	*iniquitates meæ.*
19 *he...*	*Elias...*
an hie *chamber...*	*cenaculum*
21 *he measured* the child	*expandit se atque mensus est* super puerum...

A single verse from Isaiah offers, as might be expected, a
more conclusive proof of the independence of Tindale:

My ryghteousnes is nye, and my salvacyon shall go oute, and myne armes shall iudge nacions, and ylondes shall loke for me & shall tarye after myne arme.	Prope est justus meus, egressus est salvator meus, et brachia mea populos judicabunt: me insulæ exspectabunt, et brachium meum sustinebunt.

The variations from Luther are nearly as numerous, and
still there are indications that Tindale was acquainted with
Luther's translation as he was with the Vulgate.

One continuous passage may be added as a better
sample of Tindale's work, taken from his published Pentateuch. The relation in which it stands to the Vulgate and
Luther is, as will be seen, the same as before[1]:

[1] The italics in Tindale mark what is preserved still in A.V.

VULGATE.	TINDALE.	LUTHER.

28 Et ait Moyses: In hoc scietis, quod Dominus miserit me ut facerem universa quæ cernitis, et non ex proprio ea corde protulerim :

29 Si consueta hominum morte interierint, et visitaverit eos plaga, qua et ceteri visitari solent, non misit me Dominus :

30 Sin autem novam rem fecerit Dominus, ut aperiens terra os suum deglutiat eos et omnia quæ ad illos pertinent, descenderintque viventes in infernum, scietis quod blasphemaverintDominum.

31 Confestim igitur ut cessavit loqui, dirupta est terra sub pedibus eorum :

32 Et aperiens os suum, devoravit illos cum tabernaculis suis et universa

28 *And Moses sayed: Hereby ye shall knowe that the Lorde hath sent me to doo all these workes,* and that *I haue not done them of myne awne mynde :*

29 *Yf these men dye the comon deth of all men, or yf they be visyted after the visitacion of all men, then the Lorde hath not sent me.*

30 *But* and *yf the Lorde make a new thinge, and the erth open hir mouthe and swallowe them,* and *all that* pertayne *vnto them,* so that *they goo doune quycke into* hell : *then ye shall vnderstōde, that these mē haue* rayled apon *the Lorde.*

31 *And* as soone as *he had made an ende of speakynge all these wordes, the grounde* cloue *asunder that was vnder them,*

32 *And ye erth opened hir mouthe and swalowed them and their housses and*

28 Vnd Mose sprach, dabey solt yhr mercken, das mich der Herr gesand hat, das ich alle dise werck thett, vnd nicht von meynem hertzen.

29 Werden sie sterben, wie alle menschen sterben, oder heymgesucht, wie alle menschen heimgesucht werdē, so hat mich der Herr nicht gesand.

30 Wirt aber der Herr etwas news schaffen, das die erde yhren mund auffthut, vñ verschlinget sie mit allem das sie haben, das sie lebendig hyn vntern ynn die helle faren, so werdet yhr erkennen, dass dise leut den Herrn gelestert haben.

31 Vnd als er dise wort hatte alle aus geredt, zu reyss die erde vnter yhnen,

32 vnd thet yhren mund auff vnd verschlang sie, mit yhren heusern mit

VULGATE.	TINDALE.	LUTHER.
substantia eorum;	*all the mē that* were with *Corah and all their goodes.*	allen menschen die bey Korah waren vnd mit aller yhrer habe.
33 Descenderunt-que vivi in infernum operti humo, et perierunt de medio multitudinis.	33 And *they and all that pertayned* vn*to them, went doune alyue* vn*to* hell, *and the erthe closed apon them, and they peryshed from a-monge the congre-gacyon.*	33 Vñ furen hyn vntern lebendig ynn die helle, mit allem das sie hatten, Vñ die erde decket sie zu, vnd kamen vmb aus der gemeyne.
34 At vero omnis Israel, qui stabat per gyrum, fugit ad clamorem pereuntium, dicens: Ne forte et nos terra deglutiat.	34 *And all Israel that were aboute them, fledde at the crye of them. For they sayed: The erthe* myghte happe-lye *swalowe vs also.*	34 Vnd gantz Is-rael, das umb sie her war, floh fur ihrem geschrey, denn sie sprachen, das vns die erde nicht auch verschlinge.
35 Sed et ignis egressus a Domino interfecit ducentos quinquaginta viros, qui offerebant incensum.	35 *And there came oute a fyre from the Lorde and consumed the two hundred and fyftye men that offred cens.*	35 Datzu fur das feur aus von dem Herrn, vnd frass die zwey hundert vnd funfftzig menner, die das reuchwerk op-fferten.

In his version of the New Testament we have seen that Tindale willingly faced the labour of minute correction. The texts of 1525, 1534, and 1535 are specifically distinct, and each later edition offers a careful revision of that which preceded it. Though the evidence is less extensive in the case of the Old Testament, it is evident that he expended no less pains upon this. The texts of 'the 'Epistles from the Old Testament' appended to the New Testaments of 1534 and 1535 differ in small details from the published Pentateuch of 1531 (1530)[1]; and, what is

[1] I regret that I have been unable to collate the text of the Pentateuch of 1531 (see p. 169) with that of the 'corrected' Pentateuch of 1534. The

still more interesting, from one another[1]. Thus in these, as in the New Testaments themselves, there is a double revision; and there is nothing to shew that Tindale bestowed less care upon the lessons from the Apocrypha than on those from the Canonical books[2].

This patience of laborious emendation completes the picture of the great translator. In the conception and style of his renderings he had nothing to modify or amend. Throughout all his revisions he preserved intact the characteristics of his first work. Before he began he had prepared himself for a task of which he could apprehend the full difficulty. He had rightly measured the momentous issues of a vernacular version of the Holy Scriptures, and determined once for all the principles on which it must be made. His later efforts were directed simply to the nearer attainment of his ideal. To gain this end he availed himself of the best help which lay within his reach, but he used it as a master and not as

---

Bristol Museum has only one edition, and not two, as stated in Anderson's list. Compare pp. 169, 208 notes.

In Gen. xxxvii. 6—9, the following variations occur between the 'Epistle' and the first Pentateuch:

PENT. 1531.

NEW TEST. 1534.

PENT. 1531.	NEW TEST. 1534.
this dreame *which* I *haue* dreamed	*a* dreame *that* I dreamed
makynge sheues	makynge *of* sheues
loo	se,
youres—to	*youre sheues—vnto*
because of—of	*for—for*
saynge	*and he sayd*
I *haue had one* dreame *more*	I *dreamed yet another* dreame

---

[In *Notes and Queries* for the 10th and 24th of February, 1883. Mr Fry printed a collation of the 1531 and 1534 editions of Tindale's *Genesis*. See also Dr Mombert's edition of Tindale's Pentateuch (1885), Prolegomena, pp. ciii.—cviii.]

[1] For example, in Is. liii. 6, went astraye (1534): went *all of vs* astraye (1535): 8, *whē* he *is* taken (1534): *though* he *be* taeken (1535): 12, of yᵉ *ryche* (1534): of the *mightie* (1535).

The last Epistle (for St Catharine's day) is wrongly given in 1534, Ecclus. li. 9—12. The right lesson is substituted in 1535, Ecclus. li. 1—8. [See p. 145, n. 4.]

Two most surprising misprints of 1534 are also corrected in 1535: Gen. xxxvii. 20, *a sand* pitte (some pitte, 1535). Is. liii. 2, came vp as a *sparow* (as a *spraye*, 1535).

[2] For example, in Ecclus. xxiv. 17 —22 the following corrections occur: 18, of *greatnes and* of holye hope (1534): of *knowledge* of holly hoepe (1535): 20, than honye or honye combe (1534): then honye, *and myne inheritaunce passeth honye* or honye combe (1535).

a disciple. In this work alone he felt that substantial independence was essential to success. In exposition or exhortation he might borrow freely the language or the thought which seemed suited to his purpose, but in rendering the sacred text he remained throughout faithful to the instincts of a scholar. From first to last his style and his interpretation are his own, and in the originality of Tindale is included in a large measure the originality of our English Version. For not only did Tindale contribute to it directly the substantial basis of half of the Old Testament (in all probability) and of the whole of the New, but he established a standard of Biblical translation which others followed. It is even of less moment that by far the greater part of his translation remains intact in our present Bibles[1], than that his spirit animates the whole. He toiled faithfully himself, and where he failed he left to those who should come after the secret of success. The achievement was not for one but for many ; but he fixed the type according to which the later labourers worked. His influence decided that our Bible should be popular and not literary, speaking in a simple dialect, and that so by its simplicity it should be endowed with permanence. He felt by a happy instinct the potential affinity between Hebrew and English idioms, and enriched our language and thought for ever with the characteristics of the Semitic mind[2].

[1] To take two examples about nine-tenths of the authorised version of the first Epistle of St John, and five-sixths of the Epistle to the Ephesians (which is extremely difficult) are retained from Tindale.

[2] The order of the Books in Tindale's N.T. is worth recording :—

The four Gospels
Acts
Thirteen Epistles of St Paul
(Romans—Philemon)

1, 2 Peter
1, 2, 3 John
Hebrews
James
Jude
Revelation.

This order exactly coincides with that in Luther's translation, and the books are numbered i —xxiii. up to 3 John, while the remaining four are not numbered So they stand also in Luther.

Note to p 145

In the following Table I have given the most important variations between the editions of 1535 and 1534 in a considerable number of books. The readings adopted in Matthew, 1537, are marked M.

In making the Table I have had the advantage of using a collation made by Mr F. Fry, who most generously placed it at my disposal. Where I have trusted entirely to his accuracy I feel satisfied that I have not gone wrong.

St Matthew.

	1534.	1535.
iii. 12	garner M.	graenge
ix. 31	name M.	fame
x. 5	sent	dyd. .send M.
xiii. 30	gather M.	beare ye
— 55	the c. M.	a c.
xiv. 18	hyther to me	hyther M.
xv. 3	cōmaundment M.	commaundmēts
xxi. 23	elders of the M.	rulers of the
xxiv. 19	wo be	Wo shalbe M.
— 51	There	And there M.

St Mark.

	1534	1535.
i. 31	forsoke hir by and by: and M	forsoke hyr and by, and by
— 39	throughout M.	throught
— 42	was clensed	he was clēsed (M. omits*)
ii. 23	of corne M.	of the corne
— 27	Saboth day M.	sabboth
vi. 5	coulde there M.	wolde there
— 35	nowe farre spent M.	to farre spent
vii. 32	to laye	to put M.
xii. 40	vnder coloure	vnder a coloure M.
xiii. 17	woo is	Woo shall be M.
— 30	all these thinges	these thinges M.
xvi. 11	when they herde	though they herde M.
— —	they beleved	yet they beleued M.
— 19	is set	sate him M.

St Luke.

	1534.	1535.
i. 5	kynge of	the kynge of M.
— 42	wemen	the wemen M.
— 75	that are	as are M.
ii. 7	within in	within M.
v. 10	shalt catche M.	shal taeke
vii. 19	that shall c.	that sholde c. M.
ix. 7	done of	done by M.
— 8	of other, that	of some, that M.
xvii. 1	to the disciples	to his disciples M.

[* Mark i. 42. M. omits 'and he was clensed. And he charged him.' This omission is also in Taverner.]

St John.

1534.	1535.
v. 7 sicke	sicke man M.
— 38 therto his wordes M.	thearfor his wordes
— 47 But now	But seinge M.
— — how shall	how shuld M.
vi. 23 other shippes M.	a nother shippe
— 60 Many of	Manny therfore of M.
vii. 4 knowen	knowen openlye M.
— 6 youre tyme	but youre tyme M.
— 7 Me it	But me it M.
viii. 3 and the pharises	and Pharises M.
— 16 though I M.	and yf I
— — yet is my M.	my
— 26 But he that	Ye and he that M.
— 27 They	How beit they M.
— 44 ye will folowe	ye will do M.
ix. 11 I went and	And I went & M.
x. 12 catcheth M.	taeth (for taeketh)
— 16 that ther maye be M.	that they may be
— 38 though ye beleve	then though ye beleeue M.
xi. 6 after he hearde	Then after he had harde M.
— — then aboode	yet aboode M.
xii. 34 hearde of	harde out of M.
xv. 20 his lorde	the Lorde M.
xviii. 27 denyed it	denyed M.
xix. 24 parted	departed M.
— 29 of vineger by M.	of veneger
— — And they filled a sponge with veneger	omitted

Acts.

1534.	1535.
vii. 46 desyred that he myght fynde	wolde fayne haue maede M.
viii. 3 entrynge	and entred M.
— 4 They that	How beit they that M.
xiv. 23 after they had prayde...they comended	and prayde...and comended M.
xviii. 18 had a vowe M.	had maede a vowe
xxiv. 11 yet .xii. dayes	yet but .xii. dayes M.
— 15 resurreccion from deeth	resurreccion of the dead. Cf. 1 Cor. xv. 12, 13 M.

Romans.

1534.	1535.
i. 5 obedience	the obedience M.
— 16 Iewe—gentyle M.	Iewes—Gentyles
ii. 1 the same	that same M.
— 8 yet folowe	and folowe M.
vii. 8 For	For verely M.
xii. 13 and diligently	and be readi M.

1534.	1535.
xiii. 9 these commaundementes M.	the cōmaundementes be
xv. 5 Christ	Christ Jesu M.
xvi. 5 all the company	the congregaciō M.
— — in thy	in their M.
— 12 laboured	laboured moche M.

1 Cor.

1534.	1535.
ii. 8 the worlde	this worlde M.
vii. 37 his virgin M.	his virginite
xv. 12 rose from deeth	roese from the dead M.
—12,21 resurreccion from deeth	resurreccion of the dead M.
— 13 agayne from deeth	agaeyne of the dead M.
— 20 from deeth	from the dead M.

In connexion with this edition Mr F. Fry has made a very remarkable discovery. He has found substantially the same text in an edition dated 1534 with the letters G. H. in the border of the second title, no one of the four copies which he has examined having the first title. Out of 113 readings marked as characteristic of the edition 'finished 1535' he found 102 in this edition of 1534, while it agreed only in the 11 remaining places with Marten Emperour's edition of 1534. [In Fry's *Bibliographical Description of the Editions of the New Testament, Tindale's Version*, 1878, p. 2, the number of passages in which the edition of 1535 agrees with that printed by Marten Emperour, 1534, and the G. H. edition of 1535, 4, is said to be 164, while it agrees with the edition of 1534 alone in only three passages. These figures do not correspond to Fry's original estimate.]

It seems to follow certainly from this fact that the revision was printed in the spring of 1535, *i.e.* before March 25. Thus 'finished 1535' would be reconcileable with the existence of an edition dated 1534 in the other reckoning.

At present it must remain doubtfu whether the edition of 1534 (G. H.) or that 'finished 1535' was the original. Happily this uncertainty does not affect the text which they present in common, which is the true standard of Tindale's completed work.

I learn from Mr Demaus that there is a mutilated copy of the edition of 1535 in the British Museum, and that he has ascertained with tolerable certainty that it was printed by Vorstermann of Antwerp: Demaus, *Life of Tindale*, p. 500.

§ 2. COVERDALE.

The contrast between Tindale and Coverdale has been already pointed out; and in spite of all that has been written to the contrary it is impossible to grant to Coverdale's Bible a place among independent translations. In fact Coverdale distinctly disavows the claim for himself.

I have, he writes to the king in his dedication, 'with a
'cleare conscience purely & faythfully translated this out
'of fyue sundry interpreters, hauyng onely the manyfest
'trueth of the scripture before myne eyes...[1]' 'To helpe
'me herin,' he informs the Christian reader, 'I haue had
'sondrye translacions, not onely in latyn, but also of the
'Douche [German] interpreters: whom (because of theyr
'synguler gyftes & speciall diligence in the Bible) I haue
'ben the more glad to folowe for the most parte, ac-
'cordynge as I was requyred[2].' 'Lowly & faythfully,'
he adds, 'haue I folowed myne interpreters, & that vnder
'correcyon[3].' And so it was that the title-page of his
Bible which was printed with it described it as 'faithfully
'and truly translated out of Douche and Latyn[4].'

Nothing, it might be supposed, could be more explicit
or intelligible or consistent with Coverdale's aims: but
his critics have been importunately eager to exalt his
scholarship at the cost of his honesty. If the title-page,
said one who had not seen it, runs so, 'it contains a very
'great misrepresentation[5].' To another the notice appears
to be a piece of advertising tact. Expediency, a third
supposes, led Coverdale to underrate his labours. And yet
it may be readily shewn that the words are simply and
literally true. Coverdale certainly had some knowledge

---

[1] *Remains*, p. 11 (Parker Soc. ed.).

[2] *Id.* p. 12.

[3] *Id.* p. 14.

[4] See pp. 58, 59.

[5] Whittaker, *Historical Inquiry*,
p. 59 n. In support of this bold
statement Dr Whittaker quotes four
passages from Coverdale (pp. 52 ff.),
and compares them with all the versions which, as he affirms, he could
have consulted. As Coverdale differs
from these, he is pronounced to have
translated 'from the Hebrew and from
'nothing else' (p. 50). Unhappily
Dr Whittaker was not acquainted
with the German-Swiss Version—a
sufficiently famous book—from which

they are all rendered: Ex. xxxiv. 30;
Num. x. 31; Is. lvii. 5; Dan. iii. 25.
Since this was written I find that
Dr Ginsburg has already pointed out
the falsity of Dr Whittaker's argument: Kitto's *Cyclopædia*, *s.v.* Coverdale. To him therefore belongs the
credit of having first clearly proved
the dependence of Coverdale on the
Zurich Bible. It was indeed from
the reference to Dr Ginsburg in the
Dictionary of the Bible that I was
led to examine in detail the Zurich
Versions. Henceforth it may be
hoped we shall hear no more of Dr
Whittaker's mistake.

of Hebrew[1] by which he was guided at times in selecting
his rendering; but in the main his version is based on the
Swiss-German version of Zwingli and Leo Juda (Zurich,
1524–9, 1530, 1531, 1532, 1534), and on the Latin of
Pagninus. He made use also of Luther and the Vulgate.
His fifth version may have been the Worms German Bible
of 1529, or the Latin Bible of Rudelius with marginal
renderings from the Hebrew (1527, 1529)[2], or (as is most
likely), for he does not specify that his '*five* interpreters'
are all Latin or German, the published English translations of Tindale to which he elsewhere refers.

The examination of a few chapters will place the
primary dependence of Coverdale in the Old Testament
on the Zurich Bible beyond all doubt. Thus in the four
short chapters of Malachi there are about five-and-twenty
places where he follows the German against the Hebrew
and Vulgate. Three sample instances may be quoted. In
i. 4 it is said, 'they shall be called *The border of wickedness*,'
in the Hebrew and Latin as in the Authorised Version,
but in Coverdale '*A cursed londe*,' a literal translation of
the German. Again in i. 13, 'it is *weariness* to me,'
a single word, but in Coverdale and the German we read
' It is but *laboure and trauayle*.' Once again in iii. 8, ' Will
' a man *rob* God ?' is represented in Coverdale and the
German by ' Shulde a man *vse falsede and disceate* with
' God ?' And such coincidences occur not in one book
only but throughout the Old Testament[3]. But at the
same time on rare occasions Coverdale prefers to follow
some one of the other translations which he consulted.
Thus in two passages, ii. 3 , 14, 15, of which the latter is a
very remarkable one, he adopts the renderings of Pagninus
and Luther in preference to those of the Zurich Bible.

It is not therefore surprising that notwithstanding his
acknowledged partiality for the German translators, Cover-

---

[1] Compare p. 75.

[2] *Biblia Sacra cum præfatione J.
Rudelii*, Coloniæ, Quentel, 1527. It
is unlikely that this was one of the
Latin versions consulted by Coverdale,
for the text is the Vulgate, and the
marginal renderings, which are few, do
not appear to have influenced him.]

[3] Other examples are given more at
length in § 4, and App. VII.

dale availed himself freely of the work of Tindale, as far as it was published, the Pentateuch, Jonah[1], and the New Testament[2]. His Pentateuch may, indeed, unless a partial examination has misled me, be fairly described as the Zurich translation rendered into English by the help of Tindale, with constant reference to Luther, Pagninus, and the Vulgate. In the remaining books of the Old Testament the influence of the Zurich Bible greatly preponderates[3]. In the Apocrypha, Coverdale moves with comparative freedom, and his translation has far more originality.

The New Testament is a very favourable specimen of his labour. Its basis is Tindale's first edition, but this he very carefully revised by the help of the second edition[4] and yet more by the German. Thus on a rough calculation of changes, not simply of form or rhythm, more than three-fourths of the emendations introduced by Coverdale into Tindale's version of 1 John are derived from Luther, but the whole number of changes, and they are nearly all verbal, is, if I have counted rightly, only a hundred and twenty-three.

Thus the claims of Coverdale, as far as his Bible is concerned, must be reduced to the modest limits which

---

[1] A verse from Jonah (iv. 6) may be quoted to shew the extent of the resemblance. The variations of Tindale are noted in italics and given below: 'and the Lorde *God** pre-'pared† a wylde vyne which sprange 'vp ouer Ionas, that he might haue 'shadowe *aboue*‡ his heade, to delyuer 'him out of his payne. And Ionas 'was exceadinge glad of the wylde 'vyne.'

* *om.* Tindale.   † *add* as it were. Tindale.   ‡ *ouer*, Tindale.

One singular phrase in ii. 3 common to Coverdale and Tindale may be noted, 'all thy wawes and *rowles of* '*water* went ouer me.'

[2] Like Rogers he neglected the fragmentary 'Epistles.' See p. 176.

[3] His marginal renderings throw great light on the authorities which he consulted. These are traced to their sources in App. IV.

[4] In 1 John he appears to follow the first and second editions where they differ in about an equal number of places. But it is evident that the first edition was his foundation, for he follows it in one clear mistake of reading iii. 11, that *ye* should love, and in one error of grammar, iv. 20, *hateth*, both of which were corrected by Tindale on revision, and would not have been reintroduced.

The changes are such as would easily have been made while the book was passing through the press.

he fixed himself. But though he is not original yet he was endowed with an instinct of discrimination which is scarcely less precious than originality, and a delicacy of ear which is no mean qualification for a popular translator. It would be an interesting work to note the subtle changes of order and turns of expression which we owe to him[1]. In the epistle from which most of our illustrations have been taken 'the pride of *life*' and 'the world *passeth* 'away,' are immeasurable improvements on Tindale's 'the 'pride of *goods*,' and 'the world *vanisheth* away'; and the rendering 'shutteth up his *heart*' (due to Luther) is as much more vigorous than Tindale's 'shutteth up his '*compassion*' as it is more touching than the strange combination of the Authorised Version 'shutteth up his *bowels* '*of compassion*.'

Coverdale has a tendency to diffuseness, which in some places (as Ecclus. xliv.) leads him to long paraphrases of his text. The fault is one from which the Zurich Bible also suffers, and he may have fallen into it from imitating the style of his model too closely even when he abandoned its words. But his phrasing is nearly always rich and melodious. The general character of his version as compared with that of Tindale may be very fairly represented by that of the Prayer Book Version of the Psalms as compared with the Authorised Version in the Bible. In both cases Coverdale's work is smooth rather than literal. He resolves relatives and participles and inserts conjunctions, if in that way he may make the rendering easier[2].

Just as Coverdale valued highly the existence of many translations[3], so he claimed for himself the right to extend this characteristic of diversity to his own work. He thought that he could thus attain comprehensiveness by variety, and secure in some measure for one translation the advantages which he found in many. 'Where as the 'most famous interpreters of all geue sondrye iudgmentes

---

[1] See Note at the end of the Section, p. 167.

[2] See p. 208.

[3] See p. 60.

'of the texte (so farre as it is done by ye sprete of
'knowlege in the holy goost) me thynke noman shulde
'be offended there at, for they referre theyr doinges in
'mekenes to the sprete of trueth in the congregacyon of
'god...Be not thou offended therfore (good Reader) though
'one call a scrybe, that another calleth a lawyer : or elders,
'that another calleth father & mother; or repentaunce,
'that another calleth pennaunce or amendment   And this
'maner haue I vsed in my translacyon, callyng it in some
'place pennaunce, that in another place I call repentaunce,
'and that not onely because the interpreters haue done
'so before me, but' — and this introduces a second
characteristic reason—'that the aduersaries of the trueth
'maye se, how that we abhorre not this word pēnaunce,
'(as they vntruly reporte of vs)...¹'

There may be some weakness in this, and Coverdale
suffered for it; yet it may not be lightly condemned.   In
crises of great trial it is harder to sympathize with many
views than with one.   There is a singularity which is the
element of progress ; but there is a catholicity which is
the condition of permanence, and this Coverdale felt.
'As ye holy goost then is one, workynge in y^e and me
'as he wyl, so let vs not swarue from y^t vnite, but be
'one in him.   And for my parte I ensure the I am in-
'different to call it aswell w^t the one terme as with y^e
'other, so longe as I know that it is no preiudice nor
'iniury to the meanynge of the holy goost. ²'   He may
have carried his respect for some so-called ' Ecclesiastical '
words to an excessive length, but even in this respect his
merit was substantial.   It was well that Tindale should
for a time break the spell which was attached to words
like *charity, confess, church, grace, priest,* and recall men to
their literal meaning in *love, [ac]knowledge, congregation,
favour, elder;* but it was no less well that the old words,

----

¹ [A Prologe. Myles Coverdale
vnto the Christen Reader (prefixed to
the Bible of 1535).] *Remains,* pp.
19, 20.

² [Preface to the Reader, in the
Latin-English New Testament, Nicol-
son, 1538.] *Remains,* p. 29. (*Park.
Soc.*)

and with them the historical teaching of many centuries, should not be wholly lost from our Bibles. That they were not lost was due to the labours of Coverdale; but his influence was felt not so much directly through his own first Bible, as through Matthew's Bible, in which a large portion of it was incorporated, and still more through the Great Bible, in which he revised more than once his own work and that of Tindale with which it had. been joined[1].

[1] The classification of the books in Coverdale's Bible (1535) is the following:—
(1) [The Pentateuch.]
(2) The seconde parte of the olde Testament.
Josua—1 Esdr. 2 Esdr. Hester. Job—Salomons Balettes (with no special heading).
(3) All the Prophetes in English. Esay, Jeremy, Baruch, Ezechiel—Malachy.
(4) 'Apocripha. The bokes and 'treatises which amonge the fathers of 'olde are not rekened to be of like 'authorite with the other bokes of 'the byble, nether are they foūde in 'the Canon of the Hebrue.
'3 Esdras, 4 Esdras...1 Mach. 2 'Mach.
'Vnto these also belongeth Baruc, 'whom we haue set amōge the pro-'phetes next vnto Jeremy, because he 'was his scrybe, and in his tyme.'
(5) The new testament.
iv. Gospels. Acts.
The Epistles of S. Paul. Romans—Philemon.
1. 2 S. Peter.
1. 2. 3 S. John.
Hebrews.
S. James.
S. Jude.

The Revelation of S. John.
In Nycolson's new edition of the Bible (1537) the books are arranged differently:
(1) The first part: Genesis—Ruth.
(2) The second part: 1 Samuel—Esther.
(3) The third part: Job—Salomons balletes.
(4) The Prophets: Esaias, Jeremias, Threni, Ezechiel—Malachias.
(5) The Apocrypha: 3 Esdr. 4 Esdr. ...Baruch...1 Mac. 2 Mac.
The books in the N.T. follow the same order as before.
The edition of 1550 follows the order of that of 1537.
The edition of 1537 is described as being 'newly overseen and corrected'; but as far as I have been able to compare the texts the differences which are not accidental are few and unimportant. In 1 John I have noted only the following:—
1. 1 of *the* lyfe (of life 1535).
7 is lyght (is *in* lighte).
ii. 14 *the* wycked (*that* wicked).
28 be ashamed (be *made* ashamed).
iii. 18 My children (My *litle* children).
iv. 3 *the* sprete (*that* sprete).
v. 10 because...of his sonne. Omitted in 1535.
11 *the* recorde (*that* recorde).

Note to p. 165.

The following samples taken from a single Gospel (St Matthew) will illustrate the felicity of Coverdale's minute changes.

COVERDALE, 1535.	TINDALE, 1534.
i. 25 fyrst borne sonne A.V.	fyrst sonne
ii. 2 the new borne kynge	he y^t is borne kynge
iii. 4 a lethrē gerdell A.V.	a gerdell of a skynne
— 11 to repentaunce A.V. (unto)	in tokē of repentaūce
— 14 I haue nede to be A.V.	I ought to be
iv. 8 Agayne, the deuyll toke hym vp A.V. (taketh)	The devyll toke hym vp agayne
— 14 y^t the thinge might be ful- filled A.V. (it)	to fulfill that
v. 36 one heer whyte A.V.	one white heer
— 39 the other also	the other
vi. 10 Thy kyngdome A.V	Let thy kyngdome
— 12 dettes A.V.	treaspases
— — detters	trespacers
— 32 do the heithen seke	seke the gentyls
— 34 Euery daye hath ynough of his owne trauayll	for the daye present hath ever ynough of his awne trouble
vii. 21 Lorde Lorde A.V.	Master, Master
— — the will of my father A.V.	my fathers will
viii. 9 subiect to ye auctorite of an- other	vndre power
x. 41 a righteous mans rewarde A.V	the rewarde of a righteous man
xi. 12 the violent A.V.	they that go to it with violence
xii. 4 the shew breds	ye halowed loves
— 12 to do good	to do a good dede
— 45 goeth he A.V.	he goeth
xiii. 11 Vnto you it is geuen	it is gevē vnto you A.V.
— 13 &c. parables	similitudes
— 30 tyll the haruest A.V. (until)	tyll harvest come
— 31 put he forth A.V.	he put forthe
— 58 because of their vnbeleue A.V.	for there vnbelefes sake
xiv. 24 for the winde was cōtrary A.V.	for it was a cōtrary wynde
— 28 yf it be thou A.V.	if thou be he
xv. 23 crieth after us A.V.	foloweth vs cryinge
xvi. 3 It wil be foule wedder to daye A.V.	to daye shalbe foule wedder
— — for the szkye is reed, & gloometh	& y^t because the skye is cloudy & reed
— 7 we haue takē	because we have brought
— 20 charged he A.V.	he charged
— 23 ye thinges that be of God, but of men	godly thinge᷑, but worldly thing᷑
xvii. 5 ouershadowed A.V.	shadowed
xviii. 10 do alwaye	alwayes
— 26 haue paciēce w^t me A.V	geve me respyte
— 33 shuldest not thou then A.V (also)	was it not mete also y^t thou shuldest

COVERDALE, 1535.	TINDALE, 1534.
xix. 20 All these haue I kepte fro my youth vp A.V. (things)	I have observed all these thingis from my youth
xx. 10 But whan the first came, they supposed A.V.	Then came yᵉ fyrst, supposyng
xxi. 28 But what thinke ye? A.V.	What saye ye to this?
— 42 is become the heade stone in	is set in yᵉ principall parte of
xxii. 32 the God of Abraham A.V.	Abrahams God
xxiii. 9 one is youre father A.V.	there is but one youre father
— 15 to make one Proselyte A.V.	to bringe one in to youre belefe
xxiv. 28 there wyl the Aegles be gathered together A.V.	evē thyther will the egles resorte
— 44 that ye thynke not A.V. (as)	ye thinke he wolde not
— 45 in due season A.V.	in season cōvenient
xxv. 21 entre thou in to the ioye of thy lorde A.V.	entre in into thy masters ioye
xxvi. 64 From this tyme forth	hereafter A.V.
xxvii. 6 the Gods chest	the treasury A.V.
— 62 the daye of preparynge	good frydaye

§ 3. MATTHEW.

The Bible which bears Matthew's name consists of three distinct elements. The Pentateuch and the New Testament are reprinted from Tindale's published translations with very slight variations[1]. The books of the Old Testament from Ezra to Malachi, and the Apocrypha, are reprinted in like manner from Coverdale. The remaining books of the Old Testament from Joshua to 2 Chronicles are a new translation. Nothing in the book itself indicates the sources from which it was derived, and the direct external evidence is vague and inconclusive. If it proves

---

[1] I have not collated any considerable passages of the Pentateuch with Matthew, though it would be interesting to compare a complete book in the Pentateuchs of 1531 and 1534 with Matthew (1537). [In Mombert's edition of Tindale's Pentateuch (1885) a collation of Tindale and Matthew is given, Proleg. pp. cxi—cxix.] The text of Matthew's New Testament is examined below, p. 178.

In Mr Offor's MS. Collections for a history of the English Bible (*Brit. Mus.* 26,670–3) there is a collation of Tindale's Pentateuchs of 1530 (1531) and 1534 with one another, and also with Matthew and Coverdale. Matthew appears to follow the earlier edition almost without exception: Coverdale generally the later. I have not however verified the collations.

anything it proves too much. Thus Strype, following
Bale, relates that Rogers 'translated the Bible [in this
'edition] into English from Genesis to the end of the
'Revelations, making use of the Hebrew, Greek, Latin,
'German and English (that is Tyndale's) copies.' He also
it is said·'added prefaces and notes out of Luther, and
'dedicated the whole book to king Henry, under the name
'of Thomas Matthews (*sic*) by an epistle prefixed, minding
'to conceal his own name[1].' No description could well
be more inaccurate. More than a third of the book is
certainly Coverdale's. The Preface to the Apocrypha
is translated from that in the French Bible of Olivetan[2].
The Prologue to the Romans is Tindale's. The dedication

---

[1] Strype, *Cranmer*, I. 117. With
singular inconsistency Strype elsewhere (p. 84) gives Foxe's account
(quoted below), which is different from
this in many essential particulars.

[2] This insertion is very remarkable. I have not been able to detect
any other mark of the influence of
the French translation on Matthew.
[Of the preliminary matter 'The
'Summe and Content &c.' is taken
from Lefèvre's French Bible of 1534,
as are the woodcuts in the book of
Revelation and the figure of S. Paul
in the Epistle to the Romans, &c.
The engraved title-pages to the Old
and New Testaments, the full-page
engraving before Genesis, and the
woodcut before Isaiah, are from the
Lübeck Bible of 1533-4. The headings of chapters in Matthew's Bible,
as well as the marginal notes and
references, are largely taken from
Lefèvre. See Appendix XI. The
address 'To the Chrysten Readers,'
the 'Table of pryncypall matters,'
and 'The names of all the bokes' are
from Olivetan. In the books of the
Old Testament, from Ezra onwards,
Matthew's Bible substantially follows
Coverdale, the editor making slight
changes in rendering, in which he

follows Olivetan, and in the transliteration of proper names. See, for
instance, Ezra iii. 4, 12, iv. 12, x. 17 ;
Neh. ii. 20; Job vi. 4, 6, 13, 14, xix.
22, xx. 16; Prov. ix. 2, &c Passages
omitted in Coverdale are added in
Matthew from Olivetan. See Neh.
vii. 6; Esther ii. 9. The changes in
the later books are fewer, but the
Prayer of Manasseh, as well as the
Preface to the Apocrypha, are translated literally from Olivetan. Many
of the marginal notes in Matthew are
also from Olivetan, particularly those
which refer to the Versions. See
Judg. ix. 5, 6, 14, 16, xv. 8; 1 Sam.
xii. 6, xxvi. 25; 2 Sam. xxi. 16, xxiii.
32, 33; 1 K. x. 11, &c.; Job i. 21, 22.
In Job I have traced eighteen of the
marginal notes to Œcolampadius, *In
Jobum Exegemata*, 1532.

By an Act of Parliament, 34 Henry
VIII., 1542-4, anyone who possessed
a Bible or New Testament, with
marginal notes or preambles, was
obliged, under a penalty of 40*s*., to
'cutte or blotte the same,' so as to
make them illegible. I have an imperfect copy of Matthew's Bible which
has been so treated, and there is
another in the Library of the Bible
Society. W. A. W.]

is signed by Thomas Matthew. It is evident that no
dependence can be placed on the details of such evidence.
The narrative of Foxe is not more satisfactory: 'In the
'translation of this Bible the greatest doer was indeed
'W. Tyndale, who with the help of Miles Coverdale had
'translated all the books thereof except only the Apo-
'crypha, and certain notes in the margin which were
'added after. But because the said W. Tyndale in the
'meantime was apprehended before this Bible was fully
'perfected, it was thought good...to father it by a strange
'name of Thomas Matthewe. John Rogers at the same
'time being corrector to the print, who had then translated
'the residue of the Apocrypha and added also certain
'notes thereto in the margin : and thereof came it
'to be called "Thomas Matthewe's Bible[1]."' It is unnecessary to dwell upon the errors in this account. Foxe
has evidently wrought out into a story the simple fact
that Tindale, Coverdale, and Rogers were all engaged
upon the work.

But although these original statements are thus loose,
and I have been unable to find any more trustworthy,
it can scarcely be doubted that Rogers did superintend
Matthew's Bible, and used in it the materials which Tindale
had prepared, and that these constitute the new translation
(Joshua—2 Chronicles). If he had purposed to complete
the translation himself it is not likely that he would have
paused at the end of 2 Chronicles. On the other hand,
Tindale's engagements might have allowed him to complete thus much more of his work in the interval between
the publication of his Pentateuch and his death. The
version of Jonah was an exceptional work, and furnishes
no ground for supposing that he did not intend to proceed
regularly through the Old Testament. Perhaps, too, it
was from the exceptional character of this translation,
which was as it were a text for the Prologue, that Rogers
was led to adopt Coverdale's version of Jonah as well as
of the other Prophets, though he could not have been

[1] *Acts and Monuments,* v. 410.

ignorant of Tindale's work; and the fact that Coverdale had used Tindale's rendering diligently left no over-powering reason for abandoning him[1].

We are not however left wholly to conjecture in deter-mining the authorship of the original portion of Matthew's Bible. The 'Epistles of the Old Testament' added to Tindale's New Testament of 1534, contain several passages from the Historical Books as well as from the Pentateuch; and generally it may be said that these fragments bear about the same relation to the translation in Matthew as those from the Pentateuch do to Tindale's published text. There are from time to time considerable variations between them, but still it is evident that the renderings are not independent. It is of course possible that Rogers may have consulted the fragments in the execution of his work, but, as will appear directly, this supposition is practically inadmissible, because the corresponding sections from the Prophets and the Apocrypha are completely neglected.

[1 In the year 1883 Dr Westcott received a communication from Mr Justice Bradley, a Judge of the Supreme Court of the United States, calling his attention to a passage in Hall's *Chronicle* (1548), which has a direct bearing on Tindale's share in the translation of the Historical Books of the Old Testament, as incorporated by Rogers in Matthew's Bible. The passage occurs on fol. 227a under 'The xxvij yere of Kyng Henry the '.viij.' and is as follows:

'This yere in the moneth of Sept-'ember Wyllyam Tyndale otherwyse 'called Hichyns was by the crueltie of 'the clergie of Louayn condempned and 'burned in a toune besyde Bruxelles 'in Braband called Vylford. This 'man translated the New testament 'into Englishe and fyrst put it in 'Prynt, and likewise he translated 'the .v bookes of Moses, Iosua, 'Iudicum, Ruth, the bookes of the 'Kynges and the bookes of Parali-'pomenon, Nehemias or the fyrst of

'Esdras, the Prophet Ionas, & nomore 'of ye holy scripture.'

Now bearing in mind that Richard Grafton not only printed and published Hall's *Chronicle*, but continued it from 1532 after Hall's death, and that in con-junction with Edward Whitchurch he had published Matthew's Bible in 1537, when he must have been in communication with Rogers; and moreover that Rogers returned to England in 1548, the year in which the *Chronicle* appeared, it is not unreasonable to conclude, with Mr Justice Bradley, that the paragraph in question contained information derived from Rogers, even if it were not writ-ten by Rogers himself. Tindale's com-pleted work on the Historical Books probably ended with 2 Chronicles, the rest being left unfinished, so that Rogers preferred to give Coverdale's Version of Ezra and Nehemiah with slight changes instead of attempting to supplement an imperfect work.]

Two examples will illustrate the extent of the coincidence and variations between the versions, and serve to shew how much dependence can be placed on this indication of the identity of their authorship.

TINDALE, 1534.	MATTHEW (TINDALE)
17 '*In those dayes it chaunsed* 'that the sonne of the wyfe of 'the house *was* sycke, & *the* 'syckness was so *great* that 'there *remayned no breth* in 'him. 18 Then *she sayde to* '*Helias*, what have I to do 'with the, *thou* mā of god? '*Dydest* thou come *to* me, that 'my synne shuld be *kepte in* '*mynde* & *to sle my sonne?* 19 And '*he* sayde vnto hir, geve me thy 'sonne, & he tooke him oute of 'hir lappe and caried him vp 'into *an hie chamber*, where '*he him selfe dwelt*, & layde him '*on the* bed. 20 And *he called* 'vnto the Lorde & sayde : O 'Lorde my god, hast thou *dealt so* '*cruelly with* the wydowe with 'whome I *dwell, as to kyll* hir 'sonne? 21 And he *measured* '*the chyld* .iii. tymes, & called 'vnto the Lorde & sayde : *Lorde* 'my God, let this *childes* soule 'come *agayne into him.* 22 And 'the Lorde *herkened vnto* the 'voyce of *Helias*, & *this chyldes* 'soule came *agayne vnto him*, and 'he revived.'	17 'And *after these thynges, it* '*happened* that the sonne of the 'wyfe of the house *fell* sicke. 'And *his* sicknesse was so *sore*, 'that there *was no breath left* in 'him. 18 Then *saide she vnto* '*Eliah* what haue I to do with 'the, *O thou* man of God? *art* 'thou come *vnto* me, that my 'synne shulde be *thought on* & '*my sonne slayne?* 19 And *Eliah* 'sayd vnto her : geue me thy 'sonne. And he toke him out 'of her lappe and caryed him 'vp into *a lofte* wher *he lay,* '& layde him *vpon his awne* 'beed, 20 and *called* vnto thē 'Lorde and sayde : O Lord my 'God, hast thou *bene so* euell '*vnto* the wedowe wyth whome 'I *soiourne, that thou hast slayne* 'her sonne? 21 And he *stretched* '*hym selfe vpō the lad* thre 'tymes, and called vnto the 'Lorde and sayde : *O Lorde* my 'God, let the *laddes* soule come '*into hym agayne.* 22 And the 'Lorde *heard* the voyce of '*Eliah*, and *the soule of the lad* 'came *into hym agayne*, and he 'reuiued.'

To these versions that of Coverdale[1] may be added for comparison. The differences from *both* the others are

---

[1] The text of 1537 agrees with that of 1535.

marked: '*And after these actes* the sonne of the wife of
'ye house was sicke: and his sicknes was so *exceadinge*
'sore, that there remayned no breth in him.   *And* she
'sayde vnto Elias: What haue I to do with the, thou man
'of God?   Art thou come in vnto me, y^t my sin shulde
'be kepte in *remembraunce* & *that* my sonne *shulde be*
'*slayne*?   *He* sayde vnto her: Geue me thy sonne.   And
'he toke him *frō* hir lappe, & caried him vp in to y^r
'*chamber* where he him selfe dwelt, and layed him vpō
'his bed, & called *vpon* the Lorde, and saide: O Lorde
'my God, hast thou *dealt so euell* with the wedow with
'whom I dwell, y^t thou *woldest slaye* hir sonne?   And he
'stretched *out* him selfe *over* the childe thre tymes, &
'called *vpon* the Lorde, and saide: O Lord my God, let
'*the soule of this childe* come agayne in to him.   And the
'Lorde herde the voyce of Elias.   And *the soule of the*
'*childe* came agayne *vnto* him, & he reuyued.'

The second example is similar in character:

TINDALE, 1534.	MATTHEW (TINDALE).
5 'And as he laye and slepte 'vnder *a* genaper tree: beholde, 'an angell touched him, and 'sayde *thus:* vp and eate. 6 'And he loked *vp:* and *beholde* 'there was at his heed *a cake* '*baken on the coles* and a cruse 'of water. And he ate and 'dranke, and layde him doune 'agayne. 7 And the angell of 'the Lorde came agayne the 'seconde tyme and touched 'him, and sayde: vp and eate: 'for thou hast a great waye to 'goo.'	5 'And as he laye and slepte 'vnder *the* Ginaper tree: be- 'holde, *there came* an Angell & 'touched hym, .& sayde *vnto* 'hym: vp and eate. 6 And he 'looked *aboute hym:* and *se,* 'there was *a loffe of broyled* '*breade* and a cruse of water at 'his heed. And he ate and 'drācke and layde hym downe 'agayne *to slepe.* 7 And the 'Angell of the Lorde came 'agayne the seconde tyme and 'touched hym, & sayde: vp & 'eate, for thou hast a *longe* '*Iourneye* to go.'

These versions may again be compared with Coverdale's: 'And *he layed him downe* & slepte vnder the
'Iuniper tre.   *And* beholde, y^f angell touched him, &

'sayde vnto him, *Stonde* vp, and eate. And he loked
'aboute him, & beholde at his heade there was a *bred*
'baken on the coles, & a cruse *with* water. And *whan he*
'*had eaten and dronkē, he* layed him downe agayne to
'slepe. And yᵉ angell of the Lorde came agayne the
'seconde tyme, & touched him, & sayde: *Stonde* vp, and
'eate, for thou hast a greate waye to go¹.'

It must be remembered in considering these fragments
that they are taken from simple narratives, where there is
comparatively little scope for striking variations². But
even so, as far as they go, they fall in with the traditional
belief that the new translation in Matthew's Bible is really
Tindale's and not a new work of Rogers³.

---

¹ The editions of 1535 and 1537
again agree.

² In a few verses of Genesis (xxxvii.
6–9) seven variations occur. See
p. 157, n. The passage Ex. xxiv. 12
—18, on the other hand, shews only
one variation. Ex. xx. 12—24 and
Num. xx. 2—13 are very similar in
both, but with variations.

³ I am unable to speak of the style
of the two groups of books—the Pentateuch and Joshua—2 Chron. A
careful comparison of the versions in
this respect could not fail to be fruitful; but to be of any value it must be
minute. I can find nothing but vague
generalities in the authors to whom
I have referred. [Dr Moulton, in his
History of the English Bible (pp. 128
–9), pointed out three characteristic
renderings which are found in Tindale's Pentateuch and also in the
Historical Books (Joshua—2 Chron.)
in Matthew's Bible. The Hebrew
ēlōn (A.V. plain) is represented by
'okegrove' in Tindale's Genesis, and
by 'oak' in Judges and 1 Samuel in
Matthew. *Toph* is uniformly rendered
'timbrel' by Tindale in the Pentateuch, and in the Historical Books in
Matthew, while Coverdale, except in
Ex. xv. 20, has 'tabret.' The expres-

sion 'shut up and left' (A.V.), which
occurs in Deut. xxxii. 36, is rendered
by Tindale (after Luther) 'presoned
'and forsaken,' and in the four passages in which it is found in the
Historical Books in Matthew (1 Kings
xiv. 10, xxi. 21; 2 Kings ix. 8, xiv. 26)
it is represented by 'in preson or for-
'saken,' 'presoned or forsaken,' 'the
'presoned or that is forsaken,' and
'the presoned and the forsaken.'
Dr Eadie (*The English Bible*, I. 321)
calls attention to the uniform render-
ng 'ephod' in Tindale's Pentateuch
and in the Historical Books in
Matthew, while Coverdale has 'over-
'body cote.' Tindale and Matthew
have 'Libanòn,' while Coverdale has
'Libanus.' 'Tribulation' is found as
the rendering of the same word in
Tindale, Deut. iv. 30, and in Matthew,
2 Sam. xxii. 7 and 2 Chron. xv. 4,
while in Coverdale it is different.
Coverdale always has 'the ark of the
'covenant,' while Tindale in the
Pentateuch has 'ark of the testament'
and once 'ark of the appointment,'
and both these renderings are found
in the Historical Books in Matthew.

In addition to these instances of
correspondence between the renderings of Tindale in the Pentateuch

But while Rogers thus incorporated into his Bible, as we believe, all the complete translations of Tindale, except Jonah, he took no account of the fragments which Tindale had appended to the revised edition of his New Testament as 'Epistles taken out of the Old Testament after the use 'of Salisbury.' This collection includes (if I have counted rightly) twenty-three lessons from the Prophets and six from the Apocrypha, besides others from the Pentateuch and Hagiographa. In those which I have examined Matthew's Bible coincides verbally with Coverdale, and Tindale's version is wholly different from both. Two examples will be sufficient to shew the extent of the variation, and they are the more worthy of consideration as the relation of Rogers to the two earlier translations has been commonly misrepresented. There is nothing which proves that he allowed himself more liberty in dealing with Coverdale's work than in dealing with Tindale's.

TINDALE.

'My ryghteousnes is nye, 'and my salvacyon shall go 'oute, and myne armes shall 'iudge nacions, and ylondes 'shall loke for me & shall tarye 'after myne arme.'

MATTHEW (COVERDALE).

'It is hard by, y^t my health '& my ryghtuousnesse shall 'goo forth, and the people shal 'be ordred with myne arme. 'The Ilandes (that is the Gen-'tyles) shall hope in me, & put 'their trust in myne arme.'

'She shall exalt him amonge

'She shal brynge hym to ho-

and those in the Historical Books in Matthew's Bible, I have noted the expressions 'pluck up your hearts' in Deut. xxxi. 6; Josh. x. 25, and 1 Chr. xxii. 13; 'franchised city,' Num. xxxv. 25, 'franchised cities,' Josh. xxi. 13 (Coverdale always has 'fre'); 'observe 'dismal days,' Lev. xix. 26; 2 Kings xxi. 6; 2 Chron. xxxiii. 6 (A.V. 'observe times'). For what in the A.V. is Ashdoth-Pisgah (Deut. iii. 17; Josh. xii. 3, xiii. 20), and once 'springs of Pisgah' (Deut. iv. 49),

Tindale has in Deuteronomy 'sprynges 'off Pisgah,' or 'springes of Pisga,' and Rogers in Joshua 'sprynges (or springes) of Phasgah,' this curious transliteration, which he also substituted in Deuteronomy, being taken from Olivetan. The Hebrew word, which when used in a friendly sense is rendered 'to meet,' is in Tindale (Gen. xiv. 17, xviii. 2, xix. 1, xlvi. 29, &c.) and in Matthew (Josh. ix. 11 Judg. iv. 18, 22, &c.) 'against.']

TINDALE.   MATTHEW (COVERDALE).

'his neyboures: and shall opē   'noure amonge his neyghboures,
'his mouthe evē in yᵉ thyckest   '& in the myddest of the con-
'of the congregaciō.'   'gregacyō shall she open his
                                   'mouth¹.'

It is then evident that Rogers did not undertake an
elaborate revision of the texts of Tindale and Coverdale
which he adopted. Still there are some changes in the
version which are unquestionably intentional (*e.g.* Prov. i. 1²,
Is. i. 1), and numerous various readings in the margin
(*e.g.* Ps. xlvii. f.)³. The numbering of the Psalms is ac-
commodated to the Hebrew division. The interpolated
verses in Ps. xiv., which Coverdale had specially marked
as 'wanting in the Hebrew,' are omitted. The 'Hallelujah'
in the last Psalms is nobly rendered 'Praise *the Ever-*
'*lasting*⁴.' The characters in 'Salomons Ballet' (Canticles)
are distinguished by rubricated headings⁵. But the dis-
tinguishing feature of the edition is the marginal commentary on which the chief labour of the editor was
bestowed. This however belongs rather to the history
of doctrine than to the history of the English Bible⁶
And when this is set aside the textual peculiarities of
the edition are unimportant. In itself Matthew's Bible
has had no original and independent influence upon the
authorised text. Its great work was to present the
earlier texts in a combined form which might furnish
the common basis of later revisions. But in this respect
it is most unjust to call it Tindale's Bible. If regard be
had to the books taken from each it is in its primitive
form hardly less Coverdale's than Tindale's, though (if
we except the Psalms) much more of Tindale's than

¹ [Both these are from the Zürich   ⁶ It would be an interesting and
Version of 1530.]   easy task to trace out the sources of
  ² ['Instruction' is from Olivetan.]   the commentary. Pellican was ob-
  ³ [From Lefèvre's French Bible of   viously used. Some specimens of the
1534.]   notes are given in App. v. See also
  ⁴ [From Olivetan.]   p. 71, n. 1.
  ⁵ [As in Lefèvre (1534).]

of Coverdale's work has been preserved unchanged in common use.

There is still one point in the history of Matthew's Bible which is of considerable interest. The text of the New Testament differs considerably in details from Tindale's revised edition of 1534. This fact has lent colour to the belief that Rogers revised the text of the Bible throughout, for it has been assumed that Tindale did not again revise his own work. The assumption and conclusion were equally wrong. It has been seen already that the remarkable New Testament of 1535 was again, as the title-page affirms, 'diligently corrected and com-'pared with the Greek,' and this last revision, and not that of 1534, was adopted by Rogers. The differences which exist between Matthew and this last Testament of Tindale are very slight and can be explained in most cases by the supposition of accidental errors: their agreement on the other hand extends to the adoption of some certain mistakes. A complete collation remains yet to be made, but on an examination of a large number of passages I have found scarcely any characteristic readings of the edition of 1535 which do not also appear in Matthew's Bible of 1537[1]. From internal evidence it

---

[1] The following collation of Tindale's Testaments of 1534, 1535, and Matthew of 1537 in Mark xvi. and the Epistles to the Romans and Galatians will justify in all respects the statements made in the text. The error in Mark xvi. 17 is very remarkable. The readings in ( ) are those of the Testament of 1534.

Mark xvi. 11 *though* (when 1534) they heard...and (and he 1534) had appeared...*yet* (om.) they believed it not. So Matthew (1537).

— 17 these *things* (these signs). So Matthew.

— 19 *sate him* down (*is set* down). So Matthew.

Rom. i. 5 unto + *the* obedience. So Matthew.

16 the Jews...the Gentiles... Not Matthew.

— ii. 1 in *that* (the) same. So Matthew.

8 *and* (yet) follow. So Matthew.

9 Jews...Gentiles... Not Matthew.

— iv. 10 in + *the* time of circum-, cision. So Matthew.

— vii. 8 for + *verily* without the law. So Matthew.

— viii. 3 inasmuch + *as* it was weak. So Matthew.

15 *not* (no) received. So Matthew.

30 them also he c. (them he also c.). So Matthew.

— ix. 16 *running* (cunning). So Matthew.

xii. 13 *be ready* to harbour (*diligently* to h.). So Matthew.

seems likely that both these texts were taken from the
same corrected copy of Tindale. Such a hypothesis would
account equally for the discrepancies between them, since
the New Testament at least is most carelessly printed,
and for their agreement in errors which can only have
been derived from the original copy[1].

§ 4. THE GREAT BIBLE.

Matthew's Bible was essentially a transitional work.
It had hardly passed into circulation when a careful revision of it was undertaken. This, as all evidence external
and internal goes to prove, was entrusted to Coverdale.
It was thoroughly characteristic of the man that he should
be ready to devote himself to the perfecting of another's ·

Rom. xiii. 9 *the* commandments *be*
(these c.). Not Matthew.

13 as were it in (*the* 1534) day.
Not Matthew.

— xiv. 15 with (*thy* 1534) meat.
Not Matthew.

— xv. 5 Christ + *Jesu*. So Matthew.

— xvi. 5 the *congregation* that is in
their house (all the company that is
in thy house). So Matthew.

18 preaching (preachings). Not
Matthew.

19 innocent *as* concerning (inno-
cents concerning). So Matthew.

Gal. ii. 1 thereafter (after that). So
Matthew.

2 *between ourselves* with them (apart
with them). So Matthew.

16 *can* be (shall be). So Matthew.

— iii. 4 *then* ye (there ye). Matthew omits.

9 + *the* faithful A. Not Matthew.

16 as one (as *in* one)... Not Matthew.

Prof. Moulton informs me that
there are eight differences between
the editions of Matthew of 1537 and
1551 in these passages. [If the edition

of 1551 is that printed by Daye, the
number of differences is eleven: Mark
xvi. 11 (two), 19; Rom. i. 5, vii. 8,
30, xii. 13, xvi. 5; Gal. ii. 1, 2, iii. 4.
The edition printed by Hyll in the
same year differs from Matthew in five
passages: Mark xvi. 11 (two); Rom.
xii. 13, xvi. 19; Gal. iii. 4.]

Compare also App. III. and note,
p. 158.

[1] The Books of the Bible are ar-
ranged in the following order:
The books of the Old Testament.
Genesis—The Ballet of ballets.
The Prophets: Isaiah—Malachi.
The Apocrypha: 3 Esdr. 4 Esdr....
Baruch...1 Mach. 2 Mach.
The New Testament.
The four Gospels. The Acts.
The Epistles,
¶ Romans—Philemon.
¶ 1, 2 S. Peter.
¶ 1, 2, 3 S. John.
¶ To the Hebrews.
¶ S. James.
¶ Judas.
¶ The Revelation.
The order of the books in Taverner
(1539) is the same.

labours; and he has left us an account of his method of procedure. 'We folowe,' he writes, 'not only a standynge 'text of the Hebrue, with the interpretacion of the 'Caldee, and the Greke[1], but we set, also, in a pryvate 'table, the dyversite of redinges of all textes...[2].' And again when the work had made some progress he enters into greater details: 'As touchynge the maner and order, 'that we kepe in the same worke, pleaseth your good 'Lordship to be advertised, that the merke ☞ in the text, 'signifieth, that upon the same (in the later ende of the 'booke) there is some notable annotacion; which we have 'writen without any pryvate opinion, onlye after the best 'interpreters of the Hebrues, for the more clearnesse of 'the texte.   This mark ‡ betokeneth, that upon the same 'texte there is diversitie of redynge, amonge the Hebrues, 'Caldees, and Grekes, and Latenystes; as in a table, at 'the ende of the booke, shalbe declared.   This marke ⌒✕ 'sheweth that the sentence, written in small letters is not 'in the Hebrue, or Caldee, but in the Latyn, and seldome 'in the Greke; and that we, neverthelesse, wolde not have 'it extinct, but higlye accept yt, for the more explanacion 'of the text.   This token †, in the Olde Testament geueth 'to understand, that the same texte, which foloweth it, is 'also alledged of Christ, or of some Apostle, in the Newe 'Testament.   This (amonge other oure necessarie laboures) 'is the waye that we take, in this worke...[3].'

It is obvious that a man who thus describes his plan is not the mere press-corrector of another's revision, but himself the editor of the entire work[4].   If there were any

[1] These would be accessible in the Complutensian Polyglott. A copy of this with the autograph of Cranmer [? Cranmer's secretary] is now in the British Museum. Coverdale may have used these very volumes. [The Complutensian Polyglott has only the Chaldee of the Pentateuch.]

[2] [*State Papers*, I. 576.]

[3] [*State Papers*, I. 578–9.]

[4] It is a very important confirma-tion of this view that Fulke speaks of the Bible of 1562 'most used in the 'Church Service in King Edward's 'time' as 'Doctor Coverdale's trans-'lation' (*Defence of Eng. Trans.* p. 68). This was an edition of the Great Bible. This passage also explains the anecdote which he gives of the criticism and revision of 'Coverdale's Bible.' See p. 192, n. 2.

doubt remaining it would be removed by the character of the revision. About the time when Coverdale's own Version was passing through the press a new Latin Version of the Old Testament with the Hebrew text and a commentary chiefly from Hebrew sources was published by Sebastian Münster (1534–5). It does not appear that at that time Coverdale was able to avail himself of it. The Zurich Version was sufficient. But a very slight comparison of Münster with the Zurich Bible could not fail to bring out the superior clearness of the former. Even a poor Hebrew scholar must feel its general faithfulness. Thus Coverdale found an obvious method to follow. He revised the text of Matthew, which was laid down as the basis, by the help of Münster. The result was the Great Bible.

One difficult passage given in full will be sufficient to shew the certainty of this explanation of the origin of the text of the Great Bible, and for the interest of the comparison the Zurich original of Coverdale's translation is added[1].

MATTHEW (TINDALE). '*Thorou a windowe loked* ' *Sisaras mother* and *howled* thorowe *a lattesse*, why *abydeth* 'his charet so lōge, y^t *it* cometh not, *why tarye* the wheles 'of his *waggans?*

'The wysest *of her* ladyes answered *her*: *yee & she* '*answered her awne word^r her selfe haplye* they *haue foŭde*, '& deuyde the spoyle: A mayde, *ye two mayd^t for a pece*: '*a spoyle of dyuerse coloures for* Sisara, a spoyle *of dyuerse* '*coloures wyth brodered workes, dyuerse coloured browdered* '*worck^s for* ye necke *for* a praye.'

COVERDALE.	ZURICH VERSION.
His mother loked out at the wyndowe, & *cried piteously* thorow *the trallace:* Why *tarrieth* his charet *out* so lōge,	Seyn mutter sach zum fenster ausz, vnnd schrey mit klag durchs gätter: Warūb bleibt sein wagen so lang aus-

[1] The italicised words are differently rendered in the several versions, and furnish the best means of comparison with the Greek and Latin. I have kept the spelling of the German of 1530.

COVERDALE.

that *he* cōmeth not? *Wher-fore do* the wheles of his *cha-ret make so longe tarienge?* The wysest *amōge* his ladies answered, *& sayde vnto her: Shulde* they *not finde* & deuide the spoyle, *vnto euery man a fayre* mayde *or two for a pray, & partye coloured garmētes of nedle worke to* Sissera *for* a *spoyle, partye coloured garmentes of nedle worke aboute* the necke *for* a pray?

GREAT BIBLE (1539, 1540, 1541).

The mother of Sisera loked out at a wyndowe, & cryed thorow the lattesse: Why is his charret so long *a cōmyng?* Why tarye the wheles of his *cartes?*

All the wyse ladies answered her, yee ād *her awne wordes answered hir selfe.* Surely they haue founde, they deuyde yᵉ spoyles: *Euery mā hath a dāsell* or two: *Sisera hath a praye* of diuerse coloured garmētes, *euē a praye of raymēt dyed wᵗ sōdrye coloures, & yᵗ are made* of nedle worke: rayment of diuerse coloures ād of nedle worke, *which is mete for him yᵗ is chefe in distributynge of yᵉ spoyles.*

ZURICH VERSION.

sen, das er nit kompt? Wa-rumb verziehend die reder seins wagens?

Die weysest vnder seinen frauwen antwurtet, vnnd sprach zu jr: Sollend sy nit finden vnd auszteilen den raub, eym yeglichen mann eyn schöne mätzen oder zwo zur auszbeüt, vnd Sissera bundte gestickte kleyder zur auszbeüt, gestickte bundte kleyder vmb den halsz zur auszbeüt?

MÜNSTER.

Per fenestram prospexit, et vociferata est mater Siseræ, per cancellos inquam: quare moratur currus ejus venire? ut quid morantur vestigia quadrigarum ejus? Sapientes quæque dominæ responde-bant illi, quin et ipsa sibi ipsi reddebat verba. Certe invenerunt, dividunt spolia: est puella vel duæ puellæ cui-libet viro: habet Sisera præ-dam vestium coloratarum prædam inquam vestium vario tinctarum colore et quæ acu-pictæ sunt: vestem discolorem et acupictam, quæ priori com-petit in spoliorum distributione.

The collation of a longer passage gives an exactly similar result. The Fifty-first Psalm has no especial difficulty, but Coverdale (Matthew) and the Great Bible

differ in the following places. Every change it will be
seen can be traced to Münster, except one which is
marked as coming from the Latın Vulgate[1].

1 thy goodnes Coverdale.
  thy * (*greate*) goodnes Great Bible.
— *and* acordnge vnto thy *greate*... C.
— according vnto the *multitude* of... G. B.
— secundum *multitudinem*... Münster.
2 Wash me *well* C.
  Wash me *thorowly* G. B.,
        plurimum M.
4 Agaynst the only, agaynst the... C.
  Agaynst the onely G. B.: M.
— euell C.
  this euell G. B.
  malum *hoc* M.
— in thy *saynges* C.
  in thy *sayinge* G. B.
  in *sermone tuo* M.
— shuldest *ouer coıne* C.
  [myghtest be] *cleare* G. B.
  [sis] *purus* M.
6 thou *hast a pleasure in the* treuth, and *hast shewed* me
    secrete wyszdom C.
  thou *requirest* treuth *in the inward partes,* and *shalt
    make me to vnderstōde* wisdome *secretly.* G. B.
  veritatem *exigis in interioribus,* et *in occulto* sapientiam
    me scire facies M.
7 O *reconcile* me with... C.
  [O *purge* me with... (Matt.)]
  Thou shalt pourge me with... G. B.
  Expiabis me M.
— *wash thou* me C.
  thou shalt wash me G. B.
  lavabis me M.
8 *Oh let* me heare... C.

---

[1] The initials are used for the different Bibles after the first quotation.

Thou shalt make me heare...   G. B.
Facies me audire...   M.

13   that synners maye be conuerted...   C.
and synners *shall* be cōuerted...   G. B.
ét peccatores ad te *convertentur*...   M.

14   *that* my tonge *maye prayse*...   C.
and my tonge *shall syng of*...   G. B.
et cantabit lingua mea...   M.

15   *Open*   C.
Thou shalt opē...   G. B.
aperies   M.

—   *that* my mouth *maye*...   C.
my mouth *shall*...   G. B.
os meum *annunciabit*...   M.

16   *yf* thou *haddest pleasure* in...   *I would*...   C.
thou *desyrest no*...   *els* wolde I...   G. B.
non desideras...   *alioquin* darem...   M.

18   *that* the walles of Ierusalem *maye be buylded.*   C.
buylde thou the walles of Ierusalem.   G. B.
ædifica muros J.   M.

19   *For then* shalt...   C.
Then shalt...   G. B.
Tunc acceptabis...   M.

—   laye bullockes...   C.
offre yonge bullockes.   G. B.
offerent juvencos.   M.

A complete collation of two other Psalms (xix., xlii.)
gives an equally complete coincidence of all the changes
introduced into the Great Bible with Münster's renderings. It will be enough to quote one or two of the more
remarkable :

xix. 6 there *maye no mā hyde himself* frō the heate
therof.   C.
there *is nothinge hyd* from the heate therof.   G. B.
nihil est quod absconditur a calore ejus.   M.

7 The lawe of the Lorde is a *perfecte* lawe, *it quicken-
eth* the soule.   The testimony...is *true*, & geueth
wisdome *euen* vnto *babes*.   C.

III] THE GREAT BIBLE

The law of the Lord is a *vndefyled* law *conuerting*
the soule. The testimony...is *sure*, and geueth
wisdome vnto *the symple*. G. B.

Lex domini *immaculata, convertens* animam : testi-
monium domini *firmūm*, sapienter erudiens *sim-
plicem*. M.

xlii. 4 for I wolde fayne go hence with...& passe ouer with
them vnto... C.

for I went with...& brought thē forth vnto...
G. B.

quippe qui transibam...deducens eos usque ad...
M.

8 therfore I remēbre the londe of Iordane C.

therfore *will* I remembre the *cōcernyng* the land of
Iordane G. B.

idcirco *recordabor* tui *de* terra Iordanis... M.[1]

15 I wil yet thanke him *for the helpe of his* countenaunce, and *because*... C.

I will yet thanke him *which is the helpe of my*
countenaunce, and my... G. B.

confitebor ei, *qui est salus* vultus *mei* et deus
meus.

In all the passages which have been hitherto quoted
the text of the three typical editions of the Great Bible—
Crumwell's, April 1539, Cranmer's, April 1540, Tunstall's
and Heath's, Nov. 1540—is with one exception (or at most
two) exactly identical[2]. But this is not the case in all
the parts of the Bible.

In the Prophets the revision was less complete in the
first (Crumwell's) edition, and Coverdale appears to have
gone again carefully through this part of his work at

---

[1] Here the preposition *de* of Münster has been wrongly rendered.

[2] The variations which I have observed are Ps. xlii. 12 *add* as with a
sword (Nov. 1540; May 1541 omits)
from Münster; and Ps. xix. 10 than
yᵉ *hony cōbe* and yᵉ *hony* (Nov. 1540;
as before, May 1541 follows 1539),

probably a printer's blunder.

In all the references to the Great
Bibles I have availed myself of Mr
F. Fry's exhaustive identification of
every sheet of the different editions
in his *Description of the Great Bible
of* 1539 &c. London, 1865.

least before the publication of the second (Cranmer's) edition. It is possible that the unsettled prospect of affairs in Paris may have induced him to hurry the printing of the book; or, which is not less likely, the greater difficulty of the Prophets may have hindered him from dealing satisfactorily with them on the first collation. However this may be, the text of Cranmer's Bible presents a second revision of the original Coverdale (Matthew), and that again made by a more thorough use of Münster. A single chapter of Isaiah will shew the relation of the two revisions to one another, to the original rendering (Coverdale) and to Münster. The German (Zurich) quotations determine the source of the first translation[1].

COVERDALE (MATTHEW).

1 But who *geueth credence* vnto *oure preachyng?* Or to whō is the arme of the Lorde knowne? 2 *He shall growe* before the Lorde like as a braūch, & as a rote in a drye ground, *he shall haue* nether bewtye nor fauoure. Whē *we loke* vpon him, there shalbe no fayrnesse: we shall haue no lust vnto him. 3 *He shalbe the most symple, and despysed of all, which yet hath* good experience of sorowes and infirmyties. *We shall reken him so symple & so* vile, that we *shall hyde* oure faces frō him. 4 How be it (*of a treuth*) he only *taketh awaye* our infirmite, and *beareth oure payne:* Yet we *shall* iudge him, as though he were plaged & cast downe *of God:* 5 where as he (notwithstādyng) *shall be* wounded for oure offences, & smytten for oure wickednes. For the *payne of oure punishment shalbe layde* vpon him, and with his strypes *shall we be* healed. 6 As for vs, we *go all* astraye (lyke shepe), euery one *turneth* hys awne waye. But thorowe him, the Lorde

---

[1] I have added also for comparison the renderings of Pagninus, that it may be clear that the translation is from Münster and not independently from the Hebrew.

The italics mark the words which were altered. The second English rendering is that of the Great Bible of 1539.

pardoneth all oure synnes.   7 He *shalbe payned & troubled*, *& shal not open* his mouth.   He shalbe led as a shepe to be slayne, yet shall he be as styll as a lābe before the shearer, and not open his mouth.   8 He *shall be had awaye*, his cause not herde, & without eny iudgmēt : Whose genera-cyon yet *no mā maye* nombre, *when he shalbe cut* of from the grounde of the lyuynge : Whych punishmēt *shall* go vpon him, for the transgression of *my people*.   9 His graue *shalbe* geuen him with the condempned, & *his crucyfyenge with the theues*, Where as he dyd neuer violence ner vnryght, nether hath there bene any disceatfulnesse in his mouth.   10 Yet hath it pleased yᵉ Lorde *to smyte him* with infirmyte, that when he had made hys soule an offeryng for synne, he might se *lōgelastynge sede*.   And thys deuyce of the Lorde shall prospere in his hande. 11 With trauayle & laboure of his soule, shall he obtayne *great ryches*.   My ryghtuous seruaunt shall wyth *his wys-dome* iustifye & delyuer the multitude, for he shall beare awaye their synnes.   12 Therfore wyll I geue him the multitude for his parte, & he shall deuyde the strōge spoyle because he *shal geue* ouer his soule to death, & *shalbe* rekened amonge yᵉ trāsgressours, which neuertheles *shall take* awaye the synnes of the multitude, and *make* intercessyon for the mysdoers.

1 *geueth credence*
   glaubt   Zurich.
   hath geuē credēce   1539.
   credidit   Münster (Pagninus).
   oure preachyng 1539.   *vnserem predigen Z. the thynge we*
      (*yᵗ we* Nov.) *haue hearde*   Apr. Nov. 1540.   May
      1541.   *auditui nostro*   M.
2 *He shall growe*
   er wirdt...wachsen   Z.
   For he dyd growe
   Ascendit enim   M.   (et ascendit   P.)
— he *shall haue*
   er *wirt...haben*   Z.
   he *hath*

non *est ei*   M. (P).

2 we *loke*   1539   we *shall loke*   Apr. Nov. 1540, May 1541
   videbimus   M.

3 *He shalbe the most...yet hath...*

   er wirt der aller schlächtest vnd verachtest, der doch die
   schmertzen vnnd kranckheytenn wol kennet   Z.

   He *is despysed & abhorred of men*, he is soch a man as
   hath...

   Despectus est, et devitatus ab hominibus   M.   (despectus
   est et abjectus inter viros   P.)

— as hath good experience of sorowes and infyrmities
   1539   (Z.   see before).

   as is full of sorowe & as hath good experience of
   infirmyties.   Apr. Nov. 1540, May 1541.

   homo est doloribus (plenus) et qui expertus est infirmi-
   tatem   M.

— *We shall...& so vile...shall hyde*

   wir werdend jn...vnnd verworffenn rechnen, das wir.
   verbergen werdend   Z.

   We *haue rekened* hym so vyle, that we *hyd*..
   frō hym   1539   von jm   Z.

   from him, † ye he was despised & therfore we regarded
   him not   Apr. Nov. 1540.   May 1541.

   (et quisque erat) quasi abscondens faciem ab eo: *fuit*
   enim contemptus, ideo non reputavimus eum   M.
   (despectus et non rep. eum   P.)

4 omit *of a truth.*

— *taketh awaye*

   hinnimpt   Z.

   hath taken on hym

   ipse portavit   M.   (ipse tulit   P.)

— infirmite: *infirmities*   May 1541.

— and *beareth oure payne*

   vnnd vnsere schmertzen tregt   Z.

   and *borne oure paynes*

   et *dolores nostros hos ipse sustinuit*   M.   (et dolores
   nostros portavit   P.)

— *shall* iudge

so rechnend wir   Z.
dyd iudge
reputavimus   M. (P.).
4 of God 1539 als ob er uon Gott geschlagen *vnnd*
    genideret sey Z.
of God : *and punished*   Apr. Nov. 1540, May 1541.
percussum a Deo *atque afflictum*   M.   (p. a Deo et
    humiliatum P.)
5 *shall be* wounded
verwundt...wirt   Z.
was woūded
vulneratus est   M. (P.)
— payne of oure punyshment 1539   die busz vnserer
    straaf Z.
chastysement of oure peace   Apr. Nov. 1540, May 1541.
castigatio pacis nostræ   M.   (castigatio *pro pace nostra* P.)
— *shalbe* layde
wirt jm auffgelegt   Z.
was layde
fuit...super...   M. (P.)
— *shall we be* healed
werdend wir gesund   Z.
are we healed (*we are* healed Nov. 1540)
medicatum est nobis   M.   (sanitas fuit nobis   P.)
6 we *go* all
wir alle *irrend* Z.
we *haue gone* all
omnes nos...*erravimus*   M.
— *turneth*
kert Z.
hath turned
respeximus M. (conversi sumus   P.)
— *pardoneth*
begnadet Z.
hath pardoned (M.   see below).
— But thorow hym, the Lorde hath pardoned all oure
    synnes 1539.
aber der Herr begnadet mit jm unser aller sünd   Z.

But *the Lorde hath heaped together vpon him the iniquitie of vs all*   Apr. Nov. 1540, May 1541.

et *dominus fecit concurrere in eo omnium nostrum iniquitates*   M.   (dominus pervenire fecit ad eum pænam omnium nostrum   P.)

7 He *shalbe payned...not open*

er wirt geengstiget vnd verkümmeret und wirdt...nit auffthun   Z.

He *suffred violence* and *was euell intreated,* & *dyd not yet* opē...

Vim est passus et *inique tractatus* et *tamen* non aperuit...   M.   (oppressus est et afflictus est et non *aperiet*   P.)

8 He *shall be* had awaye

er wirt vnuerhörter sach vnd on recht abgethon, des geschlächt doch niemandt erzellen mag   Z.

He *was* had awaye

sublatus est   M.

— had awaye   1539   (see above)

had awaye *from preson*   Apr. Nov. 1540, May 1541.

de carcere et de judicio sublatus est   M.   (de *clausura*...   P.)

— *no mā* maye nombre

Z.   see above.

who maye nombre?

quis enarrabit?   M. (P.)

— *when he shalbe* cut...

so er gleich...   auszgehauwen wirt   Z.

he was cut...

succisus est   M.   *abscissus est*   P.

— *shall* go

gon wirt.   Z.

dyd go   (M.   see below)

— my people   1539   meines volcks   Z.

my people, †whych in deade had deserued that punyshment   Apr. Nov. 1540, May 1541.

populi mei *quibus plaga* (*debebatur*)   M.   (Propter prævaricationem populi mei plaga fuit ei   P.)

9 *shalbe* geuen
  wirt...gegeben Z.
  was geuē
  dedit M. (P.)
— *his crucyfyenge with the theues*
  sein creützigung mit den rauberenn Z.
  wyth the ryche mā at his deeth
  apud divitem in mortibus eius M. (cum divite inter
    mortuos suos P.)

10 yᵉ Lorde to smyte 1539 so hat der Herr jnn wollen
    mit der schweche vmbringenn Z.
  the Lorde *thus to bruste* (*burste* Nov.) *hym wyth plages,*
    and to smyte Apr. Nov. 1540, May 1541
  Domino eum *sic conterere et infirmitatem inferre* M.
  (Dominus voluit conterere eum, ægrotare fecit. P.)
— lōgelastynge (a lōge lastinge Cov. 1535)
  eiñ langwirigen somen Z.
  lōnge lastynge
  quod longos viveret dies M. (prolongabit dies P.)

11 obtayne *great ryches* (optayne 1539) wirt er grosse
    hab überkommen Z.
  optayne *frute, and he shall be satisfyed* Apr. Nov.
    1540, May 1541.
  videbit (*fructum*) *et saturabitur* M. (videbit, et satura-
    bitur. P.)
— *his* wysdome
  mit *seiner kunst* Z.
  wysdome
  My ryghtuous...multitude (ryghteous 1539) Mein
    grechter knecht wirt mit seiner kunst die menge
    grecht machen vnd erlösen. Z.
— *by the knowledge of hym whych is my ryghteous seruaunt he*
    shall iustifye the multitude Apr. Nov. 1540, May 1541.
  cognitione sui qui justus servus meus est justificabit
    multos. M. (in scientia sua justificabit justus servus
    meus multos P.)

12 the strōge spoyle 1539 den starcken raub Z.
  the spoyle *wyth the strongest* Apr. Nov. 1540, May 1541.

cum robustissimis dividet spolia   M.

12 *shal geue*
vergiessen...wirt   Z.
geueth
effudit   M. (P.)
— *shalbe* rekened
gezellet wirt   Z.
is rekened
numeratus est   M. (P.)
— *shall take* awaye...*make*
hinnemmen...wirt   Z.
hath takē awaye...*made*
tulit   M. (P.)

From these collations the general character of the versions of the Old Testament in the first two editions of the Great Bible will be sufficiently clear, though a fuller examination would probably bring out some details of the method of revision into more distinct prominence. The variations from the first edition (Crumwell's 1539) in the second (Cranmer's, April 1540) are far greater in the Hagiographa and the Prophets—the part of Matthew's Bible which was Coverdale's own work—than those in the earlier books: and the variations of the text of 1539 from that of Matthew (1537) are more important throughout than the changes introduced afterwards[1]. In other words the edition of April 1540 exhibits a text formed on the same principles as that of the edition of 1539, but after a fuller and more thorough revision[2].

[1] By some incredible inadvertence Mr Anderson describes Crumwell's Bible as having Matthew's text. The edition of April 1539 and the London reprint of April 1540 (Petyt and Redman) are both carefully revised texts, as has been shewn already. The latter presents some variations from Crumwell's Bible, but they appear to be due rather to the printers than to any special revision: *e.g.* Ps. li. 14: O God, *O God* of my health: *sing thy* righteousness. 15 shew *forth*.

[2] This revision, as well as the partial one to be mentioned afterwards, was due to Coverdale, as appears from his Sermon quoted by Fulke (p. 98). 'M. Coverdale defended his trans-'lation, confessing that he did now 'himself espy some faults, which, if he 'might review it once over again, as 'he had done *twice* before, he doubted 'not but to amend.' This statement

After April 1540 the text of the Great Bible does not appear to have been systematically revised throughout, but still it is a remarkable and unobserved fact that in parts the edition of Nov. 1540 goes back from the text of April 1540 to that of 1539, so that the edition of April 1540 exhibits the greatest approximation to Münster. It is impossible to tell without a wide collation on what principle this reaction was carried out: a few examples will exhibit its reality[1].

APRIL 1539; NOV. 1540; MAY, NOV. 1541.	APRIL, JULY 1540.
Is. i. 2, *brought vp* children.	*promoted* children.
— 4, a *frowarde generacion, vnnaturall chyldren.*	a *seed of vngracious people corruptinge ther wayes.*
— 7, as *it were with enemyes in a batayle.*	as *they were subuerted y^t were alienate frō ye Lorde.*
— 8, lyke a *beseged* cytie.	lyke a *wasted* cytie.
— 11, sacryfyces vnto me.	sacrifices vnto me *saith the Lorde* (*the* om. April).
— 12, Whē ye apeare before me.	when ye *come to* apeare before me.
— — who requyreth you to treade.	who requireth *this of* you to treade
— 13, Offre me no mo oblacions.	*Therfore* offre me no mo oblaciōs.
— — your Sabbathes and solempne dayes.	your Sabbathes & *gatherīge togyther at y^e* solēpne dayes.

can only apply to Crumwell's and Cranmer's Bibles. The changes in the *one* revision of Coverdale's original Bible are not of sufficient importance to be thus described. Another passage of Fulke is itself decisive: 'the Bible 'of 1562,' he writes, 'I take to be 'that which was of Dr Coverdale's 'translation, most used in the church 'service in king Edward's time' (p. 68). This edition is a reprint of the Great Bible.

The rendering in Is. lvii. 5, 'ye 'take your pleasure under the oaks, 'under all green trees, and ye offer

'children in the valleys and dens of 'stone,' quoted in the *Hist. Account*, p. 103, to shew the existence of an independent revision in Tunstall's and Heath's edition of 1541, is found in Cranmer's (April 1540), and is of course based on Münster: 'calefacitis 'vos apud quercus sub omni ligno 'frondoso et immolatis pueros...'

[1] At first I was inclined to think that mixed sheets had been used for printer's copy in the later editions, but this hypothesis will not cover all the facts of the case.

APRIL 1539; Nov. 1540; MAY, Nov. 1541.	APRIL, JULY 1540
Is. i. 14, *Youre fastinges are also in vayne. I hate your newe holy dayes and fastyinges, euen fro my very hert. They make me weery, I cannot abyde them.*	*I hate your newe mone dayes & solẽpne feastes, euẽ fro my very hert. I can not awaye wᵗ suche vanitie & holdinge in of the people. They lye vpon me as a burthen, and I am wery of beringe thẽ* [1].
Neh. vi. 2, *come,* yᵗ we maye.	that we maye.

In other parts of the Old Testament this phenomenon is not observed, and the different editions are grouped together without any certain law. Thus, for example, the following readings occur :—

Prov. xii. 13, of parell. April 1540.	of *all* peril. Nov. 1540. May, Nov. 1541.
Jer. iv. 7, *he* maye. 1539. April 1540. May 1541. 1553.	*I* may. Nov. 1540. Nov. 1541.
— 13, *downe.* 1539 April 1540. May 1541, 1553.	*up.* July, Nov. 1540. Nov. 1541.
— 28, *purposed* ād taken -vpon me. April 1540. May 1541, 1553.	and taken vpon me. July, Nov. 1540. Nov. 1541.

The revision of the New Testament was, like Coverdale's original revision of Tindale, more independent; and based upon a careful use of the Vulgate and of Erasmus'

---

[1] In the first three chapters of Isaiah I have noted twenty other passages in which the same groups respectively agree in supporting different readings; and only five in which the November editions differ from 1539. In other parts of the book, as has been seen, the edition of Nov. 1540 follows closely that of April 1540. See pp. 187 ff.

Latin Version. An analysis of the variations in the First Epistle of St John may furnish a type of its general character. As nearly as I can reckon there are seventy-one differences between Tindale's text (1534) and that of the Great Bible[1]: of these forty-three come directly from Coverdale's earlier revision (and in a great measure indirectly from the Latin): seventeen from the Vulgate where Coverdale before had not followed it: the remaining eleven variations are from other sources. Some of the new readings from the Vulgate are important, as for example the additions in i. 4, 'that *ye may rejoice and that* your joy 'may be full.' ii. 23, '*he that knowledgeth the Son hath the* '*Father also.*' iii. 1, 'that we should be called *and be indeed* 'the sons of God.' v. 9, 'this is the witness of God *that is* '*greater.*' All these additions (like v. 7) are marked distinctly as *Latin* readings[2]: of the renderings adopted from Coverdale one is very important and holds its place in our present version. '*Hereby* we know that *he* abideth in us, '*even by* the Spirit which he *hath given* us,' for which Tindale reads: '*thereby* we know that *there* abideth in us '*of* the Spirit which he *gave* us.' One strange blunder also is corrected; 'that old commandment which ye *heard*' (as it was in the earlier texts) is replaced by the true reading: 'that old commandment which ye have *had*' (ii. 7). No one of the new renderings is of any moment (ii. 8, 18, 19, 20, 22, &c.).

As an illustration of the influence of Erasmus we may recur to the collation of his differences from Tindale in Col. ii.[3] In the following readings, nearly half of those noted, the text of the Great Bible is altered from that of Tindale (Matthew) to conformity with Erasmus (1519):

[1] The differences between the Great Bible and Matthew are about twelve [? four] fewer (see p. 178, n. 1), but I have not a complete table of them.

[2] One false rendering introduced into this version from the Latin has most unfortunately retained its place in our present Bible; 'there shall be 'one *fold* and one shepherd' (John x. 16), for 'one *flock*' of the earlier translators. The old Latin rightly distinguished between *grex* and *ovile*, but the distinction was lost in the later texts. [Corrected in the Revised Version.]

[3] See pp. 135 f.

'1 *for* I would: *how great care:* 2 *when they are* knit
'together: 6 walk...*so that ye be* rooted and built in him:
'11 *forasmuch as ye have put* off: 13 *through* sin *and*
'*through*...16 *or* of the new moon: 17 which are shadows:
'23 *by superstition and humbleness and by hurting of the*
'*body*...' Some of these renderings might have been
derived independently from the Greek or from the Vulgate; others could not, as we must believe, have occurred
to two original interpreters; and when they are taken
as a whole there can be no doubt as to their immediate
source[1].

The New Testament in the Great Bible of 1539 was
subject to a revision before the edition of 1540 no less than
the Old, and the revision was conducted on similar principles. What Münster was for the Old Testament Erasmus
was in a great measure for the New. How powerful his
influence was in the original recension has been just seen,
and the review shews additional traces of the sway which
his judgment exercised over Coverdale. One or two examples may be quoted[2]:

APRIL 1539.	APRIL, Nov. 1540.
Rom. v. 15, which was geuen by one man...	whych was of one man (quæ fuit unius hominis, *Er.*)
— i. 25, which is blessed for euer.	which is to be praysed for euer (qui est laudandus in secula, *Er.*)

[1] One or two other passages may be added in which the Great Bible certainly follows Erasmus:

Luke xix. 42...even in this thy day, *thou wouldest take heed* (Eras. 1519, *curares*).

1 Pet. i. 14...lusts *by which ye were led when as yet ye were* ignorant of Christ (Erasm. *quibus dum adhuc ignoraretis Christum agebamini*).

Col. i. 10...*that* in all things *ye* may please (Erasm. *ut* per omnia *placeatis*).

Col. iii. 9...*seeing that* ye have put off (Erasm. *posteaquam* exuistis). The

Latin New Testament of Erasmus was printed with the English of Matthew in 1538. The English Testament of 1540, said to be from the Latin of Erasmus, I have not seen. [A copy is in the Lambeth Library, and another in the Bodleian. There is no date, but the Calendar begins with 1540.]

[2] Nearly all the examples given are taken from the list of variations in Mr Fry's treatise on the Great Bibles. By using these for the analy-sis all suspicion of partial selection is removed.

APRIL 1539.	APRIL, NOV. 1540.
Phil. i. 23, is moch better.	is moche & far better (multo longeque melius est, *Er.*)
Rev. xvi. 9, repēted not.	repēted not of theyr euill dedis (neque egerunt scelerum pœnitentiam, *Er.* 1527).
— xxii. 6, the Lorde God of Saynctes and Prophetes.	the Lorde God of yᵉ holy Prophetes (Dominus Deus sanctorum prophetarum *Er.*)

No change perhaps is more remarkable than that in the difficult and famous passage of St James[1]:

APRIL 1539.	APRIL, NOV. 1540.
James i. 13. For God cannot tempte vnto euyll, because he tempteth no man.	for as God can not be tempted with euill, so nether he hymselfe tempt the [tempteth] eny man. (Nam Deus ut malis tentari non potest, ita nec ipse quemquam tentat. Er.)

In other cases the revision follows the Vulgate (with Erasmus) where the original text had deserted it, as for example:

APRIL 1539.	APRIL, NOV. 1540.
Rom. iv. 25, for to iustifie vs.	for oure iustificacyon.
Gal. i. 10, Do I now speake vnto men or vnto God? Other go I about to please...	Do I now perswade men, or God? Other do I seke to please...
Eph. ii. 12, and had no hope, & were with out...	hauynge no hope, and beynge with out...

Sometimes the turn given to the rendering appears to be original, as

Rom. i. 6, that are called of...	the electe of...
Phil. i. 10, as hurte no mannes conscyence.	as offende no mā.

But next to Erasmus the Complutensian edition con-tributed most largely to the changes in the revision. Thus

---

[1] See Fulke, *Defence of the English Translations*, pp. 559 f. (ed. P. S.).

in the Revelation the following new readings are taken
from this source:

APRIL 1539.	APRIL, NOV 1540.
x. 6, omit (1).	(*And the erth and the thynges that therin are.*)
xi. 15, for euer more (2).	for euer more (*Amen*).
xii. 4, the starres (3)	the starres (*of heauen*).
— 9, also (4).	also (*with hym*).
— 10, For *he* is (5).	For (*the accuser of our brethren*) is
xv. 2, *and of hys marke* (6).	omit.
xviii. 12, iron (7).	iron (*and marble*)
— 23, omit (8).	(*and candell lyght shalbe no more burnynge (burninge no-more* Nov.) *in the*
xxi. 16, measured the cytie w the rede (9).	measured ye cytie with the (*golden*) rede.
xxii. 9, the sayings of this book (10).	the sayinges of (*the prophecye of*) thys boke[1].

In one respect the Great Bible has an important and
lasting interest for us: the Psalter which is incorporated
in the Prayer Book is taken from it. In the first Prayer
Book of Edward VI reference is made 'to the Great
English Bible' for the numbers of the Psalms as appointed
to be read in the daily services which were necessarily
taken from it, and from that time the Psalter used in
churches has continued unchanged. No attempt seems
to have been made to substitute the Psalter of the Bishops'
Bible for that of the Great Bible; and when, upon the last
revision of the Prayer Book (1662), it was directed that
the other lessons from Scripture should be taken from the

[1] This list includes only a few very obvious differences, and makes no pretensions to completeness even in the chapters quoted. It is remarkable that all the readings are marked as Latin readings [being printed in smaller type], though 1, 3, 4, 5, 7, 8 are in the Greek text.

Mr Offor has collected all the 'in-terpolations' (Latin readings) found in the Great Bibles in his MS. collections for the history of the Bible (Brit. Mus. *Add.* 26,670, pp. 209 ff.).

For a fuller comparison of renderings of the New Testament in the different editions of the Great Bible, see Note A at the end of the Section.

royal Version, a special exception was made in favour of the Psalter. The choirs and congregations had grown familiar with it, and it was felt to be 'smoother and more 'easy to sing[1].'

A very slight comparison of the Psalter in the Prayer Book with that in the Authorised Version of the Bible will shew from what this acknowledged smoothness springs. Apart from the partial correction of errors in translation, the later version will be seen to be distinguished from the earlier by a scrupulous fidelity to the Hebrew text. Coverdale, like Luther and the Zurich translators on whose model his style was formed, allowed himself considerable freedom in dealing with the shape of the original sentences. At one time a word is repeated to bring out the balance of two clauses: at another time the number is changed: at another time a fuller phrase is supplied for the simple copula, now a word is resolved, and again a particle or an adverb or a pronoun or even an epithet is introduced for the sake of definiteness: there is in every part an endeavour to transfuse the spirit as well as the letter into the English rendering. The execution of the version undoubtedly falls far below the conception of it: the Authorised Version is almost in every case more correct: but still in idea and tone Coverdale's is as a whole superior, and furnishes a noble type for any future revision.

One or two examples will illustrate these general remarks. The materials for extending the comparison are accessible to all, and nothing throws more light on the actual history of our Bible[2].

[1] The exception was not made without an effort. The bishops concede 'that the Psalms be collated with the 'former translation mentioned in 'rubr. [? Great Bible], and printed 'according to it' (Cardwell, *Hist. of Conf.* 362). The question was again raised in 1689, and it was left to the Convocation to decide whether the Authorised Version should be inserted in the Prayer Book or the revision 'made by the Bishop of St Asaph 'and Dr Kidder' (*id.* 432).

[2] I have not ascertained from what text of the Great Bible the Psalter was taken. It contains the latest changes which I have noticed. See pp. 183 ff. For a collation of passages from the Prayer-Book Psalter with the editions of the Great Bible,

PRAYER BOOK.

1 The heavens declare the glory of God: and the firmament sheweth his handywork.

2 *One* day *telleth another:* and *one* night *certifieth another.*

3 There is *neither* speech nor language : *but* their *voices are* heard *among them.*

4 Their *sound* is gone out[1] *into* all *lands :*
and their words *into* the *ends* of the world.

5 In them hath he set a tabernacle for the sun:
which *cometh forth* as a bridegroom out of his chamber,
and rejoiceth as a *giant* to run *his course.*

6 *It goeth* forth from the *uttermost part* of the heaven, and *runneth about* unto the *end* of it *again :* and there is nothing hid from the heat thereof.

7 The law of the Lord is *an undefiled law*, converting the soul :
the testimony of the Lord is sure, *and giveth wisdom unto* the simple.

8 The statutes of the Lord are

AUTHORISED VERSION.

The heavens declare the glory of God : and the firmament sheweth his handywork.

Day unto day *uttereth speech,* and night *unto night sheweth knowledge.*

There is *no* speech nor language, *where* their *voice is* not heard.

Their *line* is gone out *through* all *the earth,*
and their words *to* the *end* of the world.

In them hath he set a tabernacle for the sun ;
which *is* as a bridegroom *coming* out of his chamber,
and rejoiceth as a *strong man* to run *a race.*

His going forth *is* from the *end* of the heaven, and *his circuit* unto the *ends* of it :
and there is nothing hid from the heat thereof.

The law of the Lord is *perfect,* converting the soul :

the testimony of the Lord is sure, *making wise* the simple :

The statutes of the Lord are

see Note B at the end of the Section.

One general change in the Prayer-Book Psalter is very greatly to be regretted, and was probably only an oversight. The insertions from the Vulgate (*e.g.* Ps. xiv. 5—7, &c.), which

were distinguished from the other parts of the translation in the Great Bible, stand unmarked in the Prayer-Book. Would it not be legitimate to print the Prayer-Book Psalter with all these insertions in Italics ?

[1] Om. *out* Nov. 1540.

right, *and rejoice* the heart .
the commandment of the
Lord is pure, *and giveth light
unto* the eyes.

9 The fear of the Lord is
clean, *and endureth* for ever :
the judgments of the Lord
are true, and righteous altogether.

10 More to be desired are they
than gold, yea than much
fine gold:
sweeter also than honey and
the honey-comb.

11 Moreover by them is thy
servant *taught :*
and in keeping of them there
is great reward.

12 Who can *tell how oft he
offendeth ?*
O cleanse thou me from *my*[2]
secret faults.

13 Keep thy servant also from
presumptuous sins, *lest they
get the* dominion over me:
so shall I be *undefiled* and
innocent from the great *offence.*

14 Let the words of my mouth
and the meditation of my
heart :
be *alway*[2] acceptable in thy
sight,

15 O Lord, my strength and
my redeemer.

1 Why do the heathen *so furi-
ously* rage *together ?* and *why*

right, *rejoicing* the heart :
the commandment of the
Lord is pure, *enlightening* the
eyes.

The fear of the Lord is clean,
enduring for ever :
the judgments of the Lord
are true and righteous altogether.

More to be desired are they
than gold, yea, than much
fine gold ;
sweeter also than honey and
the honey-comb.

Moreover by them is thy servant *warned :*
and in keeping of them there
is great reward.

Who can *understand his errors ?*

cleanse thou me from secret
faults.

Keep *back* thy servant also from
presumptuous sins ; *let them
not have* dominion over me :
Then shall I be *upright*, and
I shall be innocent from the
great *transgression.*

Let the words of my mouth,
and the meditation of my
heart,
be acceptable in thy sight,

O Lord, my strength and my
redeemer.

Why do the heathen rage, and
the people imagine a vain

---

[1] The honey-comb and the honey.
Nov. 1540, 1541.

[2] [In brackets in the Annexed Book,

which was attached to the Act of
Uniformity.]

do the people imagine a vain thing?

10 Be wise now therefore, O ye kings:
be *learned*, ye *that are* judges of the earth.

11 Serve the Lord *in* fear: and rejoice *unto him*[1] with *reverence.*

12 Kiss the son, lest he be angry, and *so* ye perish from the *right*[1] way:
if his wrath *be* kindled, (*yea*, but a little) blessed are all they that put their trust in him.

16 He clave the *hard* rocks in the wilderness:
and gave them drink *thereof*, as *it had been* out of the great *depth.*

17 He brought *waters* out of the *stony* rock:
so that it gushed out like *the* rivers.

18 *Yet for all this* they sinned more against him: *and provoked* the most *Highest* in the wilderness.

thing?

Be wise now therefore, O ye kings:
be *instructed*, ye judges of the earth.

Serve the Lord *with* fear, and rejoice with *trembling.*

Kiss the son, lest he be angry, and ye perish from the way,

when his wrath *is* kindled but a little. Blessed are all they that put their trust in him.

He clave the rocks in the wilderness,
and gave them drink as out of the great *depths.*

He brought *streams also* out of the rock,
and caused waters to run down like rivers.

And they sinned *yet* more against him,
by provoking the most *High* in the wilderness[2].

[1] [In brackets in the Annexed Book as from the Latin.]

[2] The Books are arranged in the following order in Crumwell's Bible (April 1539):
The Pentateuch.
The second part of the Bible: Josua...Esther, Job.
The third part of the Bible: The Psalter....Cantica Canticorum.
The Prophets: Esaye...Malachy.
The volume of the books called Hagiographia: 3 Esdr. 4 Esdr. ...Baruch...1 Mach. 2 Mach.

The New Testament:
The four Gospels. Acts.
The Epistles of Saint Paul: Romans ...... Philemon, Hebrews.
Epistle of St James.
1, 2 St Peter.
1, 2, 3 St John.
St Jude.
The Revelation.
In the list (but not in the text) Jude is placed before 1 John.
The order is the same in Cranmer's Bible (April 1540), and in Tunstall's

Note A.

The following comparison of readings in representative editions of the Great Bible has been based upon collations most liberally placed in my hands by Mr F. Fry. [They have all been checked and corrected.] The table will illustrate the extent of intentional and accidental variation. The notation is as follows:

1539	C
1540 April	Cr$_1$
1540 Nov.	TH$_1$
1541 Dec.	Cr$_4$

St Matthew.

iii.	4 *garment* of	C	*raiment* of	Cr$_1$ TH$_1$ Cr$_4$
v.	31 of *the* divorcement	C Cr$_1$	of divorcement	TH$_1$
vi.	29 like *unto* one	C	like one	Cr$_1$ TH$_1$ Cr$_4$
—	34 for *to* morrow *day*	C	for *the* morrow *day*	Cr$_1$ TH$_1$ Cr$_4$
vii.	16 by their *fruits*	C Cr$_1$ Cr$_4$	by their *works*	TH$_1$
ix.	21 turned him *about*	C Cr$_1$ Cr$_4$	turned him	TH$_1$
—	28 they *say* (xv. 33; xix. 10)	C Cr$_1$ Cr$_4$	they *said*	TH$_1$
x.	14 of *the* house	C	of *that* house	Cr$_1$ TH$_1$ Cr$_4$
xii.	5 *in* the temple	C Cr$_1$ Cr$_4$	*of* the temple	TH$_1$
—	23 *that* son	C Cr$_1$ Cr$_4$	*the* son	TH$_1$
xiii.	26 *then* appeared	C	*there* appeared	Cr$_1$ TH$_1$ Cr$_4$
—	31 of all seeds	C Cr$_1$ Cr$_4$	of all *the* seeds	TH$_1$
xiv.	12 buried it *&* went	C	buried it: went	Cr$_1$ TH$_1$ Cr$_4$
xv.	3 do ye *also* transgress (xvi. 18)	C Cr$_1$ Cr$_4$	do ye transgress	TH$_1$
—	17 in *at* the	C Cr$_1$	*into* the	TH$_1$ Cr$_4$
xvi.	14 John Baptist	C Cr$_1$ Cr$_4$	John *the* Baptist	TH$_1$
xxi.	42 in *your* eyes	C Cr$_1$ Cr$_4$	in *our* eyes	TH$_1$
xxii.	42 they saye	C Cr$_1$	they *sayde*	TH$_1$ Cr$_4$
—	46 that *day* forth	C Cr$_1$ Cr$_4$	that *time* forth	TH$_1$
xxiv.	32 his *branch*	C	his *branches*	Cr$_1$ TH$_1$ Cr$_4$
xxvi.	11 have *the* poor	C Cr$_1$ Cr$_4$	have poor	TH$_1$
xxvii.	19 in sleep	C	in *my* sleep	Cr$_1$ TH$_1$ Cr$_4$

Acts.

i.	19 *blood* field	C Cr$_1$ Cr$_4$	*bloody* field	TH$_1$
ii.	18 they shall prophesy	C Cr$_1$ Cr$_4$	they shall *all* prophesy	TH$_1$
iv.	30 so *that* thou	C Cr$_1$	so *shalt* thou	TH$_1$ Cr$_4$
v.	2 laid it *down* at	C Cr$_1$ Cr$_4$	laid it at	TH$_1$
xii.	23 *but* immediately	C	*and* immediately	Cr$_1$ TH$_1$ Cr$_4$
xiii.	33 in the *first* psalm	C Cr$_1$	in the *second* psalm	TH$_1$ Cr$_4$
xiv.	15 that ye *should*	C Cr$_1$ Cr$_4$	that ye *shall*	TH$_1$
xv.	31 rejoiced *of* the	C Cr$_1$ Cr$_4$	rejoiced *at* the	TH$_1$
xvi.	10 called us *for* to	C Cr$_1$ Cr$_4$	called us to	TH$_1$

and Heath's (Nov. 1540): but in Tunstall and Heath the Preface to the Apocrypha is left out, and the reverse of the title-page to that division of the book is consequently blank.

xx.	9 into a *deep* sleep	C Cr$_1$ Cr$_4$	into a *dead* sleep	TH$_1$
xxvi.	18 may *turn*	C	may *be turned*	Cr$_1$ TH$_1$ Cr$_4$
xxvii.	2 *being* with	C	*tarrying still* with	Cr$_1$ TH$_1$ Cr$_4$
xxviii.	2 the *people of the country*	C	the *strangers*	Cr$_1$ TH$_1$ Cr$_4$
—	4 this man *must needs be*	C	*no doubt* this man *is*	Cr$_1$ TH$_1$ Cr$_4$

ROMANS.

i.	6 *that are called*	C	the elect	Cr$_1$ TH$_1$ Cr$_4$
—	7 *called* saints	C	saints *by election*	Cr$_1$ TH$_1$ Cr$_4$
—	25 *turned* his truth *unto*	C	*changed* his truth *for*	Cr$_1$ TH$_1$ Cr$_4$
—	— is *blessed*	C	is *to be praised*	Cr$_1$ TH$_1$ Cr$_4$
—	30 doers of *wrong*	C	*disdainful*	Cr$_1$ TH$_1$ Cr$_4$
iv.	25 *rose* again *for to justify us*	C	*was raised* again *for our justification*	Cr$_1$ TH$_1$ Cr$_4$
vi.	14 *let not* sin *have*	C	*for* sin *shall not have*	Cr$_1$ TH$_1$ Cr$_4$
—	20 ye were *not under*	C	ye were *void of*	Cr$_1$ TH$_1$ Cr$_4$
xiv.	1 receive *unto you*	C	receive	Cr$_1$ TH$_1$ Cr$_4$
xv.	6 Lord Jesus	C	Lord Jesus *Christ*	Cr$_1$ TH$_1$ Cr$_4$
xvi.	2 in *the Lord*	C	in *Christ*	Cr$_1$ TH$_1$ Cr$_4$
—	22 chamberlain	C	treasurer	Cr$_1$ TH$_1$ Cr$_4$

1 CORINTHIANS.

iii.	18 wise among you	C	wise *to himself* among you	Cr$_1$ TH$_1$ Cr$_4$
v.	13 God *shall judge*	C	God *judgeth*	Cr$_1$ TH$_1$ Cr$_4$
ix.	5 a sister to wife	C	a woman a sister	Cr$_1$ TH$_1$ Cr$_4$

2 CORINTHIANS.

i.	11 of many occasions	C	of many persons	Cr$_1$ TH$_1$ Cr$_4$
—	— the grace given	C	the gift given	Cr$_1$ TH$_1$ Cr$_4$
iii.	15 their hearts	C Cr$_1$ Cr$_4$	their eyes	TH$_1$
vi.	3 in our office	C Cr$_1$ Cr$_4$	in your office	TH$_1$
vii.	15 is more abundant	C TH$_1$ Cr$_4$	is found abundant	Cr$_1$
ix.	6 soweth plenteously shall reap	C	soweth (in giving) largely and freely shall reap	Cr$_1$ TH$_1$ Cr$_4$
x.	2 same confidence	C	same boldness	Cr$_1$ TH$_1$ Cr$_4$
xi.	2 to make you a chaste	C	that ye should make yourselves a chaste	Cr$_1$ TH$_1$ Cr$_4$
xii.	10 in need	C	in necessities	Cr$_1$ TH$_1$ Cr$_4$
—	20 when I come	C Cr$_4$	if I come	Cr$_1$ TH$_1$
—	— and discord	C	and seditions	Cr$_1$ TH$_1$ Cr$_4$
xiii.	5 Prove yourselves	C	examine yourselves	Cr$_1$ TH$_1$ Cr$_4$
—	— examine your	C	prove your	Cr$_1$ TH$_1$ Cr$_4$

GALATIANS.

i.	10 speak unto men or unto	C	persuade men or	Cr$_1$ TH$_1$ Cr$_4$
—	— go I about to	C	do I seek to	Cr$_1$ TH$_1$ Cr$_4$

ii. 5 as concerning to be   by way of subjec-
        brought into sub-   tion   Cr₁ TH₁ Cr₄
        jection   C
— 19 unto God   C   unto Christ   Cr₁ TH₁ Cr₄
— 21 is dead   C   died   Cr₁ TH₁ Cr₄
iii. 3 so unwise   C   such fools   Cr₁ TH₁ Cr₄
— 16 in the seeds   C Cr₁ Cr₄   in thy seeds   TH₁
— 24 might be made right-   should be justified
        eous by   C   by   Cr₁ TH₁ Cr₄
iv. 11 bestowed on you   C Cr₁ Cr₄   bestowed in you   TH₁
vi. 8 soweth in his flesh C Cr₁ Cr₄ soweth in the flesh TH₁

EPHESIANS.

ii. 12 and had...and were   C   having...and being Cr₁ TH₁ Cr₄
iii. 21 all generations from time   all ages world with-
        to time   C   out end   Cr₁ TH₁ Cr₄
iv. 5 let there be but one Lord C   one Lord   Cr₁ TH₁ Cr₄
v. 10 accept that which is pleas-   searching what is
        ing unto   C   acceptable unto Cr₁ TH₁ Cr₄
— 13 are rebuked of the light C   are brought forth
                                       by the light   Cr₁ TH₁ Cr₄
— 16 avoiding occasion   C   winning occasion   Cr₁
                                     redeeming the time TH₁ Cr₄
— 33 wife fear   C   wife reverence   Cr₁ TH₁ Cr₄
vi. 4 the nurture   C   the doctrine   Cr₁ TH₁ Cr₄
—   5 be obedient unto   C   obey   Cr₁ TH₁ Cr₄
— 24 unfeignedly   C   sincerely   Cr₁ TH₁ Cr₄

PHILIPPIANS.

i. 10 as hurt no man's con-   as offend no man   Cr₁ TH₁ Cr₄
        science   C
— 29 given of Christ   C Cr₄   given for Christ   Cr₁ TH₁
ii. 5 was also in Christ   C Cr₁   was in Christ   TH₁ Cr₄
iii. 19 whose belly is their God C   whose God is their
                                       belly   Cr₁ TH₁ Cr₄
iv. 12 I can both be low and   I know how to be
        I can be high   C   low and I know
                                       how to exceed   Cr₁ TH₁ Cr₄

2 TIMOTHY.

iv. 5 do the work of   C   do the work tho-
                                       roughly of   Cr₁ TH₁ Cr₄

HEBREWS.

iv. 10 ceased also from his C Cr₁ Cr₄ ceased from all his TH₁
v.   8 by those things   C Cr₁ Cr₄ by these things   TH₁
x. 22 hearts from an evil C   hearts and the evil Cr₁ TH₁ Cr₄
xi. 16 God is not   C   God himself is not Cr₁ TH₁ Cr₄
— 40 had provided a   C Cr₁ Cr₄   had promised a   TH₁
xii. 9 of spiritual gifts C   of spirits   Cr₁ TH Cr₄
—   — lyue   C Cr₁ Cr₄   lyfe   TH₁

JAMES.

i. 13 God cannot tempt unto evil, because he tempt- eth no man C	as God cannot be tempted with evil so neither he himself tempteth (tempt the Cr_1) any man	Cr_1 TH$_1$ Cr_4
v. 17 a man mortal C	a man under infirm- ities	Cr_1 TH$_1$ Cr_4

2 PETER.

ii. 14 with covetousness C	with robbery	Cr_1 TH$_1$ Cr_4

1 JOHN.

iv. 10 to make agreement C	to be the agreement	Cr_1 TH$_1$ Cr_4

JUDE.

12 feeding themselves C	living lawless and after their own pleasure.	Cr_1 TH$_1$ Cr_4

Note B.

The following variations taken from ten Psalms collated in Crumwell (C), the Great Bible of April 1540 (Cr_1), of November 1541 (TH$_2$) and the Sealed Prayer Book of 1662, will illustrate the relation of the Prayer Book Psalter to the earlier copies. The Prayer Book never preserves the 'italics' of the Bibles. For the collations on which this table is founded I am again indebted to the kindness of Mr F. Fry.

Ps. i. 1 *stood* and *sat* (1662) for *stand* and *sit* in all the representative editions of the Great Bible, and the early Psalters.

viii. 3 *works* TH$_2$: *work* C Cr_1.

— 6 *of* the works TH$_2$: *in* the works C Cr_1.

xxvii. 1 *of* whom Cr_1 TH$_2$: *for* of whom C.

— 5 *hide* me, and Cr_1 TH$_2$: *keep* me, and C.

— 7 *an* oblation *with great gladness* Cr_1 TH$_2$: *the* oblation *of thanksgiving* C.

xxviii. 1 if thou make as though : if thou make *thee* as though C Cr_1 TH$_2$. [So Psalter bound with 4to P.B. of 1552 [? 1553] in Univ. Libr. Cambridge,' N⁰ 674.]

— — *hearest* not [so Psalter 1552] : *heardest* not C Cr_1 TH$_2$.

— 9 is *my* strength [so Psalter 1552] : is *their* strength C Cr_1 TH$_2$.

xxxiv. 16 from the earth [so Bible 1553] : from *off* the earth C Cr_1 TH$_2$. [so Psalter 1552].

xlvi. 2 *into* the midst [so Cov. and Psalter 1552] : *in* the midst C Cr_1 TH$_2$.

— 4 *tabernacle* [so Psalter 1552] : *tabernacles* C Cr_1 TH$_2$.

— 8 *destruction* [so Psalter 1552] : *destructions* C Cr_1 TH$_2$.

— 11 *refuge* : *defence* C Cr_1 TH$_2$. So Psalter 1552.

lvii. 9 awake *up* my [so Psalter 1552] : awake *O* my C Cr_1 TH$_2$.

lxv. 5 in *thy* righteousness [so Psalter 1552] : in righteousness C Cr_1 TH$_2$.

Ps. xci.   1 most *high* [so Psalter 1552] : most *highest* C Cr$_1$ TH$_2$.
—   6 in darkness : in *the* darkness C Cr$_1$ TH$_2$ [so Psalter 1552].
cxl.   6 *I said* unto the Lord Cr$_1$ TH$_2$ (so Psalter 1552) : *But my saying is* unto the Lord C.
—   8 O Lord, *let not his mischievous imagination prosper* (so Psalter 1552), lest they be too proud Cr$_1$ TH$_2$ (so Psalter 1552) : O Lord *let him not have his purpose*, lest they be too proud C.
—   11 *evil shall hunt the* wicked person *to overthrow him* Cr$_1$ TH$_2$: *a malicious and* wicked person *shall be hunted away and destroyed* C.

In no one of these examples is a rendering taken from Crumwell's Bible (C). In one case (Ps. i. 1) an archaism seems to have been removed in 1662. In ten places (xxviii. 1 (bis), 9; xlvi. 2, 4, 8; lvii. 9; lxv. 5; xci. 1, 6) changes have been introduced (apparently) without any authority. In xlvi. 11 a rendering has been adopted from the Genevan Bible [or from ver. 7]. In the American Prayer Book Psalter two other changes made (apparently) from the Genevan version have fallen under my notice: v. 6 *lies* for *leasing*); lvi. 8 *wanderings* (for *flittings*).

One of the most remarkable variations in the Psalter was due to a blunder and has been (unauthoritatively) corrected. In Ps. lxviii. 4 the Great Bible of April 1540 reads *in his name Ja and* with a ☞ in the margin to indicate a proposed note upon the sacred name. But in Nov. 1541 the curious misreading *in his name yea and* is found, and this corruption passed into the later editions of the Great Bible. (*e.g.* 1553), from which the first Psalters were taken. The error was continued throughout the 17th century even in the Prayer-Book of 1662. I do not know when the true reading was first restored[1]. The earliest Prayer Book in which I have noticed it is one printed at Oxford in 1703, while the error is found in an Oxford edition of 1698. In London editions the blunder was continued several years later (1709).

§ 5. TAVERNER.

The work of Taverner is very different from that of any of the revisers noticed before, and stamped with a very distinct individuality. Its character might be anticipated from the description of the man himself which has been already quoted[2]. Throughout he appears to aim at vigorous and idiomatic language, and his New Testament at least deserves more attention than has yet been paid to it. Probably he undertook this part of the work, for which his scholarship fitted him, first, and only afterwards extended his labours to the Old Testament, for which he had no special aptitude. As far as I have observed he

[1 It is in the Scotch Prayer Book of 1637.]   2 See p. 83.

used no help but the Vulgate in the Old Testament, and this only partially[1]. But scarcely a page perhaps will fail to shew changes which are made for the sake of clearness and force. Thus '*the child* of death' becomes '*worthye* of 'deathe' (2 Sam. xii. 5): 'of mine own *mind*' is altered to ' of myne owne *hed*' (Num. xvi. 28): 'but *and* if' is made simply 'but if': 'like *as* a branch' simply 'like a branch,' and so on. But in a passage like Is. liii. 1—5, where Coverdale is greatly at fault, he introduces no real change in the text before him[2].

In the New Testament Taverner aims equally at compression and vividness, but he was familiar with the original, and therefore could deal more happily with the translation of Tindale, which still, like Coverdale, he followed very closely. A few verses will shew the method which he followed. Thus in the beginning of St John's Gospel for '*the same*' he reads '*this*' (i. 2, 7), for to '*bear* '*witness*' simply '*witness*' (7, 15); for Tindale's '*verity*' he writes '*truth*' (14); for Tindale's 'confessed and denied 'not, and *said plainly*' he repeats the first word as in the Greek 'confessed and denyed not and *confessed*' (20). Sometimes in his anxiety to keep to the Greek text he becomes even obscure or inaccurate, as '*all were* made 'by it' (3), 'to be made the sonnes of God, *byleuynge* on 'his name' (12), '*in to* his owne (11), 'he was *fyrst er I* '*was*' (15). But he introduced substantial improvements into the translation by his regard for the article: 'that was '*the* true lyght (*a* tr. l. *Tind.*) which...'commyng in to...' (9): 'Arte thou *the* Prophet?' (21, 25): 'I am *a* voyce of 'one cryinge...' (23). Two consecutive verses of the First Epistle of St John furnish good examples of his endeavour to find English equivalents for the terms before him. All the other versions adopt the Latin '*advocate*' in 1 John ii. 1, for which Taverner substitutes the Saxon '*spokesman*.'

---

[1] A good example occurs Josh. xxiv. 27, 'leest y^t after this tyme ye 'wyll denye and lye vnto your God.'

[2] In Mr Offor's MS. collections for a history of the English Bible (Brit. Mus. 26,670-3) there is a collation of Tindale's Pentateuch (1537, 1549) with Taverner (1539, 1551), Vol. II. pp. 153—158.

Tindale, followed by Coverdale, the Great Bible, &c. strives after an adequate rendering of ἱλασμὸς (1 John ii. 2), in the awkward periphrasis 'he *it is that obtaineth* '*grace* for our sins': Taverner boldly coins a word which if insufficient is yet worthy of notice: 'he is *a mercystocke* for 'our synnes[1].'

[1] The following characteristic changes introduced by Taverner have been selected from a collation of fourteen chapters of St Matthew, most kindly placed at my disposal by Professor Moulton.

TINDALE 1534.	TAVERNER 1539.
xiii. 35 similitud⁻	parables (from Ps. ɪxxviii. 2)
— 36 to housse	home
— 41 thing⁻ that offende	griefes
— — iniquite	wickednes
— 43 iuste	ryghteous
— 45 good	fayre
— 53 finisshed	ended
— 58 for there vnbelefes sake	bicause of their vnbelefe
xiv. 5 counted	helde
— 31 thou of lytell faith	litle faythful
— 36 vesture only	garmente
xv. 2 transgresse	breake
— 6 made yᵗ...	defeated..
is with out effecte	
— 13 plantes	plantynge
— 18 procede out of	come forth of
— 22 the sonne	thou sonne
— — pytiously	soore
— 26 whelpes	dogges
— 33 as shuld suffise	to fyll
— 37 the brokē meate	the fragmētes
xvi. 3 fassion	countenaunce
— 23 godly thing⁻	thynges of God
— — worldly thing⁻	thinges of men
— 24 forsake	deny
xviii. 1 yᵉ greatest	greater
— 4 greatest	greater man
— 7 Wo be vnto	wo worth
— — because of offences	for offendynges
— 9 offende	let
— 12, 13 nynty and nyne	the .iiij. score and .xix.
— 14 perishe	be lost
— 16 all thinges	euery word
— — be stablisshed	stande
xix. 9 fornicacion	aduoutry
— — breaketh wedlocke	commytteth aduoutry
— 28 seconde generacion	newe byrth

W.   14

TINDALE 1534.	TAVERNER 1539.
xix. 28 .xii.	the twelue
xx. 25 lordes	rulers
— 34 immediatly	forthwith
xxi. 17 had his abydinge	lodged
xxii. 2 a certayne kynge	a man beynge a kynge
— 5 they made light of it	they regarded not
— — ferme place	house in the coūtrey
— 6 vngodly	fouly
— 12 was evē spechlesse	had neuer a worde to saye
— 19 tribute money	cóyne of the trybute money
— 34 yᵗ he had put the Saduces to silence	he hadde stopped the Sadduces mouthes
— 39 and ther is another	and the seconde
xxiii. 2 seate	chayre
— 3 observe	kepe
— 4 heave at	moue
— 6 synagoges	assembles
— 14 greater	the greater
— 16 he offendeth	is bounde (18)
— 22 seate	trone
— 25 brybery	rauyne
— 33 dāpnaciō	iudgement
xxiv. 12 and because iniquite shall have the vpper hande, the love of many shall abate	and because of the aboundaunce of wyckednes, the charitie of many shall waxe colde
— 24 yᵉ verie electe	euen the chosen persons
— 34 generacion	age
— 35 perisshe	passe
— — abyde	not passe
— 43 good man of the housse	housholder
— 51 will devyde him	shall hewe him
— — rewarde	part
xxv. 35 herbourlesse	a straunger (vv. 38, 43)
— 46 eternall	euerlastynge
xxvi. 2 crucified	nayled to the crosse
— 4 heelde a counsell	toke counsell
— 5 holy	feastfull
— 8 had indignacion	disdayned
— 13 memoriall	remembraunce
— 17 paschall lambe	passouer
— 24 shalbe betrayed	is betrayed (vv. 45, 46)
— 28 testament	couenaunt
— — that shalbe shedde	shedde
— — for the remission	to the forgyuenesse
— 30 sayde grace	gyuen prayses
— 41 willynge	prompte
— 42 fulfylled	done
— 45 Take hede	behold
— 52 sheathe	place
— 54 for so must it be	that so it oughte to be

It would be tempting to dwell longer on this version, but it appears to have exercised no influence whatever on the later revisions. It remains simply as a monument of one man's critical power, and in the very sharp personality of its characteristics is alien from the general history of the English Bible[1].

TINDALE 1534.	TAVERNER 1539.
xxvi. 61 felowe	man
— 63 peace	tongue
— — charge	coniure
— 64 skye	heauen
— 66 worthy to dye	gyltie of deathe
— 68 tell	Prophecye vnto
xxvii. 4 innocent	gyltles
— 24 & that ye shall se	auyse you
— 51 toppe...bottome	hygheste...loweste
— 58 begged	craued
— 62 foloweth good frydaye	folowed the daye of preparing the Sabboth
— 65 Take watche men	Ye haue a watche
xxviii. 1 The Sabboth daye at even which dauneth the mor-owe after the Sabboth	In the euenynge of the Sabboth dayes, which dawneth vnto one of the Sabothes
— 2 the angell	an aungell
— 4 be came as deed men	were as deed

Of these corrections it will be noticed that a large number exhibit an endeavour after more idiomatic or vigorous renderings: e.g. xiii. 36, 41; xiv. 31; xv. 6, 33; xvi. 23; xviii. 7, 12; xxi. 17; xxii. 34; xxiv. 43; xxv. 35; xxvi. 2; xxvii. 24; or a taste for more homely or simple or native words: e.g. xiii. 41, 43, 53; xv. 2, 18, 22; xix. 28; xxvii. 4. Some renderings shew a delicate feeling for the original : e.g. xv. 13, 22; xviii. 16; xxii. 2; xxvi. 24, 66.

[1] The Books are arranged in the following manner :

The Books of the Old Testament
   Genesis...The Ballet of balletes
The Prophets
   Isaiah...Malachi
The Apocrypha
   3 Esdras—2 Maccabees
The New Testament
   Four Gospels
   Acts
The Epistles
   13 of St Paul
   St Peter 1, 2
   St John 1, 2, 3
   Hebrews
   St James
   Jude
The Revelation.

14—2

§ 6. THE GENEVAN BIBLE.

The foundations of the English Bible were laid by exiles in a strange country; and exiles contributed the most important revision which it underwent before the final settlement of the received text. Under the influence of Calvin, Geneva had become the seat of a society of devoted Biblical students, and the results of their labours were made available for the review of the English version by the Marian persecution. The more conservative party among the refugees might have scrupled to use them without reserve, but no such feeling could hold back the seceders from Frankfurt. For the first time the task of emendation was undertaken by men who were ready to press it to the uttermost. They spoke of their position as providential, and in looking back upon the later results of their Bible we can thankfully acknowledge that it was so. They enjoyed, as they say in their preface, many advantages over earlier labourers whose renderings 'required greatly 'to be perused and reformed.' 'Not,' they add, 'that we 'vendicat any thing to our selues aboue the least of our 'brethren, (for God knoweth with what feare and trembling 'we haue bene now [April 1560], for the space of two 'yeres and more day and night occupied herein) but 'being earnestly desired......and seing the great opor- 'tunitie and occasions, which God presented vnto vs in 'this Churche, by reason of so many godly and learned 'men: and suche diuersities of translations in diuers 'tongues, we vndertoke this great and wonderful worke,.. 'which now God according to his diuine prouidence and 'mercie hath directed to a moste prosperous end.'

Some important versions indeed had been published in addition to those which have been noticed already as accessible to the first translators. Leo Juda, who had contributed greatly to the German Bible of Zurich, laboured for many years at a new Latin Version of the Old Testament. This was left unfinished at his death (1542), but the work was completed by T Bibliander and C. Pellican.

P. Cholin added a translation of the Apocrypha: R. Gualther revised Erasmus' Latin New Testament; and the whole Bible, thus finished, was printed in 1544. The version is vigorous, aiming rather at an intelligible sense, than at a literal rendering of the words of the original. Castalio (Chateillon) carried this freedom to a far greater length, and in his singularly elegant version (1551) endeavoured to make the Hebrew writers speak in purely classical Latin. In spite of Beza's vehement assaults Castalio exercised some effect on later Protestant versions; but the New Testament of his great adversary (1556) exercised a far more powerful influence than either of these complete Bibles. Beza made some use of the various readings of Greek Manuscripts which had been collected in a convenient form by Stephens in his Greek Testament of 1550 (ed. regia); but as yet, in spite of the great advances which had been made in scholarship, the true principles of Greek criticism were wholly unknown, and the text which served as the basis of translation was as faulty as before.

These Latin versions, especially Beza's New Testament, contributed important help to the English revisers, but it was of still greater moment that they were associated at Geneva with a group of scholars who were already engaged in the work of correcting the French Version of Olivetan. As early as 1545 Calvin cursorily revised this Bible, chiefly, as it is said, in points of style and expression. In 1551 he went over the work again more thoroughly; and again in 1558. The edition of 1551 contained a new version of the Psalter by Louis Budé and of the Apocrypha by Beza. But these successive revisions were confessedly provisional, and it was not till 1588 that the version appeared which, bearing the name of the venerable company of pastors at Geneva, remained for a long time the standard Bible of the French protestants[1].

---

[1] For these details I am indebted to Le Long, as I have been unable to obtain access to the editions of 1545 and 1551. [See Pétavel, *La Bible en France*, p. 171. A full account of Olivetan's version will be found in a

Thus the English exiles found themselves surrounded by those who were engaged in a task similar to their own[1]. They started indeed with a far better foundation than the French revisers, and their labours shew no impatient desire for change.   In the historical books they preserved in the main the old rendering, altering here and there an anti-quated word or a long periphrasis[2].   In the Hagiographa, the Prophets, and the poetic books of the Apocrypha, the changes were necessarily far more numerous.   An analysis of the new readings in a few representative passages will place the general character of the revision in a clear light[3].

(GREAT BIBLE.)   5 *And* in Gibeon the Lord appeared to Salomon in a dreame by night.   And God sayd : aske what *thou wilt that I maye geue it* the.

6 And Salomon sayd: thou hast shewed vnto thy seruaunt Dauid my father great mercy, when he walked before the in trueth, *in* ryghteousnesse, and in *playnnesse* of heart wyth the.   And thou hast kepte for hym thys greate mercy, *that thou* hast geuen hym a sonne to syt on his *seat* : as *it is come to passe* this daye.

7 And now, O Lord my God, *it is thou that* hast made thy seruaunt kynge in steade of Dauid my father.   And I am but *younge,* and *wot* not howe to go out and in.

8 And thy seruaūt is in the myddest of thy people, whyche thou hast chosen.   *And verelye the people are so manye that they* cannot be tolde nor nombred for multitude.

9 Geue therfore vnto thy seruaunt an vnderstandynge hert, to iudge *the* people, that I maye decerne betwene good

series of articles by Reuss in the *Revue de Théologie*, 3me série, voll. III and IV, Strasburg, 1865–6.]

[1] A revised Italian version of the Bible appeared also [probably] at Geneva in 1562.

[2] A small sign will shew the scho-. lar's instinct, and this is found in the spelling and *accentuation* of the He-brew names which is characteristic of the edition of 1560, as Iaakób, Izhák,

Rebekah, Joshúa, Zebulún, Abimé-lech, &c.   Mr Aldis Wright called my attention to this significant pecu-liarity.

[3] The text of the Great Bible is taken from the edition of 1550, which the revisers were most likely to use. The words altered in the Genevan version are italicized : those substi-tuted for them are given afterwards.

and bad.   For who is able to iudge thys, thy *so myghty a* people?

10 And thys pleased the Lorde well, that Salomon had desyred thys thynge.

5 *And :* om. So Pagninus, French 1556. visus*que* Münster. *autem* Leo Juda. (1)

— *thou...it* (so M.): *I shal giue* Postula quod dem tibi J. (2)

6 *in* (M. J.)*: & in* P. Fr. (3)

— *playnnesse: vprightnes* rectitudine P. M. J. d'vn cœur droit enuers toy Fr. (4)

— *that thou* (ut M. J.)*: and* P. (5)

— *seat: throne* super thronum P. (6)

— *it...passe: appeareth* (in ital.) il appert Fr. (secundum diem hanc P. ut est dies hæc M. ut hæc dies [declarat] J.) (7)

7 *it...that: thou* tu m'as fait regner Fr. (Similarly P. M. J.) (8)

— *younge: a yong childe* puer parvus P. M. J. un petit iouuenceau Fr. (9)

— *wot: knowe* (10)

8 *And verelye...they: euen a great people which...* populi multi qui... P. et quidem populus est multus qui M. J. qui est vn grand peuple qui... Fr. (11)

9 *the: thy* ton peuple Fr. (So 1539, P. M. J.) (12)

— *so myghty a: mighty.* (13)

Of these thirteen changes one seems to come from the French (7), two are different readings adopted from Pagninus (1, 3), seven are renderings closer to the Hebrew, chiefly from Pagninus (2, 4, 5, 8, 9, 11, 12), and three are simply linguistic changes (6, 10, 13).

In a passage from Job there is on the other hand considerable originality.

(GREAT BIBLE). 23 O that my wordes were nowe written: O that they were *put* in a boke:

24 *wolde God they were* grauen with an yron penne in leade, or in stone *to continue.*

25 For I am sure, that my redemer lyueth, and *that I shall ryse out of the earth in the latter daye:*

26 *that I shall be clothed agayn with this skynne, and* se God in my flesh.

27 *Yea, I my selfe shal behold him, not with other, but with these same eyes.*

28 *My reines* are consumed within me, *did not ye saye:* why *doth he suffre persecuciō? Is there found an occasion in me?*

23 *put: writen euen*   describerentur P. exarentur J.   (1)

24 *Would...were* (utinam P.): *And* (in italics) stilo*que* J.   (2)

— *to continue: for euer*   ut sint in perpetuum P. ut in perpetuum sint M. quo perpetuo durent J.   (3)

25 *that I...daye: and he shal stand the last on the earth* (novissimus resurget in pulvere M. alternative rendering).   (4)

26 *that...and* se: *And thogh after my skin* wormes *destroy this* bodie, *yet shal I* se (et post pellem meam contritam vermes contriverunt hanc carnem et de carne mea videbo deum P.   Et postquam corroserint (vermes) corpus istud videbo deum de carne mea M.: otherwise J.)   (5)

27 *Yea,...eyes: Whome I my self shal se, and mine eies shal beholde and nonother* for me (quem ego visurus sum mihi, et oculi mei videbunt et non alienus P.   Similarly M. and J.)   (6)

28 *My reines:* thogh *my reines* (none)   (7)

— *did...saye: But ye said* (none)   (8)

— *why doth...persecution:* Why *is he persecuted?* (ob quid patitur persecutionem M.)   (9)

— *Is there...in me?: And there was a depe matter in me* (none)[1]   (10)

Throughout these verses the French rendering is widely different; and of the ten changes introduced into the text

---

[1] The margin of the French Bible of 1559 has *Cause bien fondée.*

of the Great Bible three of considerable importance are
apparently original (7, 8, 10). Of the remainder one
perhaps comes from the version of Leo Juda (2), four
from Pagninus (1, 3, 5, 6), one from Münster (4), and one
is linguistic (9).

The revision of the Prophets is similar in kind to that
of the historical books though the changes are far more
numerous:

(GREAT BIBLE.) 2 The people that *walke* in darckenes
haue sene a greate lyght. *As for them that dwell* in the
lande of the Shadowe of death, vpon them hath the
lyght shyned.

3 Thou hast multyplyed the *people*, & not increased theyr
joye. They *reioyse* before the, *even as men make mery* in
harueste, and as men *that have gotten the victory*, when
they *deale the* spoyle.

4 *For thou hast broken the* yocke of *the peoples* burthen:
the staff of *hys* shoulder and the rod of *his oppressoure*, as
in the *dayes* of Madian.

5 *And trulie* every batayll *that the warryour accomplissheth
is done with confused* noyse, & *defylynge ther* garmentes
with bloude: But *this batayle* shall be with burnynge &
consumynge of fyre.

6 For vnto vs a childe is borne & vnto vs a sonne is geuen.
Vpon hys shoulder doth the kyngdome lye, and *he is called
with hys awne name*, wonderfull: *The geuer of councell*,
the myghtie God, the euerlasting father, the prince of
peace,

7 *he shall make no ende to encrease the kyngdome & peace, &
shall* syt vpon the *seate* of Dauid & *in* his kyngdome, to
set vp the same, & to stablish it with *equytie* and *ryghteousnesse* from hence forth *for euermore.*

2 *walke* (M. J.): *walked* P.   (1)
— *As...dwell: thei that dwelled* habitantibus P. J.   (2)
3 *people: natiō* gentem P. M. J.   (3)
— *reioyse: haue reioyced* lætati sunt P. M. J.   (4)

3 *even...mery: according to the ioye* secundum lætitiam
   P. M. (5)

— *that...victory: reioyce* quemadmodum (sicut M.)
   exultant P. M. J. (6)

— *deale the: diuide a* (7)

4 *For thou...the: For the* (8)

— *the peoples: their* ejus P. M. J. (9)

— *the* (P.): *& the* P. M. J. (10)

— *hys: their* (bis) (11)

— *oppressoure: oppressour hast thou broken* (8)

— *dayes* (temporibus J.)*: day* P. M. (12)

— [*Madian: Midian* P. M. (13)]

5 *And trulie: Surely* (equidem J.) (14)

— *that...accomplissheth* (quod fit per præliantem M.): *of
   the warriour* (profligantis J.) (15)

— *is...confused noyse* (fit strepitu tumultuoso J.): *is with
   noise* So P. M. (16)

— *defylynge ther: with tumbling of* volutatione vest.
   M. J. (17)

— *with: in* So M. J. (18)

— *this batayle* (hoc vero bellum M.): *this* (ital.) (19)

— *consumynge: deuouring* M. J. (20)

6 *Vpon...lye: & the gouernement is vpō his shulder* fuit
   (factus est M.) principatus super humerum ejus P. M.
   otherwise J. (21)

— *he is...name: he shal call his name* (none) (22)

— *The geuer of councell: Coūseller* consiliarius P. M. J.
   Conseillier Fr. (23)

7 *he shall...peace: The increase of his gouernement and peace
   shal haue none end* (Multiplicatio principatus et pax
   (erunt) absque fine M.) (24)

— *& shall: he* shal So J. (25)

— *seate: throne* So P. M. J. (26)

— *in: vpon* So P. M. J. (27)

— *set...same: order it* ut disponat M. (28)

— *equytie: iudgement* judicio P. M. J. jugement Fr. (29)

— *ryghteousnesse: with iustice* justitia P. M. J. justice
   Fr. (30)

7 *for euermore*: euen *for euer* et usque in seculum
    P. M. (31)

Of these thirty-one alterations by far the largest part is
due to the desire of greater literality: no less than fifteen
can be traced to Pagninus (1—6, 9, 10, 12, 13, 16, 21, 23,
27, 31), five to Münster (17, 18, 20, 24, 28), three perhaps
to Leo Juda (14, 15, 25), two are original (19, 22), and six
changes are linguistic (7, 8, 11, 25, 28, 29).

In the Apocryphal books the influence of the French
translation, which was due as we have seen to Beza, is
unmistakeable.   One example may suffice:

GREAT BIBLE, 1550.	GENEVA, 1560.	FRENCH BIBLE (Lyons), 1556[1].
15 God hath graunted me to *talke wisely, and cōueniently to hādle the thinges that he hathe graciouslye lent me.* For *it is he, that leadeth* vnto wisdome, and *teacheth to vse wisdom a right.*	God hathe granted me to *speake according to my minde, and to iudge worthely of the things, that are giuen* me: for *he is the leader* vnto wisdome, and *the director of the wise.*	Et Dieu m'ha donné *de parler à ma volunté, & de presumer choses dignes de celles qui me sont donnees: car cestui est le conducteur* de sapience, & *le correcteur des sages.*
16 In his hande are bothe we and oure wordes: *yea,* all *our* wisdome, *oure vnderstandinge* and knowledge of *all oure* workes.	*For* in his hand are bothe we and our wordes, *and* all wisdome, *& the* knowledge of *the* workes.	*Car* nous sommes en la main d icelui, nous & noz paroles, & aussi toute sapience *& discipline des œuures* de science.
17 For he hathe gyuen me the true *science* of *these* thinges: so that I knowe howe the worlde was made,	For he hathe giuē me the true *knowledge* of *the* things *that are*, so that I knowe how the worlde was made,	Car cestui m'ha donné la vraye *science* des choses *qui sont:* à fin que ie sache la disposition de toute la terre, &

---
[1] I have endeavoured to preserve the original spelling.

GREAT BIBLE, 1550.

GENEVA, 1560.

FRENCH BIBLE (Lyons), 1556.

and the powers of the elementes :

18 the beginninge, endinge, and middest of the times : *how the times altre, howe one goeth after an other, and how they are fulfilled,*

19 the course of the yere: the *ordinaunces* of the starres :

20 the nature *and kyndes of beastes :* the furiousnesse of beastes : the power of the windes : the ymaginacyons of men : the diuersities of *yonge* plantes : the vertues of rootes,

21 and al *such* thinges *as are secrete and not looked for,* haue I learned : For *the workemaster of all thinges hath taught me wisdome...*

27 And *for so muche as she is* one, she *may* do all thinges, and *beinge stedfast* her selfe she renueth all : and *amonge the people*

and the powers of the elements,

The beginning *and the* end, & the middes of the times: how the times alter, *and the change of the seasons;*

The course of the yere, the *situacion* of the starres,

The nature of *liuing things, and* the furiousnes of beasts, the power of ye windes, and the imaginacions of men, the diuersities of plants, *and* the vertues of rootes.

And all things *bothe secret and know-en* do I knowe: for *wisdome the worker of all things, hathe taught me it...*

And *being* one, she *can* do all things, and *remaining in* her self, renueth all, and *according to the ages she entreth* into the holie soules, *and*

les vertus des elemens,

le commencement, *la* consommation & *le* milieu des temps, changemens des mutations, *& les diuisions des temps,* les decours des annees, les *dispositions* des estoilles,

les natures *des animaux, &* les corroux des bestes, la force des vēts, & les cogitations des hommes, les differences des plantes, *&* les vertus des racines: & ay apprins toutes choses *secrettes & manifestes.* Car *l'ouurier de toutes choses m'ha enseigné par sapience*[1]....

Et *combien qu'elle soit* seule, elle *peult* toutes choses, & *estant* en soy *permanente,* elle renouuelle toutes choses, & *par les nations descendant*

---

[1] The revision of 1588 has as a marginal rendering 'car la Sapience   'qui est l'ouvrier de toutes choses 'm'a enseigné.'

GREAT BIBLE, 1550.	GENEVA, 1560.	FRENCH BIBLE (Lyons), 1556.
conueyeth she her selfe into the holy soules. She maketh Gods frendes and prophetes :	*maketh them the friends of God* and Prophetes.	es saintes ames, *elle ordonne les amis de Dieu* & les prophetes.
28 for God loueth *noman but him in whom wisdome dwelleth.*	For God loueth none, *if he dwell not with wisdome.*	Car Dieu *n'* ayme *personne fors que celui, qui habite auec sapience.*
29 For she is more beautyfull then the Sunne & *giueth more light then* the starres, and the *daye* is not to be compared vnto her :	For she is more beautiful then the sunne, and *is aboue all the order of* the starres, and the *light* is not to be compared unto her.	Car icelle est plus belle que le Soleil, & *par dessus toute la disposition* des estoilles, elle comparée à *la lumiere* est trouuée la premiere :
30 for *vpon the day commeth night.* But wickednesse cannot ouercome wisdome, *and foolishnesse maye not be with her.*	For *night cometh vpō it,* but wickednes can not ouercome wisdome.	car *à ceste succede la nuict,* mais malice ne vaincra point sapience.

Conversely the same books shew that the English version influenced the later French revision :

LYONS, 1556.	GENEVA, 1560.	GENEVA, 1588.
19 I'estoye aussi vn enfant ingenieux, & *auoye d'auenture trouué vne bonne ame.*	*For* I was a wittie childe, and *was of a good spirit.*	*Or* estoy-ie aussi vn enfant ingenieux & *m' estoit escheute vne bonne ame :*
20 *Mais estant vn peu meilleur,* ie *vins à* vn corps sans souillure.	*Yea, rather being good,* I *came to* an vndefiled bodie.	*Ou plutost, estant bon, i'estoye venu* en vn corps sans souillure.
21 *Et* quand ie	*Neuertheles, when*	Quand *donc* i'eu

LYONS, 1556.	GENEVA, 1560.	GENEVA, 1588.
congnu *que autrement ne pouuoye estre continent*, si Dieu ne *le* donnoit, & que celà mesmes estoit *souueraine sapience* de sauoir de qui estoit ce don: ie m'en allay *au* Seigneur, & le priay, *& lui dis* de tout mon cœur...	I perceiued *that I colde not enioye her*, except God gaue *her* (and that was *a pointe of wisdome* also, to knowe whose gifte it was) I went *vnto* the Lord, and besoght him, *and* with my whole heart *I said*...	cognu *que ie n'ē pourroy' iouïr*, si Dieu ne me *la* donnoit, & que cela mesme estoit *prudence*, de sauoir de qui estoit ce don, ie m' en allai *supplier le* Seigneur, & le priai, *disant* de tout mon cœur...

The examples which have been given exhibit very fairly the method of revision which was adopted by the Genevan translators in the Old Testament. In all parts they took the Great Bible as their basis and corrected its text, without ever substituting for it a new translation. Even where the changes are greatest the original foundation can still be traced, and the new work fairly harmonizes with the old. One chief aim of the revisers seems to have been to make the translation as nearly verbal as possible, and consequently in a great number of passages they replace the renderings of the Zurich scholars (Coverdale) or Münster by those of Pagninus. At the same time there is abundant evidence to shew that they were perfectly competent to deal independently with points of Hebrew scholarship; and minute changes in expression shew that they were not indifferent to style.

The history of the Genevan New Testament is simpler than that of the Old. It is little more than the record of the application of Beza's translation[1] and commentary to Tindale's Testament in three successive stages, first in the separate New Testament of 1557 (Gt)[2], next in the Bible of 1560 (G), and lastly in the New Testament of

---

[1] [In quoting Beza's translation I have only referred to the editions of 1556 and 1559 by which alone the Genevan version of 1560 could be influenced. W. A. W.]

[2] See p. 223, n. 4.

L. Tomson in 1576[1] (T). The revisers undoubtedly exercised an independent judgment in following his renderings. They did not adopt all the alterations which he suggested; and at times they introduced original phrases; but by far the greater part of the changes which were made in the text of Tindale were simply due to Beza[2].

An analysis of the changes in one short Epistle will render this plain. Thus, according to as accurate a calculation as I can make, more than two-thirds of the new renderings in 1 John introduced into the revision of 1560 are derived from Beza, and two-thirds of these then for the first time. The rest are due mainly to the revisers themselves[3], and of these only two are found in the revision of 1557. Tomson adds barely five or six closer approximations to Beza, of which one is important (v. 4 'hath overcome'); and once he definitely goes against him (iv. 9 'Herein was that love of God made manifest 'amongst us').

The general conclusion thus indicated will be made still clearer by an examination of two short continuous passages. The differences between the first New Testament and the New Testament in the Bible (1560) will thus appear, and it will be seen that the revision in the latter extended to points of language as well as to points of interpretation[4]:

---

[1] Tomson's New Testament presents the fullest form of Beza's influence. One peculiarity is characteristic of Tomson alone. In his anxiety to express the emphatic force of the Greek article he constantly renders it by 'that' or 'this,' and in many cases the effect is almost grotesque. One example will suffice: 'He that hath 'that Son hath that life: and he that 'hath not that Son of God hath not 'that life' (1 John v. 12).

[2] The basis of the Genevan Testament was certainly Tindale's (the last text, i.e. Matthew) and not the Great Bible. See for instance Gal. i. 10, 14, 15, 19, 21: ii. 1, 2, 5, 6, 9, 10, 11, &c. The corresponding coincidences of the Genevan Testament with the Great Bible against Tindale are very few: Gal. i. 9, 12: ii. 4.

[3] The most striking are: ii. 18, 19, 20, 29: iv. 5: v. 6.

[4] It is very greatly to be regretted that the New Testament of 1557 and not the New Testament of the Bible has been reprinted in Bagster's Hexapla as the Genevan version. The confusion which has resulted from this error of judgment has led to end-

(TINDALE, 1534.)   12 *Remēber I saye, y^t ye were at* that
tyme w^t oute Christ, & were *reputed* aliantes from
the cōmen welth of Israel, & were straũgers[1] frō the
testament of promes, & had no hope, & were with out
god in *this* worlde.

13 But now in Christ *Iesu*, ye which *a whyle agoo*[2] were
farre of, are made *nye* by ye bloude of Christ.

14 For he is oure peace, whych hath made of both one,
·and hath *broken doune the wall y^t was a stoppe bi-
twene vs,*

15 *and hath also put awaye* thorow his flesshe, the *cause of*
hatred (that is *to saye*, the lawe[3] of commaundementes
contayned in the lawe written) for to make of twayne
one newe mā in him silfe, so makynge peace:

16 and *to* recōcile both vnto god in one body *thorow* his
crosse, and *slewe* hatred therby:

17 and came and preached peace to you which were a farre
of, and to them that were *nye.*

18 For thorow him we both have an *open waye in, in one
sprete vnto the father.*

12 *Remēber...at* Gt: *That yē were*, I say, G. T.[4]   (*vos
inquam...fuisse* B.)   (1)

— *reputed* Gt: om. G. T. (so B.)   (2)

— *testamentes : couenants* Gt. G. T.   (pactis B. 1556,
      1559)   (3)

— *this* Gt: *the* G. T.   (in mundo B.)   (4)

13 *Iesu : Iesus* Gt. G. T.   (5)

— *a whyle agoo : once* Gt. G. T.   (olim B.)   (6)

---

less mistakes in discussions on the
Authorized Version.   The Testament
of 1557 has had no independent influence on the A.V. as far as I can
see.   Compare Mr F. Fry on *The
English New Testament of the Genevan Version* in the *Journal of Sacred
Literature*, July, 1864.

[1] The Great Bible reads : being
aliantes from...and straungers...

[2] somtyme (G. B.).

[3] euen the lawe (G. B.).

[4] The Testament of 1557 is marked
by Gt and quoted from Bagster's
Hexapla : G represents the first edition of the Bible 1560 : T, Tomson's
Testament quoted from the Bible of
1576.   The rendering of Beza is
marked B.   G gives the following
words in italics : Eph. ii. 2 *I say, were*
1°;   15 *that is, which standeth, so* ;
16 *his.*   Rev. ii. 9 *I knowe, are* 2°.

13 *nye* Gt: *nere* G. T.   (7)

— *the bloude* I say *of Christe* Gt.   (inquam B. 1556, 1559)
G. omits *I say*.   (8)

14 *broken...vs : broken the stoppe of the particion wall* Gt.
G. T. (intergerini parietis septum B.)   (9)

15 *and...awaye: In abrogating* Gt. G. T.   (inimicitiis...
abrogatis B. 1556, 1559)   (10)

— *cause of* om. Gt. G. T.   (so B.)   (11)

— *to saye* Gt: om. G. T.   (so B.)   (12)

— *contayned...written:* which standeth *in ceremonies* (*or-
dinances* G. T.) Gt. G. T.   (quæ in ritibus posita
est B.)   (13)

16 *to : that he myght* Gt. G. T.   (ut conderet...et ut recon-
ciliaret B.)   (14)

— *thorow : by*   Gt. G. T.   (per B.)   (15)

— *slewe : slaye*   Gt. G. T.   (16)

17 *and to them that were nye* (*and nye* Gt): *& to them
that were nere* G. T.   (17)

18 *open waye in, in* (*by* Gt) *one sprete vnto the father :
entrance* (so Great Bible) *vnto the Father by one
Spirit* G. T.   (aditum per unum Spiritum ad Patrem
B.)   (18)

Thus it will be seen that the Testament (Gt 1557)
differs from the Bible (1560) in nine places, half of the
whole number (1, 2, 4, 7, 8, 12, 13, 17, 18), and of these
variations two are of considerable importance (2, 17).   In
one case the Bible deserts Beza where the Testament
followed him (13), one change is simply linguistic (7), but
in the other seven cases the Bible is supported by Beza.
Of the remaining nine changes common to the Testament
and Bible five are in accordance with Beza (3, 9, 11, 14,
15), one is perhaps independent of him (6), and the remaining three are changes of expression (5, 10, 16).   In this
passage Tomson agrees with the Bible.

(TINDALE, 1534.)   8 And unto the angell of the *congregacion* of *Smyrna* wryte: These thynges sayth he

that is fyrste, and *the* laste, which was deed and is alive.

9 I knowe thy workes and tribulacion and poverte, but thou art ryche: And I knowe the blaspemy of them whiche *call them selves* Iewes, and are not: but are the *congregaciō* of sathan.

10 Feare none of thoo thynges which thou shalt soffre. Beholde, *the devyll* shall caste *of* you into preson, *to tempte you*, and ye shall have tribulacion .x. dayes. *Be* faythfull vnto the deeth and I will geve thee *a* crown of lyfe.

11 Let him that hath *ears* heare, what the sprete sayth to the *congregacions*: He that overcōmeth shall not be hurte of the seconde deeth.

8 *congregacion* of *Smyrna*: *Church* of *the Smyrnians* Gt. G. T. (Smyrnæorum B. 1559) (Smyrnæ Ecclesiæ B. 1556) (1)

— *the*: om. Gt. G. T. (2)

9 *call them selves* Gt.: *say they are* G. T. (se dicunt... esse B.) (3)

— *congregacion*: *Synagogue* Gt. G. T. (synagoga B.) (4)

10 *the devyll*: *it shall come to passe, that the d.* Gt. G. T. (futurum est ut...B.) (5)

— *of*: *some of* (so Great Bible) Gt. G. T. (6)

— *to...you*: *that ye may be tryed* Gt. G. T. (ut exploremini B. 1559   ut tentemini B. 1556) (7)

— *Be* Gt.: *be thou* G. T. (8)

— *a*: *the* Gt. G. T. (9)

11 *ears*: *an eare* Gt. G. T. (aurem B.) (10)

— *congregacions*: *Churches* Gt. G. T. (ecclesiis B.) (11)

In this passage again Tomson's text agrees with that of the Bible[1]. The Testament differs from it twice (3, 8), and in both cases the Bible agrees with Beza. The remaining nine changes are all, as far as the Latin can express them, in accordance with Beza, and one is evidently due to him (5).

[1] An important example of his disagreement is given below, p. 228, n. 1.

It is of more importance to place in a clear light the real origin of the changes in the English Genevan New Testament, because very many of them have passed from that into our own Bible, and it has been forgotten to whom the renderings are due. Thus Archbp Trench quotes five passages to shew[1] 'the very good and careful scholarship 'brought to bear upon this [the Genevan] revision,' in which 'it is the first to seize the exact meaning...which 'all the preceding versions had missed.' They are all derived from Beza. In one case the English translator has adopted his alternative rendering; in the four others he simply takes Beza's translation:

Luke xi. 17 one housse shall (doth *Great Bible*) fall upon another (*Tindale G.B.*).
　　domus super domum cadit (*Erasmus*).
　　domus adversus se partita cadit (*Beza* 1556, 1559).
　　a house deuided against it self (an house G. T.) falleth (Gt).

Acts xxiii. 27 cam I...and rescued him, and perceaved that he was a Romayne (*Tind. G.B.*).
　　superveniens...exemi, cognito quod Romanus esset (*Beza* 1556, 1559).
　　I came...& rescued him, perceauing that he was a Romaine (Gt).

Acts xxvii. 9 because also that we (they *G.B.*) had over-longe fasted (*Tind. G.B.*).
　　quod jam etiam jejunium [tempus designat Lucas ex more Judaici populi] praeteriisset (*Beza*).
　　because also ye tyme of (om. the time of G. T.) the Fast was now passed (Gt).

James i. 13 God tempteth not (cannot tempt *G.B.*) unto evil (*Tind. G.B.*).
　　Deus tentari malis non potest (*Beza*).
　　God cannot be tempted with euyl (Gt)[2].

---

[1] *On the Authorized Version*, p. 113 n.
[2] This rendering (as we have seen, p. 197) is found in the Great Bible after the first edition.

Mark xiv. 72 [he] began to weep (*Tind. G.B.*).
    animum adiiciens flevit (*Beza* 1556, 1559 *not.*).
    waying that with himselfe, he wept (Gt).

The credit of recognizing the right turning remains, but the Genevan translator can have no claim to original sagacity on this evidence.

To place the relation of the Genevan translator to Beza in a still clearer light it will be worth while, though it is an ungracious task, to quote an equal number of cases where under the same influence the Genevan version first goes wrong.

Matt. i. 11 Iosias begate *Iacim And Iacim begate Iechonias*.
Luke ii. 22 When the tyme of *Maries* purification...was
    come.
Luke iii. 36 (Sala) which was the sonne of Arphaxad...
Rev. xi. 1 Then was geven me a rede, lyke vn to a rodde,
    and the Angel stode by, saing...
Hebr. x. 38 But if *any* withdraw him selfe.
Mark xvi. 2 When the sunne *was yet rysing*.

Of these, which include four arbitrary corrections of the text, the second and fourth and fifth have been incorporated in our present version: the first was abandoned by Beza in his third edition: the sixth is suggested in a note[1] and has modified the received rendering.

A comparison of the two groups of passages will shew at once the strength and the weakness of Beza, and so of the revisions which were moulded after him. In the interpretation of the text he was singularly clear-sighted: in the criticism of the text he was more rash than his contemporaries in proportion as his self-reliance was greater. But though it is a far more grievous matter to corrupt the text than to misinterpret it, the cases in which Beza has corrected the renderings of former translators

---

[1] One still more surprising change has been adopted in A.V. though it is not in 1557, $\dot{\alpha}\pi o\theta\alpha\nu\acute{o}\nu\tau os$ for $\dot{\alpha}\pi o$- $\theta\alpha\nu\acute{o}\nu\tau\epsilon s$ in Rom. vii. 6 (He being dead in whom we were holden, T.).

are incomparably more numerous than those in which he has introduced false readings; and on the whole his version is far superior to those which had been made before, and so consequently the Genevan revisions which follow it[1].

The notes of the Genevan Version contributed so greatly to its influence that some examples of them may be added which will be sufficient to shew the general character and scope of the commentary.

'Thogh we prouoke God iustly to angre, yet he wil 'neuer reiect his.

'God repeteth this point because the whole keping of 'the Lawe standeth in the true vse of the Sabbath, w^c is to 'cease from our workes. & to obey the wil of Ged.

'For finding nothing in mā that cā deserue mercie, he 'wil frely saue his.

'Hereby it appeareth that Naomi by dwellīg amōg 'idolaters was waxen colde in ye true zeale of God, w^c 'rather hathe respect to the ease of ye body than to y^e 'comfort of ye soule.

'Herein he shewed y^t he lacked zeale: for she oght to 'haue dyed bothe by the couenant, and by the Lawe of 'God: but he gaue place to foolish pitie, & wolde also 'seme after a sorte to satisfie the Lawe.

'Tabór is a moūtaine Westwarde frō Ierusalē, & 'Hermón Eastwarde: so the Prophet signifieth y^t all 'partes & places of the worlde shal obey Gods power for 'the deliuerance of his Church.

'He speaketh this for two causes: ye one, because 'he y^t was a mortal creature, and therefore had more nede 'to glorifie God then the Angels, did it not: and the other, 'because ye more nere y^t man approcheth to God, the more 'doeth he knowe his owne sinne, & corruption.

---

[1] The books of the Bible are thus arranged:
'The Names and order of all the 'Books of the Old and New Testa-'ment...' ['Genesis...Malachi.
'The Books called Apocrypha. 1 'Esdr. 2 Esdr.—1 Macc. 2 Macc.
'The Books of the New Testa-'ment. Matthew...The Epistle of 'Paul to the Romans...Titus, Phile-'mon. To the Ebrewes. James... 'Jude. Revelation.'

'If the sunne, moone, and starres can not but giue
'light according to mine ordinance, so long as this worlde
'lasteth, so shal my Church neuer faile, nether shal anie
'thing hinder it: and as sure as I wil haue a people, so
'certeine is it, that I wil leaue them my worde for euer to
'gouerne them with.

'He deuided the law of nature corrupt into vngodlines,
'& vnrighteousnes. Vngodlines conteineth the false wor-
'shiping of God: vnrighteousnes, breache of loue towarde
'man.

'As the onelie wil & purpose of God is the chief cause
'of election & reprobacion, so his fre mercie in Christ
'is an inferior cause of saluacion, & the hardening of the
'heart, an inferior cause of damnacion.

'Open that w^c greueth you, y^t a remedie may be
'founde: and this is cōmanded bothe for him y^t com-
'plaineth, & for hī that heareth y^t the one shulde shew his
'grief to the other.

'The soules of the Saintes are vnder the altar which
'is Christ, meanīg that they are in his safe custodie in the
'heauens.

'Locustes are false teachers, heretikes, and worldlie
'suttil Prelates, with Monkes, Freres, Cardinals, Patriarkes,
'Archebishops, Bishops, Doctors, Baschelers & masters
'which forsake Christ to mainteine false doctrine[1].'

§7. THE BISHOPS' BIBLE.

The correspondence on the subject of the Bishops'
Bible which has been already quoted explains the general
design of the revisers[2].   It was their object to remove
from the Great Bible all errors which seemed to impair
the sense, and at the same time to produce a popular
and not a literary version. In both respects—in the
alteration of the renderings and in the alteration of the

---

[1] In the New Testament the notes
in the Bible (1560) differ from those
in the Testament of 1557 (e.g. Matt.
xxviii. 15; Mark i. 1; Rom. xvi. 7),
but chiefly by additions made in the
Bible.

[2] See pp. 96 ff.

language—they proposed at least in the first instance to confine themselves to necessary changes, for the revision was essentially conservative in its conception. But in the execution of the plan some of the revisers certainly made use of far wider liberty than the original scheme permitted.

The execution of the work is indeed, if a very partial examination may be trusted, extremely unequal; and the Greek scholarship of the revisers is superior to their Hebrew scholarship. How far the separate sections are marked by the special characteristics of the men engaged upon them I cannot say, and the inquiry is not one which would reward the labour which it would cost. Still the revision has received far less attention than it deserves, and in the New Testament it shews considerable vigour and freshness.

The historical books of the Old Testament follow the text of the Great Bible very closely[1]. The Hagiographa, as far as I have examined them, are corrected with considerable freedom. The Prophets are altered very frequently, but in these the new renderings can generally be traced to some other source. The influence of the Genevan revision is perceptible throughout, but it is more obvious in the Prophets than elsewhere. Castalio was certainly consulted and had some influence with the revisers, but with the exception of the Genevan version itself no fresh sources were open to them in addition to those which the Genevan exiles had used[2].

One or two passages will illustrate what has been said[3].

---

[1] [This is not strictly accurate. The changes may not be important, but they are numerous. In Gen. i. out of 31 verses 22 are altered. In Gen. ii. out of 25 verses 17 are altered. In Gen. xiv. out of 24 verses 17 are altered. In Gen. xxii. out of 22 verses 12 are altered. In Gen. xxiv. out of the first 14 verses 8 are altered. In Ruth iii. out of 18 verses 8 are altered. These instances are taken from the narrative portions of the historical books. In the poetical parts, such as Gen. xlix., Ex. xv., Num. xxiii., xxiv., Deut. xxxii., xxxiii., Judg. v., 1 Sam. ii., 2 Sam. i., xxii., xxiii., 1 Chr. xvi., the changes are equally numerous.]

[2] See pp. 212, 213.

[3] The passages are taken from the Great Bible of 1550. The readings of the Bishops' Bible are from the first edition of 1568.

GREAT BIBLE, 1550[1].   1 But who hath geuen credence vnto *the thing we haue heard?*   Or to whom is the arme of the Lorde knowne?

2 For he dyd grow before the Lord lyke as a braunch and as a rote in a drye groūd.   He hath nether bewtye nor fauour.   When we *shall loke* vpon him, there shalbe no fayrnesse : we shal haue no lust vnto him.

3 He is despysed and abhorred of men, he is suche a mā as *is full of sorowe and as hath good experience of infirmyties.* We haue rekened him so vyle, that we hyd oure faces from him, *yee he was dispysed & therfore we regarded him not.*

4 Howebeit he only hath taken on him our *infirmities* & borne our paynes.   Yet we dyd iudge him, as though he were plaged & cast downe of God : *& punished*

5 where as he (*not with standinge*) was woūded for our offences, & smyttē for our wickenes.   For the *chastisemēt of our peace* was layde vpon him, and with his stripes are we healed.

6 As for vs, we *haue* gone all astray (lyke shepe) euery one hath turned his owne waye.   But the lorde hath *heaped together* vpon him *the iniquitie of us all.*

7 He suffered violence and was euel intreated : and dyd not *yet* opē his mouth.   He shall be led as a shepe to be slayne, yet shal he be as styl as a lambe before the shearer, and not open his mouth.

8 *He was had awaye frō prison: his cause not hearde and without any iudgement.   Whose generation yet who may numbre?   he* was cut of from the grounde of the lyuinge : whiche punishment dyd go vpon him for the transgression of my people, *which in dede had deserued that punishement.*

9 His graue was geuen him with the condempned, and with the ryche man at his death,   Where as he did neuer violence : nor vnright, neyther hath there bene any disceatfulnesse in his mouth.

---

[1] The italics, as before, indicate words and phrases which were changed in the revision.   The renderings substituted are given in detail afterwards.

10 Yet hath it pleased the Lorde *thus, to bruste him with plages, and to smite* him with infirmitie, that when he had made his soule an offeringe for sinne, he might see longe lastinge sede. And this deuyce of the Lorde shall prosper in his hande.

11 *With trauayle and laboure of his soule, shall he optayne fruyte, and he shalbe* satisfied *by the knowledge of him whiche is my righteous seruaunte: he shal* iustifie the multitude, for he shall *beare awaye* their sinnes.

12 Therfore will I geue him *the multitude for* his parte: and he shall deuyde the spoyle with the *strongest,* because he geueth ouer his soule to death: And is rekened amonge the transgressours, which neuertheles hath taken away the sinnes of the multitude, and made intercession for the misdoers.

1 *the thinge we haue heard: our preaching* (our reporte Geneva 1560) prædicationi nostræ Leo Juda[1] (1)

2 *shall* loke. (shall se G.) : *loke* videmus J. (2)

3 as *is full...infirmyties:* as *hath good experience of sorowes and infirmities.* homo dolorum ægritudinisque gnarus C. (3)

— *yee he was dispysed & therfore we regarded him not* (similarly G. and all) : *omit* (4)

4 *infirmities* (so all) : *infirmitie* (5)

— *& punished* (and humbled G., similarly all) : *omit* (6)

5 *not with standinge:* (in brackets and smaller type). (*om.* G.) (7)

— *the chastisemēt of our peace* (so P. M. G.) : *the payne of our punishment* mulcta correctionis nostræ J. (8)

6 we *haue* gone all (G.) : we *are* all gone (9)

— *heaped together...all* (hathe layed vpon hym the iniquitie of vs all G.) : *throwen* vpon hym *all our sinnes* in eum omnium nostrum crimen conjecit C. (10)

7 dyd not *yet* (similarly M. J. G.) : dyd not P. (11)

8 *He was had awaye.. iudgement: From the prison and*

---

[1] The translation of Leo Juda will be indicated by J. The Geneva version and the versions of Pagninus, Münster, and Castalio are indicated by G, P, M, C.

iudgement was he taken (he was taken out from prison
and from judgment G.): so P. C. otherwise J.   (12)

8 *Whose* generation...*numbre: and his* generation who *can
declare?* (and who shall declare his age? G.) genera-
tionem ejus quis enarrabit P. M.   (13)

— *he* was : *for he* was (so P. M. J. G.)   (14)

which...punishement (M): *om.* (so P. J. G.)   (15)

10 *thus, to bruste him with plages, and* to smite (somewhat
similarly P. M. G.): to smite (infirmando atterere
J.) (libuit autem Jovæ eum ægritudine contun-
dere C.)   (16)

11 *With trauayle...shalbe...*: *Of the* trauayle and labour of
his soule *shall he see the fruite & be...*so M. (he shal
se of the trauayl of his soule, (and) shalbe...G.)   (17)

— *by the knowledge...shal* iustifie (M.): *My righteous seruaunt shall with his knowledge* iustifie (by his knowledge shall my righteous servant justify many G.)
cognitione sui multos justificabit justus servus meus J.
similarly C.   (18)

— *beare awaye...*: beare.. (so P. M. J. C.)   (19)

12 *the multitude for* his parte.... *among the great ones* his
part... (give him a portion with the great G.) similarly
P. M. C. otherwise J.   (20)

— the *strongest* (M): the *mightie* (the strong G.) fortibus
P. J.   (21)

Thus of the twenty-one corrections five are due to the
Genevan version (7, 12, 18, 20, 21): five more agree with
Pagninus (11, 13, 14, 15, 19): three with Leo Juda (1, 2, 8):
three with Castalio (3, 10, 16); and one with Münster (17).
One change is simply linguistic (9), and three are apparently
original (4, 5, 6).

In a passage from the Psalms the reviser shews far
greater originality and the influence of the Genevan revision
is considerably less[1]:

[1] [The original version of the Psalms
in the Bishops' Bible of 1568 was reprinted in the quarto edition of 1569
and in the folio of 1572, where it was
accompanied by the Great Bible version printed side by side with it. It
only appeared once more, in the Bible
of 1585. One peculiarity of this ver-

GREAT BIBLE 1550. 1 The heauens declare the glory of God, & the firmamente sheweth his handy worcke.

2 *One day telleth another: and one nighte certifieth another.*

3 *There is nether speache ner langage, but their voyces are heard amonge them.* Their sounde is gone out (*gone* May 1541) into all lādes : & their wordes īto the endes of the world.

4 In them *hath he* set a tabernacle for the sunne, whiche commeth forth as a brydgrome out of his chaumbre, and reioyseth as a giaunt to runne his course.

5 *It goeth furthe* from the vtmost parte of *the* heauen, and *runneth about* vnto the *ende of it agayne,* and there is nothinge hid from *the heate therof.*

6 The lawe of *the Lord* is *an vndefiled law* cōuerting the soule. The testemony of *the Lorde* is sure, and geueth wisdome, vnto the simple.

7 The statutes of *the Lorde* are righte and reioyse the herte, the commaundement of *the Lorde* is pure and gyueth lighte vnto the eyes.

8 The feare of *the Lorde* is *cleane,* and endureth for euer, the iudgementes of *the Lorde* are *true and righteous all together.*

9 *More to be desired are they* then golde, ye then much fine golde : *sweter also* then honye, and the hony combe.

10 Moreouer, by thē *is* thy seruaunt *taught,* and in kepinge of them there is *greate* rewarde.

11 Who can *tell, how ofte he offendeth?* Oh clense thou me frō (*my*) secrete fautes.

12 Kepe thy seruaunte also from presumptuous *sinnes, Lest they get the dominion* ouer me: so *shal I* be *vndefiled,* and *innocente frome the greate* offence.

13 Let the wordes of my mouth and the meditacyon of my herte be (alwaye) acceptable in thy sight. O *Lorde,* my strength and my redemer.

2 *One...another:* A day occasioneth talke therof vnto a day: and a night teacheth knoweledge vnto a nyght.*

sion is that the words 'God' and 'Lord' are almost uniformly inter- changed, as will be seen in the examples here given.]

(Daie vnto daie vttereth the same, and night vnto night teacheth knowledge **G.**) similarly P. M.   (1)

3 *There is...gone out: No language, no wordes, no voyce of theirs is hearde: yet their sounde goeth* (non est [illis] sermo, non verba, neque auditur vox eorum, in omnem tamen... J.)   (2)

4 *hath he: he hath*   (3)

5 *It...furthe: His settyng foorth is* egressus ejus **M.**   his going out is **G.**   (4)

— *the:* om.   (5)

— *runneth about: his circuite* revolutio ejus P. M.   his compas **G.**   (6)

— *ende of it agayne: vtmost part therof* ad extrema eorum M. J.   (7)

— *the* heate *therof: his* heat   (8)

6 *the Lord: God* (so throughout), not P. M. J. G. C.   (9)

— *an vndefiled law: perfect* **G.**   (10)

8 *cleane* (P. J. G.): *sincere* sincerus **M.**   (11)

— *true* (J.): *trueth* P. M. G.   (12)

— *and...all together: they be iust in all poyntes* (justificata pariter P. M.   simulque justa J.)   (13)

9 *More...they: They are more to be desired...*   (14)

— *sweter also* (G.): *they are also sweeter*   (15)

10 *is...taught:* thy servaunt *is well aduertised.*   (perspicue admonetur J.)   (16)

— *greate* (G): *a great*   (17)

11 *tell...offendeth: knowe his owne errours* (errores quis intelligit M.   errores quis animadvertat J.)   (18)

— *(my) secret faults: those that I am not priuie of*   (19)

12 *sinnes:* [*sinnes*]   (20)

— *Lest...dominion: let them not raigne*   So **G.**   (ne dominentur mihi   P. M. J.)   (21)

— *shal...vndefiled: I shall be perfect* perfectus ero P.   (22) *innocente...greate: voyde from all haynous* (innocens a quovis grandiori scelere J.)   (23)

13 (alway): *omit.*   So **G.**   (24)

— *Lorde: God*   (25)

Of these changes one-fifth appear to be original (1, 5, 13, 20, 25): seven more are linguistic (3, 8, 9, 14, 15, 17, 19): three are coincidences with Pagninus (6, 12, 22): five with Leo Juda (2, 7, 16, 18, 23); four with the Genevan version (4, 10, 21, 24): and one with Münster (11).

There is but little to recommend the original renderings of the Bishops' Bible in the Old Testament. As a general rule they appear to be arbitrary and at variance with the exact sense of the Hebrew text[1]. The revision of the New Testament however will repay careful study.

Among the revisers was Lawrence, 'a man in those 'times of great fame for his knowledge in the Greek[2],' of whose labours Strype has preserved a singularly interesting memorial in a series of 'notes of errors in the 'translation of the N. T.[2]' Some of these are worthy of quotation.

Matt. xxi. 33. '*There was a certain man, an house-* '*holder, which made a vineyard.* ὅστις ἐφύτευσεν ἀμπε- 'λῶνα (that is) *which planted a vineyard.* The word '(made) is too general...I allow not such generalities in 'translation when our tongue hath as apt words as the ' Greek, *ib.* he putteth (made) for ὤρυξεν (that is) he *digged.* 'The first error is amended in the Geneva Bible; the 'second is noted in the margin.'

Matt. xxv. 20. '*I have gained with them five talents* '*more:* ἄλλα πέντε τάλαντα ἐκέρδησα ἐπ' αὐτῇ, signifieth '*over* and *besides* them...'

---

[1] It is possible that I have been unfortunate in the parts which I have examined; for what I saw did not encourage me to compare very much of the Bishops' text with the other versions.

[2] Strype's *Parker*, ii. 223. [There is no reason to suppose that Lawrence was a reviser. He seems to have criticised certain passages in the translation of the New Testament of 1568, and his notes were at one time in the possession of Strype. It has been conjectured that he was Thomas Law-rence, who was headmaster of Shrewsbury School, but this is impossible. Strype says the writer of the notes was an eminent Greek scholar who had taught Greek to Lady Burghley, once Mildred Cooke. Now Mildred Cooke was married in 1545, when Thomas Lawrence, who took his degree in 1566, must have been an infant. It was no doubt Giles Lawrence, Professor of Greek at Oxford, to whom Strype referred.]

[3] Strype, App. LXXXV. Lawrence notices twenty-nine passages.

Matt. xxviii. 14. '*We will save you harmless:* ἀμερίμ-
'*νους* (that is,) *careless:* ἀβλαβής or ἀζήμιος is *harmless:*
'*ἀμέριμνος, careless.* I may be *harmless* in body and
'goods, and yet not *careless.* This is not considered in
'the Geneva Bible.'

Luke i. 3, 4. '*I determined also, as soon as I had searched*
'*out diligently all things from the beginning that then I*
'*would write unto thee...that thou...hast been informed.*'
This Lawrence translates: '*It seemed good to me having*
'*perfect understanding* [as they that follow foot by foot]
'*of all things from the beginning to write to thee in order...*
'*that thou...hast been taught by mouth.*'

Mark xv. 3. 'These words αὐτὸς δὲ οὐδὲν ἀπεκρίνατο
'be omitted both here and in the Geneva translation. Yet
'the Greek printed by Stephanus hath it.'

Mark xiii. 16. '*Let him that is in the field not turn*
'*back again unto the things which he left behind him.* For
'all these words there be no more in the Greek but, ὁ εἰς
'τὸν ἀγρον ὤν, μὴ ἐπιστρεψάτω εἰς τὰ ὀπίσω (that is) *he*
'*that is in the field let him not turn back.* εἰς τὰ ὀπίσω
'signifieth no more but *back:* John vi. 66...This superfluity
'is in the Geneva translation.'

It is not known how far Lawrence's labours extended,
but an examination of a difficult passage of an Epistle will
prove that the reviser who corrected it was not deficient
in originality and vigorous scholarship[1]:

GREAT BIBLE, 1550. 7 *Vnto* euery one of vs is geuen
grace, accordyng to the measure of the gifte of
Christ.

8 Wherfore he saith: when he wente vp on hye, he led
captuitie captiue and gaue giftes vnto men.

9 *That* he ascended: what *meaneth* it? but that he also
descended fyrst into the *lowest* partes of the erthe?

10 He that descended, is euen the same also that ascended
vp, *aboue* all heauens, to fulfill al thinges.

11 And *the very same made* some Apostles, *some* Prophetes,
some Euangelistes, *some* Shepherdes and Teachers:

[1] The text is taken as before from the Great Bible of 1550.

12 to the *edifyinge* of the saynctes, *to* the worke *and* ministracion, *euen to* the edifyinge of the bodye of Christe,

13 till we all *come to* the vnitie of faith, and knowlege of the sonne of God, vnto a perfect man, vnto the measure of the *full perfite age* of Christ.

14 That we hence forthe *shoulde* be nomore children, wauerynge and caryed aboute with euery wynde of doctrine, *by* the wilynes of men, *thorowe* craftynes *whereby they laye a wayt for vs to deceaue vs.*

15 But *let vs folowe the* trueth in loue, *and in all thynges growe in him*, which is the head, *euen* Christ,

16 in whome *if* all the bodye *be* coupled and knet together *thorowe oute* euery ioynt *wherwith one ministreth to another* (according to the *operacion as euery parte hath his measure*) *he* icreaseth the body, vnto the edifyinge of it self *thorowe* loue.

7 Vnto: *But* vnto G.[1] (1)

9 That: *But* that (Now, in that G.) (2)

— *meaneth: is* G. (3)

— *lowest* G.: *lower* (4)

10 aboue: *farre* aboue G. (5)

11 *the very...made: he gaue* G. (6)

— some (three times): *and* some G. (7

12 *edifyinge: gatheryng together* G.: that the Saincts myght be gathered together Gt. for the repairing of the saints T. (8)

— *to: into* (9)

— *and: of* (10)

— *euen to: into* (11)

13 *come to: meete together into* (meet together, in G.) (12)

— *full...age: age of the fulnesse* G. (13)

14 shoulde: *omit* G. (14)

— *by: in* (15)

---

[1] The notation is the same as before. The Testament of the Genevan Bible (1560) is represented by G, the Genevan Testament by Gt, Tomson's revision by T. The readings of the Bishops' Bible are taken from the first edition of 1568. See p. 241.

14 *thorowe: in* (16)

— *whereby...vs* (whereby they laye in waite to deceiue G.):
    to the laying wayte of deceyte (17)

15 *let vs folowe* G.: *folowyng* (18)

— *and in...him: let vs growe vp into him in all thynges*
    (and in all things growe vp into him G.) (19)

— euen: *om.* (20)

16 if: *om.* G. (21)

— *be: beyng* G. (22)

— *thorowe oute...another: by euery ioynt of subministration*
    (by euerie ioynt, for the furniture thereof G.) (23)

— *operacion...measure: effectuall power in* y^e *measure of*
    euery part (effectual power, which is in &c. G.)
    (24)

— *he icreaseth: maketh increase of* (receiueth increase of
    G.) (25)

— *thorowe: in* G. (26)

Of these twenty-six variations no less than sixteen are
new, while only ten are due to the Genevan version; and
the character of the original corrections marks a very close
and thoughtful revision based faithfully upon the Greek.
The anxiously literal rendering of the particles (2) and
prepositions (9, 11, 12, 15, 16) is specially worthy of notice:
so too the observance of the order (19), and of the original
form of the sentences (17, 18, 20, 23, 24), even where some
obscurity follows from it. In five places the Authorised
Version follows the Bishops' renderings (3, 4, 10, 25, 26);
and only one change appears to be certainly for the worse
in which the rendering of the Genevan Testament has been
followed (8 Beza *ad coagmentationem*). The singular independence of the revision as compared with those which
have been noticed before is shewn by the fact that only
four (3, 10, 11, 18) of the new changes agree with Beza
and at least nine are definitely against him (4, 12, 15, 16,
17, 20, 23, 24, 25)[1].

[1] According to Mr Offor (MS.
Collections, III. 54 ff.) the New Testament in the Bishops' Bible is taken
from a revision of Sir J. Cheke's (?)
New Testament published by Jugge
in 1561. The collations which he

In 1572 a new edition of the Bishops' Bible was published. In this the translation of the Old Testament, as far as I have been able to examine it, is unchanged, but that of the New Testament is carefully revised. The later editions follow this revision with very few intentional variations; and I am not aware that the text of 1568 was ever reprinted. As was natural this second edition was taken as the basis of the Authorised Version, though there are numerous cases in which the rendering of the edition of 1568 is restored there[1]. The collation of a single epistle will shew the extent of the differences, and the proportion in which the respective readings were preferred by King James' revisers[2].

BISHOPS' BIBLE 1568.	BISHOPS' BIBLE 1572, 1578.
Eph. i. 2 Grace be...& from	grace [be]...and [from] A.V. 1569 (1)
— 5 predestinate 1569	predestinated A.V. (2)
— 10 heauen A.V.	heauens 1569 A.V. mg. (3)
— 13 In whom also ye	In whom also ye [hoped] 1569 (similarly A.V.) (4)
— 21 not in this worlde only 1569	not only in this worlde only (1572) (5)
	not onely in this world (1575—1602) A.V.
ii. 1 And you	And [he quickened] you 1569 (similarly A.V.) (6)
— 5 by grace are ye saved (A.V. ye are)	by [whose] grace ye are saued 1569 (7)
— 6 in the heauenly	in heauenly thynges 1569 (8)

gives of John i., Acts i., Rom. i., Rev. i., certainly go far to establish the statement, but I have not been able to consult the edition referred to. The Testament which answers to it in Dr Cotton's list is described as 'Tindale's.' Mr F. Fry has taken great pains to ascertain the truth of this statement, but has not been able to find the least trustworthy evidence in support of it. [I have not been able to verify all the statements in this paragraph with regard to Beza. They do not agree with the editions of 1556 and 1565. W.A.W.]

[1] Mr F. Fry has shewn (*N. & Q.* 4th S. vii. Jan. 28, 1871) that the edition used by the Revisers of K. James was probably that of 1602.

[2] [To shew the intermediate character of the edition of 1569 I have indicated the renderings found in it.]

BISHOPS' BIBLE 1568.	BISHOPS' BIBLE, 1572, 1578.
ii. 7 in kyndnesse	in [his] kyndenesse 1569 A.V. (9)
— 10 hath ordeyned 1569	hath before ordeyned A.V. (10)
— 14 the wall 1569	the mydle wal A.V. (11)
— 17 preached 1569 A.V.	preached the glad tidinges of (12)
— — you which were A.V.	you [whiche were] 1569 (13)
— 18 both haue 1569 A.V.	haue both (14)
— 19 citezins 1569	fellowe citizens A.V. (15)
— 22 ye also A.V.	also ye 1569 (16)
iii. 3 shewed he	shewed [God] 1569 (17)
— 6 That the A.V.	[That] the 1569 (18)
— 7 am made 1569	was made A.V. (19)
— 8 Vnto me the least 1569	vnto me whiche (who, A.V.) am lesse then the least A.V. (20)
— 12 confidence which is by	confidence by 1569 A.V. (21)
— 13 in my	for my 1569 (22)
— 19 knowledge A.V.	[al] knowledge 1569 (23)
— 21 Be praise 1569	Be glory A.V. (24)
iv. 14 in the wylynesse 1569	and in the wylynesse (25)
— 15 Christ	[euen] Christe 1569 A.V. (26)
— 16 beyng coupled 1569	being conueniently coupled (27)
— — ioynt of subministration 1569	ioynt, yeeldyng nourishment (28)
v. 13 rebuked of the lyght, are manifest 1569	rebuked, are made manifest of the light (29) mg. some reade, rebuked of ye light, are made manifest
— 15 howe ye walke	that ye walke A.V. (30)
— 24 to Christ	vnto Christ 1569 A.V. (31)
— 26 clensyng [it] 1569	when he had cleansed [it] (32)
— 27 To make it vnto 1569	That he might present it vnto (to A.V.), A.V. (33)
vi. 1 your fathers and mothers 1569	your parentes A.V. (34)
— 5 your bodyly	[your] bodily 1569 (similarly A.V.) (35)
— 9 threatnyng A.V.	threatenynges 1569 (36)

BISHOPS' BIBLE 1568.	BISHOPS' BIBLE 1572, 1578.
vi. 12 rule 1569	rules (37)
— spiritual craftynesse	spiritual wickednesse 1569 A.V. (38)
— 14 loynes 1569	your loynes A.V. (39)
— — putting on 1569	hauyng on A.V. (40)
— 15 hauyng your feet 1569	your feete A.V. (41)
— 18 watche thervnto 1569 A.V.	watching for the same purpose (42)
— 23 Peace [be] vnto (to A.V.) the brethren A.V.	peace [be unto you] brethren 1569 (43)
— 24 Grace be	Grace [be], A.V. 1569 (44)

Of the changes introduced in 1572, 1, 6, 7, 21, 26, 30, 34, 38, 39, 40, 41, 44 appear to be due to the Genevan version; but the revision generally bears the same mark of independent judgement as that of 1568.

The notes in the Bishops' Bible differ generally in their character from those in the Genevan. They are shorter and more epigrammatic, and deal more frequently with the interpretation than with the application of the text. Yet there are in them, as will be seen even in the following examples, many dogmatic statements which are of importance in estimating the standard theology of the age. The chief part of the commentary on a single chapter will shew the general range of the notes: a few detached specimens will illustrate their doctrinal nature.

'Naturall sorowe yf it be in measure, is not to be 'reprehended.

'*to embalm:* This was to the godly then an out-'warde token of incorruption: but to ye ignoraunt a vayne 'ceremonie. ['but...ceremonie' omitted in 1569.]

'*Am I God?* Or, *In the place of God.*

'That is, he woulde not turne that to their shame, 'which God had disposed to their wealth.

'*kindly. To their heartes.*

'*born* Or, *brought vp, or nourished.*

'The trueth of gods promise is immortall which men

16—2

'must loke for patientlye, and not prescribe God a
'tyme[1].'

4   'his name Everlasting.   Iah, a name of God that
'signifieth hym to be alwayes, and other thinges to be
'of hym.

11   '*preachers*   The women that tolde it abroade.

12   '*the ornament of an house divided the spoil.*   That is,
'a woman, meanyng Debora.

14   '*in it.*   In the lande of promise.

30   '*the people lyke vnto calues.*   Calues of the people.

31   '*princes.*   Embassadours.   [In the text in 1569.]

33   '*the most hyghest eternall heauens.*   Vpon the heauens,
'the heauens of eternitie.'

'Satan betrayeth hymselfe, shewing his bold sacralege,
'vsurping the empire of the earth.

'The misterie of mans redemption & saluation, is per-
'fected by the only sacrafice of Christ: the promise to the
'fathers fulfylled : the ceremonies of the law ended.'

'The wyll and purpose of God, is the cause of the
'election and reprobation.   For his mercie and callyng,
'through Christe, are the meanes of saluation: and the with-
'drawyng of his mercie, is the cause of damnation.'

'Our health hāgeth not on our workes : & yet are they
'sayd to worke out their health, who do run in ye race
'of iustice.   For although we be saued freely in christ
'by fayth, yet must we walk by the way of iustice vnto
'our health.'

'They that sticke to the ceremonies of the law, can not
'eate, that is, can not be partakers of our aulter, which
'is thankesgeuyng and liberalitie, whiche two sacrifices or
'offeringes, are nowe only left to the Christians[2].'

---

[1] [Omitted in 1569.]

[2] [Omitted in 1569.] The books
are arranged in the following manner
in the table òf contents :

'The ordėr of the bookes of the
'Old Testament.'

'The first part :' Genesis—Deuteronomy.

'The seconde part :' Joshua—Job.

'The thirde part of the Bible :'
The Psalter—Malachi.

'The fourth part of the Bible called
'Apocryphus :' 3 Esdr.—1 Macc.,
2 Macc.

'The order of the bookes of the
'newe Testament.'

§ 8. The Rhemes and Doway Bible.

The Rhemish Bible, like Wycliffe's, lies properly outside the line of English Bibles, because it is a secondary translation based upon the Vulgate. But it is nevertheless of considerable importance in the internal history of the authorised text, for it furnished a large proportion of the Latin words which King James' revisers adopted; and it is to this rather than to Coverdale's Testaments that we owe the final and most powerful action of the Vulgate upon our present Version.

The Rhemish translators give a very interesting and ingenious defence of their method, but they express no obligation to the earlier English translations which still formed the groundwork of their version[1]. They take the current Latin Vulgate for their güide, and expressly disclaim the intention of acting as interpreters where that is obscure. What they say upon each point is well worth quoting, and may serve as a commentary on Romish views of Scripture at the end of the 16th century.

'We translate the old vulgar Latin text, not the 'common Greeke text, for these causes.

'1. It is so auncient, that it was vsed in the Church 'of God above 1300 years agoe.

'2. It is that (...by al probabilitie) which S. Hierom 'afterward corrected according to the Greeke, by the 'appointment of Damasus then Pope...

'The fifth part.'
The four Gospels. The Acts.
St Paul's Epistles: Romans—He-brews.
St James.
1, 2 St Peter.
1, 2, 3 St John.
St Jude.
Revelation.

[1] This will appear, at least in the New Testament, by a comparison of any chapter in the Rhemish Version with the earlier English translations

The coincidences with the Genevan revision alone (1560) in a single chapter are striking. Rom. i. 6 *the called of* Jesus Christ; 10 *haue a prosperous journey*; 12 be *comforted* together in you; 17 *revealed*; 23 *corruptible*; 28 a *reprobate* sense; id. *are not convenient*. Some of these words may have come independently from the Vulgate, but a comparison with Wycliffe shews that it is unlikely that all did. Cf. ii. 5, 17; iv. 14; vii. 6, &c.

'3.   Consequently it is the same which S. Augustine
'so commendeth...

'4.   It is that, which for the most part euer since hath
'been vsed in the Churches seruice.,.

'5.   The holy Councel of Trent, for these and many
'other important considerations, hath declared and de-
'fined this onely of al other latin translations, to be
'authentical...

'6.   It is the grauest, sincerest, of greatest maiestie,
'least partialitie, as being without all respect of contro-
'uersies and contentions, specially these of our time...

'7.   It is so exact and precise according to the Greeke,
'both the phrase and the word, that delicate Heretikes
'therfore reprehend it of rudenes...

'8.   The Aduersaries them selues, namely Beza, pre-
'ferre it before al the rest...

'9.   In the rest, there is such diuersitie and dissension
'and no end of reprehending one an other, and translating
'euery man according to his fantasie, that Luther said,
'If the world should stand any long time, we must receiue
'againe (which he thought absurd) the Decrees of Councels,
'for preseruing the vnitie of faith, because of so diuerse
'interpretations of the Scripture...

'10.   It is not onely better than al other Latin trāsla-
'tions, but then the Greeke text it self, in those places
'where they disagree...

This last statement is supported by the argument that
as the first heretics were Greeks, the Greek Scriptures
suffered much at their hands.   Further, it is shewn that
many Latin readings are supported by ancient Greek
authority ; but it is also allowed that some errors had crept
into the current text by the fault of scribes as *in fide* for
in fine (I Pet. iii. 8), *præscientiam* for *præsentiam* (2 Pet. i. 16),
placuerunt for *latuerunt* (Hebr xiii. 2)[1].

In the Preface to the translation of the Old Testament
the same arguments are repeated briefly.   The Hebrew
text is said to have been 'fouly corrupted by Iewes,' as

[1] Preface to the New Testament.

the Greek by heretics. But in the interval between the
publication of the New and Old Testaments an authoritative
text of the Vulgate had been printed (by Clement VIII.
1592), and the English version of the Old Testament was
made to agree with this. 'Only one thing we haue donne,'
the editors say, 'touching the text...We haue againe con-
'ferred this English translation, and conformed it to the
'most perfect Latin Edition[1].'

Their choice of a text being thus defended[2], the translators explain also the principles on which they rendered
it. They claim for themselves absolute impartiality. Their
utmost desire was to reproduce the Vulgate in English
without removing its technicalities or its obscurity. 'We
'haue vsed no partialitie for the disaduantage of our
'aduersaries, nor no more licence then is sufferable in
'translating of holy Scriptures : continually keeping our
'selues as neere as is possible, to our text & to the very
'wordes and phrases which by long vse are made venerable,
'though to some prophane or delicate eares they may
'seeme more hard or barbarous, as the whole style of
'Scripture doth lightly to such at the begining : ac-
'knowledging with S. Hierom, that in other writings it is
'ynough to giue in trãslation sense for sense, but that in
'Scriptures, lest we misse the sense, we must keepe the
'very wordes.' They add, 'but to the discrete Reader
'that deepely weigheth and considereth the importance
'of sacred wordes and speaches, and how easily the
'voluntarie Translatour may misse the true sense of the
'Holy Ghost, we doubt not but our consideration and
'doing therein, shal seeme reasonable and necessarie : yea
'and that al sortes of Catholike Readers wil in short

[1] The delay in the appearance of the Old Testament is set down by the editors to 'one general cause, our 'poore estate in banishment.' When they published the New Testament (1582) the Old Testament was lying by them, 'long since translated.'
I do not know what edition of the Vulgate they followed in the New Testament. It was probably one by Hentenius. The text differs from the Complutensian (Apoc. xvi. 7) and the Clementine (Apoc. xxii. 9).

[2] It may be noticed that the trans-lators retain without comment the in-terpolations in 1 Samuel; e.g. iv. 1 ; v. 6 ; x. 1 ; xiv. 22 ; xv. 12 ; xvii. 36.

'time thinke that familiar, which at the first may seeme
'strange, & wil esteeme it more, when they shal otherwise
'be taught to vnderstand it, then if it were the common
'knowen English.'

Thus they retain *Amen, Amen* and *Alleluia* 'for the
'more holy and sacred authoritie thereof.' In the same
way they keep *Corbana, Parasceue, Pasche, Azymes, the
bread of Proposition,* just as we retain Pentecost. *Neophyte*
(1 Tim iii. 6) they defend by *Proselyte; Didragmes, Pre-
puce* and *Paraclete* by *Phylacteries.* 'How is it possible,'
they ask, 'to expresse *Euangelizo,* but as we do, *Evan-*
'*gelize?*...Therfore [also] we say *Depositum* (1 Tim. vi. 20)
'and, He *exinanited* him self, (Phil. ii. 7), and, You haue
'*reflorished* (Phil iv. 10) and, to *exhaust,* (Heb. ix. 28),
'because· we can not possibly attaine to expresse these
'wordes fully in English, and we thinke much better, that
'the reader staying at the difficultie of them, should take
'an occasion to looke in the table following[1], or otherwise
'to aske the ful meaning of them, then by putting some
'vsual English wordes that expresse them not, so to de-
'ceiue the reader...The *aduent* of our Lord, and, *Imposing*
'of handes ..come out of the very Latin text of the
'Scripture. So did *Penance, doing penance, Chalice, Priest,*
'*Deacon, Traditions, aultar, host,* and the like...'

From these principles it followed consistently that the
translators did not scruple to leave the version unintelligible
or ambiguous where the Latin text itself was so.   This
they distinctly profess:

[1] In this table, which contains fifty-five terms, the following words occur as 'not familiar to the vulgar 'reader:'

acquisition, getting, purchasing Eph. i. 14.

advent, The coming Matt. xxiv. 28.

adulterating, corrupting 2 Cor. ii. 17.

allegory, a mystical speech Gal. iv. 23.

cooperate, signifieth working with others Rom. viii. 28.

evangelize.

holocaust, a kind of sacrifice...Hebr. x. 6.

paraclete, John xiv. 16.

prescience, foreknowledge Acts ii. 23.

resuscitate, raise, quicken, renew 2 Tim. i. 6.

victims, sacrifices Acts vii. 42.

The list is a singular commentary on the large infusion of classical words into common language since the beginning of the xviith century. Comp. p. 253.

'Moreouer, we presume not in hard places to mollifie 'the speaches or phrases, but religiously keepe them word 'for word, and point for point, for feare of missing, or 'restraining the sense of the holy Ghost to our phantasie. 'as Eph. 6 [12], *Against the spirituals of wickednes in the* '*celestials*...James 4, 6, *And giueth greater grace*, leauing 'it indifferent to the *Scripture*, or to the *holy Ghost*, both 'going before...'

In itself then the Version has no independent merit as a version of the original texts. It is said indeed to have been compared with the Hebrew and Greek, but the collation must have been limited in scope or ineffectual, for the Psalter (to take one signal example) is translated, not from Jerome's version of the Hebrew, but from his revision of the very faulty translation from the Septuagint, which commonly displaced it in Latin Bibles. As it stands, the Doway Bible is simply the ordinary, and not the pure, Latin text of Jerome in an English dress. Its merits, and they are considerable, lie in its vocabulary. The style, so far as it has a style, is unnatural, the phrasing [as a rule] is most unrhythmical, but the language is enriched by the bold reduction of innumerable Latin words to English service[1].

One or two examples will be sufficient to indicate its merits and defects:

DOWAY.	VULGATE.
18 Incline my God thine eare, & heare: open thine eyes, and see our desolation, & the citie *vpon which thy name is inuocated:* for neither in *our iustifications doe we prostrate prayers* before thy face, but in thy manie commiserations.	Inclina Deus meus aurem tuam et audi; aperi oculos tuos et vide desolationem nostram et civitatem *super quam invocatum est nomen tuum;* neque enim *in justificationibus nostris prosternimus preces* ante faciem tuam, sed in miserationibus tuis multis.
19 Heare ô Lord, be pacified ô	Exaudi, Domine, placare, Do-

[1] I am not aware that English lexicographers have examined this subject, but it would repay examination.

Lord: attend & doe, delay not for thine owne sake my God: because thy name is inuocated vpon thy citie, & vpon thy people......

24 Seuentie weekes are abbridged vpon thy people, & vpon thy holie citie, *that preuarication may be consummate,* and sinne take an end, & iniquitie be abolished; and euerlasting iustice be brought; & vision be accomplished, and prophecie; & the Holie one of holies be anointed.

25 Know therfore, & marke: From the going forth of the word, that Ierusalem be built againe vnto Christ the prince, there shal be seuen weekes, and sixtie two weekes, & the streete shal be built againe, & the walles in straitnes of the times.

26 And after sixty two weekes Christ shal be slaine: *and it shal not be his people, that shal denie him.* And the city, & the sanctuary shal the people dissipate with the prince to come: *& the end therof waste,* & after the end of the battel the appoynted desolation.

mine, attende et fac: ne moreris propter temetipsum, Deus meus: quia nomen tuum invocatum est super civitatem et super populum tuum......

Septuaginta hebdomades abbreviatæ sunt super populum tuum, et super urbem sanctam tuam, *ut consummetur prævaricatio* et finem accipiat peccatum et deleatur iniquitas, et adducatur justitia sempiterna et impleatur visio et prophetia et ungatur sanctus sanctorum.

Scito ergo et animadverte: ab exitu sermonis ut iterum ædificetur Jerusalem usque ad Christum ducem, hebdomades septem et hebdomades sexaginta duæ erunt; et rursum ædificabitur platea et muri in angustia temporum.

Et post hebdomadas sexaginta duas occidetur Christus *et non erit ejus populus qui eum negaturus est.* Et civitatem et sanctuarium dissipabit populus cum duce venturo, et *finis ejus vastitas* et post finem belli statuta desolatio.

The correspondence with the Latin text is thus absolutely verbal, and it is only through the Latin that the English in some places becomes intelligible. But on the other hand Jerome's own greatness as a translator

is generally seen through the second version. A very
familiar passage will shew how closely the rendering can
approach our own even in the Prophets :

6 For a little childe is borne to vs, and a sonne is geuen
 to vs, and principalitie is made vpon his shoulder :
 and his name shal be called, Meruelous, Counseler,
 God, Strong, Father of the world to come, the Prince
 of peace.
7 His empire shal be multiplied, and there shal be no
 end of peace ; he shal sit vpon the throne of Dauid,
 and vpon his kingdom : that he may confirme it,
 and strengthen it in iudgement and iustice, from
 this time & for ever : the zeale of the Lord of hostes
 shal doe this.

The Psalter is the most unsatisfactory part of the
whole book. Even where the sense is sufficiently clear to
remain distinct through three translations, from Hebrew
to Greek, from Greek to Latin, from Latin to English, the
stiff, foreign style sounds strangely unsuited to words of
devotion ; and where the Latin itself has already lost the
sense, the English baffles understanding. One specimen
of each kind may be added :

8 The Law of our Lord is immaculate conuerting soules :
 the testimonie of our Lord is faithful, geuing wise-
 dome to litle ones.
9 The iustices of our Lord be right, making hartes ioy-
 ful : the precept of our Lord lightsome ; illuminating
 the eies.
10 The feare of our Lord is holie, permanent for euer
 and euer ; the iudgmentes of our Lord be true.
 iustified in themselues.
11 To be desired aboue gold and much precious stone :
 and more sweete aboue honie and the honie combe.
12 For thy seruant keepeth them, in keeping them is
 much reward.
13 Sinnes who vnderstandeth ? from my secrete sinnes
 cleanse me : and from other mens spare thy seruant.

This is not what a translation of the Psalms should be, but the following passage is positively painful from the ostentatious disregard of meaning in the words[1]:

9 As waxe that melteth, shal they be taken away: fyre hath falne on them, and they haue not seene the sunne.

10 *Before your thornes did vnderstand the old bryar: as liuing so in wrath he swalloweth them.*

11 The iust shal reioice when he shal see reuenge: he shal wash his handes in the bloud of a sinner.

12 And man shal say: If certes there be fruite to the iust: there is a God certes iudging them on the earth.

The translation of the New Testament is exactly similar to that of the Old; and next to the Psalter the Epistles are most inadequately rendered. Neither the Psalter, indeed, as translated by the Rhemists, nor the Epistles had the benefit of Jerome's independent labour. He revised the Latin texts of both hastily and imperfectly, but in both he left much which he would not himself have written. A few isolated quotations will be enough to shew the character of the Rhemish Version:

Rom. v. 18 Therfore as by the offence of one, vnto al men to condemnation: so also by the iustice of one, vnto al men to iustification of life.

vi. 13 Exhibite your selues to God as of dead men, aliue.

vii. 23 I see another law in my members, repugning to the law of my minde, and captiuing me in the law of sinne that is in my members.

viii. 18 I thinke that the passions of this time are not condigne to the glorie to come.

ix. 28 For, consummating a word, and abbridging it in equitie: because a word abbridged shal our Lord make vpon the earth.

[1] The translation follows the Gallican Psalter verbally. Jerome's own translation is wholly different.

Eph. vi. 12 Our wrestling is...against Princes and Potestats, against the rectors of the world of this darkenes, against the spirituals of wickednes in the celestials.

Heb. xiii. 16 Beneficence and communication do not forget: for with such hostes God is promerited[1].

Such translations as these have no claim to be considered vernacular renderings of the text: except through the Latin they are unintelligible.   But still they only represent what there was in the Vulgate incapable of assimilation to an English version.   And on the other hand a single Epistle furnishes the following list of Latin words which King James' translators have taken from the Rhemish Testament: *separated* (Rom. i. 1), *consent* (mg.) (i. 32), *impenitent* (ii. 5), *approvest* (ii. 18), *propitiation* (iii. 25), *remission* (id.), *grace* (iv. 4), *glory* in tribulations (v. 3), *commendeth* (v. 8), *concupiscence* (vii. 8), *revealed* (viii. 18), *expectation* (viii. 19), *conformable* (viii. 29), *confession is made* to salvation (x. 10), *emulation* (xi. 14), *concluded* (xi. 32), *conformed* (xii. 2), *instant* (xii. 12), *contribution* (xv. 26)[2].

But at the same time it must be added that the scrupulous or even servile adherence of the Rhemists to the text of the Vulgate was not always without advantage. They frequently reproduced with force the original order of the Greek which is preserved in the Latin; and even while many unpleasant roughnesses occur, there can be little doubt that their version gained on the whole by the faithfulness with which they endeavoured to keep the original form of the sacred writings.   Examples of this simple faithfulness occur constantly, as for instance: Matt. xviii. 9, *hauing one eye to enter into life;* id. 27, *the dette*

---

[1] All the quotations are made from the first editions.   In the later (Challoner's and Troy's) editions of the Rhemes and Doway Bible and New Testament there are considerable alterations, and the text is far nearer to that in the A. V.   Examples are given by Dr Cotton, *Rhemes and*

Doway...Oxford, 1853, pp. 183 ff.

[2] [But *consent* is found in the Genevan margin, *revealed* in the Genevan text of i. 17, 18, viii. 19; *impenitent* is in Coverdale, and *propitiation*, *grace*, *instant* are in the Bishops' Bible in the passages quoted. W.A.W.]

he forgaue him; xx. 12, *the burden of the day and the heates;* id. 23, *My cuppe in deede you · shal drinke of;* xxi. 41, *The naughtie men he wil bring to naught;* xxiii. 13, *those that are going in, you suffer not to enter;* xxvi. 11, *the poore you haue.*

The same spirit of anxious fidelity to the letter of their text often led the Rhemists to keep the phrase of the original where other translators had unnecessarily abandoned it: *e.g.* Matt. xviii. 1, *houre;* id. 6, *it is expedient;* id. 9, *the hel of fire;* xx. 20, *the sonnes of Z.;* xxii. 2, *likened;* id. 44, *the foote stole of thy feete;* xxvi. 25, *Is it I Rabbi?* (contrasted with v. 22) and so v. 49.

When the Latin was capable of guiding them the Rhemists seem to have followed out their principles honestly; but wherever it was inadequate or ambiguous they had the niceties of Greek at their command. Their treatment of the article offers a good illustration of the care and skill with which they performed this part of their task. The Greek article cannot, as a general rule, be expressed in Latin. Here then the translators were free to follow the Greek text, and the result is that this critical point of scholarship is dealt with more satisfactorily by them than by any earlier translators. And it must be said also that in this respect the revisers of King James were less accurate than the Rhemists, though they had their work before them. For example the Rhemish version omits the definite article in the following passages where it is wrongly inserted by A.V. and all earlier versions: Matt. ii. 13 (*an angel*); Luke ii. 9 (*an angel*); John vi. 26 (*signes*, not *the miracles*). Much more frequently it rightly inserts the article where other versions (including A.V.) omit it: *e.g.* Matt. iv. 5 (*the pinnacle*); vi. 25 (*the meate, the rayment*); xiv. 22 (*the boate*); xxv. 30 (*the vtter darknesse*); xxviii. 16 (*the mount*); John v. 35 (*the lampe*); 1 Cor. x. 5 (*the more part*); Gal. iii. 25 (*the faith*); Apoc. vii. 13 (*the white robes*)[1].

[1] For most of these and of the other references to the Rhemish Version, I am indebted to the kindness of Prof. Moulton, who placed at my

There are also rarer cases in which the Rhemists furnish a true English phrase which has been adopted since, as *felow seruant* (Matt. xviii. 28), *kingdom against kingdom* (Matt. xxiv. 7), *faile* (Luke xvi. 9), *darkened* (Rom. i. 21), *foreknewe* (Rom. xi. 2). Elsewhere they stand alone in bold or idiomatic turns of expression: *thratled him* (Matt. xviii. 28), *workemen* (Matt. xx. 1), *stagger not* (Matt. xxi. 21), *vipers broodes* (Matt. xxiii. 33), *bankers* (Matt. xxv. 27), *ouergoe* (1 Thess. iv. 6).

§ 9. THE AUTHORISED VERSION.

The Rhemish Version of the New Testament, supported by Martin's attack on the English Bible, had once again called attention to the importance of the Latin Vulgate before the revision of King James was undertaken. During the sixteenth century this had been in a great degree thrust out of sight by the modern translations of Erasmus and Beza, which had influenced respectively the Great and the Genevan Bibles. At the same time the study of Hebrew and Greek had been pursued with continued zeal in the interval which had elapsed since the publication of the Bishops' Bible; and two important contributions had been made to the interpretation of the Old Testament.

In 1572 Arias Montanus, a Spanish scholar not unworthy to carry on the work of Ximenes, added to the Antwerp Polyglott, which he edited by the command of Philip II., an interlinear Latin translation of the Hebrew text, based on that of Pagninus, whose readings he added to his own. The translation is rigidly verbal, but none the less it helped to familiarize ordinary scholars with the exact forms of Hebrew idioms which were more or less hidden in the earlier versions. Seven years afterwards Tremellius, by birth a Jew, published an original Latin translation of the Old Testament (1579), with a commentary, which rapidly obtained a very extensive currency.

disposal a most exact collation of the   portion of the Gospels.
English versions, reaching over a large

His son-in-law Junius added a translation of the Apocrypha. The whole Bible was completed by a translation of the New Testament by Tremellius from the Syriac; but for this the New Testament of Beza was frequently substituted[1].

Besides these works, which were designed for scholars, three important vernacular versions also had been published. In 1587–8 an authoritative revision of the French Bible was put forth by the venerable company of Pastors at Geneva, which was based upon a careful examination of the original texts. The chief part of the work is said to have been executed by C. B. Bertram, a Hebraist of distinguished attainments, and he was assisted by Beza, Goulart and others. An Italian translation was printed in the same city in 1607 by J. Diodati, who was a professor of Hebrew there. This translation has maintained its place to the present day, and though it is free, it is of very great excellence. In the mean time two Spanish versions had appeared, the first at Basle in 1569 by Cassiodoro de Reyna, and the second, which was based on Reyna's, at Amsterdam in 1602 by Cipriano de Valera. All these versions have an independent value, and when King James' revisers speak of their pains in consulting 'the Spanish, French and Italian translators,' there can be no doubt that it is to these they refer[2].

Thus King James' revisers were well furnished with external helps for the interpretation of the Bible, and we have already seen that they were competent to deal independently with questions of Hebrew and Greek scholarship. Like the earlier translators they suffered most from the corrupt form in which the Greek text of the New Testament was presented to them. But as a whole their work was done most carefully and honestly. It is possible to point out inconsistencies of rendering and other traces of

---

[1] [In the edition of 1585 the versions of the New Testament by Beza and Tremellius are printed in parallel columns.]

[2] The French version [1566] of Réné Benoist (Renatus Benedictus) is said to have no independent value.

compromise, but even in the minutest details the translation is that of a Church and not of a party. It differs
from the Rhemish Version in seeking to fix an intelligible
sense on the words rendered: it differs from the Genevan
Version in leaving the literal rendering uncoloured by any
expository notes[1]. And yet it is most worthy of notice
that these two Versions, representing as they do the
opposite extremes of opinion, contributed most largely of
all to the changes which the revisers introduced.

The important use which was made of the Rhemish
and Genevan Versions shews that the revisers did not hold
themselves to be closely bound by the instructions which
were given them. The Rhemish Version was not contained
in the list which they were directed to consult[2]; and on
the other hand the cases are comparatively rare in which
they go back from the text of the Bishops' Bible to an
earlier English rendering. If indeed they had not interpreted liberally the license of judgment which was given
them, they could not have accomplished their task. As it
is, their work is itself a monument of the catholicity of
their design.

An examination of the chapter of Isaiah which has

---

[1] The most extreme form in which
Calvinistic opinion appears in the
translation of the Bible is in the
French translation of 1588, which has
been severely criticized by P. Coton
in his *Genève plagiaire* in connexion
with the other Genevan versions. One
or two examples may be quoted:

Rom. v. 6 desnués de toute force...du
tout meschans.

—— x. 15 Sinon qu'il y en ait qui
soyent enuoyés.

Acts x. 35 qui s'addonne à justice
(cf. Coton, p. 2091).

Phil. ii. 12 employez vous à...(Coton,
p. 1746).

John vi. 50 qui est descendu (Coton,
p. 158).

—— 51 viuifiant (Coton, p. 174).

In all these places the English

Genevan version is unobjectionable;
but in other places an unfair bias
appears:

Acts iii. 21 contain (cf. Coton, p.
255).

1 Cor. ix. 27 reproved (Coton, p.
1718).

1 Cor. iv. 6 that no man presume
above that which is written (Coton, p. 1486).

And to this must be attributed the
avoidance of the word. 'tradition' in
1 Cor. xi. 2; 2 Thes. ii. 15; iii. 6.

One notable phrase at least has
passed from the French through the
Genevan Bible into our own: Jerem.
xvii. 9 Le cœur est cauteleux, & des-
esperémēt malin par dessus toutes
choses (cf. Coton, 1926).

[2] See p. 116.

been traced through the earlier versions will exhibit more clearly than a general description the method by which the revision was guided and the extent to which it was modified by the different authorities which the revisers consulted. The text of the Bishops' Bible is of course taken as the basis.

BISHOPS' BIBLE, 1568, 1572. 1 *But who* hath geuen *credence vnto* our *preaching? or* to whom is the arme
2 of the Lorde *knowen?* For he *dyd growe* before *the Lorde like* as (om. 1602) a *braunche,* and as a roote *in* a drye grounde, he hath *neither beautie* nor *fauour: when* we *loke vpon* hym, there *shalbe* no *fairenesse, we shall haue*
3 *no lust vnto* him. He is dispised and *abhorred* of men, *he is such a man as hath good experience of sorowes and infirmities: We haue reckened hym so vile, that we* hyd
4 our faces from hym. *Howbeit,* he *only* hath *taken on him* our *infirmitie,* and *borne* our *paynes:* Yet we dyd *iudge* hym *as though he were plagued, and cast downe* of
5 God. *Wheras* he [*notwithstandyng*] was wounded for our *offences, and smitten* for our *wickednesse: for the payne* of our *punishment* was *layde* vpon hym, and with
6 his stripes *are we* healed. *As for vs* we *are all* gone astray lyke sheepe, euery one *hath* turned his owne way:
7 *but* the Lord hath *throwen* vpon hym *all our sinnes.* He *suffered violence,* and *was euyll intreated, and dyd not open* his mouth: He *shalbe led* as a *sheepe* to. *be slayne, yet shall he be as styll* as a *lambe* before *the shearer, and*
8 *not open* his mouth. From *the* prison *and* iudgement *was he* taken, and *his* generation who *can* declare? for he was cut of *from the grounde* of the lyuyng, *which punishment dyd go vpon hym* for the transgression of
9 my people. His graue *was geuen hym* with the *condempned,* and with the riche *man at* his death, *wheras* he *did neuer* violence *nor vnright,* neither *hath there ben*
10 any disceipt*fulnesse* in his mouth. Yet *hath* it pleased the Lord to *smite* hym *with infirmitie, that* when *he had made* his soule an offeryng for sinne, he *might* see *long lastyng* seede: and *this deuice* of the Lorde shall prosper

11 in his hande (hands 1602). Of the trauayle and labour
of his soule, *shall he see the fruite* & *be* satisfied: My
righteous seruaunt shall *with his* knowledge iustifie *the*
12 *multitude*, for he shall beare their *sinnes*. Therfore
wyll I *geue* hym *among* the great *ones his part*, and
he shall deuide the spoyle with the *mightie*, because
he *geueth ouer* his soule *to* death, and *is reckened among*
the transgressours: *which neuerthelesse hath taken away*
the *sinnes* of *the multitude*, and made intercession for the
misdoers.

1 *Who* hath *believed* our *report*[1] (wil beleue our *report*
Genevan). *credidit* Pagninus. credit Tremellius (1)
— *and* so G. P. Tr. (2)
— *revealed* so G. *revelatum est* P. revelatur Tr. (3)
2 *shall grow up* before *him* as a *tender plant* (*shall* growe
...as a branche G.) (*tenera planta* Tr.) (4)
— *out of* a so G. Tr. (5)
— *no form* nor *comeliness* (nether *forme* nor beautie G.)
non est forma ei neque decor P. Tr. (6)
— *and when* we *shall see* him so G. (omitting *and*)
(*vidimus* P. quando intuemur Tr.) (7)
— there *is* no *beauty that we should desire* him. (there
shalbe no forme *that...him* G.) et non erat aspectus
ut desideraremus eum P. *non inest species* cur de-
sideremus eum Tr. (1593) (8)
3 *rejected* of so G. (abjectus inter viros P. desiit viris
Arias Montanus. abjectissimus virorum Tr.) (9)
— *a man of sorrows and acquainted with grief*. (a man
ful of sorows and hathe experience of infirmities
G.)
vir dolorum et expertus infirmitatem (notus ægritudine
A. M.) P. otherwise Tr. (10)
— *and* we hid *as it were* our faces from him; *he was
despised and we esteemed him not* so G. and P.
otherwise Tr. (1593), velut homo abscondens faciem
a nobis... (11)

[1] The renderings given are those of   to the italicised words in the text of
the Authorised Version corresponding   the Bishops' Bible.

4 *surely* he hath *borne* our *griefs* (infirmities G. languores
    P.) and *carried* our *sorrows*   so G. P. Tr.   (12)

— *esteem* him *stricken, smitten* of God, *and afflicted*
    (judge hī, as plagued, and *smitten* of God, &
    humbled   G.)   et nos reputavimus eum plagatum,
    percussum a Deo (Dei A. M.) et humiliatum (*afflic-
    tum* Tr.)   P.   (13)

5 *But* he was...   so G.   (14)

— *transgressions*   so G.   (15)

— *he was bruised* (broken G.) for our *iniquities*   (so G.)
    (16)

— *the chastisement* of our *peace* was upon him   G. P. Tr.   (17)

— *we are*   G.   (18)

6 *All* we, like sheep, *have* gone astray   G.   (19)

— *we have turned* every one *to* his...   G.   (20)

— *and*   G.   (21)

— *laid* on (upon G.) him *the iniquity of us all*   G. (Vulg.)
    (22)

7 He *was oppressed* and *he was afflicted, yet he opened not*
    (did he not opē G.)...   so G.   (23)

— he *is brought* as a *lamb* (shepe G.) to *the slaughter,
    and* as a *sheep* before *her shearers* (shearer G.) *is
    dumb, so he openeth not*...   so G. Tr.   (ducetur...non
    aperiet P.)   (24)

8 He *was taken* from (out from G.) prison *and from* judg-
    ment *and who shall* declare his generation (age G.)
    so G. P. Tr.   (25)

— cut off (cut G.) *out of the land* of...   so G.   (26)

— for the tr. of m. p. *was he stricken* (plagued G.)   so G.
    (27)

9 And *he made* (dedit P.) his grave with the *wicked.*
    G. P. Tr.   (populus exposuit improbis sepulchrum
    ipsius Tr.)   (28)

— the rich *in*...   G.   (29)

— *because* he *had done no* violence...   (thogh *he had done
    no* wickednes G.)   eo quod non iniquitatem (in-
    juriam A. M.) fecerit P.   *eo quod non fecit violen-
    tiam*... Tr.   (30)

9 neither *was* any *deceit*...   G. (31)

10 Yet it pleased the Lord to *bruise* him; *he hath put him to grief*: (Yet the Lord wolde breake him, & make him subiect to infirmities G.) *Et Dominus voluit conterere eum, aegrotare fecit* P. similarly Tr. (32)

— when *thou shalt make* his... (whē he shall make his... G.) si posuerit seipsam pro delicto (posuerit delictum A. M.) anima eius P. (quandoquidem exponebat se ipse sacrificium pro reatu, dicens Tr. 1593) (33)

— *he shall* see *his* seed, *he* (& G.) *shall prolong his days*, and *the pleasure* (wil G. P.) of...   so G. P. Tr. (34)

11 *He shall see* of the travail of...   and *shall be*...   so G. (35)

— *by his* knowledge shall my righteous servant justify *many* G. P. Tr. (36)

— *iniquities* G. P. Tr. (37)

12 *divide* (giue G. dabo Tr.) him *a portion with* the great... (so G.) (cum multis P. pro multis Tr.) (38)

— *strong* G. P. Tr. (39)

— *hath poured out...unto...* G. P. Tr. 1593 (40)

— *he was numbered* (counted G.) *with*... (so G.) P. Tr. (41)

— *and he bare* the *sin* of *many*...   so G. P. Tr. 1585 (42)

— *transgressors* (trespassers G.) (43)

Thus as far as the variations admit of being reduced to a numerical form about seven-eighths are due to the Genevan Version, either alone or in agreement with one or both of the Latin Versions. Two renderings appear to be due to Tremellius (4, 30): the same number to Pagninus (10, 32), including the noble rendering 'a man 'of sorrows and acquainted with grief.' Three times the Genevan translation is abandoned (30, 32, 33); and once the rendering appears to be independent (33). But throughout the most delicate care is given to the choice of words, and there is scarcely a verse which does not bear witness to the wisdom and instinctive sense of fitness by which it was guided, e.g. 2 no *beauty*... (3 *a man of sorrows*...) 4 our *griefs...stricken*... 5 *bruised*... 7 as a *lamb*... 16 *put him to grief*... 12 *transgressors*. Even subtleties of rhythm are not to be disregarded, as 7 he *opened not*... 8 *from* prison... 12 *numbered*...; nor yet the endeavour after a more exact representation of the original, as 10 *he* shall... 12 *divide*...

The example which has been taken is undoubtedly an extreme one, but it only represents on an exaggerated scale the general relation in which the Authorised Version stands to the Genevan and Bishops' Bibles in the Prophetical books In the Historical, and even in the Poetical books, it is far less divergent from the Bishops' Bible. In the Apocrypha it is, as far as I can judge, nearer to the Bishops' Bible than to the Genevan, but marked by many original changes. A passage from Wisdom, which has been already examined[1], will be sufficient to shew the character of the revision in this part of the Bible, and the independent freedom with which the reviser performed his work.

BISHOPS' BIBLE, 1568, 1572. 15 God hath graunted me to speake *what my mynde conceaueth*, and to *thynke* as is meete for the thynges that are geuen me: *For* it is he that leadeth vnto wisdome, and *teacheth to vse wisdome a ryght*.

16 For in his hande are both we and our wordes, *yea* all *our* wisdome and knowledge of [*his*] *workes*.

17 For he hath geuen me *the true science* of the thinges that are, *so that I* knowe howe the worlde was made, and the *powers* of the elementes:

18 The begynnyng, endyng, and myddest of the tymes, *howe the tymes alter, howe one goeth after another, & howe they are fulfylled*,

[1] p. 219.

19 The *course of the yere, the ordinaunces of the* starres,

20 The natures of lyuyng *thynges, the furiousnesse* of *beastes,* the *power of the* wyndes, *the imaginations* of men, the diuersities of *young* plants, *the* vertues of rootes ;

21 And all such thynges as are either secrete or manifest, them *haue I learned...*

27 And beyng [but] one, she (wisdom) can do all thinges : and remaynyng in her selfe she *renueth all,* and in all ages of tymes entryng into holy soules, she *maketh Gods friendes,* and prophetes,

28 For God loueth none, *if he dwell not* with wisdome.

29 For she is more beautifull then the sunne, and *geueth more lyght then the* starres, *and the day is not to be compared vnto her.*

30 For *vpon the day* commeth nyght : but *wickednesse can not ouercome* wisdome.

15 *what...conceaueth: as I would   ex sententia* Junius (1)
— *thynke: conceive* (Greek) (2)
— *For* G. : *because* (3)
— *teacheth...a ryght: directeth the wise.* (directer of the wise G.) (4)
16 *yea all our* wisdome : all wisdome *also* (5)
— [*his*] *workes : workmanship* (opificiorum scientia J.) (6)
17 *the true science: certain knowledge cognitionem certam* J. (7)
— *so that I* G. : *namely to* (8)
— *powers* G. : *operation* (Gr. ?) (9)
18 *howe...fulfylled: the alterations of the turning of the sun and the change of seasons* (how the times alter, *and the change of the seasons* G.) *solstitiorum mutationes et varietates temporum* J. (10)
19 *course...of the : the circuits of years and the positions of : anni circuitus, et stellarum situs* J. (11)
20 *thynges* G. : *creatures* (12)
— *the...beastes* G. : the *furies of wild* beasts (Gr.) (13)
— *power of the* G. : *the violence of* (Gr.) (14)

20 *the imaginations* G.: *and the reasonings* (Gr.) (15)

— *young*: om. so G. J. (Gr.) (16)

— *the · and the* G. J. (Gr.) (17)

21 *haue I learned: I know* G. J. (18)

27 *renueth all* G.: *maketh all things new* (19)

— *maketh Gods friends: maketh them friends of God* (*the friends* G.) (20)

28 *if...not* G.: *but him that dwelleth   nisi cum qui habitat* J. (Gr.) (21)

29 *geueth...the: above all the order of* (G. *is* aboue...the starres) (22)

29 *and the...her: being compared with the light, she is found before it   cum luce comparata prior esse deprehenditur* J. (Gr.) (23)

30 *vpon the day: after this*   (24)

— *wickednesse...ouercome* G.: *vice shall not prevail against sapientiæ non est prævalitura malitia* J. (25)

Of these changes three seem to be due to Junius (10, 11, 25), and perhaps four others (1, 6, 7, 23): two to the Genevan Version (4, 18), and perhaps two others (16, 17): the remainder are either linguistic (3, 5, 8, 12, 19) or closer renderings of the Greek (2, 9, 13—15, 20—22, 24).

The marginal renderings offer a certain clue to the authorities on which the revisers chiefly relied; and an analysis of those given in Malachi fully confirms the conclusions which have been already obtained.

Malachi i. 1 by: *Heb.* by the hand of.   per manum M.

5 from: *or* upon *Heb.* from upon.

7 ye offer: *or* bring unto &c. (1)

8 for sacrifice: *Heb.* to sacrifice.

9 God: *Heb.* the face of God.

— by your means: *Heb* from your hand.

13 and ye have snuffed at it (Münster, Genevan): *or* whereas you might have blown it away, quum id vel difflare possitis Castalio; quum exsufflare possetis illud Tremellius. (2)

i. 14 which hath in his flock (G.): *or* in whose flock is. (quum sit in grege ipsius Tr.) (3)

ii. 3 corrupt (G.): *or* reprove increpabo Leo Juda. (4)

— spread: *Heb.* scatter spargam M. J. (5)

— *one* shall take you away with it: *or* it shall take you away to it. (et tollet vos ad se M. Similarly Pagninus, J.: otherwise G.) it shall take you with it Douay. ut abripiat vos ad se Tr. (6)

8 stumble at the law: *or* fall in the law (fall by...G.) (impingere in lege M. J.) (7)

9 have been partial in (G.): *or* lifted up the face against *Heb.* accepted faces. attollitis faciem contra legem Tr. (8)

11 loved (G. and all except Tr.): *or* ought to love amaturus fuerat Tr. (9)

12 the master and the scholar: *or* him that waketh and him that answereth, so M. Tr. (10)

15 residue: *or* excellency, so P. (11)

— a godly seed: *Heb.* a seed of God.

— treacherously: *or* unfaithfully. (12)

16 that he hateth putting away (so Fr. 1588. Sibi odio esse dimissionem ait Tr.): *or* if he hate *her*, put *her* away (similarly P. M. J. C. G.) *Heb.* to put away. (13)

iii. 4 former: *or* ancient P. (14) .

5 oppress: *or* defraud fraudant C. (15)

10 pour you out: *Heb.* empty out.

11 destroy: *Heb.* corrupt.

14 his ordinance: *Heb.* his observation.

— mournfully: *Heb.* in black.

15 are set up: *Heb.* are built.

17 jewels (mes plus précieux ioyaux Fr. 1588): *or* special treasure. peculium M. J. C. Tr. (16)

Thus of the sixteen alternative renderings four are found in Tremellius (2, 3, 8, 9), four in Münster with Leo Juda or Tremellius or both (5, 7, 10, 16), two in Pagninus (11, 14), one in Castalio (15), one in the Genevan (13), the Douay (6) and Leo Juda's Version (4) respectively; while two alone cannot be certainly referred to any one of these authorities (1, 12)[1].

The revision of the New Testament was a simpler work than that of the Old, and may be generally described as a careful examination of the Bishops' Version (1572) with the Greek text, and with Beza's, the Genevan, and the Rhemish Versions[2]. Examples of words derived from the Rhemish Version have been given already, but the use of this version is so remarkable that it may be well to add more unequivocal proofs of its reality. Thus in the Epistle to the Romans the following phrases are found which are common, I believe, to the Rhemish and Authorised Versions alone; and it is impossible that the coincidences can have been accidental[3].

i. 10 *if by any means*
— 13 I would *not have you ignorant*

[1] [The first of these is from Münster.]

[2] See note at the end of the chapter for a collation of some chapters of the Bishops' Bible with the Authorised Version.

[3] Some of the phrases, it may be noticed, are found also in Wycliffe, and these may be taken to represent the amount of natural coincidences in two versions made independently from the Latin.

A still more certain proof of the influence of the Rhemish Version (Vulgate) on A.V. is found in changes of words and phrases in the earlier version which had been objected to by Romish controversialists. Thus, among renderings identical with, if not adopted from, those of the Rhemish Version in passages objected to by Martin, the

following may be mentioned:
Matt. ii. 6 *rule.*
— xxvi. 26 *blessed.*
John ix. 22 *put out of the synagogue.*
Acts i. 26 *numbered with.*
— iii. 21 heaven must *receive* (so Bishops').
— xiv. 23 *ordained* (*for* ordained *by election*).
James v. 16 *confess.*
2 Cor. ii. 10 *person.*
— iv. 17 *worketh.*
2 Thess. ii. 15 *traditions.*
Tit. iii. 5 *regeneration* (so Bishops').
Hebr. xii. 23 *Church.*

Other passages objected to, as Eph. v. 5, Col. iii. 5, Tit. iii. 10, were altered already in the Genevan Version: others, as 2 Thess. ii. 15, were altered independently in the Authorised Version.

i. 23 *changed* the glory (so 25)
— 28 did not *like* (*liked* not Rh.)
ii. 5 *revelation* of the
— 10 *glory, honour and peace to every* man *that worketh good*
— 13 *for not the hearers of the law are just*
— 15 *the work* of the law
iii. 7 *why* yet *am I also judged as a sinner*
v. 3 *and not only* so
— 15 *but not as the offence so also*
xi. 14 *provoke to emulation*
xii. 16 be not wise *in your own conceits*
xiii. 4 minister un*to thee for good*
— 8 owe *no man anything*

The relation in which the different authorities stand
to one another in the execution of the revision will appear
from an analysis of the changes in a passage of moderate
difficulty.

BISHOPS' BIBLE, 1572.   5 Let your conuersation be without couetousnesse, *beyng* content with suche things as
ye haue.   For he hath sayde, I wyl *in no case* (*not* 1568,
1569) *fayle* thee, *neyther* forsake thee.
6 So that we may boldely say, The Lord is my helper,
and I wyl not feare what man *may* doe vnto me.
7 Remember them whiche haue the *ouersight of* you,
whiche haue spoken vnto you the worde of God : whose
ende of conuersation ye consydering, folowe their fayth.
8 Jesus Christ *yesterday* and today, and *the same* for
euer.
9 Be not caried about with diuers and strange doctrines :
For it is a good thing that the hart be *stablished* with
grace, *and* not with meates, whiche haue not profited
them that haue benne occupied therein.
10 We haue an aulter, whereof they haue no right to eate,
which serue in the tabernacle.
11 For the bodies of those beasts, whose blood is brought
into the *holye place*, by the hygh priest for sinne, are
burnt without ye *tentes.*

12 *Therfore* Jesus also, that he myght sanctifie the people
with his owne blood, suffered without the gate.

13 Let us goe foorth therefore vnto hym *out of the tentes*,
bearyng his reproche.

14 For here haue we no continuing citie: but we seeke
one to comme.

15 By hym therefore let vs (*do we* 1568, 1569) offer *sacrifice*
of *laude alwayes to God*, that is, the fruite of *lippes confessing* his name.

16 *To doo* good and to *distribute* forgeat not, for with suche
sacrifice God is wel pleased.

5 *beyng: and be* Genevan   (1)

— *in no case* (not 1568, 9) *fayle. never leave* (*not leaue*
Rhemish)   (2)

— *neyther* G.: *nor*   (3)

6 *may: shall* Rh. (*can* G.) *facturus est* Tremellius
(4)

7 *ouersight of* G.: *rule over* (gubernatorum Tr.)   (5)

— *whiche* G.: *who* (6)

— *ende...fayth: whose faith follow considering the end* (*what
hathe bene* the end G.) *of their conversation*   (7)

8 yesterday G.: *the same* yesterday (Rh. different)   (8)

— *the same* (*the same also is* G.): omit   (9)

9 *stablished* G.: *established* Rh.   (10)

— *and* G.: omit, so Rh.   (11)

11 *holye place* G.. sanctuary (*sacrarium* Beza)   (12)

— *tentes: camp* G.   (13)

12 *Therfore* G.: *wherefore* (*quapropter* B.)   (14)

13 *out...tentes: without the camp* Rh. (*out of the campe* G.)
(15)

15 sacrifice: *the* sacrifice G.   (16)

— *laude alwayes* to God: *praise* to God *continually* (*praise
alwayes to God* G. Rh.)   (17)

— lippes: *our* lips (*the* lippes G.)   (18)

— *confessing: giving thanks to* (*quæ gratias agunt* Tr.)
(*whiche confesse* G.)   (19)

16 To doo G.: *but* to do (*beneficentiæ vero* B.)   (20)

III] THE AUTHORISED VERSION

16 *distribute* G.: *communicate* (communication Rh. B.)
  (21)
— *sacrifice* 1569: *sacrifices* 1568 G. (22)

Thus about seven changes are due to Beza (12, 14, 20), or the Genevan version (1, 7, 13, 16); nearly an equal number to the Rhemish (2, 4, 10, 11, 15, 21); two were perhaps suggested by Tremellius' version of the Syriac (5, 19); and six are original, reckoning three linguistic variations (3, 6, 17).

The chief influence of the Rhemish Version was on the vocabulary of the revisers, that of Beza and the Genevan Version on the interpretation. But still our revisers exercise an independent judgment both in points of language and construction. Thus in the latter respect they often follow Beza, rightly and wrongly, when the Genevan Versions do not; and again they fail to follow him where these had rightly adopted his rendering. In the former class such passages as these occur:

Mark xi. 17 called *of* all nations.
  ab omnibus gentibus (*Beza* 1565).
Rom. vii. 6 that being dead wherein...
  mortuo eo in quo... (*Beza*).
Hebr. xi. 13 and *embraced* them.
  postquam...et ea *amplexi* fuissent (*Beza*).
1 John ii. 19 *they went out* that...
  egressi sunt ex nobis ut... (*Beza* 1585).

On the other hand the Authorised Version retains (by no means unfrequently) the old rendering of the Great Bible when it had been rightly corrected from Beza in the Genevan revisions:

Matt. xxviii. 14 if this come to the governor's ears.
  come *before* the Gouernour (Gt.), if *yᵉ gouernour
  heare of this* (G.).
  Quod si hoc auditum fuerit apud præsidem (*Beza*
  1585).

periculum erat ne hoc nomine milites apud
Pilatum *deferrentur* (*Beza note*).

Acts xxviii. 4 *suffereth* not to live.

hath not suffered (*Gen.*) non *sivit* (*Beza*): ser-
vanda præteriti temporis significatio. Comp.
I John v. 4 *vicit.*

Eph. iv. 18 *blindness.*

hardness (Gen.).

obduratione (*Beza*, 1556, 1559).

I Pet. i. 17 If ye *call on the* Father...

If ye *call him* Father... (*Gen.*).

Si patrem *cognominatis eum* qui... (*Beza*).

And still further, some right renderings of Beza are
neglected both by the Genevan revisers and by our own:

Mark vii. 4 *tables.*

lectorum (Beza: so Vulg.: *beds Wycl. Rh.* and
A.V. marg.).

I Tim. vi. 5 that *gain is godliness.*

quæstui habent pietatem (*Beza*)[1].

If we apply the same test as before and examine the
sources of the various renderings given in St Mark, the
same authorities, as we have already noticed, reappear, and
not disproportionately distributed.

Mark i. 4 for: unto Rhemish (1)

— 10 opened: cloven Genevan (2) *or* rent (se fendre
Fr. 1588) (3)

— 34 to speak because they knew him: to say that
they knew him (to speak that Rh.) G. so
Beza, 1598 and Fr. (4)

ii. 14 at the receipt of custom: at the place where

---

[1] Archbp Trench, to whom I owe
the references to most of the examples just given, has collected some
very instructive instances of improvements (p. 121): Hebr. iv. 1: Acts
xii. 19 (Beza's note): John i. 3, 4:
Acts i. 4 (Beza); and striking phrases
(p. 37): Acts iii. 15; Hebr. ii. 10;
xii. 1. The list might easily be increased. It is unfortunate that Archbp Trench, like many other writers,
confounds the Genevan Testament of
1557 with the New Testament of the
Genevan Bible.

the custom was received (au lieu du peage Fr.) (5)

ii. 21 new: raw Rh. (6) *or* unwrought (new and un-dressed Gt. escru Fr.) (7)

iii. 5 hardness: blindness Tindale, Great Bible, Rh. (8)

— 10 pressed: rushed (Vulgate and Erasmus *irruerent*) (9)

— 19 into an house: home G. (10)

— 21 friends: kinsmen (kinsfolkes G.) (11)

iv. 29 brought forth: ripe (adolevit Castalio) (12)

vi. 19 a quarrel: an inward grudge (en auoit à lui Fr.) (13)

— 20 observed him: kept him Rh. (le gardoit en prison Fr. mg.) (14) *or* saved him (15)

— 27 an executioner: one of his guard (erant spiculatores principum satellites *Beza note*) (16)

— 45 unto Beth.: over against Beth. Beth. oppositam B. (1598) (17)

— 56 him: it (so B. as alternative) (18)

vii. 2 defiled: common Ti. G. B. Gen. Rh. (19)

— 3 oft: diligently (summo studio *B. note*) *in the original*, with the fist: Theophylact [quoted by B.] up to the elbow. (20)

— 4 tables: beds Rh. B. (21)

— 9 reject: frustrate Rh. (22)

— 26 Greek: Gentile Rh. (23)

ix. 16 with them: among yourselves G. (24)

— 18 teareth him: dasheth him Rh. (25)

— 43, 47 offend thee: cause thee to offend G. (26)

x. 42 are accounted (qui reputantur Tremellius): think good (qui font estat Fr., quibus placet B.) (27)

— 52 made thee whole: saved thee Ti. G. B. Gen. (28)

xi. 22 Have faith in God: have the faith *of* God (have faith in God Rh.) (29)

— 29 question: thing Ti. B. Gen. (30)

xiv. 3 spikenard: pure nard (nard that was pure...
Ti. G. B. Gen.) (31) *or* liquid nard (so B.)
(32)
— 15 killed: sacrificed G. (33)
— 26 hymn: psalm G. (34)
— 72 he wept: he wept abundantly (35) *or* he began
to weep Ti. G. B. Rh. (36)
xvi. 14 at meat: together G. (37)

Thus of the thirty-seven alternative renderings nearly
one-half agree with the Genevan Version (2, 7, 10, 11, 24,
26, 33, 34, 37) or Beza's (4, 16—18, 20, 21, 27, 32); seven
agree with the Rhemish Version (1, 6, 14, 22, 23, 25, 29);
three more or less with the French (3, 5, 13); seven with
the earlier English versions (8, 19, 28, 30, 31, 35, 36); one
with Castalio (12); and one with the Vulgate (9).

Once again: the examination of the first Epistle of
St John will shew very fairly how far K. James' revisers
generally availed themselves in the New Testament of
earlier labours, and how far they impressed a special
character upon the Version.   In six (four) places, if I
reckon rightly, they have altered the construction of the
text:

1 John i. 3 'and *truly* our fellowship *is* with...
for '*that* our fellowship *may be* with...'
(ii. 19 'they went out that they might be...' so
Beza 1585)
(ii. 29 '*ye know* that...' B.)
for '*know ye* that...' G. so A.V. *marg.* 'ye
haue knowen' (Gt.)
iii. 16 'Hereby perceive we the love of God, because...' (B.)
for 'hereby perceive we (haue we perceiued
G.) love, that' (because Great Bible)...
iv. 17 'Herein is our love (love with us *marg.* so B.
1598) made perfect, that...'
for 'Herein is the love perfect in us, that...'

v. 6 'This is he that came by water and blood, even Jesus Christ...' (so B.)
  for 'This Iesus Christ is he that cam...'
  (Tindale, G. B.)
  or 'This is that Iesus Christ that came...
  (G.)

The changes of words are far more frequent, and of these a large number introduce phrases identical with those used in the Rhemish Version. Examples occur i. 9 *'confess'* for *'[ac]knowledge'*: ii. 2 (iv. 10) 'he is the *propitiation for...'* for 'he *it is that obtaineth grace for...'*: iv. 10 *'to make agreement for...'* (*propitiatio* Vulg.): ii. 17 'he that *doeth...'* for 'he that *fulfilleth...'*: ii. 20 'an *unction'* for 'an *ointment'*: ii. 26 *'seduce'* for *'deceive'* (*seducunt* Vulg.): ii. 28 (iii. 21, v. 14) 'have *confidence'* for *'be bold'* (*habeamus fiduciam* Vulg.): iii. 15 *'murderer'* for *'manslayer'*: v. 20 'an *understanding* that...' for *'a mind to...'* (*sensum ut* cognoscamus Vulg.)[1].

In other cases the revisers aimed at a more literal exactness, as in iii. 14 *'have passed'* for *'are translated'*: iv. 18 *'is made* perfect' for *'is* perfect': iii. 1 *'bestowed'* for *'shewed'*: iii. 9 *'doth not commit sin'* (committeth not sinne Rh.) for *'sinneth not'*: ii. 22 (article): v. 9, 10 (tense); or at consistency of rendering, as ii. 27 *'abideth'* for *'dwelleth'*: iii. 10 *'manifest'* for *'known'*[2]; or at clearness, as ii. 24, iii. 8 'that he might destroy the works of the devil' for *'to loose...'*; or at emphasis, as ii. 3 *'do* know...' Once an unhappy combination of renderings is attempted, iii. 17 *'Bowels of compassion...'* (*Bowels* Rh. compassion Tind. &c.): once a neater word is introduced, iii. 3 *'purifieth'* for *'purgeth'*[3].

---

[1] Other coincidences are found: ii. 8 *which thing...*: ii. 9 until *now...*: ii. 10 occasion of *stumbling* (marg. *scandal*): iv. 15 *shall* confess.

[2] The converse change of 'record' to 'witness' in v. 8 is quite inexplicable.

[3] The substitution of 'torment for 'painfulness' in iv. 18 is less completely successful: neither word renders κόλασις.

The scrupulous and watchful care with which the revisers worked is nowhere seen more remarkably than in their use of italics to mark the introduction of words not directly

This analysis, in which I have endeavoured to include all the variations introduced into the Authorised Version, will shew better than any description the watchful and far-reaching care with which the revisers fulfilled their work. No kind of emendation appears to have been neglected, and almost every change which they introduced was an improvement. They did not in every case carry out the principles by which they were generally directed; they left many things which might have been wisely modified, they paid no more attention than was commonly paid in their time to questions of reading[1]; but when every deduc tion is made for inconsistency of practice and inadequacy of method, the conclusion yet remains absolutely indisputable that their work issued in a version of the Bible better—because more faithful to the original—than any which had been given in English before[2].

represented in the original. The detail may seem at first sight trivial, and Luther neglected it entirely; but in reality it involves much that is of moment.   It is of importance as marking distinctly that the work is a translation; and yet more the use distinguishes in many cases an interpretation from a rendering : e.g. Hebr. x. 38. This question has been exhaustively treated by Dr Turton in his pamphlet on The Text of the English Bible (1833), who shews conclusively that the Cambridge text of 1638 bears clear marks of representing very exactly the true form of the Authorised Revision. In the use of italics it is far more consistent than the editions of 1611, which seem to have been hastily printed.

[1] I have given an account of the Greek text followed by the revisers in Smith's Dictionary of the Bible, II. 524 n. But the question is of no real importance, as they do not appear to have been influenced by any consistent critical views, and the variations are too superficial to admit a general classification or discussion.

An examination of the headings of the chapters, the running headings, and the marginal references does not fall within my scope, though in itself interesting. Some remarks on these points will be found in a paper by Mr Kegan Paul in the Theological Review for 1869, pp. 99 ff.

[2] It is impossible to enter here upon the question of the language of the Authorised Version.   Linguistic changes were common in each successive revision, as has been already noticed; but it does not at once follow that no archaisms were retained. The following examples of old words contained in the Genevan Bible and altered in A.V. are interesting. I am indebted for them to an anonymous [by the Rev. J Gurnhill] Essay called English retraced (Cambridge, 1862), which contains many excellent criticisms on the English of the Genevan Version. The readings of A. V. are given in ( ). The other notation is as before.

Ex. xxviii. 8 garde   Genevan   (girdle so Matthew, Bishops')
1 Sam. ii. 26 profited and grewe   M. G. Bp.   (grew on)
1 Sam. xxx. 18 frailes (*mg.* clusters)   G. Bp.   bondelles   M.   (clusters. *mg.* lumps)
1 K. xx. 39 be lost, and want   G.   be missed   M.   be myssed or lost   Bp. (be missing)
2 K. xix. 24 plant   G.   soles M.   steppe of my goyng   Bp.   (sole)
Ps. cxxxvi. 23 in our base estate   G.   when we were brought lowe   Bp. (in our low estate)
Ps. cxlii. 7 art beneficial vnto   G.   (shalt deal bountifully with)
Prov. xxii. 6 in the trade of his way   G.   (in the way he should go.   *mg.* in his way)
Is. xxiii. 8 chapmen   G.   factours   Bp.   (traffickers)
Mark v. 35 diseasest   Tindale, Great Bible, G.   Bp.   (troublest)
Mark x. 41 disdaine at   Ti. G. B. G. Bp.   (be much displeased with)
Mark xii. 42 quadrin   G.   (farthing   Ti. G. B. Bp.)
Mark xv. 26 cause   Ti. G. B. G. Bp. Rh.   (accusation)
Acts xxi. 15 trussed up our fardeles   G.   made ourselves ready   Ti.   toke vp oure burthens   G. B. Bp.   (took up our carriages)
Acts xxi. 35 a grece   Ti.   a stayre   G. B.   the grieces   G.   (the stairs so Bp.)
Acts xxv. 18 crime   G.   (accusation)   so Ti. G. B. Genevan Test. Bp.
Rom. xiv. 16 treasure   Ti. G. B.   commoditye   G.   (good   so Bp.)
2 Cor. ix. 9 sparsed   Ti. G. B. G. Bp.   (dispersed   so Bp.)
2 Cor. xii. 17 pill   Ti. G. B. G. Bp.   (make a gain of)
2 Tim. iv. 2 improue   Ti. G. B. G. Bp.   (reprove)
Tit. i. 8 herberous   Ti.   harberous   G.   a keper of hospitalite   G. B.   (a lover of hospitality   so Bp.)
Heb. viii. 2 pight   Ti. G. B. G. Bp.   (pitched)
1 Pet. iv. 9 Be ye herberous   Ti. G. B. G. Bp.   (use hospitality)   See above, Tit. i. 8.

The valuable *Bible Word-Book* (1866) of Mr Eastwood and Mr Aldis Wright [second edition, 1884] furnishes an admirable foundation for a study of the English of A. V. There can hardly be a more instructive lesson in English than to trace to their first appearance a number of the archaisms there noticed. It will appear that not a few of them are due to K. James' revisers themselves and not to the earlier texts. The charges brought by the Rhemists against the language of the earlier English Versions are all summed up by Martin and met by Fulke, *Defence of the English translations*, pp. 218, 569 (ed. P. S.). The argument of Martin, it will be seen, loses all its point, when applied to the Authorised Version.

Note to p. 266.

The following selection of variations in some chapters of St Matthew will give a fair idea of the relation of A.V. to the Bishops' Bible.

BISHOPS' BIBLE, 1568, 1569, 1572.	AUTHORISED VERSION, 1611.
i. 18 The birth	Now the birth Comp. vv. 21, 22; ii. 1, 13; iii. 15; iv. 12; vii. 3; viii. 18; x. 2; xi. 2, &c.
— — betrouthed	espoused
— 23 is by interpretation	being interpreted is
ii. 1 (a citie) of Iurie	of Judæa
— 10 excedyngly with great ioy	with exceeding great joy
— 12 after they were	being Comp. ver. 22; iv. 13, 21; viii. 5.
— 13 it wyll come to passe, that Herod shall	Herod will
— 16 as many as were	from
— — searched out	enquired
— 23 Nazarite	Nazarene
iii. 7 anger	wrath
— 9 be not of suche mynde, that ye woulde	think not to
— 11 I baptize you in	I indeed baptize you with
— 16 (John) sawe	he saw
iv. 10 Auoyde 1568, 1569: get thee hence behind me 1572	get thee hence
— 12 delyuered up *mg.* That is, *cast in pryson*	cast into prison *mg. delivered up*
— 21 the shippe	a ship Comp. xiii. 2.
v. 6 satisfied	filled
— 10 which suffer persecution 1568, 1569; which have been persecuted 1572	which are persecuted
— 11 lying, shall say all maner of euyll saying agaynst you	shall say all manner of evil against you falsely
— 12 be glad	be exceeding glad
— 22 vnaduisedly	without a cause
— 44 hurt	despitefully use
— 47 singuler thyng do ye	do ye more than others
— 48 Ye shall therfore be	Be ye therefore
vi. 7 babble not much much bablinges sake	use not vain repetitions much speaking
— 19 Hoorde	lay
— 25 be not carefull	take no thought Comp. vv. 27, 28, 34.
— 28 weery not [them selues] with labour	toil not
— 29 royaltie	glory

BISHOPS' BIBLE, 1568, 1569, 1572.	AUTHORISED VERSION, 1611.
vii. 4 suffer me, I will plucke (caste 1572) out a mote	Let me pull out the mote
— 24 of me these sayinges	these sayings of mine Comp. ver. 26.
— 29 power	authority
viii. 7 when I come, I wyll	I will come and
— 11 rest	sit down
— 32 russhed headlong	ran violently down a steep place
— 33 done of	befallen to
ix. 21 touche but euen his vesture only	but touch his garment
— 36 were destitute	fainted
x. 9 Possesse not	Provide neither
— 15 easier	more tolerable Comp. xi. 22.
— 18 in witnesse to	for a testimony against
— 21 their fathers, and mothers	their parents
— — put them to death	cause them to be put to death
— 29 litle sparowes	sparrows Comp. xi. 16; xv. 26.
— — light	fall
xi. 12 plucke it [vnto them]	take it by force
— 19 and wisdome is (was 1572)	but wisdom is
— 26 was it thy good pleasure	it seemed good in thy sight
— 28 labour sore	labour
— — laden	heavy laden
— — ease you	give you rest
xii. 18 childe	servant
— — well delighteth	is well pleased
— 23 Is not this that	Is this the
— 41 in the iudgement	in judgment
xiii. 11 secretes	mysteries
— 19 that euyll	the wicked one Comp. ver. 38.
— 28 the malicious man	an enemy
— 32 make their nestes	lodge
— 46 precious pearle	pearl of great price
— 54 commeth this wysdome and powers (1568, 1569: mighty woorkes 1572) vnto him	hath this man this wisdom and these mighty works
xiv. 8 platter	charger
— 15 let the people depart	send the multitude away Comp. xv. 32.
— 30 a myghty wynde	the wind boisterous
xv. 5 by the gyft that [is offered] of me, thou shalt be helped	It is a gift by whatsoever thou mightest be profited by me
— 13 Euery plantyng 1568: All maner plantyng 1569, 1572	every plant
— 39 parties	coasts
xvi. 3 lowryng redde	red and lowring
— — outwarde appearaunce	face
— 17 happy	Blessed Comp. xi. 6.
— 18 congregation	church

BISHOPS' BIBLE, 1568, 1569, 1572.	AUTHORISED VERSION, 1611.
xvi. 20 Iesus Christe	Jesus the Christ
— 22 Lorde, fauour thy selfe	Be it far from thee, Lord
— 23 go after me	Get thee behind me
— 24 forsake	deny
— 26 for a raunsome of	in exchange for
xvii. 16 heale	cure Comp. ver. 18.
— 22 were occupyed (1568, 1569 : were conuersant 1572)	abode
— 25 tribute or toule	custom or tribute
— 27 peece of twenty pence	piece of money

CONCLUSION.

THUS step by step and in slow degrees, under every variety of influence, the English Bible assumed its present shape; and the record of its progress is still partially shewn in our public services. Among its other manifold memorials of the past, the Book of Common Prayer preserves clear traces of this eventful history. Some of the Scriptural translations which it contains are original, some are from the Great Bible, some from the Authorised Version. The Offertory sentences and the 'comfortable 'words' are not taken from any version, but are a rendering of the Latin, made probably by Cranmer. The same independence is found in the Evangelic Hymns, the *Benedictus*, the *Magnificat* and the *Nunc dimittis*, which differ more or less from the Great Bible and the Authorised Version. But even here the labour of correction was not neglected; for after their introduction into the first Prayer-Book of 1548 these Hymns were elaborately revised in 1549 and again in 1552. So also the *Benedicite* was revised in 1549, and the burden of the Hymn was altered throughout in 1552.

The Psalms *Venite*, *Jubilate*, *Cantate*, *Deus misereatur*, agree almost literally with the Great Bible (April, 1540), though even in these there are traces of a minute and careful revision; and the same remark holds true also of the Psalms and the Occasional Services[1].

[1] Two changes of tense are worthy of notice. In the *Cantate* (Ps. xcviii. 9) 'he *cometh*' is read for 'he *is* '*come*'; and in Ps. cxvi. 4 (The Churching of Women) 'I *found*,' 'I '*called*' for 'I *shall find*,' and 'I *will* '*call*.'

But the great and enduring monument of the earlier Version of Coverdale and Cranmer[1] is the Psalter itself, which had, as we have seen, become so completely identified with the expression of religious feeling that it was felt to be impossible to displace it[2]. When the last changes in the Prayer-Book were made it was found, it is said, smoother to sing; but this is not a full account of the matter, and it cannot be mere familiarity which gives to the Prayer-Book Psalter, with all its errors and imperfections, an incomparable tenderness and sweetness. Rather we may believe that in it we can yet find the spirit of him whose work it mainly is, full of humility and love, not heroic or creative, but patient to accomplish by God's help the task which had been set him to do, and therefore best in harmony with the tenour of our own daily lives.

But when the Psalter and the Hymns were left unaltered in 1662, the Introductory Sentences and the Epistles and Gospels were at last taken from the Authorised Version. Up to that time the Epistles and Gospels had been printed from the Great Bible with a few, perhaps unintentional, discrepancies, and the Introductory Sentences, like those at present in the Communion Service, had been an original translation. Thus the cycle was completed, and each great stage in the history of our Bible represented in the Prayer-Book.

Whatever else may be thought of the story which has been thus imperfectly told, enough has been said to shew that the history of the English Scriptures is, as was remarked by anticipation, unique. The other great vernacular

---

[1] [It may be confidently stated that the Prayer-Book Version of the Psalms is due to Coverdale alone. If all the words which are taken from Coverdale (1535) be underlined with red, those from the Great Bible of 1539 with blue, and those from the edition of April 1540 (Whitchurch) with black, it will be found that there remain only slight verbal changes, with some errors, which have been made in later editions. There is no reason to suppose that Cranmer had anything to do with the translation of the Psalter, though he wrote the Prologue to the Bible of April 1540.]

[2] See p. 199.

versions of Europe are the works of single men, definitely stamped with their impress and bearing their names. A German writer somewhat contemptuously remarks that it took nearly a century to accomplish in England the work which Luther achieved in the fraction of a single lifetime. The reproach is exactly our glory. Our version is the work of a Church and not of a man. Or rather it is a growth and not a work. Countless external influences, independent of the actual translators, contributed to mould it; and when it was fashioned the Christian instinct of the nation, touched, as we believe, by the Spirit of God, decided on its authority. But at the same time, as if to save us from that worship of the letter, which is the counterfeit of true and implicit devotion to the sacred text, the same original words are offered to us in other forms in our Prayer-Book, and thus the sanction of use is distinguished from the claim to finality. Our Bible in virtue of its past is capable of admitting revision, if need be, without violating its history. As it gathered into itself, during the hundred years in which it was forming, the treasures of manifold labours, so it still has the same assimilative power of life.

One Version only in old times, the Latin Vulgate, can in this respect be compared with it. This also was formed by private efforts silently and slowly till it was acknowledged by the acceptance of the Western Church. One supremely great man, Jerome, partly revised and partly renewed it, and by a strange coincidence even he could not displace the old Psalter which had been adopted for public use. But the English Bible has what the Latin Bible, as far as we know, had not. It has not only the prerogative of vitality while the other has been definitely fixed in one shape, but it has also the seal of martyrdom upon it. In this too it differs from the other great modern versions. Luther defied his enemies to the last. Lefevre in extreme old age mourned that when the opportunity was given him he had not been found worthy to give up his life for Christ. Calvin died sovereign at

Geneva. But Tindale, who gave us our first New Testament from the Greek, was strangled for his work at Vilvorde: Coverdale, who gave us our first printed Bible, narrowly escaped the stake by exile: Rogers, to whom we owe the multiform basis of our present Version, was the first victim of the Marian persecution: Cranmer, who has left us our Psalter[1], was at last blessed with a death of triumphant agony.

The work was crowned by martyrdom and the workmen laboured at it in the faith and with the love of martyrs. The solemn words in which they commend the Bible to their readers, the prayers which they offer for the spiritual enlightenment of their countrymen, the confessions which they make of their own insufficiency, have even now lost nothing of their eloquence. These are the moral of the story.

'I haue here translated,' writes Tindale, and these were his first words, '(brethern and susters moost dere and 'tenderly beloued in Christ) the newe Testament for youre 'spirituall edyfyinge, consolacion, and solas: Exhortynge 'instantly and besechynge those that are better sene in 'the tonge then y, and that have hyer gyfte of grace to 'interpret the sence of the scripture, and meanynge of 'the spyrite, then y, to consydre and pondre my laboure, 'and that with the spyrite of mekenes. And yf they 'perceyve in eny places that y have not attayned the 'very sence of the tonge, or meanynge of the scripture, 'or haue not geven the right englysshe worde, that they 'put to there hande to amende it, remembrynge that so 'is there duetie to doo. For we have not receyved the 'gyfte of god for oure selues only, or forto hyde them: 'but forto bestowe them vnto the honouringe of god and 'christ, and edyfyinge of the congregacion, which is the 'body of christ.'

'As for the commendacyon of Gods holy scripture,' writes Coverdale, 'I wolde fayne magnifye it as it is 'worthy, but I am farre vnsufficiēt therto. & therfore

[1] But see note 1, p. 280.

'I thoughte it better for me to holde my tonge, then
'with few wordes to prayse or commēde it : exhortynge
'yᵉ (most deare reader) so to loue it, so to cleue vnto it,
'& so to folowe it in thy daylye conuersacyon, yᵗ other
'men seynge thy good workes & the frutes of yᵉ holy
'goost in the, maye prayse the father of heauen, & geue
'his worde a good reporte . for to lyue after the lawe of
'God, and to leade a vertuous conuersacyon, is the greatest
'prayse yᵗ thou canst geue vnto his doctryne...'

    'Euery man,' writes Cranmer, 'that commeth to the
'readynge of thys holy booke ought to brynge wyth him
'fyrst and formoste thys feare of almyghtye God, and
'then nexte a fyrme and stable purpose to reforme hys
'awne selfe accordyng ther vnto, and so to continue,
'procede, and prospere frō tyme to tyme, shewynge hym
'selfe to be a sober and frutefull hearer ād learner, whych
'yf he do, he shall proue at the length well able to
'teache, though not wyth his mouth, yet with his liuynge
'and good example, whych is suer the moost lyuely, and
'effecteouse forme and maner of teachyng.'

    'It remaineth, that we commend thee to God, and to
'the Spirit of his grace, which is able to build further
'than we can aske or thinke. Hee remoueth the scales
'from our eyes, the vaile from our hearts, opening our
'wits that we may vnderstand his word, enlarging our
'hearts, yea correcting our affections, that we may loue
'it aboue gold and siluer, yea that we may loue it
'to the end. Ye are brought vnto fountaines of liuing
'water which yee digged not : doe not cast earth into them
'with the Philistines, neither preferre broken pits before
'them with the wicked Iewes. Others haue laboured, and
'you may enter into their labours ; O receiue not so great
'things in vaine, O despise not so great saluation !......
'It is a fearefull thing to fall into the hands of the liuing
'God ; but a blessed thing it is, and will bring vs to
'euerlasting blessednes in the end, when God speaketh
'vnto us, to hearken ; when he setteth his word before vs,

'to reade it ; when he stretcheth out his hand and calleth,
'to answere, Here am I ; here we are to doe thy will,
'O God.   The Lord worke a care and conscience in vs to
'know him and serue him, that we may be acknowledged
'of him at the appearing of our Lord Iesus Christ, to
'whom with the holy Ghost, be all prayse and thankes-
'giuing.   Amen.'

APPENDICES.

I. SPECIMENS OF THE EARLIER AND LATER WYCLIFFITE VERSIONS.

II. CHRONOLOGICAL LIST OF EDITIONS OF BIBLES AND OF PARTS OF THE BIBLE OF CRITICAL IMPORTANCE IN THE HISTORY OF THE AUTHORISED VERSION.

II. COLLATION OF 1 JOHN IN THE THREE TEXTS OF TINDALE.

IV. AN EXAMINATION OF THE SOURCES OF COVERDALE'S NOTES.

V. SPECIMENS OF THE NOTES OF TINDALE AND MATTHEW.

VI. SPECIMENS OF THE LATIN-ENGLISH TESTAMENTS OF COVERDALE.

VII. PASSAGES FROM THE PENTATEUCH AND HISTORICAL BOOKS IN TINDALE, COVERDALE, &c.

VIII. THE RELATION OF THE WYCLIFFITE TO THE LATER VERSIONS.

IX. THE REVISION OF THE AUTHORISED VERSION.

X. PHRASES IN THE PSALMS MARKED IN THE PSALTER OF THE GREAT BIBLE AS ADDITIONS FROM THE VULGATE.

XI. SOURCES OF THE NOTES IN MATTHEW'S BIBLE.

XII. NOTES ON THE TRANSLATORS OF THE AUTHORISED VERSION.

XIII. RULES FOR THE TRANSLATION OF THE AUTHORISED VERSION AS REPORTED TO THE SYNOD OF DORT.

APPENDIX I.

Specimens of the earlier and later Wycliffite Versions.

WYCLIFFE.

Lord oure Lord; hou myche meruei-lous is thi name in al the earthe.

For rerid vp is thi grete doing, ouer heuenes.

Of the mouth of vnspekende childer and soukende thou performedist preis-ing, for thin enemys; that thou destroʒe the enemy and the ven-iere.

For I shal see thin heuenes, the werkis of thi fingris; the mone and the sterris, that thou hast found-id.

What is a man, that myndeful thou art of hym; or the son of man, for thou visitist hym?

Thou lassedest hym a lytil lasse fro aungelis; with glorie and worshipe thou

VULGATE.

Domine Dominus noster, quam admi-rabile est nomen tuum in universa ter-ra!

Quoniam elevata est magnificentia tua super cælos.

Ex ore infantium et lactentium perfe-cisti laudem propter inimicos tuos, ut de-struas inimicum et ultorem.

Quoniam videbo cælos tuos, opera di-gitorum tuorum : lu-nam et stellas, quæ tu fundasti.

Quid est homo, quod memor es ejus? aut filius hominis, quoniam visitas eum?

Minuisti eum pau-lo minus ab angelis, gloria et honore co-ronasti eum :

PURVEY.

Lord *thou art* oure Lord; thi name is ful wonderful in al erthe.

For thi greet doyng is reised, aboue he-uenes.

Of the mouth of ʒonge children, not spekynge and souk-ynge mylk, thou ma-dist perfitli heriyng, for thin enemyes; that thou destrie the enemy and avengere.

For Y schal se thin heuenes, the werkis of thi fyngris; the moone and sterris, whiche thou hast foundid.

What is a man, that thou art myndeful of hym; ethir the sone of a virgyn, for thou visitist hym?

Thou hast maad hym a litil lesse than aungels; thou hast corouned hym with

WYCLIFFE.	VULGATE.	PURVEY.
crounedest hym, and settist hym ouer the werkis of thin hondys.	et constituisti eum super opera manuum tuarum.	glorie and onour, and hast ordeyned hym aboue the werkis of thin hondis.
Alle thingus thou leidest vnder his feet, shep and oxen alle; ferthermor and the bestis of the feeld;	Omnia subjecisti sub pedibus ejus, oves et boves universas : insuper et pecora campi ;	Thou hast maad suget alle thingis vndur hise feet; alle scheep and oxis, ferthermore and the beestis of the feeld ;
the foulis of heuene, and the fishis of the se; that thurȝ gon the sties of the se.	volucres cæli, et pisces maris, qui perambulant semitas maris.	the briddis of the eir, and the fischis of the see ; that passen bi the pathis of the see.
Lord, oure Lord ; hou myche merueilous is thi name in al erthe.	Domine Dominus noster, quam admirabile est nomen tuum in universa terra!	Lord, *thou art* oure Lord ; thi name is wondurful in al erthe.
For which thing he seith, He styȝinge into hiȝ, ledde caitifte caytif, *or prysonynge prisoned,* he ȝaf ȝiftis to men.	Propter quod dicit : Ascendens in altum captivam duxit captivitatem : dedit dona hominibus.	For which thing he seith, He stiyinge an hiȝ, ledde caitifte caitif, he ȝaf ȝiftis to men.
Forsoth that he assendide, what is it, no but for he dessendide first into the lowere partis of the erthe?	Quod autem ascendit, quid est, nisi quia et descendit primum in inferiores partes terræ ?	But what is it, that he stiede vp, no but that also he cam doun first in to the lowere partis of the erthe?
He it is that cam down, and that stiȝede vp on alle heuenes, that he schulde fulfille alle thingis.	Qui descendit, ipse est et qui ascendit super omnes cælos, ut impleret omnia.	He it is that cam doun, and that stiede on alle heuenes, that he schulde fille alle thingis.
And he ȝaf summe sotheli apostlis, summe forsoth prophetis, othere forsothe euangelistis, othere forsoth schepherdis and techeris,	Et ipse dedit quosdam quidem apostolos, quosdam autem prophetas, alios vero evangelistas, alios autem pastores et doctores.	And he ȝaf summe apostlis, summe prophetis, othere euangelistis, othere scheepherdis, and techeris,
to the ful endynge	ad consummatio-	to the ful endyng

WYCLIFFE.

of seyntis, into the work of mynisterie, into edificacioun of Cristis body,

til we rennen alle, in vnyte of feith and of knowynge of God-dis sone, into a parfyt man, into the mesure of age of the plente of Crist;

that we ben not now litile children, mouynge as wawis, and be borun aboute with al wynd of tech-inge, in the weyward-nesse of men, in sutil witt, to the discey-uynge of errour.

VULGATE.

nem sanctorum in opus ministerii, in ædificationem corpo-ris Christi:

donec occurramus omnes in unitatem fidei, et agnitionis Fi-lii Dei, in virum per-fectum, in mensuram ætatis plenitudinis Christi:

ut jam non simus parvuli fluctuantes, et circumferamur om-ni vento doctrinæ in nequitia hominum, in astutia ad circum-ventionem erroris.

PURVEY.

of seyntis, in to the werk of mynystrie, in to edificacioun of Cristis bodi,

til we rennen alle, in to vnyte of feith and of knowyng of Goddis sone, in to a parfit man, aftir the mesure of age of the plente of Crist;

that we be not now litle children, mo-uynge as wawis, and be not borun aboute with ech wynd of teching, in the wei-wardnesse of men, in sutil wit, to the dis-seyuyng of errour.

APPENDIX II.

Chronological List of Editions of Bibles and of parts of the Bible of critical importance in the History of the Authorised Version.

In the following list I have only included those editions which have a direct literary bearing on the history of the Authorised Version. It has no bibliographical object whatever. In foreign versions it has generally seemed sufficient to mark the *first* edition of each work. In the case of rare books I have indicated the copies which I have been allowed to use. The principal sources of the several English versions are added in brackets.

Foreign Translations.

1516 Erasmus' first Edition of the Greek Testament with a new Latin Translation.
1519 Erasmus' second Edition.
1520 The Complutensian Polyglott, Hebrew, Chaldee, Greek and Latin texts.
1522 ERASMUS' THIRD EDITION.
—— LUTHER'S GERMAN NEW TESTAMENT (Sept. and Dec.)
1523 LUTHER'S PENTATEUCH.
1524 LUTHER'S HISTORICAL AND POETICAL BOOKS OF THE OLD TESTAMENT.
—— ZURICH VERSION OF THE PROPHETS.

English Translations.

1525 Tindale's New Testament in two shapes.
[Erasmus, Luther.]

Foreign Translations.

1527-29. ZURICH VERSION finished.

1528 SANCTES PAGNINUS' Latin Version of the Bible.

1532 LUTHER'S VERSION finished.

1534 LUTHER'S BIBLE published.

1534-5 SEB. MÜNSTER'S Latin Version of the Old Testament.

1534 Lefèvre's French Version.

1535 Olivetan's French Version.

English Translations.

1530 Tindale's Pentateuch.

1534 Tindale's New Testament revised[1].

[First edition, Luther, Complutensian readings, Erasmus.]

—— Tindale's Pentateuch revised.

1535 Tindale's New Testament again revised[2]. [See p. 161.]

1535 Coverdale's Bible[3].

[Vulgate, Luther, Zurich, Pagninus, Tindale.]

1536 Coverdale's Bible, second edition[4].

[1] The newe Testament, dylygently corrected and compared with the Greke by Willyam Tindale: and fynesshed in the yere of oure Lorde God A. M. D. &. xxxiiii. in the moneth of Nouember.

Second title.

The newe Testament. Imprinted at Anwerp by Marten Emperowr. Anno .M.D.xxxiiij.

[Univ. Libr. & Trin. Coll. Cambridge. Brit. Mus.]

[2] The newe Testament, dylygently corrected and compared with the Greke by Willyam Tindale: and fynesshed in the yere of oure Lorde God A. M. D. and xxxv.

No imprint. [Probably pirated.]

[Univ. Libr. Cambridge.]

[3] The following are the title-pages of the different issues of the first edition of Coverdale's Bible.

(a) Biblia The Bible, that is, the holy Scripture of the Olde and New Testament, faithfully and truly translated out of Douche and Latyn in to

Englishe. M.D.xxxv.

Colophon:

Prynted in the yeare of oure LORDE M.D.xxxv. and fynished the fourth daye of October.

[Earl of Leicester. British Museum (not quite perfect).]

(β) Biblia The Byble : that is, the holy Scrypture of the Olde and New Testament, faythfully translated in to Englyshe. M.D.xxxv.

[Marquess of Northampton.]

(γ) Biblia The Byble : that is, the holy Scrypture of the Olde and New Testament, faythfully translated in to Englyshe. M.D.xxxvi.

[Earl of Jersey (now in the Earl of Carysfort's Library). Gloucester Cathedral Library.]

[4] Bible The Byble, that is the holy Scripture of the Olde and New Testament, faythfully translated in Englysh, and newly ouersene & corrected. M.D.xxxvii.

Imprynted in Sowthwarke for Iames Nycolson.

English Translations.

1537 Matthew's Bible[1]
[Tɪndale, Coverdale.]

1538 Coverdale's Latin-English
Testaments.

1539 Aprıl.   First Edition of the
Great Bible[2].
[Matthew, Münster, Erasmus,
Complutensian Polyglott.]

1539 Taverner's Bible[3].
[Matthew's, Vulgate, Greek
text.]

1540 April.   Second Edition of
the Great Bible[4].
[First   Edition,   Münster,
Erasmus, Complut. Pol.]

1540 Nov.   Fourth   Edition   of
the Great Bible[5].
[First and second editions.]

[Baptist College, Bristol.   Lincoln
Cathedral Library.   British Museum
(imperfect).]

[1] The Byble, which is all the holy
Scripture: In which are contayned
the Olde and Newe Testament truely
and purely translated into Englysh
by Thomas Matthew .M,D,xxxvii,
Set forth with the Kinges most gracyous lycēce.
Colophon:
To the honoure and prayse of God
was this Byble prynted and fynesshed,
in the yere of oure Lorde God a,
M,D,xxxvii.

[2] The Byble in Englyshe, that is
to saye the content of all the holy
scrypture, bothe of yᵉ olde and newe
testament, truly translated after the
veryte of the Hebrue and Greke
textes, by yᵉ dylygent studye of dyuerse excellent learned men, expert
in the forsayde tonges.   Prynted by
Rychard Grafton & Edward Whitchurch.   Cum priuilegio ad ımpri-
mendum solum.   1539--- Fynisshed
in Apryll, Anno .M.CCCC.XXXIX.   *A
Dño factū est istud.*

[British Museum.   Baptist College,

Bristol.]

[3] The most sacred Bible, Whiche
is the holy scripture, conteyning the
old and new testament, translated in
to English, and newly recognised
with great diligence after most fayth-
ful exemplars, by Rychard Taverner.
Prynted at London. .by Iohn Byd-
dell, for Thomas Barthlet.   Cum
Priuilegio ad imprimendum solum.
M.D.xxxix.

[4] The Byble in Englyshe testament, with a prologe therinto, made
by the reuerende father in God,
Thomas archbysshop of Cantorbury,
This is the Byble apoynted to the
vse of the churches.   Cum privilegio M.D.XL.   *Colophòn:* Fynisshed in Apryll, Anno M.CCCC.XL.   *A
dño factū est istud.*

[British Museum.   Baptist College,
Bristol.]

[5] The Byble in Englyshe of the
largest and greatest volume, aucto-
rysed and apoynted by the com-
maundemente of oure moost redoubted
Prynce and soueraygne Lorde Kynge
Henrye the viii. supreme heade of
this his churche and realme of Eng-

Foreign Translations.

1543 LEO JUDA'S Latin Version.
1550 Stephens' third edition of the Greek Testament (ed. regia).
1551 CASTALIO'S Latin Version.
1556 Beza's Latin Version of the New Testament.

1558 Revised edition of the Bible of Olivetan.
[1559 Beza's first edition of the Greek Testament with Latin Version.]

[1565 Beza's second edition.]

[1569 Spanish Version of the Bible by Cassiodoro de Reyna.]
1572 ARIAS MONTANUS' interlinear translation of the Hebrew text with Pagninus' Version.

English Translations.

1557 Genevan Testament[1].
[Tindale, Beza.]

1560 Genevan Bible[2].
[Original texts, Great Bible, Leo Juda, Beza, French Version.]

1568 The Bishops' Bible[3].
[Great Bible, Genevan, Original texts, Castalio.]

1572 The Bishops' Bible, second edition.
[First edition, Greek Testament.]
1576 Tomson's revised Genevan Testament.
[Genevan Bible, Beza, Greek text.]

lande : to be frequented and vsed in euery churche wᵗ in this his sayd realme, accordynge to the tenour of his former Iniunctions geuen in that behalfe. Ouersene and perused at the cōmaundemēt of the kynges hyghnes, by the ryghte reuerende fathers in God Cuthbert bysshop of Duresme and Nicolas bisshop of Rochester. Printed by Edwarde Whitchurch. Cum priuilegio ad imprimendum solum. 1541. Fynyshed in Nouember anno M CCCCC XL. *A Dn̄o factū est istud.*

[British Museum.]
[1] The Newe Testament of our Lord Iesus Christ...
Colophon: Printed By Conrad Badius, M.D.LVII. this x. of Iune.
[2] The Bible and Holy Scriptures conteyned in the olde and newe Testament. Translated according to the Ebrue and Greke, and conferred with the best translations in diuers langages... At Geneva. Printed by Rouland Hall. M.D.LX.
[3] The Holie Bible.

Foreign Translations.	*English Translations.*
1579 TREMELLIUS' Latin Version of the Old Testament, and version of the Syriac New Testament.	
—— JUNIUS' Latin Version of the Apocrypha.	
1582 Beza's third edition of the Greek Testament.	1582 Rhemish New Testament[1] [Vulgate, Genevan.]
1588 FRENCH BIBLE revised by the Pastors at Geneva.	
1602 Cypriano de Valera's Spanish Version.	
1607 Giovanni Diodati's Italian Version.	
	1609–10 Douai Old Testament[2]. [Vulgate, Genevan.]
	1611 Authorised Version. [Original texts, Bishops' Bible, Genevan, Rhemish, Tremellius, Beza and earlier Latin Versions.]

---

[1] The New Testament of Iesus Christ, translated faithfully into English, out of the authentical Latin... 1582. Cum privilegio.

[2] The Holie Bible faithfully translated into English, out of the authentical Latin...Tom. I. M.DC.IX. Tom. II. M.DC.X.

APPENDIX III.

Collation of 1 *John in the editions of Tindale's New Testament,* 1525, 1534, 1535.

The reading of Tindale's revision of 1534 (T₂) is given first: that for which it is substituted is the reading of the original translation (T₁, 1525). Where the reading of the revision of 1535 (T₃) is not specified it agrees with T₂. When the reading of T₃ alone is given T₁ and T₂ agree against it.

i. 1 om. '*declare we unto you*' after 'beginning' (1)

T₁T₃ om. '*concerning*' before '*which*' (33). So Matthew.

 4 '*oure* ioye' for '*youre* ioye' (2). Not Matthew.

 7 '*Iesus* Christ' for 'Christ' (3)

 8 'yf we saye' for 'yf we *shall* saye' (4)

ii. 1 'synne not' for '*shulde* not sinne' (5)

— 'yf...yet' for '*and* yf...yet' (6)

 2 T₃ '*youre* synnes' for '*oure* synnes' (34). Not Matthew.

 3 'we *are sure*' for 'we *knowe*' (7)

— '*knowe* him' for '*have knowen* him' (8)

 5 '*therby*' for '*therin*' (9)

 9 'the light' for 'the *true* light' (10)

 11 T₃ '*the* darkness' for '*thatt* darknes' (35). Not Matthew.

 13 T₃ 'ye *know*' twice for 'ye *have knowen*,' and so ver. 14 (36). So Matthew.

 17 T₃ 'abideth *euer*' for 'abydeth *for ever*' (37). So Matthew[1].

 21 T₃ '*know* not' for '*knewe* not' (Matthew) (38)

 22 '*the same* is *the* Antichrist' for '*he* is Antichrist' (11)

[1 But T₁ T₂ T₃ all read 'abideth ever.' The error is in Bagster's Hexapla.]

iii. 1   T₃ 'on *to* us' for '*on* us' (Matthew) (39)

—   '*knoweth* not him' for '*hath* not *knowen* him' (12)

  2   '*dothe* not *appere*' for '*hath* not *apered*' (13)

  4   '*for* synne is' for '*and* synne is' (14)

11   'that *we* shuld' for 'that *ye* shulde', which is also in T₃ (15)

15   T₃ '*hate*' for '*hateth*' (Matthew) (40)

16   'and *therfore*' for '*and*' (16)

—   'ought we' for 'we ought' (17)

17   '*have neade*' for '*in necessitie*' (18)

18   T₃ 'with *the* dede' for 'with dede' (41). So Matthew.

19   '*for therby*' for '*and hereby*' (19)

—   '*can* before him *quiet* our hertes' for '*will* before hym *put* oure hertes *out of dout*' (20)

20   '*But*' for '*For*' (21)

21   'Beloved' for '*Tenderly* beloved': comp. iv. 1, 7, 11 (22)

24   '*therby*' for '*herby*' (23)

iv. 1   '*Ye* beloved' for '*Derely* beloved' (24)

—   T₃ 'or *not*' for 'or *no*' (42). So Matthew.

  3   T₃ '*that* confesseth' for '*which* confesseth' (Matthew) (43)

  5   '*and* therfore' for '*therfore*' (25)

—   T₃ 'and *that* world' for 'and *the* worlde' (Matthew) (44)

  7   'Beloved' for '*Derely* beloved,' so iv. 11 (26)

  8   '*knoweth* not' for '*hath* nott *knowen*' (27)

20   '*hate*' for '*hateth*' (28)

—   '*For* how' for '*Howe*' (29)

v. 1   T₃ 'that Jesus Christ' for 'Iesus *is* Christ' (Matthew) (45)

  7   'for there'...'are one.' In smaller type and in brackets. In T₃ the words are in ( ). In the first edition no difference is marked (30)

  8   '*For*' for '*And*' (31)

15   '*desire*' for '*desired*' (32)

In this list 1, 4, 5, 10, 11, 18, 22, 24, 26, 29 are closer renderings of the Greek text.

On the other hand 6, 9, 14, 16, 19, 21, 25, 31 are instances of the abandonment of the more literal renderings in order (as it seems) to bring out the argument with greater distinctness.

The aorist which was first rendered by a perfect form is rendered by an indefinite present in 8, 12, 13, 27: a mode of rendering adopted for the perfect in 32. The change in 7 seems to be a consequence of the change in 8 to avoid repetition.

An error of grammar is corrected in 28, and an improvement of rhythm is introduced in 17. .

Two false readings are corrected in 3, 15 ; and a new reading adopted in 2. The spurious passage in v. 7 is marked (30).

The changes are more frequently away from Luther than to Luther ; but it is impossible not to think that Luther suggested the longest change of rendering (20), for which he has (1534) 'dass wir, *können* vnser Hertz fur ihm *stillen*[1].'

Of the renderings first introduced in 1535 three are improved translations (33, 35, 38): two are worse renderings for emphasis (41, 44): one is a false reading [? a misprint] (34): one is a substitution (as before) of an indefinite present for a perfect (36): two appear to be indifferent (42, 43): three are probably misprints (39, 40, 45).

In the Epistle to the Ephesians the changes generally are of the same character. Two of these very worthy of notice have influenced our present text, of which one is the singularly beautiful '*making melody* in your hearts' (v. 19) for '*playing*': and the other the strange substitution of 'which before *believed* in Christ' (i. 12) for 'before *hoped* in Christ', which is altered into 'trusted' in A.V.

[The edition of 1534–5, printed by G. H., agrees with that of 1535 except in 1 John ii. 9, 11, 21, iii. 1, 15, iv. 5, v. 1.]

---

[1] The rendering for which it is substituted was also due to Luther (1522): ' vnd bereden vnser hertz fur yhn.'

APPENDIX IV.

*An Examination of the sources of the Notes in Coverdale's
Bible of* 1535.

ii. 12¹ Some call it *Schoham*.   So Zurich   (1)
  18   to *beare him cōpany*
     Some reade : to *stōde nexte by him*
     Luther (1523): *gegen yhm*
     Luther (1534): *die sich zu jm hielte*
     Zurich (1530): *der zunächst bey jm stunde*   (2)
     Pagninus : quod sit coram eo
     Tindale : to *beare him companye*
     Vulgate : simile sibi

iii. 6   a pleasaunt tre *to make wyse*
     Some reade : *whyle it made wyse*
     L. (1523) *weyl er klug mechte*   (3)
     Z. *dieweil er k. m.*
     P   concupiscibilis arbor ad intelligendum
     T   a pleasant tre for *to make wyse*
     V   aspectu delectabile
  16   *thy lust shal pertayne vnto* thy huszbande
     Some reade : *Thou shalt bowe downe thy self before* thy
        husbande
     L. (1523) *du solt dich ducken fur deynem man*   (4)
     Z. *zu deinem mañ deine gelüst* oder begird
     P   ad virum tuum erit desiderium tuum
     T. *thy lustes shall pertayne vnto* thy husbond
     V   sub viri potestate eris

¹ In some cases I have given only
the Versions from which Coverdale's
renderings are derived   in others I
have thought it worth while to add
parallel renderings for comparison and
contrast.   Simply explanatory notes
as 2 Sam. xvi. 22, 1 K. ii. 17 are
neglected, and one or two others ;
but the list of various renderings is
nearly complete.

iv. 7   *Shal he then be* subdued vnto the? *and wilt thou rule him?*

Some reade: *Let it be* subdued vnto the, and *rule thou it*

L. (1534) Las du ir nicht jren willen, sondern *herrsche vber sie*

Z. *Stadt dañ sein aufsehen zu dir, vnd wilt über in herrschen?*

P. in te erit appetitus ejus et dominaberis ei

T. *Let it be* subdued vnto the, ād see thou *rule it*   (5)

V. sub te erit appetitus ejus et dominaberis illius

viii. 7   came agayne

Some reade: came *not* agayne

so Vulgate   (6)

xi. 2   *towarde* the East   (L)

Some reade: *frō* the East   (T)

so Vulgate   (7)

xvii. 2   I am the *allmightie* God   (V. L. P. T.)

Some reade I am the God *Schadai* (*that is : plenteous in power, abundaunt, sufficiēt, and full of all good*)

so Z. (1530) (*das ist, ein vollmächtiger, vnnd ein über-flüssige genugsamme vnnd volly alles gutenn*)   (8)

xviii. 10   aboute this tyme twolue moneth, (*yf I lyue*)

Some reade: *As soone as the frute cā lyue*

L. (1523) *nach der zeyt die frucht leben kan*

L. (1534) *so ich lebe*

Z. so ich läb

P. revertar ad te secundum tempus vitæ

T. *as soone as the frute can lyue*   (9)

V. Revertens veniam ad te tempore isto, vita comite

xxiii. 4   bury my coarse *by me*

Some reade: my coarse *that lyeth before me*

L. (1523) der fur mir legt   (10)

Z. *mein leych bey mir*

xxiv. 31   thou *blessed* of the Lorde   (V. L. P. T.)

Some reade thou *beloved*

Z. *du geliebter*   (11)

xxvii. 25   that my *soule maye blesse the*   (V. L. P. T.)
            that my *hert maye wysh the good*
            Z. *das ich von hertzen dir guts wünsche*   (12)

xxviii. 1   *blessed him*   (V. L. P. T.)
            Some reade : *talked louīgly with him*
            Z. *redt freüntlich mit jm*   (13)

xxxiii. 19 *an hundred pence*   (L., Z. *vmb hundert grosschen*)
            Some reade : *an hūdreth lābes*   (So V. P. T.)   (14)

xli. 44   called him *Zephnath Paena*
            Zaphnath Paena, that is to saye   *An expoūder of
               secrete thinges,* or *a man to whō secrete thīges are
               opened*
            L. (1534) *Den heimlichsten Rat*
            Z. Zaphnath Paena; L. (1523) *Zaphnath paenea*
            P *vir cui abscondita revelata sunt,* vel *absconditorum
               expositor*   (15)
            V. *Salvatorem mundi*

ix. 16   haue I *stered yᵉ vp*
            Some reade : I haue *holden the vp*
            L. (1523) *hab ich dich erweckt*
            Z. *hab ich dich aufrecht behalten*   (16)
            P. *Stare feci te*
            V. *posui te*

xvi. 15   *This is Mā*   (So L. Z. *Das ist Man.   Man est* P.)
            Some reade . *What is this?*   (So V T.)   (17)

xvii. 15   The Lorde Nissi   (L.)
            That is : *The Lord is he that lifteth me vp*
            P. *dominus elevatio mea*   (18)

xxix. 28   in their *deade offrynges*
            Some call thē *peace offeringes*   (So T.)
            L. (1534) *an jren danckopffern*
            Z. an jren *tödopffern*   (So L. 1523)
            P. De sacrificiis *pacificorum suorum*   (19)
            V. *de victimis eorum pacificis*

iii. 15   full of all maner waters *of the londe*
            Some reade : *of the harvest*
            L. (1524) *vol an allen seynen vffern von allerley gewesser
               der erndten*   (20)

iii. 15 Z. voll an allen seinen gstadē, *von allerley gewässer der erden*
P. *omnibus diebus messis*
V. *tempore messis*

iii. 3 *moffell* the
Some reade : *Anoynte* the
Z. *verhülle* dich (So L.)
P. *unge te* (21)

xxiii. 28 Sela Mahelkoth (L. Z.)
The rocke of *partinge asunder*
P. petra *divisionum* (So L. marg.) (22)

viii. 18 *prestes* (So V. L. Z.)
Some reade : *rulers*
P. *principes* (23)

xxv. 6 And *he gaue* iudgmēt *vpon him*
Some reade : And *they talked with hī of* iudgmēt
L. (1534) sie sprachen ein vrteil vber jn
Z. *sy redtend mit jm vom rechten* (So L. 1523) (24)
V. *locutus est cum eo judicium*
P. *locuti sunt cum eo judicium*
Matthew, they reasoned with hym

vii. 20 rote *you* out
Some reade : *them*
L. (1523) sie aus wurtzelen
Z. *sy auszwurtzlē*
P. evellam *eos* (25)
V. evellam vos

ix. 10 so madest thou *the* a name
Some reade: *them*
Z. *jnenn* (26)
L. (1523) *yhn* L. (1534) *jnen*

xiv. 5—7 These thre verses are not in the Hebrue (27)

xxxvi. (xxxvii.) 21 *The vngodly boroweth and paieth not agayne*
(So V. L. P. Z. (1530))
Some reade thus : *The vngodly lēdeth vpon vsury and not for naught*
Z. (1531, 1534, 1536) *Auff wücher leicht der Gottlos, nit vm̄ sunst* (28)

xxxix. (xl.) 7 but *a body hast thou ordeined me* (Hebr. x. 5)
Some reade thus : but *myne eares hast thou opened*
(So L. Z.)   (29)
P. *aures fodisti mihi*
V. *aures autem perfecisti mihi*

vii. 7 *a masons trowell*
Some call it *a lyne*
L. (1532) *eine bleischnur*   (30)
Z. ein *maurerkellen*
P. *perpendiculum*

ii. 14 So dyd not the one
The one.   This the interpreters rekē to be spoken
of Abraham
L. (1532) Also thet der Einige nicht
Z. er hat nit allein einen menschen gemachet
P. nec unus quidem *Abraham* fecit ut facitis   (31)

iv. 52 as touchinge yⁱ life[1]
Some rede, *my* life
Z. (1530) *dein* läbenn
Z. (1531, 1534, 1536) *mein* läben   (32)
V de vita *tua*

xii. 1 yᵉ heade
Rede, I sawe, and beholde
Z. do hab ich gesehen   (33)

xv. 55 receaue *rewarde*
Some rede, *no rewarde*   (Z. 1531, 1534, 1536)   (34)

i. 14 hauynge ten talētes of *syluer*   (V.)
Some reade : ten talētes of *golde*
Z. zähennt Talent *golds*   (35)

iv. 10 delyuereth *frō death*
Some reade : frō *all synne & from death*
P. ab *omni peccato et a* morte   So L. (1534)   (36)

xii. 6 shewed his mercy vnto *vs*   (P. Z.)
Some reade, vnto *you*   So V. L. (1534)   (37)

---

[1] [Bagster's reprint has yᵉ.]

iii. 23   curious in many of *his* workes (P.)
        Some rede, *thy* workes
        Z. *deiner* wercken (38)

xxxiii. 15   there are euer two agaynst *two* (P.)
        Some reade : two agaynst *one*
        Z. zwey gegen *einen* (39)

ii. 13   wrytynges of *Ieremy*
        Some reade : *Nehemias*
        Z. *Ieremie*
        L. (1534) *Nehemias*
        P. *Nechemiah* (40)

xii. 43   *two* thousande drachmas
        Some reade : *twolue* thousande
        Z. zweytausent So L. (1534)
        P. *duodecim* milla (41)

i. 18   before they *came together*
        Some reade : before they *sat at home together*
        L. (1534) ehe er sie heim holet
        Z. *ee sy miteinanderen zu hausz sassend* (So L. 1522)
            (42)
        Erasmus : priusquam congressi fuissent
        Tindale : cam *to dwell* to gedder

xi. 11   *lesse* (T. 1534)
        Some reade : *least*
        L. (Sept. 1522) der *kleynist* (43)

xvi. 13   y^t ye sonne of mā *is*
        Some reade that *I the* sonne of man *am* (T.)
        L. (Sept. 1522) *das da sey des menschen son*
        L. (Dec. 1522) *das des menschen son sey* (44)
        Z. (1531) *das da sey dess menschen sun*

xx. 25   the greatest *exercise power* (T.)
        Some reade, The greatest *deale with violence*
        L. (1534) *haben gewalt*
        L. (Sept. 1522) die vberherrnn *faren mit gewalt* (So Z.)
            (45)

xxiii. 25   *excesse* (T)
        Some reade : *vnclennes*
        L. (1534) frasses

xxiii. 25.   L. (1522) vnreynes
             Z. *vnreyns* (46)
             P. injustitia
             E. intemperantia

xxvi. 7   a boxe with precious *oyntment*
             Some reade : *A glas with precious water*
             L. (1522) *eyn glas mitt kostlichem wasser* (47)
             T an *alablaster* boxe of precious oyntment

   i. 11   in whom I *delyte* (T.)
             Some reade : In whō I *am pacified*
             L. (1522) *ynn dem ich eyn wolgefallen habe*
             Z. in dem ich zu friden bin (48)

 iii. 21   he *taketh to moch vpon him*
             Some reade . He *wil go out of his witt*
             L. (1534) *er wird von Sinnen komen* (49)
             Z. *Er thut jm zu vil* So L. (1522)
             P. in stuporem versus est
             E. in furorem versus est
             T. (1534) he had bene beside him selfe

 xiii. 9   *councels* (T.)
             Some reade : *coūcell-houses*
             L. (1522) *radtheuser* So Z. (50)

  ix. 40   she sat *hir downe agayne*
             Some reade : She sat *vp* (T.) (51)
             L. (1522) *satzt sie sich widder*

  xv. 3   *conuersation* (T. 1525)
             Some reade : *conuersion* (T.)
             L. *wandel*
             V. *conversionem* (52)

 xvii. 18   new *goddes*
             Some reade : *deuyls* (T.)
             L. *Götter*
             V. *dæmoniorum* (53)

 iii. 28   by faith (T.)
             Some reade : By faith *onely*
             L. (1522) *alleyn durch den glawben* So Z. (54)

x. 17 by *hearynge* (T.)
   Some reade : By *preachinge*
   L. aus der *predigte* So Z. (55)

Thus of the whole number (54) of alternative renderings twelve (3, 4, 5, 10, 29, 42, 43, 47, 49, 50, 54, 55) agree with Luther nineteen (1, 2, 8, 11, 12, 13, 16, 24—6, 28, 32, 33, 34, 35, 38, 39, 46, 48) with the Zurich Version : ten with Pagninus (15, 18, 21—3, 30—1, 36, 40—1) : nine with the Vulgate (6, 7, 14, 17, 19, 20, 37, 52, 53) ; and four with Tindale (9, 44—5, 51). Of these the most remarkable coincidences with Luther are 3, 4, 10, 42, 47, 54, 55; with the Zurich Version 8, with Pagninus 15, 31, with Tindale 9, 52, 53. Of the readings adopted the most singular are 17, 19 (Luther) and 10, 20 (Zurich); 24 is apparently adapted from the Vulgate.

Nothing could sum up the internal history of Coverdale's Bible more accurately than this analysis.

W.   20

APPENDIX V.

Specimens of Notes from Tindale and Matthew.

Tindale (Cologne), 1525. Iesus is asmoche to saye as a saver, for he onli saveth all men from their synnes bi his meretes with oute there deserving.

Tindale, 1534. *None.*

Matthew. Messiah, it sygnifyeth, annoynted. Iesus Christ then is the earnest & pledge of Goddes promes, by whom yᵉ grace and fauoure of God is promesed to vs, wyth the holy goost: whych illumineth lyghteth & renueth oure hertes to fulfyll the lawe. [From Lefèvre's French Bible of 1534.]

Tindale, 1525. Of mathew they ar callid Magi, & in certeyne coūtreis ī the est, philosophers conynge in naturall causes & effectes, and also the prestes, were so callyd.

Tindale, 1534. *None.*

Matthew. These were nother kynges nor princes, but as Strabo saith (whych was in their tyme) sage men amōge yᵉ Persiens as Moses was amonge the Hebrues, he sayth also yᵗ they were the prestes of yᵉ Persiens. [From Lefèvre's French Bible of 1534.]

Tindale, 1525. Put youre truste ī goddes wordes only, & not ī abraham. Let saynctes be an ensāple vnto you & not youre truste & cōfidence For then ye make Christ of them.

Tindale, 1534. *None.*

Matthew. None.

Tindale, 1525. Trouble, is the dayly laboure. He wil hit be ynough that we laboure dayly wyth oute forther care.

Tindale, 1534. *None.*

Matthew. It is cōmaunded vs ī in the swet of oure face to

winne our bred, that trauayle must we dayly, dilygently & ernestly do: but not be carefull what profet shall come vnto vs therof, for that were to care for to morow: we must therfore cōmytt that to God, which is readye to prospere oure laboures wyth his blessyng, and that aboundaūtly, so that most shall we profet when we are lest carefull.

Tindale, 1525. Compare dede too dede, so ys one greater then another: but cōpare them to god, so are they all lyke, ād one as good as another even as the spyrite movyth a mā, & tyme & occasiō gevyth.

Tindale, 1534. Couenanus.
Matthew. None.

Tindale, 1525. Tradicions of men muste fayle att the last: god word bydeth ever.

Tindale, 1534. Mennes preceptes. What defileth a man. Plantes. Blynde leaders. With what a mā is defiled.

Matthew ver. 13. Origen and Chrisostom vnderstande thys of the Pharises because of their euell opinions. Hilarius And Erasmus vnderstand it of mennes tradicions.

Tindale, 1525. Stronge feyth requyreth fervent prayer, & prayer requyreth fastyng to subdue the bodye, that lustes vnquyet nott a mānes mynde.

Tindale, 1534. Prayer & fastynge.
Matthew. None.

Tindale, 1525. By this similitude maye ye pceave that no similitude serveth throwgh out, but sū one thyng cōteyned ī the similitude. As this lōge parable pteyneth butt here vnto, that werke holy shall despise weeke synners, which same werke holy shall not there have ther rewarde as these which come fyrst have here butt shalbe reiecte & put awaye, because they chalenge hit of meritt & nott of mercy & grace.

Tindale, 1534, ver. 5. The Iewes reken one, whē the sonne is vp an houre.

Matthew. None.

APPENDIX VI.

Specimens of the Latin-English Testaments of Coverdale.

(COVERDALE'S BIBLE.)

1 That which was from ye begynnynge, *which* we ·haue herde, *which* we haue sene with oure *eyes, which* we haue *loked vpon,* and oure handes haue handled *of* the worde of life : 2 and the life *hath appeared,* and we haue sene, and *beare wytnes,* and shewe vnto you ye life *that is euerlastinge,* which was *with* the father, and *hath apeared* vnto vs. 3 *That* which we haue sene & *herde, declare we* vnto you, that ye also maye haue fellishippe with vs, and that oure fellishippe *maye be* with the father and with his sonne Iesus Christ. 4 And *this wryte we* vnto you, that *youre* ioye maye be full. 5 And this is the tydinges *which* we haue herde of him, & *declare* vnto you, that God is lighte, and *in him is no darknes at all.* 6 Yf we saye that we haue fellishippe with him, and *yet walke* in darknes, we lye, and do not the trueth. 7 But yf we walke ɪn lighte, *euen, as he* is in lighte, *then haue we* fellishippe together, and the bloude of *Iesus Christ his sonne* clenseth vs from all synne. 8 Yf we *saye* that we haue no synne, we disceaue oure selues, and the trueth is not in vs. 9 *But yf* we knowlege oure synnes, he is faithfull and *iust to* forgeue vs oure synnes, & *to clense* vs from all *vnrighteousnes.* 10 Yf we *saye, we* haue not synned, we makè him a lyar, and his worde ɪs not in vs.

v. 1 *that* which (3) Nicolson. Hollybushe
  eyen N. H.
  beholden N. H.
  cōcerning Regnault. *of* N. H. (*de* Vulgate)

2 *is manifest* N. H.
  testify N. H. R.
  euerlastyng N. H. R. (*vitam æternam* V.), omitting *that is by* N. H.
  appeared N. H.

3 *Euē that* R. (*Quod vidimus* V.)
  haue heard N. H.
  do we shew N. H.
  be N. H.

4 *these thynges* N. R. (*hæc* V.)
  do I write N. *do we wryte* H.
  ye may reioice and (*that* R.) *your* N. H. R. (ut gaudeatis et gaudium vestrum V.)

5 *that* N. H.
  do shewe N H.
  ther is no darkenesse in hym N. H.

6 *walke* N. H. R.

7 *as he also* N. H. R. (*sicut et ipse* V.)
  we haue N. H.
  hys sonne Iesus Christe N. H.

8 *do saye* N. H.

9 *if* N. R. *Yf* H.
  ryghteous that he do N. H.
  clense N. H.
  wyckednesse N. H.

10 *do saye* N. H.
  that we N. H. R. (*quoniam* V.)

v. 16 *Yf eny man se* his brother *synne* a synne not vnto death, let him axe, and *he shal geue him life, for thē* yᵗ synne not vnto death. There is a synne vnto death, *for the which saye I not* that *a* man shulde praye. 17 *All vnrighteousnes* is synne, and there is *synne not* vnto death. 18 We knowe, that *whosoeuer* is borne off God, *synneth not*: but *he that is begottē* of God, kepeth *himselfe*, & yᵗ wicked toucheth him not. 19 We knowe that we are of God, & the *worlde* is set *alltogether* on *wickednes*. 20 *But* we knowe, that the sonne of God is come, and hath geuen vs a *mynde, to* knowe *him*

which is true: and *we are in him* y*ᵗ* *is true*, *in his sonne*
Iesu Christ.   This is the true God, and euerlastinge life.
21 *Babes* kepe *youre selues* from ymages.   *Amen.*

16   *He that knoweth* N. H. R.
    to synne N. H. R.
    lyfe shalbe geuen vnto hym that synneth (*synninge* N. H.)
        N. H. R.
    I saye not that *any* man shulde (*do* N.) praye *for that* (N.)
        R. H.

17   *Euery wyckednesse* N. H.
    a synne N. H. R.   omit *not* N. H. R.

18   *euery one that* N. H.
    doth not synne N. H. R.
    the generacion N. H. R.
    hym N. H. R.
    the N. H. R.

19   the *whole* worlde is set on (*in* N.) *myschefe* N. H. R.

20   *And* N. H. R.
    vnderstandynge, that we maye N. H. R.
    the true God N. H. R.
    be (*we are* N. H.) *in hys true sonne* N. H. R.
    The (This N. H.) *same* N. H. R.

21   *Little children* N. H.   Lytle chyldren H.
    you N. H. R.
    om. *Amen* N. H. R.

APPENDIX VII.

Collation of Passages from the Pentateuch and Historical Books in Tindale, Coverdale, Matthew, the Great Bible, the Genevan Bible, and the Bishops' Bible.

COVERDALE. *I will* synge vnto yͤ LORDE, for he *hath done gloriously*: horse & *charet* hath he ouer throwne in the see.

The LORDE is my strength, and my songe, and is become my saluacion.

This is my God, I wil *magnifie* him: He is my fathers God, I wil *exalte him.*

ZURICH VERSION. Ich wil dem Herren singē, da͠n er hat herrlich gehandlet, rossz vnnd wagen hat er gestürtzt ins Meer.

Der Herr ist mein stercke, vn̄ lobgesang, vnd ist mein helffer worden.

Das ist mein Gott, ich wil jn beherbergen. Er ist meines vatters Gott, ich wil jn erheben[1].

TINDALE (1530). *Let vs* synge vnto the Lorde, for he *is become glorious, the* horse and *him that rode vpon him* hath he ouerthrowne in the see.

The Lorde is my strength ād my songe, ād is become my saluation.

He is my God *and* I will *gloryfie* him, he is my fathers God *and* I will *lifte him vp an hie*[2].

MATTHEW agrees verbally with TINDALE.

TAVERNER agrees verbally with TINDALE.

[1] Luther's Version (1534), with the Latin Version of the Wittenberg Bible (1829), may be added for comparison:
Ich wil dem Herrn singen, denn er hat eine herliche that gethan, Ros vnd wagen hat˜er ins meer gestortzet.
Der Herr ist mein sterck vnd lobsang, vnd ist mein Heil. Das ist mein Gott, ich wil jn preisen, Er ist meines vaters Gott, ich wil jn erheben.
In the Wittenberg Bible the passage runs:

Cantemus Domino, gloriose enim *egit*, equum et ascensorem deiecit in mare.

Fortitudo mea et *carmen meum* Dominus, *qui* factus est mihi in salutem.

Iste *est* Deus meus, et *ornabo* eum, Deus patris mei, et exaltabo eum.

This is nearer to the Vulgate than to Luther, and differs from it only in the italicized words.

[2] The italics mark variations between Tindale and Coverdale.

GREAT BIBLE (1539, 1540, 1541). I wyll...hath *triūphed* gloriously: the horse & hym that rode vpon him :...my strength and *prayse*, and *he* is...He is...glorifye him : my fathers God, and I wyll exalte hym.

[MÜNSTER. ...*triumphando* magnifice egit...Fortitudo mea et *laus* dominus, *factusque est*... Iste Deus meus et *decorabo* eum : deus patris mei, et exaltabo eum.]

GENEVA. I will...hathe triūphed · gloriously : yᵉ horse and him that rode upon him....

The Lord *is* (ital.)...praise, and he is...He is,..*prepare him a tabernacle : he is* (ital.)...exalt him.

BISHOPS' agrees verbally with GREAT BIBLE.

COVERDALE. And Moses sayde: Hereby *shal ye* knowe that the LORDE hath sent me, to do all these workes, and that I haue not done them of myne awne *hert*. Yf these men dye the comon death of all men, or be vysited *as all men are vysited*, then *hath not the* LORDE sent me. But yf the LORDE make a new thinge, and the earth open hir mouth, and swalowe them *with* all *that they haue*, so that they go downe quycke in to hell, thē *shal ye knowe*, that these men haue *blasphemed* tħe LORDE.

LUTHER (1534). Vnd Mose sprach, Dabey solt jr mercken, das mich der Herr gesand hat, das ich alle diese werck thet, vnd nicht aus meinem hertzen. Werden sie sterben, wie alle menschen sterben, oder heimgesucht wie alle menschen heimgesucht werden, so hat mich der Herr nicht gesand. Wird aber der Herr etwas newes schaffen, das die erde jren mund auff thut, vnd verschlinget sie mit allem das sie haben, das sie lebendig hinunter jnn die Helle faren, so werdet jr erkennen, dass diese leute den Herrn gelestert haben[1].

TINDALE. And Moses sayed : Hereby *ye shall* knowe that the Lorde hath sent me to doo all these workes, and that I haue not done them of myne awne *mynde :* Yf these men dye the comon deth of all men or *yf they* be visyted *after the visitacion of all men*, then the Lorde hath not sent me. But *and* yf the Lorde make a new thinge, and the erth open hir mouthe and swalowe them *and* all that *pertayne vnto them*, so that they goo doune quycke in to hell : then ye shall *vnderstōd*, that these mē haue *rayled vpon* the Lorde.

[1] The Wittenberg Bible differs from the Vulgate only by rendering *universa opera hæc et non ex proprio corde* for *universa quæ cernitis et non ex proprio ex corde protulerim*, and by adding *viri isti* after *blasphemaverint*. The Zurich Bible simply differs by dialectic peculiarities.

Matthew agrees verbally with Tindale.

Taverner agrees verbally with Tindale except in reading: of myne own *hed*: But yf (*om.* and).

Great Bible (1539, 1540, 1541) agrees with Tindale except: swalowe them *vp* with all that they haue, *and* they go...*prouoked.*

A note is indicated (in 1539, 1540) by ☞ to 'visited.'

[Münster. devoraverit eos una cùm omnibus quæ habent et descenderint...: *irritarint*...dominum.]

Geneva. for *I haue* (ital.) not *done them* (ital.)...: the Lord (*om.* then): but if: swalowe...go downe quicke into y^e *pit.*

Bishops' agrees with Great Bible except in reading: for I have not done them (Gen.): into *the pit* (Gen.).

Coverdale. And Iosua wrote *this acte* in the boke of the lawe of God, and toke a greate stone, and *set* it *vp there* vnder an oke, *which was* in ye Sanctuary of ye Lorde, and sayde vnto all the people: Beholde, this stone shall be witnesse *ouer you;* For it hath herde all the wordes of the Lorde, which he *hath spoken vnto* us, *and* shall be a witnesse *ouer* you, *that ye denye not* youre God. So Iosua let the people *go* euery *one* to his inheritaūce.

Luther. Vnd Josua schreib dis alles jns Gesetzbuch Gottes, vnd nam einen grossen stein, und richtet jn auff daselbs vnter einer Eiche, die bey dem Heiligthum des Herrn war, vnd sprach zum gantzen volck. Sihe, dieser Stein sol zeuge sein zwisschen vns, denn er hat gehöret alle rede des Herrn, die er mit vns geredt hat, vnd sol ein zeuge vber euch sein, das jr ewrn Gott nicht verleuck[n]et. Also lies Josua das volck, einen jglichen inn sein erbteil[1].

Matthew. [Tindale.] And Iosua wrotte *these wordes* in the boke of the lawe of God, and toke a great stonne & *pitched* it *on ende in ye sayde pláce euen* vnder an ocke *that stode* in the sanctuarye of the Lorde. And *Iosua* sayde vnto all the people: beholde, thys stone shalbe *a* witnesse *vnto vs,* for it hath hearde all the wordes of the Lorde whych *he spake wyth vs. It* shalbe *therfore* a wytnesse *vnto* you, *lest ye lye vnto* youre God. *And* so Iosua let the people *departe* euery *man vnto* hys enherytaunce.

[1] The Wittenberg Bible differs from the Vulgate only in reading *grandem* (pergrandem), *audivit* (audierit), and *locutus est nobis, et erit testis* (loc. est vobis).

The Zurich Bible has the following significant variations:— ...schreyb *disen handel...* die *inn* dem Heyligthumb... zeüg *über euch sein...*

TAVERNER agrees verbally with [TINDALE] MATTHEW except in reading: spake with *you*: leest y^t after this tyme ye wyll denye and lye vnto your God (Vulg. see below).

GREAT BIBLE (1539, 1540, 1541) agrees with TINDALE except by reading: (1) that *was*: and (2) lest *ye denye** (*and dissemble with*).

[MÜNSTER. (1) quæ *erat* (2) ne forte *abnegare velitis* deum vestrum (*Vulg.* ne forte postea negare velitis et mentiri Domino Deo vestro).]

GENEVA agrees with TINDALE except by reading: pitched it *there:* that *was:* a witnes *against* you: lest ye deny your God: *Thē* Joshua....

BISHOPS' agrees with GREAT BIBLE exactly, only omitting the added clause '*and dissemble with.*'

COVERDALE. There were two men in one cite, *the one* riche, *the other* poore. The riche *man* had *very many* shepe and oxen: but the poore *man* had nothinge saue one litle *shepe* which he *had* boughte and norished *it, so that* it grewe vp with him and his children *together. It* ate of his *bred,* and dranke of his cuppe and slepte in his *lappe,* and *he helde it* as *a* doughter. *But whan* there came a straunger vnto the riche man, he *spared* to take of his awne shepe & oxen (to *prepare oughte* for the straunger that was come vnto him) *and* toke the poore mans *shepe,* and *prepared* it for the man that was come vnto him. *Thē was* David wroth *with greate displeasure agaynst that* man, and sayde unto Nathan: As *truly* as the LORDE liueth, the *man* that hath done this, is the childe of death.

LUTHER. Es waren zween menner inn einer stad, einer reich, der ander arm. Der reich hatte seer viel schafe vnd rinder, aber der arme hatte nichts, deñ ein einigs kleins scheflin, das er gekaufft hatte, vnd er neerete es, das es gros ward, bei jm vnd bey seinen kindern zu gleich, Es ass von seinem bissen vnd tranck von seinem becher, und schlieff jnn seinem schos, vnd er hielts wie eine tochter. Da aber dem reichen man ein gast kam, schonet er zu nemen von seinen schafen und rindern, das er dem gast etwas zurichtet, der zu jm komen war, vnd nam das schaf des armen mans, vnd richtet zu, dem man der zu jm komen war. Da ergrimmet Dauid mit grossem zorn wider den man, vnd sprach zu Nathan, So war der Herr lebt, der man ist ein kind des tods, der das gethan hat[1].

[1] The Wittenberg Bible agrees with the Vulgate, except in reading *et creverat* (om. quæ), *ut pararet* (*ut exhiberet*), and in one or two transposi-tions, &c. which are probably various readings of the Vulgate text. The Zurich text has only two unimportant verbal differences.

MATTHEW [TINDALE]. There were two men in one citie, *a* (1) ryche and *a* (1) poore. *And* the ryche (2) had *excedyng great aboundaunce of* (3) shepe and oxē. But the poore had nothyng saue one lytle *lambe* (4) whych he bought (5) & norysshed *vp*. *And* it grew vp with hym and hys children (6), *and did* eate of his *awne meate* and drancke of his *awne* cuppe, & slept in his *bosome*, & *was as dere vnto hym* as *his* daughter (7). *And* there cam a straūger vnto the ryche man. *And* he *coulde not fynde in his heart* to take of his awne shepe *nor of hys beestes* (8) to *dresse* for ẙe straunger ẙt was come vnto him. *But* toke the poore mānes *lambe* (4) & *dressed* it for the mā that was come to him. *And* Dauid *was excedyng* wroth *wt the* man, and sayd to Nathan: as *surely* as ẙe Lorde lyueth ẙe *felow* (9) ẙt hathe done this *thyng*, is ẙe chylde of deeth....

TAVERNER agrees verbally with Matthew except by reading: to *make* of his own (error): to *prepare* for the s.: is *worthye of deathe*.

GREAT BIBLE (1539, 1540, 1541) agrees with TINDALE except (1) *the one—the other* (Cov.): (2) *The* ryche *man* (C): (3) excedyng many: (4) shepe (C): (5) had b. (C): (6) *wyth* his ch. *also:* (7) was unto him as his d.: (8) *and of his own* oxen: (9) *man*. Before 'the child of death' stands (in 1539, 1540) a ☞ to indicate an intended note, such as is given in Matthew. [That is, is worthye to dye.]

[MÜNSTER. (1) *unus—alter* (2) *Dives* (3) *multos valde* (4) *ovis* (5) *emerat* (6) *apud* filios ejus *pariter* (7) *eratque ei quasi filia* (8) *atque de bobus suis*.]

GENEVA agrees with the GREAT BIBLE except in reading: had *none at all*: his own *morsels*: *Now* there came: *who refused* to take: As the Lord liueth: *shall surely dye*.

BISHOPS' agrees with the GREAT BIBLE except in reading: he *spared* to take: as the Lord liveth (Gen.).

To the phrase 'The child of death' a note is added: 'that is *shall surely die*' (Gen.).

APPENDIX VIII.

The Relation of the Wycliffite to the later Versions.

The History of our English Bible begins with the work of Tindale and not with that of Wycliffe. Every step in the descent of our present Authorised Version, from Tindale's first New Testament and Matthew's composite Old Testament and Apocrypha, is clearly made out; but neither Tindale's nor Coverdale's translation has any direct filiation on Wycliffe's. As far as Tindale is concerned, his own explicit statement leaves no room even for raising the question: 'Them that are learned Christenly, 'I beseche: for as moche as I am sure, ād my conscience beareth 'me recorde, that of a pure entent, singilly and faythfully I have 'interpreted itt [the New Testament] as farre forth as god gave me 'the gyfte of knowledge ād vnderstondynge: that the rudnes off 'the worke nowe at the fyrst tyme, offende them not: but thatt 'they consyder howe that *I had no man to counterfet, nether was* '*holpe with englysshe of eny that had interpreted the same, or soche* '*lyke thīge ī the scripture beforetyme.*' And on the other hand Coverdale is equally explicit (see p. 162) as to the sources from which he himself derived help for his first great work. At the same time the words of Tindale imply that he knew of the Wycliffite versions (nor could it have been otherwise), and admit the supposition that he had used them, though he deliberately decided that he could not (1) 'counterfeit' them, that is follow their general plan, as being a secondary translation only, or (2) adopt their language. It is possible however that some of the earlier renderings may have obtained a traditional currency, and in this way have affected Tindale's or Coverdale's own work. But coincidences which can be referred to this origin are very rare in Tindale, and the fact that they are much more frequent in Coverdale's Latin-English Testaments appears to shew that they were really due to the immediate influence of the Vulgate and not to the Wycliffite translation of it.

A few specimens will place the relations between the earlier and later works in a clear light.

PURVEY.

3 Blessid ben pore men in spirit, for the kyngdom of heuenes is herne.

5 Blessid ben mylde men, for thei shulen welde the erthe.

4 Blessid ben thei that mornen, for thei schulen be coumfortid.

6 Blessid ben thei that hungren and thristen riȝtwisnesse, for thei schulen be fulfillid.

7 Blessid ben merciful men, for thei schulen gete merci.

8 Blessid ben thei that ben of clene herte, for thei schulen se God.

9 Blessid ben pesible men, for thei schulen be clepid Goddis children.

9 Oure fadir that art in heuenes, halewid be thi name;

10 Thy kyngdoom come to; be thi wille don in erthe as in heuene;

11 Ȝyue to vs this dai oure breed ouer othir substaunce;

12 And forȝyue to vs oure dettis, as we forȝyuen to oure dettouris;

13 And lede vs not in to temptacioun, but delyuere vs fro yuel. Amen.

24 Therfor ech man that herith these my wordis, and doith hem, schal be maad lijk to a wise man that hath bildid his hous on a stoon.

25 And reyn felde doun, and flodis camen, and wyndis blewen, and russchiden in to that hous;

TINDALE (1534).

3 Blessed are the povre in sprete: for theirs is the kyngdome of heven.

4 Blessed are they that morne: for they shalbe conforted.

5 Blessed are the meke: for they shall inheret the erth.

6 Blessed are they which honger and thurst for rightewesnes: for they shalbe filled.

7 Blessed are ye mercifull: for they shall obteyne mercy.

8 Blessed are the pure in herte: for they shall se God.

9 Blessed are the peacemakers: for they shalbe called the chyldren of God.

9 O oure father which arte in hevē, halowed be thy name.

10 Let thy kyngdome come. Thy wyll be fulfilled, as well in erth, as it ys in heven.

11 Geve vs this daye oure dayly breede.

12 And forgeve vs oure treaspases, evē as we forgeve oure trespacers.

13 And leade vs not into tēptacion: but delyver vs frō evell. For thyne is ye kyngedome and ye power, & ye glorye for ever. Amen.

24 Whosoever heareth of me these sayinges and doethe the same, I wyll lyken hym vnto a wyse man which bylt hys housse on a rocke:

25 & aboundance of rayne descended, & the fluddes came, & the wyndes blewe and bet

PURVEY.

and it felde not doun, for it was foundun on a stoon.

26 And euery man that herith these my wórdis, and doith hem not, is lijk to a fool, that hath bildid his hous on grauel.

27 And reyn cam doun, and floodis camen, and wyndis blewen, and thei hurliden aȝen that house; and it felde doun, and the fallyng doun therof was greet.

TINDALE.

vpon that same housse, and it fell not, because it was grounded on the rocke.

26 And whosoever heareth of me these sayinges & doth them not, shalbe lykened vnto a folysh man which bilt hys housse apō the sonde:

27 & abundaūce of rayne descended, & the fluddes came, and yᵉ wyndes blewe and beet vpon that housse, and it fell and great was the fall of it.

In the whole of the Sermon on the Mount I have only noted the following coincidences in which the Wycliffite rendering may have suggested that of Tindale:

vii. 3 litil mote W. (*festucam*)	moote T.
— 6 al to tere ȝou W.	all to rent you T.
— 16 breris W. (*tribulis*)	bryres T.
— 23 knouleche to W.	knowlege vnto T.

In the whole of the first Epistle of St John I have observed only one coincidence in any way remarkable: iii. 15 *mansleere* W., T., a common rendering which recurs in 1 Tim. i. 9 (so also A.V.), while elsewhere Tindale uses *murderers*, and Purvey sometimes *mansleere* and sometimes *manquillere*. The differences on the other hand are very striking:

PURVEY.

The world schal passe, and the couetise of it; but he that doith the wille of God, dwellith with outen ende.

Ech man that dwellith in hym, synneth not; and ech that synneth, seeth not hym, nether knew hym.

He that woot that his brother synneth a synne not to deth, axe he, and lijf schal be ȝouun to hym that synneth not to deth. Ther is a synne to deth; not for it Y seie, that ony man preie.

TINDALE.

The worlde vannyssheth awaye, and the lust therof: but he that fulfilleth the will of god abydeth ever.

As many as byde in him synne not: whosoever synneth hath not sene him, nether hath knowen him.

Yf eny man se his brother synne a synne that is not vnto deeth, let him axe, and he shall geve him lyfe for them that synne not vnto deeth. Ther is a synne vnto deeth, for which saye I not that a man shuld praye.

In the Epistles of St Paul the differences between Purvey and Tindale are even greater. Thus the only two striking phrases common to them in Romans viii., *trauelith with peyne* (ver. 22 W., *travayleth in payne* T.) and *tribulacioun, or anguysch* (ver. 35), seem to be due to the Latin *parturit* (συνωδίνει) and *tribulatio an angustia*.

A comparison of the Wycliffite versions of Ps. viii. given in App. 1. with the same Psalm in the Prayer-Book Psalter will shew the wide difference between the Old Versions and Coverdale's work.

APPENDIX IX.

The Revision of the Authorised Version.

The question of the revision of the 'Authorised Version' of the Bible was discussed more or less seriously at various times after the abortive attempt under the Commonwealth (see p. 120), but did not take any practical shape till the present generation. It is unnecessary to notice here the different private attempts at revision, which at least kept the way open for a more complete solution of the problem and furnished materials for the work. The question assumed a new character when at length in the year 1870 it was brought before the Convocation of the Province of Canterbury. On Feb. 10th the Bishop of Winchester (S. Wilberforce) submitted the following motion to the Upper House: 'That a Committee of both Houses be appointed, with 'power to confer with any Committee that may be appointed by 'the Convocation of the Northern Province, to report upon the 'desirableness of a revision of the Authorized Version of the New 'Testament, whether by marginal notes or otherwise, in all those 'passages where plain and clear errors, whether in the Hebrew '(*sic*) or Greek text originally adopted by the translators, or in the 'translation made from the same, shall, on due investigation, be 'found to exist[1].'

In the course of the discussion which followed, the Bishop of Llandaff (A. Ollivant) proposed to include the Old Testament in the scope of the inquiry; and the motion was agreed to with the addition of the words 'Old and' before 'New Testaments.' Upon this the Bishops of Winchester, Bath and Wells (Lord

[1] *Chronicles of Convocation*, 1870, p. 74. The words, 'Hebrew or' seem to be either a relic of an original motion of a wider scope, or an anticipation of the motion as afterwards amended.

A. C. Hervey), St David's (C. Thirlwall), Llandaff, Gloucester and Bristol (C. J. Ellicott), Ely (E. H. Browne), Lincoln (Chr. Wordsworth) and Salisbury (G. Moberly) were appointed members of the Committee to represent the Upper House. The resolution was at once communicated to the Lower House; and the following members of that House were nominated to serve upon the joint Committee. The Prolocutor (E. Bickersteth), the Deans of Canterbury (H. Alford), Lincoln (J. A. Jeremie) and Westminster (A. P. Stanley), the Archdeacons of Bedford (H. J. Rose), Exeter (P. Freeman) and Rochester (A. Grant), Chancellor Massingberd, Canons Blakesley, How, Selwyn, Swainson, Woodgate, Drs Kay and Jebb and Mr De Winton.

The Convocation of York, however, declined to meet the advances of the Southern Province. A resolution was adopted by that body in which they stated that 'although blemishes existed 'in [the text of the Authorized Version] such as had from time 'to time been pointed out, yet they would deplore any recasting 'of the text. [They did not] accordingly think it necessary to 'appoint a Committee to co-operate with the Committee appointed 'by the Convocation of Canterbury, though favourable to the 'errors being corrected[1].'

In spite of this disappointment the Committee of the Convocation of Canterbury proceeded with their work.

On May 3rd, 1870, a report which 'was unanimously agreed 'to by all the members of the Committee who were present' was laid before the Upper House by the Bishop of Winchester and before the Lower House by the Prolocutor[2]. This report was embodied in the following resolutions:

1. 'That it is desirable that a revision of the Authorized 'Version of the Holy Scriptures be undertaken.

2. 'That the revision be so conducted as to comprise both 'marginal renderings and such emendations as it may be found 'necessary to insert in the text of the Authorized Version.

3. 'That in the above resolutions we do not contemplate 'any new translation of the Bible, or any alteration of the lan-'guage, except when in the judgment of the most competent 'scholars such change is necessary.

4. 'That in such necessary changes, the style of the language employed in the existing version be closely followed.

[1] *Chronicles of Convocation*, p. 210.   [2] *Ib.* pp. 209 ff., 234 f., 328 ff.

5.   'That it is desirable that Convocation should nominate
'a body of its own members to undertake the work of revision,
'who shall be at liberty to invite the cooperation of any eminent
'for scholarship, to whatever nation or religious body they may
'belong.

This report was adopted in the Upper House without any
amendment having been proposed; and it was at once resolved,
without any opposition, 'That a committee be now appointed to
'consider and report to Convocation *a scheme of revision* on the
'principles laid down in the report now adopted.

'That the Bishops of Winchester, St David's, Llandaff, Glou-
'cester and Bristol, Salisbury, Ely, Lincoln, and Bath and Wells
'be members of the Committee.

'That the Lower House be directed to appoint an equal
'number from their own body as members of the Committee[1].

'That the Committee be empowered to invite the cooperation
'of those whom they may judge fit from their Biblical Scholarship
'to aid them in their work.'

These resolutions were communicated to the Lower House
on the same day; and the report and resolutions were discussed
in that House on May 5th.   Various amendments were proposed
to the different sections of the report, but met with little support,
and the report was adopted without change.   There was, however, considerable opposition to the direction which fixed the
representatives of the Lower House at the same number as those
of the Upper House.   It was urged that the usual practice of
Convocation with respect to joint Committees, according to which
the Lower House is represented in the proportion of two of its
members to one of the Upper House, ought to be observed in
this case.   A resolution embodying this opinion was communicated to the Upper House, which however again affirmed its
judgment, still leaving to the Lower House the power of asking
for a larger number of representatives, if after this second expression of opinion they thought it well to do so.   The subject was
again debated in the Lower House, but it was finally decided,
by 27 voices to 25, to accept the number suggested by the Upper

---

[1] *Chronicles of Convocation*, pp.
227 ff., 269 f. In the first place referred to the third paragraph does
not appear, and there is no indication in the published records of
Convocation as to its introduction
into the resolution agreed to by the
Upper House.

House. On this the Prolocutor, in virtue of his office, nominated the following members of the House to act on the joint Committee: the Prolocutor [apart from all other considerations 'it was judged necessary for the Prolocutor to be on the Committee'], the Dean of Canterbury, the Dean of Westminster, the Archdeacon of Bedford, Canon Selwyn, Canon Blakesley, Dr Jebb (Canon of Hereford), and Dr Kay.

In the course of the debates some doubt was expressed as to the exact duty of the joint Committee which was described by the phrase 'considering and reporting *a scheme of revision.*' The phrase was interpreted by some as if it were equivalent to drawing up a plan for making a revision; but this interpretation was overruled. It was laid down that 'the scheme of revision' necessarily included those changes by the adoption of which it was proposed that the revision should be carried out[1].

At this point then the action of Convocation as to the work of revision was for a time ended. Thenceforward the joint Committee had to carry out on their own responsibility the instructions which they had received, and whenever 'the scheme 'of revision' is completed they will present it with their report to Convocation according to the laws of that body. It will then rest with Convocation to adopt or reject or modify 'the scheme of 'revision' offered to them.

The Committee lost no time in carrying out the work with which they were entrusted. 'At the first meeting [May 25th, 1870] 'the following Resolutions and Rules were agreed to, as the 'fundamental principles on which the Revision is to be con-'ducted:

'RESOLVED,—

'I. That the Committee, appointed by the Convocation of Canterbury at its last Session, separate itself into two Companies, the one for the revision of the Authorized Version of the Old Testament, the other for the revision of the Authorized Version of the New Testament.

'II. That the Company for the revision of the Authorized Version of the Old Testament consist of the Bishops of St David's, Llandaff, Ely, Lincoln, and Bath and Wells, and of the following Members from the Lower House, Archdeacon Rose, Canon Selwyn, Dr Jebb, and Dr Kay.

---

[1] *Chronicles of Convocation*, pp. 400 ff.

'III. That the Company for the revision of the Authorized Version of the New Testament consist of the Bishops of Winchester, Gloucester and Bristol, and Salisbury, and of the following Members from the Lower House, the Prolocutor, the Deans of Canterbury and Westminster, and Canon Blakesley.

'IV. That the first portion of the work to be undertaken by the Old Testament Company, be the revision of the Authorized Version of the Pentateuch.

'V. That the first portion of the work to be undertaken by the New Testament Company, be the revision of the Authorized Version of the Synoptical Gospels.

'VI. That the following Scholars and Divines be invited to join the Old Testament Company :—

Alexander, Dr W. L.[1]
Chenery, Professor[2]
Cook, Canon[3]
Davidson, Professor A. B.[4]
Davies, Dr B.[5]
Fairbairn, Professor[6]
Field, Rev. F.[7]
Ginsburg, Dr[8]
Gotch, Dr[9]

Harrison, Archdeacon[10]
Leathes, Professor[11]
McGill, Professor[12]
Payne Smith, Canon[13]
Perowne, Professor J. S.[14]
Plumptre, Professor[15]
Pusey, Canon[16]
Wright, Dr (British Museum)[17]
Wright, W. A. (Cambridge)[18]

[1] Professor of Theology to the Congregationalists of Scotland.
[2] Lord Almoner's Professor of Arabic, Oxford.
[3] Canon of Exeter.
[4] Professor of Hebrew in New College, Edinburgh.
[5] One of the Tutors at the Baptist College, Regent's Park. [d. 1875.]
[6] Principal of the Free Church College, Glasgow. [d. 1874.]
[7] Formerly Fellow of Trinity College, Cambridge. Editor of the *Hexapla of Origen*, &c.
[8] Translator and Editor of *Ecclesiastes*, &c.
[9] Principal of the Baptist College, Bristol.
[10] Archdeacon of Maidstone.
[11] Professor of Hebrew in King's College, London.
[12] Professor of Oriental Languages in the University of St Andrew's.
[13] Regius Professor of Divinity, Oxford. [Dean of Canterbury, 1871.]
[14] Canon of Llandaff: Professor of Hebrew and Vice-Principal of St David's College, Lampeter. [Prælector in Divinity, Trinity College, Cambridge, 1872. Afterwards Hulsean Professor of Divinity, Dean of Peterborough, and Bishop of Worcester.]
[15] Formerly Fellow of Brasenose College, Oxford. Professor of Divinity, King's College, London. [Resigned 1874.]
[16] Regius Professor of Hebrew, Oxford.
[17] [Professor of Arabic, Cambridge, 1870.]
[18] Bursar (formerly Librarian) of Trinity College, Cambridge.

'VII. That the following Scholars and Divines be invited to join the New Testament Company :—

Angus, Dr[1]	Newman, Dr J. H.[10]
Dublin, Archbishop of	Newth, Professor[11]
Eadie, Dr[2]	Roberts, Dr A.[12]
Hort, Rev. F. J. A.[3]	Smith, Rev. G. Vance[13]
Humphry, Rev. W. G.[4]	Scott, Dr (Balliol Coll.)[14]
Kennedy, Canon[5]	Scrivener, Rev. F.[15]
Lee, Archdeacon[6]	Tregelles, Dr[16]
Lightfoot, Dr[7]	Vaughan, Dr[17]
Milligan, Professor[8]	Westcott, Canon[18]
Moulton, Professor[9]	

'VIII. That the General Principles to be followed by both Companies be as follows :—

1. To introduce as few alterations as possible into the Text of the Authorized Version consistently with faithfulness.

2. To limit, as far as possible, the expression of such alterations to the language of the Authorized and earlier English versions.

3. Each Company to go twice over the portion to be

---

[1] President of the Baptist College, Regent's Park, London.

[2] Professor of Biblical Literature in the Divinity Hall of the United Presbyterian Church, Glasgow. [d. 1876.]

[3] Formerly Fellow of Trinity College, Cambridge. [Fellow of Emmanuel College, Cambridge, 1872. Afterwards Hulsean Professor and Lady Margaret's Reader in Divinity.]

[4] Formerly Fellow of Trinity College, Cambridge. Rector of St Martin's in the Fields.

[5] Canon of Ely and Regius Professor of Greek, Cambridge.

[6] Archdeacon of Dublin. Archbishop King's Lecturer in Divinity in the University of Dublin.

[7] Fellow of Trinity College, and Hulsean Professor of Divinity, Cambridge. [Canon of St Paul's, 1871.]

[8] Professor of Biblical Criticism, Aberdeen.

[9] Professor of Classics. Wesleyan College, Richmond.

[10] Formerly Fellow of Oriel College, Oxford.

[11] Professor of Classics, New College, London [Principal 1872].

[12] Professor of Humanity, St Andrew's [1871].

[13] Minister of St Saviour's-gate Chapel, York.

[14] Master of Balliol College, and Professor of Exegesis, Oxford. [Dean of Rochester, 1870.]

[15] Editor of the *Codex Bezæ*, &c.

[16] Editor of the New Testament in the original Greek.

[17] Formerly Fellow of Trinity College, Cambridge. Master of the Temple [and Dean of Llandaff].

[18] Canon of Peterborough. [Regius Professor of Divinity, Cambridge, 1870.]

revised, once provisionally, the second time finally, and on principles of voting as hereinafter is provided.

4. That the Text to be adopted be that for which the
evidence is decidedly preponderating; and that when the Text
so adopted differs from that from which the Authorized Version
was made, the alteration be indicated in the margin.

5. To make or retain no change in the Text on the second
final revision by each Company, except *two-thirds* of those present
approve of the same, but on the first revision to decide by simple
majorities.

6. In every case of proposed alteration that may have
given rise to discussion, to defer the voting thereupon till the
next Meeting, whensoever the same shall be required by one-
third of those present at the Meeting, such intended vote to be
announced in the notice for the next Meeting.

7. To revise the headings of chapters, pages, paragraphs,
italics, and punctuation.

8. To refer, on the part of each Company, when considered desirable, to Divines, Scholars, and Literary Men, whether
at home or abroad, for their opinions.

' IX. That the work of each Company be communicated to
the other as it is completed, in order that there may be as little
deviation from uniformity in language as possible.

' X. ·That the Special or Bye-rules for each Company be as
follows :—

1. To make all corrections in writing previous to the
Meeting.

2. To place all the corrections due to textual considerations on the left-hand margin, and all other corrections on the
right-hand margin.

3. To transmit to the Chairman, in case of being unable
to attend, the corrections proposed in the portion agreed upon
for consideration.

> S. WINTON, *Chairman.*'

May 25, 1870.

Of the scholars who were invited to take part in the work,
in accordance with this resolution, Canon Cook, Dr Newman,
Dr Pusey, and Dr W. Wright declined the invitation; and Dr
Tregelles was unable from ill health to take his seat among the

revisers. Dr Alford and Professor McGill were removed by death in 1871 from a work to which they had already rendered important services. The Bishop of Lincoln and Dr Jebb resigned their places on the original Committee of Convocation, shortly after their labours had commenced[1]. On the other hand the following new members were appointed :—

(1) For the Old Testament Company :

Mr R. L. Bensly, Assistant University Librarian, Cambridge.

Dr Douglas, Professor of Hebrew, Free Church College, Glasgow.

Rev. J. D. Geden, Professor of Hebrew, Wesleyan College, Didsbury.

Dr Weir, Professor of Oriental Languages in the University of Glasgow [d. 1876].

(2) On the New Testament Company :

Dr Charles Wordsworth, Bishop of St Andrews.

Dr David Brown, Professor of Divinity in the Free Church College, Aberdeen.

Dr C. Merivale, Dean of Ely. [Resigned 1871.][2]

The Companies entered upon the work as soon as they were organized. The New Testament Company met for the first time on June 22nd (1870), in the Jerusalem Chamber, Westminster Abbey : the Old Testament Company on June 30th.

---

[1] [The Bishop of Llandaff resigned in 1875, but continued a corresponding member of the Company till his death in 1882. Archdeacon Rose died in 1873 ; Canon Selwyn and Bishop Thirlwall in 1875.]

[2] [To these were added to the Old Testament Company in 1874 :

The Rev. C. J. Elliott, Vicar of Winkfield,

The Rev. J. R. Lumby, afterwards Norrisian Professor and Lady Margaret's Reader in Divinity, Cambridge,

The Rev. J. Birrell, Professor of Oriental Languages, St Andrew's,

The Rev. A. H. Sayce, Fellow of Queen's College, Oxford ; now Professor of Assyriology,

The Rev Professor W. Robertson Smith, Free Church College, Aberdeen :

and in 1875 :

The Rev. T. K. Cheyne, Fellow of Balliol College, Oxford ; now Professor of Exegesis and Canon of Rochester,

Dr William Wright, Professor of Arabic, Cambridge,

Mr S. R. Driver, Fellow of New College, Oxford ; now Regius Professor of Hebrew and Canon of Christ Church,

F. Chance, M.B., of Trinity College, Cambridge.

To the New Testament Company was added in 1873, in place of the Bishop of Winchester,

The Rev. Edwin Palmer, Professor of Latin, Oxford, and afterwards Archdeacon of Oxford.]

Before the first Session (June 22nd) a large number of the revisers joined in the Holy Communion, which was celebrated by the Dean of Westminster in Henry VIIth's Chapel. From that time the Companies have continued their work regularly, except during the summer vacation, the Old Testament Company in bi-monthly sittings of ten days, and the New Testament Company in monthly sittings of four days each.

Shortly after the work was commenced negotiations were opened by the Committee of Convocation with the two Universities of Oxford and Cambridge on the subject of the copyright of the revised Version [*i.e.* the Authorised Version amended according to the scheme of revision prepared by the Companies]. These negotiations led to an arrangement in 1872, by which the Presses of the two Universities undertook to provide a sum probably sufficient to pay the bare expenses of the production of the work (travelling expenses, printing, &c.) in return for the copyright. The revisers, it need scarcely be added, offer their time and labour as a free contribution to the great work in which they have been allowed to join. In the course of these negotiations it was for the first time laid down that the Apocrypha should be included in the scheme of revision, the two Companies combining to produce this part of the work.

When the revision was fairly in progress in England, the Committee of Convocation, according to the tenor of their instructions, and a more specific resolution of July 7th[1], opened communications with Biblical scholars in America. Dr Angus arrived in New York in August 1870 and conferred with Dr Ph. Schaff (a pupil of Neander, who stands in the foremost rank among American theologians), and after the negotiations thus commenced were brought to an end, the following groups of scholars were organized to assist the English Companies by their criticisms and suggestions.

THE OLD TESTAMENT COMPANY.

Prof. Thomas J. Conant, D.D. (Baptist), Brooklyn, N.Y.
 „ George E. Day, D.D. (Congregationalist), New Haven, Conn.
 „ John De Witt, D.D. (Reformed), New Brunswick, N.J.
 „ Wm. Henry Green, D.D. (Presbyterian), Princeton, N.J.
 „ George Emlen Hare, D.D. (Episcopalian), Philadelphia, Pa.

[1] *Chronicles of Convocation*, 1870, p. 565.

Prof. Charles P. Krauth, D.D. (Lutheran), Philadelphia, Pa.
„ Joseph Packard, D.D. (Episcopalian), Fairfax, Va,
„ Calvin E. Stowe, D.D. (Congregationalist), Cambridge, Mass.
„ James Strong, D.D. (Methodist), Madison, N.J.
„ C. V. A. Van Dyck, M.D.[1] (Missionary), Beyrut, Syria.
„ Tayler Lewis, LL.D. (Reformed), Schenectady, N.Y. [d. 1877][2].

THE NEW TESTAMENT COMPANY.

Bishop Alfred Lee, D.D. (Episcopalian), Wilmington, Delaware.
Prof. Ezra Abbot, LL.D. (Unitarian), Cambridge, Mass.
Rev. G. R. Crooks, D.D. (Methodist), New York [resigned].
Prof. H. B. Hackett, D.D. (Baptist), Rochester, N.Y. [d. 1875].
„ James Hadley, LL.D. (Congregationalist), New Haven, Conn. [d. 1872].
„ Charles Hodge, D.D., LL.D. (Presbyterian), Princeton, N.J. [d. 1878].
„ A. C. Kendrick, D.D. (Baptist), Rochester, N.Y.
„ Matthew B. Riddle, D.D. (Reformed), Hartford, Conn.
„ Charles Short, LL.D. (Episcopalian), New York.
„ Henry B. Smith, D.D., LL.D. (Presbyterian), New York, attended only one session [resigned, and died, 1877].
„ J. Henry Thayer, D.D. (Congregationalist), Andover, Mass.
„ W. F. Warren, D.D. (Methodist), Boston, Mass. [resigned].
Rev. Edward A. Washburn, D.D. (Episcopalian), New York.
„ Theo. D. Woolsey, D.D., LL.D. (Congreg.), New Haven, Conn.
Prof. Philip Schaff, D.D. (Presbyterian), New York[3].

[1] Dr Van Dyck. the distinguished translator of the Arabic Bible, cannot be expected to attend the meetings, but may be occasionally consulted on questions involving a thorough knowledge of Semitic languages.

[2] [To these were added :
Professor Charles A. Aiken, D.D., Theological Seminary, Princeton, N.J.
The Rev. T. W. Chambers, D.D., Collegiate Reformed Dutch Church, N.Y.
Professor Charles M. Mead, D.D., Theological Seminary, Andover, Mass.

Professor Howard Osgood, D.D., Theological Seminary, Rochester, N.Y.]

[3] [Besides these were:
The Rev. J. K. Burr, D.D., Trenton, N.J.
President Thomas Chase, LL.D., Haverford College, Pa.
Chancellor Howard Crosby, D.D., LL.D., New York University, New York.
Professor Timothy Dwight, D.D., Divinity School of Yale College, New Haven, Conn.]

'In the delicate task of selection, reference was had (so Dr
'Schaff writes), first of all, to ability, experience, and reputation
'in Biblical learning and criticism; next, to denominational con-
'nection and standing, so as to have a fair representation of the
'leading churches and theological institutions; and last, to local
'convenience, in order to secure regular attendance. Some
'distinguished scholars were necessarily omitted, but may be
'added hereafter by the committee itself.

'So far as I know, the selection has given general satisfaction.
'A few gentlemen (not included in the above list) declined the
'invitation for personal reasons, but not from any hostility to
'the pending revision. One of these, a learned bishop of the
'Protestant Episcopal Church, wrote to me: "Let me assure
'you, it is from no feeling that a revision is not needed, nor yet
'from any unwillingness to invoke aid in making it from others
'than members of the Church of England, that I have been led
'to this view of my duty." Another wrote: "Respecting the
'success of the enterprise I have little doubt. The result of the
'best scholarship of the Church in England and America will
'command assent, and the opposition will speedily subside." And
'a third one, likewise a bishop, who is esteemed by all denomina-
'tions, expresses himself in this way: "I am glad that, as the revision
'in England was set on foot by a Convocation of the Church of
'England, and is proceeding mainly under such guidance and
'control, in constituting an American Committee, to co-operate,
'the work of formation has been given by the British Committee
'to a *non-Episcopalian* and to *you*[2]. This will greatly help not
'only the *all-sidedness* of the work, but, in case it shall be desir-
'able to introduce it into substitution for the present revision, will
'very materially prepare the way for such result."'

Meanwhile Dr Schaff visited England in 1871, and was present
by a special vote at one of the Sessions of the New Testament
Company. Having thus become familiar with the method of
procedure, he was able to make provision for the efficient
co-operation of the American Companies. The result was that in
December 1871 the following constitution was adopted for their
guidance:

'I. The American Committee, invited by the British Com-

[1] Preface to 'Lightfoot *On Re-*   [2] 'The italics are the Bishop's.'
vision.'

mittee engaged in the revision of the Authorized English Version of the Holy Scriptures to co-operate with them, shall be composed of Biblical scholars and divines in the United States.

'II. This Committee shall have the power to elect its officers, to add to its number, and to fill its own vacancies.

'III. The officers shall consist of a President, a Corresponding Secretary, and a Treasurer. The President shall conduct the official correspondence with the British revisers. The Secretary shall conduct the home correspondence.

'IV. New members of the Committee, and corresponding members, must be nominated at a previous meeting, and elected unanimously by ballot.

'V. The American Committee shall co-operate with the British Companies on the basis of the principles and rules of revision adopted by the British Committee.

'VI. The American Committee shall consist of two Companies, the one for the revision of the Authorized Version of the Old Testament, the other for the revision of the Authorized Version of the New Testament.

'VII. Each Company shall elect its own Chairman and Recording Secretary.

'VIII. The British Companies will submit to the American Companies, from time to time, such portions of their work as have passed the first revision, and the American Companies will transmit their criticisms and suggestions to the British Companies before the second revision.

'IX. A joint meeting of the American and British Companies shall be held, if possible, in London, before final action.

'X. The American Committee to pay their own expenses.'

In the summer of 1872 Dr Schaff again visited England and had further conference with members of the Revision Companies. In July of that year all the details of co-operation between the English and American Companies were arranged, the copies of the 'first and provisional revision,' so far as it was then completed, were forwarded to the American revisers for their private and confidential use.

[The Revised New Testament was published in May, 1881, and the Old Testament in May, 1885. The Revision of the Apocrypha was undertaken by four Committees, three formed by members of the New Testament Company and one by members of the Old Testament Company. Of the former, one, called the London Committee, consisted of the Bishops of Gloucester and Bristol, Salisbury, and St Andrew's, the Deans of Rochester and Lichfield, the Master of the Temple, Dr Angus and Prebendary Humphry. The Bishops of Salisbury and St Andrew's were unable to attend. This Committee undertook the revision of Ecclesiasticus. To the second, called the Westminster Committee, were nominated the Archbishop of Dublin, the Dean of Westminster, the Archdeacons of Dublin and Oxford, Dr Scrivener, Dr Brown, Principal Newth, and Dr Vance Smith. Dr Brown declined to serve. They revised the books of Tobit, Judith, and 1 Maccabees.

The third Committee, which met at Cambridge, consisted originally of the Bishop of Durham (Lightfoot), the Dean of Lincoln (Blakesley), Professors Hort, Kennedy, and Westcott, Dr Milligan, Dr Moulton, and Dr Roberts. The Bishop of Durham, the Dean of Lincoln and Professor Kennedy were unable to attend, and Dr Roberts was a corresponding member. They revised the books of Wisdom and 2 Maccabees. It does not appear from the minutes of the Committee that Dr Milligan took any part in the revision.

The fourth Committee, consisting of members of the Old Testament Company, also met at Cambridge. The following were appointed to serve. The Dean of Peterborough (Perowne), Professors Lumby and Robertson Smith, Mr (afterwards Professor) Bensly, Mr Cheyne, and Mr W. A. Wright. Dr Field was invited to assist in the formation of the text. The Dean of Peterborough and Mr Cheyne were unable to take part in the work, and the death of Dr Field in 1885 deprived the Committee of his assistance. They revised the following books : 1 and 2 Esdras, Esther, Baruch, Song of the Three Children, Susanna, Bel and the Dragon, and the Prayer of Manasses.

The Revised Version of the Apocrypha was published in 1896. In 1898 the Revised Version of the Old and New Testaments and Apocrypha was issued with marginal references. After the publication of the English edition of the Revised Version the American Revision Committee continued their organization in order to prepare an American recension of the English Revision. The result of their labours appeared in 1901.]

APPENDIX X.

Phrases in the Psalms marked in the Psalter of the Great Bible in smaller type as additions from the Vulgate.

Some of the additions made to the text of the Psalter from the Vulgate Latin are of interest: and, as copies of the Great Bible are not always accessible, it will be worth while to give a list of them. The fact that these additions form an integral part of the text in the Prayer-Book Psalter has frequently led to error; and even a writer who proposes to discuss the relation of the Bible and Prayer-Book Psalters as a scholar (Sir L. C. Lee Brenton), appears to be wholly ignorant of the original notation, which ought not indeed to have been abandoned in the reprint.

Ps. i.   5   from the face of the earth.
     ii. 11 unto him.
     —   12 right.
     iii. 2   his.
     iv. 8   and oil.
     vii. 12 strong and patient.
     xi. 5   the poor.
     xii. 1   me.
     xiii. 6 Yea, I will praise the name of the Lord the most
                 highest.
     xiv. 2   no not one.
     —   5—7 Their throat......eyes.
     —   9   even where no fear was.
     xviii. 6 holy.
     —   49 cruel.
     xix. 12 my.
     —   14 alway.
     xx. 9   upon thee.

xxii.	1	look upon me.
—	16	many.
—	31	my.
—	32	the heavens.
xxiii.	6	thy.
xxiv.	4	his neighbour.
xxviii.	3	neither destroy me.
xxix.	1	bring young rams unto the Lord.
xxx.	7	from me.
xxxiii.	3	unto him.
—	10	and casteth out the counsels of princes.
xxxvii.	29	the unrighteous shall be punished.
—	37	his place.
xxxviii.	16	even mine enemies.
—	22	God.
xli.	1	and needy.
xlii.	12	that trouble me.
xlv.	10	wrought about with divers colours.
—	12	God.
xlvii.	6	our (1°).
xlviii.	3	of the earth.
l.	21	wickedly.
li.	1	great.
lv.	13	peradventure.
—	25	O Lord.
lxv.	1	in Jerusalem.
lxvii.	1	and be merciful unto us.
lxxi.	7	that I may sing of thy glory.
—	18	again.
lxxiii.	12	and said.
—	27	in the gates of the daughter of Sion.
lxxvii.	13	our.
lxxxv.	8	concerning me.
xc.	6	dried up.
xcii.	12	of the house.
xcv.	7	the Lord.
cviii.	1	my heart is ready (2°).
[cxi. end.		Praise the Lord for the returning again of Aggeus and Zachary the prophets. The heading of Psalm cxii. in Vulg.],

cxv.	9	house of.
cxviii.	2	that he is gracious and.
—	25	me.
cxix.	97	Lord.
cxx.	6	unto them.
cxxxii.	4	neither the temples of my head to take any rest.
cxxxiv.	1	now.
—	2	even in the courts of the house of our God.
cxxxvi.	27	O give thanks to the Lord of Lords, for his mercy endureth for ever. [In April 1540. Not in 1539.]
cxxxvii.	1	thee, O.
cxlv.	15	O Lord.
cxlvii.	8	and herb for the use of men.
cxlviii.	5	he spake the word and they were made.

It may be added that Ps. lxxii. 20 (Here end the prayers of David the son of Isai) and Ps. cxiii. 1a (Praise the Lord) are omitted in the Prayer-Book Psalter as well as the addition to Ps. cxi. (cxii.). [But they are in the Bible of 1539.]

Other additions of the nature of glosses have been introduced from Münster [in April 1540]:

xx.	9	heaven.
xxxix.	4	at the last.
—	12	fretting a garment.
l.	21	the things that thou hast done.
lxviii.	4	as it were upon a horse.
cii.	20	(children) appointed (unto death).
cix.	30	unrighteous (judges).
cxxxvi.	5	excellent (wisdom).

APPENDIX XI.

Sources of the notes in Matthew's Bible (p. 72).

(p. 72).

LEFÈVRE, 1534.

MATTHEW, 1537.

Gen. i. 22. Beneir po᷑ augmenter & multiplier.

Here is blessynge takē for encreasynge & multiplyenge.

ii. 17. Telles repetitions de parolles signifient aucunesfois hastiuete ou vehemence, aucunesfois certitude, cōme Pseau. 117. c.

Soche rehersalls of wordes dothe sygnifye somtyme an hastynes or vehemēce, somtyme an assewrance that the thinge shalbe performed that is promysed, as it is Psal. cxvii. c.

Ex. xi. 8. Soudaine mutation de parler en diuerses personnes, cōme Ps. 15. a. & ce est referre a la fin du chapitre precedent.

A soudayne chaunge of speakyng to dyuerse personnes, as in the Psal. xv. a., and thys is referred to the ende of the chapter that goeth before.

Lev. xxii. 29. Action de graces, est quant les benefices de dieu sont recite3, par quoy la foy en Dieu est confermee de tant plus confidentemēt àttendre ce que lon desire. Ephe. 5. a. 1. Timot. 4. a. b.

Thankes geuynge is when the benefytes of God are recyted, wherby the fayth to Godward is strēgthened the moare fastly to loke for the thyng that we desyre of God. Ephe. v. a. 1. Timo. iiij. a. & b.

Num. v. 22. Amen est vng mot Hebrieu, qui signifie, aïsy soit faict, ou ce soit ferme, approuuāt la parolle precedente : & quāt il est double il augmēte la confirmation, cōme en plusieurs pseaulmes, & en Jeā 5 & 6.

Amen is an Hebrew word & sygnifyeth, euen so be it, or be it fast and sewer, approuynge & alowing the sentēce going before : and when it is doubled it augmenteth the confyrmacyon, as in many Spalm. & Iohn v. & .vi.

Deut. i. 27. Le seigneur est dict hair aucun, quant il le met hors de sa cure, & quil ne luy fait pas de grace. Pseaulme 5. b. & 30. b.

God is sayd to hate a man whē he putteth him forth of hys hert, & geueth him not of his grace. Psal. v b and .xxx. b.

LEFÈVRE, 1534.

Josh. ii. 12. Iurer par le Seigneur & iurer au Seigneur sont differens, cōme est dict. 2. Paralip. 15. c.

Judg. iii. 9. Par ces saluateurs sont entenduȝ les Ducȝ ou iuges, lesquelȝ en Luc. 22. sont appelleȝ bienfaicteurs ou beneficieȝ. 2. Esd. 9. c.

Ruth iv. 1. La porte es escriptures signifie souuent le lieu publique ou le peuple se rassemble, & ou les iugemens se font & les causes. Car iadis se faisoiēt les iugemens es portes, cōe maintenāt es maisons de la ville. 2. des Roix. 15. a.

1 Sam. xv. 11. La repentance de dieu est seullemēt la mutation du faict. Et comme affection de misericorde & de paternelle beneuolence est attribuee a Dieu, aussy attribue lescripture a dieu selon sa maniere de parler affection de ire & de fure': car autrēmēt ne peullent les hōes parler de Dieu, Genese. 6. a.

2 Sam. i. 11. Rōpre ses vestemens estoit signe de grosse tristresse, & aussy de gros courroux por le zele du Seigneur, cōme Matthieu. 26. g. & ī. 3. f. & 13. f.

1 Kings i. 13. Cy apert cōmēt souuēt estre assis signifie regner & auoir domination ou iudicature, cōme en plusieurs lieux cy apres, & Matthieu. 19. d.

2 Kings i. 6. Lescripture a de coustume de nōmer les dieux des gētilȝ de nōs infames, comme pseau. 105. e. Aussy Beel-
w.

MATTHEW, 1537.

To sweare by the Lorde & to the Lord are ij. thinges as it is sayd. ij. Paralip. xv. c.

By these sauers are vnderstāded Rulars or iudges : which in Luke xxij. are called graciouse Lord⸜ ij. Esdr. ix. e.

The Gates in the scripture do oft tymes signifye the places where the people dyd cōmenlye assemble, and where Iudgementes were geuē and causes determyned : for in olde time were soche thynges done in the Gates. ij. Re. xvi. a.

The Repentaunce of God, is onely the chaungynge of the deade. And as the affeccion of mercy & of fatherly loue is attrybute to God : euen so dothe the scripture attribute to God after his maner of speache the affeccyon of Anger and of furye & of repētaunce also : for men can not other wise speake of God. Gene. vi. a.

The rentyng of his clothes was a signe of great sadnesse, & also of great anger for the ȝele of the Lorde, as in Mat. xxvi. g And beneth iij. f. and xiij. f.

Here it apereth that to be sett vpon the seate, sygnifyeth to bere rule and to haue dominyon or iurisdiccion, as in many places here after and Matth. xix. d.

The scripture of custome nameth the Goddes of the gentyles by infamouse names as in the Psal. cv. e. Beelȝebub sygnifyeth yᵉ God of

22

LEFÈVRE, 1534.

zebub signifie le dieu de la mousche. Luc 11. c.

1 Chron. xxviii. 2. La scabelle, &c. estoit le propiciatoire auq̄l & sus leq̄l Dieu auoit promis aux Hebrieux de les exaucer & parler a eulx leq̄l estoit sus larche, cōme appert Exo. 25. b.

2 Chron. vii. 2. La maieste du Seigneur rēplissant la maison, estoit cōme vne nuee visible prefigurant q̄ Dieu deboit estre presche, loue, & annōce par tout le mōde en la cōgregation des fideles, comme il dit Nōbre. 14. d. & Pseaulme. 7. d.

Ezra viii. 13. Les iunes dōt le-scripture fait mention, ont este publiques humiliatiōs auec sup-plicatiōs faictes deuant Dieu, ou poʳ quelque grande tribula-tion soufferte ou eminente, ou poʳ singuliere penitēce des pecheȝ, cōme est escript. 1. roix 7. b. & 31 d. 2 Esdras. 1. a. &c.

Neh. ix. 25. Ceste grasse terre signifie terre fertile & abond-ante en to' biēs cōme est dict du paī gras de Aser Genese. 49. c.

Esther iv. 3. Les Iuifȝ premiere-ment estoient appelleȝ He-brieux, de Heber premier filȝ de Sale filȝ de Arphaxat, cōme appert Genese. 11. b. & 1. Para-lip. 1. b. puis furēt appelleȝ Israel de Iacob, puis furent appelleȝ Iuifȝ de lung des filȝ de Iacob, ascauoir Iudas.

Psalm v. 3. Il dit au matin, pour le tēps conuenable a oraison & a ouyr la parolle de Dieu, auquel tēps conuenoit & au tabernacle,

MATTHEW, 1537.

a flee Luc. xi. c.

The fotestole &c. was yᵉ mercye seate at which and on which God had promesed yᵉ Hebrues to heare thē and speake vnto thē: which was vpon the Arcke, as it ap-peareth Exodi. xxv. b.

The glorye of God fyllyng the house, was as a vysyble cloude prefiguryng that God ought to be preached praysed & magnifyed thorow the whole worlde in yᵉ congregacion of yᵉ faythfull, as he sayth Nume. xiiij. d.

Fastynges, as the scripture maketh mēcyon, haue bene com-men humilyacions & supplycaciōs done before God: other for some great trybulacyon suffered or cōmyng at hād, or for a syngular repētaunce & ernest forthynckynge of their synnes, as it is wrytten 1. Reg. vii. b. and .xxxi. d. ij. Esdr. i. a. &c.

This fat lāde signifieth a frute-full grounde that aboūdeth wyth all. good thinges as it is sayd of fat bred of Aser. Gene. xlix. c.

The Iewes were fyrst called Hebrues, of Heber the eldest sonne of Sale sone of Arphaxat, as it appeareth. Genes. xi. b. & 1. Paral. 1. c. after were they called Israel of Iacob, & after Iewes of one of the sonnes of Iacob that is to wete of Iuda.

He sayth betymes & early in the morning because yᵗ tyme is con-uenyent to praye and to heare the word of God in: at which

LEFÈVRE, 1534.

& au tēple de Dieu.

MATTHEW, 1537.

tyme also they customably came together both to the tabernacle and vnto the tēple of God.

xxxvi. 4. Couche selon les escriptures, signifie les secretȝ du cueur, cōme Pseaul. 4. b. & Ecclēs. 10. d.

Bedde after the scripture sygnifieth ye secretes of the herte, as in the Psal. iiij. b. & Ecclē. x. d.

Prov. iv. 27. Par la dextre est entendue faulse confidence & mauvaise seurete : & par la senestre desperation. Ou decliner a la dextre est adiouster aux parolles de Dieu & decliner a la senestre est y diminuer, cōe est escript Deut. 18. b. & Iosue. 23. b.

By the right hand is vnderstande the false & wycked confidence in worckes, & by yᵉ left, desperacyō. To turne asyde or adde to yᵉ right hand is, to adde that to the worde of god, which God neuer cōmaunded. To turne a syde or bowe to the left hande is, to take awaye frō the worde of God, or to do that which is forbiddē. As it is written in Deuter. xxviii. b. & Iosue. xxiij. b.

Eccles. iv. 17. car dieu est pres plus pour ouyr ta parolle, q̄ pour receuoir le sacrifice que les folȝ donnent.

Canticles.

Some reade : For he is readier to heare (vnderstād, thy worde) thā to reseaue the sacrifices that foles geue.

The headings of the chapters are taken almost literally from Lefèvre.

Isaiah x. 12. Visiter souuēt signifie prendre vengeance, cōme Exode. 32. g.

To vyset doth often synifye for to take vengeaunce, as in Exodi. xxxij. g.

Jer. vii. 31. Ceste vallee estoit le lieu ou les corps mortȝ & les ordures de Hierusalem estoient portees, la ou les ydolatres immoloient leurs enfans a Moloch.

Topheth is a valleye wher vnto all yᵉ deed bodyes & fylthines of Ierusalem were caried & where Idolatrers offred their chyldren to Moloch.

Lam. iii. 5. Fiel pour amertume, maledictions ou iniures. Pseaulme. 68. e.

Gall, for soroufulnes : as in the Psalme lxix. e.

Ezek. xxxiii. 27. Ie suis viuāt, est le sermēt que fait le Seigneur en promettant quelque chose, cōme Nom. 14. d. e.

As truely as I lyue, is an othe which the Lorde comenly vseth, when he promeseth any thyng. Nume. xiiij. d. e.

Daniel.

No notes borrowed.

Hosea ii. 2. Mere icy signifie par

Mother here sygnifieth the

LEFÈVRE, 1534.

figure la Sinagogue des Iuifʒ ou leglise & la congregatiō du peuple. Esaie 50. a.

Joel i. 1. Saĩct Hierome dit au Prologue sus Osee, que les Prophetes qui ne mettēt point le tēps de leur prophetie, ont prophetise au mesme temps que le precedent Prophete qui declaire le tēps de sa prophetie.

Amos vi. 12. Changer le iugement. &c. est deliurer le coulpable, & oppresser linnocēt. Deuterono. 27. c.

Obad. 20.

Jonah ii. 2. Lescripture parle denfer cōmunement pour le lieu commun a tous descendant en la terre, come aueʒ es Pseaulmes & en Genese.

Micah vii. 2. Aguatter apres le sang est faire la vie des homes laborieuse & angoisseuse p menasses, murdres & rapines, cōme il declaire....Prouerbes i. b.

Haggai i. 14. Susciter lesperit de lhome, est quãt Dieu p son esperit conforte & anime les cueurs pour sans crainte entreprēdre quelque grand affaire.

Zechar. v. 2. Volume volant estoit vng rollet q' se tournoit autour dung bastō: ce q̄ encoire ceulx Dorient appellent liure, & en vsent de telʒ.

Malachi i. 7. Offrir le pain pollut est faire quelque chose par hypocrisie & nō pour la gloire de Dieu, cōme est dict Osee. 9. a.

MATTHEW, 1537.

Synagoge of the Iewes, or the churche or congregaciō of the people, as in Esai. l. a.

S. Hierome sayth in the prologe of Osee, yᵗ those prophet͛ which shewe not the tyme of their prophecye, dyd prophecy in the tyme of the prophet that standeth next before thē, which declareth the tyme of hys prophecye.

To turne iudgement is to delyuer yᵉ fautie, & to oppresse the innocent. Deu. xxvij. c.

The marginal notes are from Olivetan.

The scripture speaketh of hel comēly as of a place comē for al thē that go doune in to the earth, as in to a graue, or to the depe of yᵉ see &c. as ye haue in Genesi and in the Psalmes.

To labour to shede bloude, or to lye in wayte for bloude, is, to make mennes lyues laborous & miserable, by threatnynges, murthers, & violēce. Prouer. i. b.

To wake vp the sprete of a man is, when god by his sprete comforteth & boldeneth the hert to take vpon him without feare any acte or deade of great importaunce.

This flying boke was a rolle turned roūd aboute a staffe, which the inhabyters of the east part of the worlde do yet call a boke, and do also vse them.

To offer defyled bredde is, to do any thing by hypocrysye, & not to gloryfye God, as he hath commaunded in hys worde, but accordyng to the inuencions and dreames of men. Osee. ix. a.

LEFÈVRE, 1534.

MATTHEW, 1537.

Matthew ii. 1. Ceste Euangile mōstre asseʒ q̄ ces sages icy nestoiēt ne roix ne Princes : mais cōme dit Strabo, q̄ estoit de leur tēps estoient gens sages q' enseignoiēt aux gētilʒ les diuīs enseignemēs cōme estoit Moyse aux Hebrieux & dit que cestoiēt les Prestres des Perseens.

These were nother kynges nor princes, but as Strabo saith (whych was in their tyme) sage men amōge yᵉ Persiens as Moses was amonge the Hebrues, he sayth also yᵗ they were the prestes of yᵉ Persiens.

Mark vi. 48. De ceste quatriesme veille est dict Matth. 14. c.

The fourth quarter is the iiij. watche as in Mat. xiij. c.

Luke vi. 20. Christ appelle icy poures ceulx q' le sont desperit ascauoir qui ne se confient en nulle chose de ce monde, delaisseʒ & mespriseʒ des autres, & aucunement affligeʒ, poures & contritʒ de cueur, desquelʒ leurs choses ne vont guieres biē : & ne se adherent que a Dieu, qui leur est tout en tout. Mat. 5. a.

Christ calleth them here poore whych are poore in spirit : yᵗ is, which trust in no worldly thyng-ᵗ and are forsakē and despysed of other, beynge poore & cōtryte in hert, whych often do not prospere in the worlde because they leade a godly lyfe & put their hole trust and cōfydence in God, as in Matth. 5. a.

John xiv. 13. Le pere est glorifie au filʒ quāt on cōgnoit & quō luy rend' grace de ce quil a dōne son filʒ poʳ nous sauuer.

The father is glorified by the sonne, whe we knowledge and geue thanckes that he gaue hys sonne for vs to saue vs.

Acts xiii. 9. Du nom de Paul plusieurs en dispuēt, mais suyuant la plus saine opinion est q̄ par les Hebr. estoit appelle Saul : & selon la maniere de parler des gentilʒ & Romains estoit appelle Paul.

Of the name of Paul do many dispute, but the most alowed opyniō is, that of the Hebrues he was called Saul : & after yᵉ maner of speache of yᵉ Gentyles and Romaynes he was called Paul.

Romans vii. 4. Estre mort a la loy est estre faictʒ libres de la loy & de sa charge, & receuoir lesperit p lequel nous puyssions faire selon la loy. Et ce mesme est estre deliure de la loy de mort. Gala. 2. d.

To be deed concernīg the lawe is to be made fre frō the lawe and from the burthē therof : & to receaue the spirite, by which we may do after yᵉ law. And the same, is to be delyuered from the lawe of deeth. Galat. ij. d.

1 Cor. i. 24. Les Grecʒ aucunesfois signifiēt seullement leur natiō, cōme Acte. 6. a. & au

The Grekes sygnyfye some time their awne nacyon onely, as in the Actes. vi. a. Some tyme all the

LEFÈVRE, 1534.

cunesfois tous gentilȝ, cõme icy, & Romains. i. b.

2 Cor. i. 17. Ouy & non icy est mis pour instabilite, vanite, inconstance, & diuersite de pler.

Gal. i. 16. Chair & sang signifie icy les homes ou humaĩ conseil, cõe Matthieu.

Eph. ii. 21. Tẽple es escriptures Apostoliques signifie le peuple sainct assemble, ou le cuer dung chascun Chrestien, cõme 2. Corinth· 6. d. & 1. Corint. 3. & 6. d.

Phil. iv. 3. De ce livre de vie est dict en la Pseaulme. 68 f.

2 Thess. ii. 4. Estre assis au temple de Dieu, est regner & commander sus les consciences des homes, selon ce qui est dict. 1 Corint. 3. c. du tẽple de Dieu.

Hebrews v. 13, 14. Par le laict est entendue la parolle non difficile a entendre, & par la ferme viande les choses plus difficiles & haultaines.

James i. 4. Entier selon les Hebrieux, signifie celuy q' en delaissant la prudence des filȝ de ce mond & la finesse por son proffit vit de vie simple & sans macule. Tel que estoit Iacob, du q̄l est dict Gen. 25. d.

1 Peter i. 3. Viue esperãce est celle par laquelle nous sommes certains de la vie eternelle.

2 Peter i. 10. Combien q̄ la vocatiõ de Dieu soit ferme & certaine: neant moins veult Lapostre q̄ par oeuvres declairions aux hões icelle estre vraye, comme est dict.

MATTHEW, 1537.

Gentyles, as here, and Rom. i. b.

Yee yee, and Naye naye is here put for vnstablenes, incõstãtnes, faynĩg or flyttynge of with wordes.

Flesshe and bloudde here signifie men or mennes coũsell.

Temple in the Epystles of the Apostles sygnyfyeth the congregacyon of faythfull holy & vertuouse men. Sometyme it sygnyfyeth the hert of euery Christian: as in ij. Corint. vj. d. & 1 Corin. iij. and vj. d.

Of the boke of lyfe is spokẽ in ye Psal. lxviij. f.

To syt in the temple of God, is, to rule in the cõsciences of men, and thére to cõmaunde, &c.

By mylck are vnderstãde thynges easye to perceaue, by stronge meate soche as are harde & obscure

Sounde after ye Hebrues sygnifieth him which in leuĩg the wisdome of the chyldren of thys worlde, & the procuryng for hys awne profet, lyueth a symple life and with oute blame. Soche a one was Iacob of whõ Genes. xxv d.

A lyuely hope is that wher by we be certertayne of euerlastyng lyfe.

Al though ye callyng of God be stable & suer, neuerthelesse ye Apostle wyll, yt oure workes shulde declare vnto men that we are called.

APPENDIX XII. (p. 117.)

Gibson Papers, Vol. 5, No. 41 (Lambeth Palace Library).

1. Dn. Westminster was Lancelot Andrews, borne in London, brought up in Ratcliffe Schole under Mr. Mulcaster; sent to Pembroke Hall, was yᵉ first who had exhibitiō of Dr. Watts schollerships. He was Mʳ of Pembroke, D.D. 1590 (I thinke) Exceedingly commended by Dr. Whitaker. He wrote divers things. Was

Bishop of { Chichester / Ely / Winchester } and { (? King's) Almoner / Dean of the Chappell.

Died 1626, Septemb. 21, aged 71.

2. John Overall Dn. of Paulᵗ, was borne at Hadleigh, Suffolke: of Trinity Colledge. Mʳ of Catherine Hall. Regius Professor of Divinity, when Dr. Whitaker died about 1596. Bishop of { Coventry / Norwich } Died 1618. I have not seen anything of his in print. Both these at Hamptō Court Conference. Neither of thē appeared against Barret 1595, when all the Heads (but these 2 and the Mʳ of Clarehall whyther Dr. { Bing or / Smith }) did.

3. Dr. Adrian Saravia was a French man bornę (as I have heard): Prebend in Westminster.

Wrote { Of yᵉ divers degres of yᵉ ministers of yᵉ gospell. / Of yᵉ Honour due to priests and prelates. / Of sacriledge.

Since his works new printed in Latin ad annum 1611, as Jus Divinū page 17 tells us. He was a married mā, but never had child. His wife was remaried to Dr. Robt. Hill. Francis Dee

Bp. of Peterboroug was his foster-son (as I haue heard), i.e. the
Dr. put him to Westm. Schole. Jno. Theme (?) procured him
chosen into your Trinity Colledge.

4. Dr.   Clarke Cant. His workes I have seene in a thin
folio. I take it his name was Richard, but—quaere.

5. Dr. John Layfeild was D.D. 1603 (I take it), $\begin{cases} \text{preacher} \\ \text{parson} \end{cases}$
at Clement Danes.

6. Who is not in yours is Dr. Teigh. I have a catechism
made by Williā Tye dedicated to Prince Henry 1612, wherein
he mentiōs that Christopher Tye his grandfather was Tutour to
Edw. 6. Christopher Tye was Dr. Musick 1545. This is all of
him. I suppose Will Tye might be chaplein to yͤ Prince, quaere
tom . . . (illegible.)

7. Mr. Francis Burleigh. There was a B.D. 1594 of this
name; after D.D. 1607, but whyther the same or not I know not.

8. Mr. Jeffery King, Sussex Coll. Regall. There was one
Mr. King a Cambridge-mā, parson of Warbleton, 4 miles from
Battell Abbey to yͤ west. Mr. Joseph Bennett of my yeare, whē
he came to cōmence told me that he maried Mr. King's Dᵗᵉʳ, and
that he was at Harlletō for his father in law. Mr. King was
Yorkshire borne as he told me also.

9. Mr Richard Tomsō, Clare hall. There was a B.D. 1593.
Noe more doe I know.

10. Mr.   Bedwell. I never heard of him in any
place but in this besines.

_____

1. Dr. Richardson was Dr. John Richardsō borne at Lintō
7 miles from Cambridge, to which he gaue yͤ old pulpit at
Sᵗᵉ· Maryes whē that which now stands was set up in August 1618.
Of him see *Catalog. Mss. Peterhouse and Trinity.* He died
Aprile 21, 1625. Dr. Walford preached his funerall sermō, buried
in your Chappell. Gave part of his Library to Emā Colledg.

My copy places this mā in yͤ second place after Mr. Lively,
and calls him Mr. and not Dr. Richardson. If myne be him, thē
there might be some other Mr. Richardson, and thē why not
Mr. Alexander Richardsō? quaere.

2. Mr. Edward Lively, Coll. Trin. fellow, profess^r Hebrew.

3. Mr. Laurance Chadertō, Cheshire borne, came to Cambridge aged 20 years, 7th of the queen of X^{ts} Colledg, fellow there. Made Master of Emā by the Founder himselfe (who (as Mr. Acknell told v̄s in his sermō 2 Oct. 1622, the day they chose Dr. Prestō M^r Emā) the founder told him, that if he would not be M^r and take that charge, He would desist frō his purpose of Founding the Colledge. He was lecturer a long time at Clements, till he was D.D. 1613. Then succeeded by Mr. Bentley. He was one of the 4 at Hampton Court Conference for ye ministers who petitioned ye King; but with noe satisfactiō to thē. I have heard, Mr. Humphrey Fen wrote to him, not to betray their cause, as Mr. Fen told a friend of mine, and he told mee: who also (Mr. Fen I mean) lamented that they should have 4 men to act for thē, whereof 3 never tooke the cause to Heart. Dr. Chadertō died Nov. 1640.

4. Mr. Francis Dillingham Soc. Coll. Chr. There was one of this name B.D. 1599. I make account that this mā you seeke for was he who was psō of Dean in Bedfordshire. He died 1648. In my Catalogue of silenced ministers I find one Mr. Dillingham in Lincolne Diocese, whyther this or some other man I cannot tell, but I am informed his name was Thomas, younger brother To Francis. Francis was psō of Wildon in Bedfordsh., a single man all his time: gave his estate to his brother Mr. Thomas He died 30 years ago. Wrote divers bookes. The father of Mr. Dillingham of Barnwell, and Bartō Segrave was a 3rd brother to Francis and Thomas.

5. Mr. Thomas Harrisō, fellow and vice-M^r of Trinity. B.D. but what yeare I dare not say, there were 2 or 3 of that name about his standing. He lived all his time in ye Colledge. I have heard that when Robt Earle of Essex came to Trinity Colledge, as a student, That this Mr. Harrisō was father of the Freshmē that yeare, and cōmended that son of his. quaere.

6. Mr. Robt. Spalding. Fellow Coll. Johan. B.D. 1600. Hebrew Professor.

7. Mr. Roger Andrews, Brother to Launcelot Andrews, borne in Londō. Fellow Pembroke.

Vicar of { Chigwell in Essex. } Prebend. { Chichester } B.D. 1604.
{ Cowfeild in Sussex. } { Southwell. }

D.D. 1609. Master of Jesus Colledg. Put out there as I take it vpō complaint of yᵉ fellows to yᵉ King.

8. Mr. Bridges, as your copy hath it. Mine reads him Bing, and well as I conceive, This was Mr., or rather Dr. Andrew Bing, 1603 D.D. Whē I came to Cambridge He was professʳ Heb. of Trinity Colledg. He used to sit next to Dr. Richardson, a tall mā of a smiling countenance. Archdn. Norwich. He was living in the beginning of the Parlemᵗ. Left Cambridge 1621.

Whē we sate in the Scholes for Bachelers { Mr. Medcalfe) \
Mr. Cheney } stood \
Mr. Creiton)

to be Hebrew Lecturers, This man was 1617 parsō of Broughton in Buckinghamshire, but he left it before his death.

----

1. Dr. John Harding was parsō of Halsey in Oxfordsh, 4 miles frō Oxon. toward yᵉ east. Hebrew professor, and 6 or 7 yeares before his death president of Magdalene. He was maried. His wife died July last in Dr. Reignolds' lodgings in Corpus Christi, Mrs. Reignolds was their only daughter. The Dr. died 1617.

2. Dr. John Reignolds, Devonsh. of Corpus Xᵗⁱ Coll. Fellow. Thē upon exchange with Dr. Will. Cole, who was president, he succeeded him in yᵉ Colledg and Dr. Cole was Dn. of Lincolne. He wrote divers things. A sermon of his I haue, wherein I perceive he had knowledge of the Italiā and French tongues besides his vniversity languadges. He died May 21. 1607, buried May 25 with much honour and lamentation. *See Abel redivivus.* A letter of his to Sʳ Francis Knowles that noe Scripture makes difference betw. a Bp. and presbiter ag. Dr. Bancroft's sermō is famous.

3. Dr. Thomas Holland, Shropshire, of Exeter Colledg. fellow, then Rectour. Regius professour of Divinity above 20 years, that is frō Dr. Humphreys death, 1589, till he died himselfe, 1612. He was noe man for episcopacy. In the Act 1608 he concluded, quòd episcopatus nō sit ordo distinctus a presbiteratu, eoq superioʳ jure divino. He was succeeded in his 2 Universitye preferments by 2 most learned mē, Dr. Robt. Abbot in the chaire, and Dr. John Prideaux in his rectorship and after in the chaire. *See more of him Abel redivivus: Mr. Sam. Clerk's lives: and Mr. Hugh Holland's lives.*

4. Dr. Rich. Killby, Leicestersh., is omitted in your copy. He was D^n. D. fell. of Lincolne Coll. Hebrew profess^r after Dr. Harding; was Rector of Lincol. Colledg. Died about such time that King James did. Dr. Bret preached his funerall.

5. Mr. Miles Smith, against whose name you write Hereford, I thus make it out; Mr. Miles Smith, Canon Residentiary in Hereford. I have heard that he was of Corp. X^{ti} Collē. quaere comē. He was 1612 made Bp. Gloster. *See Goodwin de presulibus title Gloster.*

6. Mr. Bret was borne in London, son of Robt. Bret. Sir John Bret was Mr. Bret's elder brother. fellow of Lincoln Colledg; tutour to our Mr. Robt. Boltō. He proceeded D.D. whē he left Oxford he was made psō of Quaintō in Buckinghamshire. He was a maried mā, daughters of his 2 or 3 I have seen. His wife was a citizē's daughter of Oxford. After her Husband's death (which was about Easter 1636,) she came and lived in Northamton. If you remember: you, Mr. Encen (?) and she were susceptores to Sam. Ball, 1642. She died 1643 in Northampton, caried to be buried by her husband. Dr. Bret reported that the Bps. altered very many places that the translaters had agreed upō: He had a note of ye places.

7. Mr. Faireclough. Enquiring after him, I find by two Oxford mē that Dr. Hen. Fearley was called Fearley alias Farclough. The Dr. cannot be the man you seeke. He was too young. He proceeded Dr. 1617, and therfore was little above 20 years old, when the Bibles Translation was put forward. Therfore Ile tell you what I met with all els where, viz. in my wiues Brother's House, in a little Booke which relates ye County of Suffolke divided into 12 or 14 Classes. In Clare or Sudbury Classis there is mentiō of Mr. Faireclough. He is Minister of Kattō, or as in the mapp it is writtē Kediton, 2 miles frō Haverill to ye north, the same Town where Sir Nathan^l. Barnardiston lives. He had (it may be hath) sons, scholars in Cambridge as I heard.

---

1. Dr. John Duport, Lecestershire borne. He died a little before I came to Cambridge. Dr. Bollē died Jan. 28, 1617. This Dr. made verses for Bollen, but fell sicke, died, and was

buried himselfe before the other, as I heard in Emā Collē. One sermon of this Dr. I have heard of, but never saw it.

2. Dr. Will. Brainthwait. Norwich mā borne. fellow of Emā B.D. 1593. M[r] of Caius Colledg. He was the 2nd Dr. for seniority whē I came to Cambridg. Died Vice-Chancellor Feb. 15. 1618.

3. D[r] Jeremy Ratcliffe, Col. Tr. C. Soc. I find nothing of him but that a D.D. cōmencē 1588.

4. Mr.   Wood, Immanuel. It should be as mine hath it Mr. Sam. Ward, Immanuel. Who was borne in the Bp[rick] Durham. Fellow Emā. B.D. 1603. M[r] of Sidney. To speake of him to you, is nedlesse for me. Yet one small thing I wil add, that is this, He made y[e] Diall over the great gate in Eman. Colledg. He died 1644.

5. Mr. Andrew Downes. fellow Johns Coll. greek profess[r] all my time, and long before, for there is but one between him and Mr. Barthol. Doddingtō, who was professour in y[e] very beginning of queen Elisab.

6. Mr. John Boyse, C. Joh. This mā was neither Will. Boys, Proctor of Clarhall, 1599; nor yet elegant Dr. Boyse, D[n] of Canterbury; but a 3[d] B.D. 1590. Mr. Palmer tells me that this Mr. Boys was prebend in Ely, and that he lived in y[e] isle. Was living till within these 5 or sixe yeares.

7. Mr. Robt. Ward. Coll. Regall. I have nothing of him. and Kgs. Col. Catal. A. 1588.

---

1. D[n] of X[t] X[h] was Thomas Ravis D.D., borne he was at Maldon in Surrey. a Westminster scholler, frō thence sent to Oxford. He took all Academicall degres, and enjoyed all Collegiat dignityes, *ōnibus perfunctus est dignitatibus*, i.e. was student, canon, and D[n] of X[t] X[h]. Chaplein to ArchBp. Whitgift. ViceChancellor of Oxford twise. Bp. of Gloster 1604, and of London 1607. He died Decemb. 14, 1609, as appears by his monument in Pauls, where he lies buried. He was a great mā ag. y[e] ministers who petitioned King James.

2. Dn. Winchester was Dr. George Abbot borne in Surrey at Guilford; younger Brother to Robt. Abbot. Chaplein to Thom. Earl Dorset 1de Tresurer. Master of University Coll. Vice-Chancellor 1603. Bp. of Coventry, of London, and ArchBp. all in a yeare and quarters space. He made a chorographicall descriptiō of ye world. He wrote ag: Dr. Hill a papist. He died August 4, 1633. A sermon of his at ye Earle of Dorsets funerall I have: not anything els.

4. Dn. of Winsor was Giles Tomsō D.D., all these three at Hamptō Court Conference. He was made Bp. of Gloster 1611, but sate not above a yeare. of C. C. C. in Oxford but quaere.

3. Dn. of Worcester. Is not in my Copy at all, but in yours it is as it seemes. Ag. the title you write Dr. Lake. Here I have a doubt (though I grant that ye Dn. of Worster was employed) that Dr. Lake was not ye man. I deny not but Dr. Lake might be Dn. Vigorn. but at this time, 1603 or 1604, I cānot see how possible. Reason is, 1597, Dr. Rich. Eedes was Dn.; whē he died Dr. Henry Parry succeeded; when he preferred Dr. James Montague came; when he made Bp. Aprill 19, 1618, Then came Dr. Lake. I take it Dr. Henry Parry was Dn. at this time. He was Corp. X^{ti} Coll. Chaplein to Henry Earl Pembroke, to whō he dedicated his translation of Vrsins Catechisme. He was after Chaplein to the Queene, wayted that very March whē she died. *See Coṁ. Prefer. to Q. Elis.* Made Bp. Gloster 1607, and then of Worster 1610.

Dr. Arthur Lake was Warden of New Colledg. Master of the Hospitall of Crosse near Winchester. Vice-Chancell. Oxford that yeare when Wadham Colledg was built. He layd the first stone and 2 Halfe-penies under it, made a taking speech, sayth my Authour who heard it, in cōmendatiō of good workes. 1616 He was Bp. of Bath and Wells. My Tutour Dr. Stoughtō had institution into Artus (?) frō him and much respect as he reported, whē he came back to ye Colledge. 1624 in August.

5. Mr.   Savill, was suerly Sr Henry Savill, who might be fellow of New Colledg, but not Warden. He was anno 1598 Warden of Mertō Colledg I am sure. A great greciā witnes his editiō of Chrysostome, and a mathematiciā. He erected 2 Mathematical lectures in Oxford; read thē both himselfe awhile. His first lecturers were Dr. Bambridge and Mr. Brigs. Mr. John

Wallis of Emā Coll. is now Savile geometry reader. Sir Henry
Savill was also Provost of Eaton Colledge, wherein he was
succeeded by Sir Henry Wotton.

6.   Mr.   Harman.   My copy calls him Mr. Harmer.
There was one Harmā vnder scholm^r in Magdalene, but he will
be too young to be the man you seeke for.

7.   Dr.   Perin was canō X^t X^h, D.D. greek Professor.
Died an old mā in Oxford.

8.   Mr. Ravins, or as mine hath him Mr. Ravens.   I haue
nothing of him.

---

1.   Dn. Chester was Dr. Will. Barlow B.D. 1594, D.D. 1599
of Trinity Colledg, Camb. I think.   He was Chaplen to ArchBp.
Whitgift: wrote the Hampton Court Conference.   Translated
several feuelyes (? feuilles) of Lavater which I have.   Wrote
some thing to ye disparadgment of ye silenced Ministers, whereof
they complaine to K. James in a supplicatiō of theirs to ye King
which I have.   He was Bp. Rochester, thē of Lincolne, died
1613.   His father was Bp. of Chichester, of whō that place in
Ascham's preceptor I thinke ment, p. 51, "A Bp. that now
liveth, a good mā, whose Judgment in religiō I better like thā
opinion in pfectness in other learning."   However this Dr. was
well seene in greek as his father little.   He was a mā of strong
memory.

2.   Dr.   Hutchinson.

3.   Dr. J. Spencer. Author geneal. There was a Dr. Spencer
who succeeded Dr. Reignolds in Corp. X^{ti} Coll. presidentship,
who had some publick place in ye Vniversity, Lady Margaret
professor, I suppose.   Author geneal.   I understand not what
that means.   The genealogicall....

[The rest of the document is missing.]

APPENDIX XIII. (p. 118.)

ACTA SYNODI NATIONALIS...DORDRECHTIANAE
HABITAE 1618.

DORDRECHTI. 4to, 1620.

Sessione Septima
xx Novembris die Martis ante meridiem.

[ACCOUNT BY SAMUEL WARD.]

Modus quem Theologi Angli in versione Bibliorum sunt
secuti :

Theologi Magnae Britanniae, quibus non est visum tantae
questioni subitam & inopinatam responsionem adhibere, officii
sui esse judicârunt, praematura deliberatione habita, quandoquidem facta esset honorifica accuratissima translationis Anglicanae
mentio, à Serenissimo Rege Jacobo, magna cum cura, magnisque
sumptibus nuper editae, notum facere huic celeberrimae Synodo,
quo consilio, quaque ratione sacrum hoc negotium a Serenissima
ejus Majestate praestitum fuerit.

Primo, in opere distribuendo hanc rationem observari voluit.
Totum corpus Bibliorum in sex partes fuit distributum : cuilibet
parti transferendae destinati sunt septem vel octo viri primarii
Linguarum peritissimi.

Duae partes assignatae fuerunt Theologis quibusdam Lon-
dinensibus ; quatuor vero partes reliquae divisae fuerunt aequa-
liter inter utriusque Academiae Theologos.

Post peractum a singulis pensum, ex hisce omnibus duodecim
selecti viri in unum locum convocati integrum opus recognoverunt
et recensuerunt. Postremo Reverendissimus Episcopus Wintonensis, Bilsonus, una cum doctore Smitho, nunc Episcopo Glocestrensi

viro eximio et ab initio in toto hoc opere versatissimo, omnibus mature pensitatis et examinatis, extremam manum huic versioni posuerunt.

Leges Interpretibus praescriptae fuerunt hujus modi :

Primo, cautum est vt simpliciter nova versio non adornaretur, sed vetus, & ab Ecclesia diu recepta ab omnibus naevis & vitiis purgaretur ; idque hunc in finem, ne recederetur ab antiqua translatione, nisi originalis textus veritas, vel emphasis postularet.

Secundo, ut nullae annotationes margini apponerentur : sed tantum loca parallela notarentur.

Tertio, vt ubi vox Hebraea vel Graeca geminum idoneum sensum admittit; alter in ipso contextu, alter in margine exprimeretur. Quod itidem factum, ubi varia lectio in exemplaribus probatis reperta est.

Quarto, Hebraismi et Graecismi difficiliores in margine re positi sunt.

Quinto, in translatione Tobit et Judithae, quandoquidem magna discrepantia inter Graecum contextum et veterem vulgatam Latinam editionem reperietur, Graecum potius contextum secuti sunt.

Sexto, ut quae ad sensum supplendum ubivis necessario fuerunt contextui interserenda, alio, scilicet minusculo, charactere, distinguerentur.

Septimo, ut nova argumenta singulis libris, & novae periochae singulis capitibus praefigerentur.

Denique, absolutissima Genealogia et descriptio Terrae sanctae, huic operi conjungeretur.

Then followed a discussion.

Sententiam suam...prolixe exposuerunt.

INDEX.

Ales, A., 64 f.

Anderson's Annals of the English Bible quoted, 27, 32, 35, 36, 38, 39, 42, 47, 48, 52, 55, 67, 76, 78, 86, 92, 107, 109, 110, 111, 112, 114, 118, 126, 131, 138, 192

Anglo-Saxon versions of Scripture, 4 ff.

Anne of Bohemia, Q., studied the Scriptures, 18 n.

Anne Boleyn's, Q., copy of Tindale's New Testament, 48

Arber's edition of Tindale's quarto fragment, 30, 34, 35, 36, 54 ff.

Arias Montanus' Latin Version, 255

Arundel, Abp, condemns Wycliffe's writings and version of Scripture, 17

Authorised Version, scholars engaged on, 112, 113
—— rules for its execution, 114 ff.
—— published, 119
—— relation to earlier versions, 257 ff.
—— use of italics, 273 n.
—— character of the language, 274 n.
—— compared with the Latin Vulgate, 281 f.
—— revision of, 320 ff.

Bancroft, Archbp, takes part in the preparation of A.V., 109 ff.

Barnes circulates Tindale's New Testament, 37
—— attacks Wolsey: does penance at St Paul's, 38 f.

Bede translates St John's Gospel: his death, 5

Beza's New Testament, 213, 222, 227 ff.

Bible, study of, 20, 24, 80, 86, 94, 101
—— new version proposed under the Commonwealth, 120
—— destroyed, 18, 35 ff., 86 f.

Bible, quotations from, by Elizabethan divines, 107 n.
—— Society, Catalogue of Bibles in the Library of the, 93

Bilney, anecdote of, 27 n. : his Latin Bible, ib.

Bishops' Bible, The, 95
—— scholars engaged on it, 99 ff.
—— specimens of the translation, 233, 235, 239, 258, 262, 267, 276 ff., 311 ff.
—— enjoined to be used, 101
—— specimens of the notes, 243 f.
—— Bodleian copy of, 118 n.
—— version of the Psalms in, 234 n.

Bodley, J., assists in bringing out the Genevan Bible, 92

Bonner's, Bp, admonition on the reading of the Bible in St Paul's 79

Bradshaw, Henry, on English copies of Latin Bibles, 15 n.: on Tindale's New Testament of 1536, 49 n.

Broughton's, H., translations of Scripture, 121 n.

Bülbring, Dr Karl, *The earliest complete English Psalter*, 12 n.

Carleton, Dr J. G., on the Rheims Version, 103 n.

Castalio's version of the Bible, 213

Chaucer's English quotations of Scripture, 19 n.

Cheke's, Sir J., translation of St Matthew, 88

Cochlæus' account of the preparation of Tindale's first New Testament, 31 f.

Complutensian Edition used by Coverdale in the Great Bible, 197
—— Polyglott, 197: Cranmer's copy, 180 n.

Conference at Hampton Court, 108

Cook, A. S., Biblical Quotations in Old English Prose Writers, 7 n.

Coton's, P., Geneve plagiaire, 257 n.

Coverdale intimate with Crumwell, More, Tindale, 55 f.

—— the first edition of his Bible, 56; different title-pages, &c., 57, 167 n., 291 f.

—— his description of his work as a secondary translation, 59, 162, 165

—— his Latin-English Testaments, 62, 308 ff.

—— second edition of his Bible, 66, 167 n.

—— superintends the preparation of the Great Bible, 74 ff.

—— specimens of his translation, 168, 174, 176, 181, 186, 311 ff.

—— sources of his alternative renderings, 298 ff.

Cox, Bp, on the revision of the Great Bible, 98

Cranmer rejoices on receiving a copy of Matthew's Bible, 69

—— prepares a preface for the second edition of the Great Bible, 77

—— engages Bucer and Fagius upon the Bible, 87 f.

Crumwell furthers Coverdale's translation of the Bible, 56

—— his views on the authority of Scripture, 65

—— obtains the king's sanction for the sale of Matthew's Bible, 70

—— enjoins that a Bible be set up in each church, 76

Dalaber's account of the first English Testament at Oxford, 40 ff.

Demaus' *Life of Tyndale*, 26 n.

Edward VI.'s zeal for the Bible, 86

Elizabeth, Q., on the English Bible, 96

Erasmus at Cambridge, 25

—— his New Testament, 27, 196 n.

—— used by Tindale, 135

—— used by Coverdale in the Great Bible, 196 ff.

Fisher, Bp, attacks Luther, 39

Fox, Bp, at the Council held by Crumwell, 64

Foxe, John, quoted, 20, 24, 26, 27, 29, 30, 35, 39, 42, 43, 55, 65 f., 79, 80, 171

Francis I. licenses the printing of the English Bible at Paris, 74

French translations of Scripture, 71 n., 130, 256

—— specimens of the versions, 219 ff.

Froude's, Mr, estimate of Tindale, 27 n.

Fry, Mr F., 26 n., 33 n., 44 n., 54, 56 n., 57 n., 58 n., 72 n., 91 n., 107 n., 185 n.

Fryth at Oxford, 126

—— does penance there, 42

—— works with Tindale, 52 n.

Fulke, *Defence of the English Translations of the Bible*, 63 n., 75 n., 106 n., 192 n., 275 n.

Gardiner, Bp, prevents a translation of the New Testament being undertaken, 85

Garret's story told by Dalaber, 40 ff.

Gasquet, Abbot, his theory on the Wycliffite Versions, 20 n.

Genevan Testament, 91, 223 ff.

—— Psalms, 91 n.

—— Bible, 90 ff., 212; woodcuts in, 93 n.

—— specimens of the translation, 215 ff., 311 ff.

—— specimens of the notes, 229 ff.

German Versions of Scripture, 129 f.

Ginsburg, Dr, 57 n., 162 n.

Grafton, with Whitchurch, defrays the expense of Matthew's Bible, 68

—— seeks Crumwell's protection, 72

—— examined as to the proposed notes to the Great Bible, 78

Great Bible, The, 73 ff., 179 ff.

—— successive revisions, 185, 192 ff.

—— specimens of the translation, 182, 214 ff., 232, 311 ff.

—— analysis of the changes introduced in it, 183 ff., 187 ff.

—— Crumwell's copy of, 75 n.

—— varieties in different editions of, 203 ff.

Greek, the study of, in England, 25 n., 126, 127
—— on the Continent, 127
Guest, Bp, on the revision of the Great Bible, 97

Hebrew, study of, 127
Henry IV. takes severe measures against the Wycliffites, 17
Henry VI. gave a copy of Wycliffe's Bible to the Charterhouse, 18
Henry VIII., Coverdale's Bible dedicated to, 61
—— Matthew's Bible dedicated to, 69
—— declaration as to reading the Bible, 79

James I. presses forward a new version of the Bible, 110 f.
John of Gaunt favoured Wycliffe, 18 n.
Joye revises Tindale's New Testament, 45, 144 n.
—— specimen of his work, 46
—— Tindale's comments on it, 53
Juda's, Leo, version of the Bible, 212, 215 ff.
Junius' translation of the Apocrypha, 256

Lawrence works on the New Testament in the Bishops' Bible, 237
Lee's, Archbp, letter to Henry VIII. on Tindale's New Testament, 33
Lewis' History of Translations, 120 n.
Lollard opinions in Purvey's Prologue, 14 n.
Luther's New Testament used by Tindale, 132 f.
Luther's writings adapted freely by Tindale, 146 ff.

Maldon's narrative, 81 f.
Marler, A., defrays the expense of the Great Bible, 78 n.
Matthew's Bible, 67 n., 169 f.
—— the New Testament from Tindale (1535), 178 f.
—— notes, 71 n., 306 f.
Meteren, Jacob von, and Coverdale's Bible, 57 n.

More, Sir T., attacks Tindale's translation, 35
Munmouth's account of Tindale, 28 f.
Münster's, S., Latin translation of the Old Testament used for the Great Bible, 181 ff., 186 ff., 311 ff.

Nix, Bp, complains of the circulation of the English Testament, 42

Offor's, Mr, manuscript collections for a history of the English Bible, 169 n., 208 n., 240 n.

Pagninus' Latin Version of the Bible, 128, 215 ff.
Parker's, Archbp, judgment on the Genevan Bible, 94
—— plans the Bishops' Bible, 94
Paues, Miss, A Fourteenth Century English Biblical Version, 12 n.
Prayer-book, variety of translations in, 279 f.
Psalter, the Prayer-book, 200 ff., 206, 280 n., 333 ff.
—— the Canterbury, 7 n.
Purvey revises Wycliffe's Version, 13
—— Lollard opinions in his Prologue, 14 n.

Reynolds, Dr, proposes a new Version at the Hampton Court Conference, 108
Rheims and Doway Bible, 102
—— method of translation, 247 ff.
—— specimens of the translation, 249 ff.
—— influence on the A.V., 257, 266, 269, 273
Rogers (see Matthew's Bible), 89, 171
Rolle, Richard, of Hampole, 11 n.
Roye, W., his Rede me and be nott wrothe, 35 n.
Rudelius, Latin Bible edited by, 163 n.

Sandys, Bp, on the revision of the Great Bible, 97
Scriptures, translation of, interrupted by national causes, 4, 7
—— zeal in studying, 20

Scriptures, perils of possessing, 24
—— burnt, 36, 39, 42
Selden's criticism on the A. V., 117 n.
Smith's, Bp Miles, Preface to the Authorised Version, 108 n., 116 f.
Spalatinus' account of Tindale's New Testament, 35
Stevens, Henry, of Vermont, on Coverdale's Bible, 57 n., 58 n.

Taverner at Oxford, 126
—— doing penance there, 42
—— his Bible, 84, 207 ff., 311 ff.
Tindale, birth and early life, 25 f.; visit to London, 27 f.; exile, 29; his first *New Testament*, 29 ff., 137; pirated editions, 45 n.; translates the *Pentateuch*, 44; *Jonah*, 44, 68 n.; revises his New Testament, and adds 'the Epistles out of the Old Testament,' 47, 156 ff., 172 ff.; revises his New Testament for the last time, 50, 144 ff.; his martyrdom, 50; his character and spirit, 51 ff.
—— leaves a manuscript translation of part of the Old Testament (Josh. —2 Chron.), 67, 172 n., 175 n.
—— independence of his translations, 132 ff., 152
—— glosses on the New Testament of 1525, 306 f.
—— glosses on the New Testament of 1534, 141 ff., 306 f.
—— influence of Luther on his writings, 146 ff.
—— his prologues to the books of the N. T., 149 ff.
—— specimens of his translation, 133 ff., 155 ff., 173 f., 176, 181, 224, 225, 311 ff.
—— comparison of the three texts of his New Testament in 1 John, 295
—— his translation of St Matthew compared with Coverdale's, 167 n.
—— his translation of Jonah compared with Coverdale's, 68 n.

Tomson's, L., New Testament, 94 n., 223 ff.
Tremellius' Latin Version of Old Testament, 255
Trench, Archbp, on A. V., 270 n.
Tunstall, Bp, declines to receive Tindale, 27
—— orders the destruction of Tindale's New Testament, 35; preaches against the book, 35
—— sanctions the third edition of the Great Bible, 77
Turton, Dr, on The Text of the English Bible, 274 n.
Tyball's account of the circulation of Tindale's New Testament, 37

Warham, Archbp, orders the destruction of Tindale's Testaments, 35
—— calls an assembly to discuss the use of Scripture, 43
Whittaker, Dr, on Coverdale, 162
Whittingham engaged on the English Bible at Geneva, 90 ff.
—— his wife, 90 n.
Wright's, Mr A., Bible Word-book, 275
Wycliffe's translation of Scripture, 12 f.
—— from the Vulgate, 13
—— opposition to his work, 15
—— remaining manuscripts, 18 ff.
—— disputed by Abbot Gasquet, 20 n.
—— not used by Tindale, 130 n., App. viii. p. 316
—— specimens of the Versions (see Purvey, Arundel, John of Gaunt, Anne of Bohemia), 287 ff.
—— printed editions, 20 n.

Zurich Bible, 130 f.
—— one of the chief sources of Coverdale's, 163
—— specimens of the translation, 181, 311 ff.